Piracy: Leakages from Modernity

Piracy: Leakages from Modernity

Martin Fredriksson and James Arvanitakis, Editors

Litwin Books
Sacramento, CA

Published by Litwin Books in 2014

Litwin Books
PO Box 188784
Sacramento, CA 95818

http://litwinbooks.com/

Layout by Christopher Hagen.

This book is printed on acid-free, sustainably-sourced paper.

Library of Congress Cataloging-in-Publication Data

Piracy : leakages from modernity / edited by James Arvanitakis and Martin Fredriksson.
pages cm
Includes bibliographical references and index.
Summary: "A collection of texts that takes a broad perspective on digital piracy and attempts to capture the multidimensional impacts of digital piracy on capitalist society today"-- Provided by publisher.
ISBN 978-1-936117-59-8 (alk. paper)
1. Computer crimes. 2. Piracy (Copyright) 3. Internet--Social aspects. I. Arvanitakis, James, editor of compilation. II. Fredriksson, Martin, editor of compilation.
HV6773.P57 2014
364.16'62--dc23

2013048073

Table of Contents

Part III - Practices

On Piracy

The image of 'the pirate' is an ambiguous figure in contemporary culture: the romanticized hero of Johnny Depp's 'Jack Sparrow', the portrayal of anarchism of the seas controlled by the Somali pirates, the illegal goods that we are told fund terrorism and child labor, and the members of national Pirate Parties across the world. Contemporary piracy is also associated with the file-sharer: generally a young white man hiding behind a computer screen somewhere in Europe or North America, downloading movies and music, or anonymously trolling online conversations, or hacking into large and powerful computer systems – banks and other corporates, governments and international bodies. This is indeed a wide spread form of piracy that deserves more serious, and unbiased, attention from scholars and researchers. It is however also an image that tends to limit the understanding of piracy to a matter of intellectual property, and digital distribution of entertainment.

Until recently, a large part of the research about digital piracy has been initiated by the entertainment industry, and the independent research that challenges the claims made by media companies and copyright organizations has still had to address the problems and questions formulated by that industry. Research on digital piracy has consequently – with a few exceptions – come to focus on piracy as a problem to be solved: how to put a stop to it or how the artists, producers and copyright holders can be compensated if we accept a certain level of file-sharing? While illegal copies of all sorts of cultural products have been produced since the advent of the printing press, these issues become more complex in a digital environment where media companies are trying to find ways to keep on selling products that are infinitely reproducible.

This question is particularly poignant for those who try to make a living from selling the products of their artistic labor, but piracy has implications far beyond the sphere of the media economy. After the rise and fall of the music-sharing site, Napster, but before the file-sharing architecture known as BitTorrent really exploded with sites like The Pirate Bay, William Uricchio (2004, 139) pointed to the social and political potentials of digital piratical technologies:

> In the case of aforementioned peer-to-peer (P2P) networks, the implications of this shift range from the reconsideration of how we define and interact with certain cultural texts, to how collaborative communities take form and operate, to how we understand our rights and obligations as citizens – whether in the political, economic, or cultural sphere.

This implies that peer-to-peer (P2P) networks not only present a new way for individuals to interact with commodities, but also to interact with each other and with society as a whole. From newspapers to universities, record labels to textbooks, independent musicians to pornography, the monopolistic linear or vertical distribution model has been irrevocably changed. We now live in a global distribution system that has moved beyond 'the network' to be 'a constellation'. Like the constellations in the sky that we stare at in wonder, the connections are often not visible and can be incredibly difficult to understand.

The starting point for this book is how acts of piracy, understood in a wider sense, can redefine or confirm such interactions: that is, how does piracy open up spaces and create leakages of culture, knowledge and capital between different political, organizational and geographical spheres?

Piracy here is understood in a way that includes but is not limited to file-sharing and other technologies for unauthorized distribution of media and information. Researchers such as Ravi Sundaram (2010) and Lawrence Liang (2005) – working within the broader interdisciplinary Sarai Network that studies cultural and urban commons in the developing world – have begun to explore how piracy is intertwined with unauthorized use of urban space in third world cities. Pirated products are widely circulated in the ungovernable slums and shantytowns of cities like Delhi. New research demonstrates the parallels between the distribution of pirated software, films and books and the various practices that provide illegal access to public spaces such as squatting and tapping into networks for water and electricity (Liang 2005; Sundaram 2010). In this context, piracy can be envisioned as struggles over resources that are located in the borderlands between the public and the private: struggles that create and exploit leakages between enclosed properties and the commons. This interplay, or 'wrestle', demands that we re-imagine cultural and geographical space.

Piracy thus also touches on one of the crucial questions in the construction of modern capitalist societies: what is a common right and what is a commodity? This balance is currently under (re)negotiation, from debates over access to knowledge versus the rights of authorship, to the reorganization of national health insurance, social security and rights and freedoms around labor and labor migration. In this way, we can understand contemporary debates over piracy as a continuation of the struggles over the commons and enclosure of societies since the middle ages. The enclosure-fuelled emergence of the economic machine resulted in immeasurable innovations and allows those of us belonging to mainstream Western societies to live the lifestyle we enjoy today. But the destruction it caused displaced millions. With an eye to this history of the commons-commodity struggle, we choose not to see piracy as a revolutionary moment, or as simply something illegal – for it can be neither and both in one simultaneous act. We do not romanticize piracy but rather see it as representing a complex interplay between claims of rights, knowledge systems, technology and ontological positions.

Piracy not only actualizes structural changes in the Western world, it also relates to ongoing postcolonial transformations. The work undertaken at the Sarai Network can be seen as one example of new research that contextualizes piracy in different ways and looks at it from geographical, geopolitical and thematic perspectives other than those articulated by the media industry. As Joe Karaganis (2011) points out in his introduction to the report *Media Piracy in Emerging Economies* – derived from comprehensive fieldwork done by local researchers in six countries across South America, Asia and Eastern Europe – most research on media piracy has been formulated by American actors with the interests of their national industries in mind (also see Drahos and Braithwaite 2003). It unilaterally focuses on how piracy affects American copyright holders, while rarely discussing how changing laws and technologies of distribution affect consumers, citizens and informal economies in the third world. The privilege to formulate the problem has rested with the corporations and governments of the Western world. Like many emerging research networks, this book challenges this dominant perspective.

Leakages and innovations

This book, then, connects with and reflects the changing agenda of piracy research by opening up the field to a wide range of new thematic, disciplinary and geographical points of view that take piracy seriously as a global, social, political and cultural phenomenon. The geographic and thematic diversity of this collection reflects that development and gives a glimpse into the wider field of inquiry that takes the issue of piracy beyond the narrow focus on sales and business models. This is not to say that sales and business models are not important, but a discussion about the media economy has to be situated in a broad social context; and acknowledge other interests in order to be relevant. The readers will indeed find discussions about digital piracy and media economies in this book, but contextualized in a way that highlights more fundamental social, political and cultural aspects and consequences of piracy.

The point of departure for this anthology is to approach piracy not as an abnormality that needs to be rectified or a problem that needs to be solved, but as something inherent to modern, capitalist society. Piracy, we argue, is a phenomenon that actually teaches us something about contemporary society if we are prepared to learn from it.

In *The Cultural Commons of Hope,* Arvanitakis (2007) details the history of counter movements as opening up new commons as well as protecting existing ones, while capital moves to enclose and commodify these spaces. This has occurred in different phases, with different kinds of resources: the common lands, the environment more generally, the institutions of the welfare state, the human body, the intellect, and ultimately cultural practices. The ability to place definable private property rights around each of these is at the very core of capitalism and modernity. But property rights are never that easy to define: even in something as obvious as a car you may own, there are many obligations associated with those rights – from needing insurance and registration to wearing a seatbelt and driving within the speed limit. This ambiguity of property rights becomes even more immediate when it comes to the more slippery resources that are systematically commodified under intellectual property rights regimes and continuously challenged by piracy.

In many ways, this focus on piracy contributes to articulating a new way of understanding the very processes of modernity. If we understand modernity as a series of institutional developments accompanied by changing social and cultural practices, piracy allows us to re-examine historical and contemporary developments. The emergence of capitalist economies is inextricably linked with the changing nature and definition of property rights: something that had to be defined to respond to what were being identified as 'acts of piracy'. Likewise, the modern split between private and public spheres is continuously redefined as authorities attempt to deal with 'piracy'. In the cultural sphere, as various authors in this collection note, the norms among 'pirate' file-sharers can, in some aspects, actually align with the values and norms that hold the ideology of copyright together.

Piracy thus creates a gap or leak from the processes of modernity, while at the same time meeting the capitalist economy's need for interventions and innovations. In contemporary terms, Internet piracy is founded on countless innovations that create a 'leak' from the globalized capitalist economy, where profits, control and the monopoly on distribution is dispersed beyond the existing property regimes. Authorities tend to respond to these developments with stricter enforcement of intellectual property rights, while corporations attempt to enclose and commodify innovations created by the very same outlaws it rails against. These legal, technological, political and economic changes seek to reinforce the capitalist system that piracy potentially destabilizes.

This complex interplay creates a dance of power, control, innovation, confrontation, leakage and enclosures. Moreover, this leads to a contestation of rhetorical devices, as claims of piracy are matched by declarations of freedom: after all, what may be considered an act of piracy by one person, community or nation, may well be seen as a form of resistance by others.

It is here that piracy has the potential to help us gain new insights into the processes of modernity. Specific forms of piracy often emerge in the margins of innovative processes and transformations: but these innovations are at the core of modernity, not at the periphery. As such, we return to our first point: piracy *must* be understood as part of the everyday.

Structure

This book is structured according to three themes. Since nothing piratical should be taken for granted, we begin by discussing the *ontological* basics: *What is piracy?* Or more precisely, *What can piracy be made to be?* These questions reflect a fundamental aspect of our approach: piracy is neither homogenous, nor essential. As noted, 'piracy' is a label that certain actors slap on others for specific reasons. How this label is distributed tells us a great deal, about the alleged pirates, about those who have the power and desire to stick on labels, and the social context of both. We then move on to chapters that discuss the *politics* of piracy from a macro perspective, analyzing how piracy relates to structures of power and processes of transformation. Finally, we present a selection of texts that focus more closely on piratical *practices* and show how acts of piracy, whether street-vending or file-sharing, carry different meanings and have shifting implications in various contexts.

Part 1. Ontology

The opening text is **James Meese's** *The Pirate Imaginary and the Potential of the Authorial Pirate.* Meese sets the scene by discussing how various discourses struggle to position the pirate either as a criminal, a rebel or a mundane media consumer. At the end, however, Meese challenges this kind of polarization with which piracy is so often associated. Importantly, the first chapter raises the question as to whether we should abandon the term 'piracy', as it tends to evoke a 'criminal/hero dichotomy' that 'reinforces unequal institutional structures, at the expense of a fully realized understanding of how we all engage with, create and reproduce cultural artifacts'. This excellent starting point for this collection asks what we mean when we say 'piracy', as well as why the word is used to describe certain acts.

Virginia Crisp addresses the same fundamental question of how the image of the pirate is constructed, but she approaches it from the perspective of the assumed perpetrators. In her chapter, *To Name a Thief: Constructing the Deviant Pirate*, Crisp examines how certain groups of file-sharers relate to the concept of piracy and to what extent they identify themselves as pirates. The chapter raises important questions about identity: If you have ever read a newspaper over someone's shoulder, would you consider yourself to be taking content illegally?

The following chapter entitled *'You Can't Change Our Ancestors Without Our Permission': Cultural Perspectives on Biopiracy*, is in many ways, also about naming a thief. Here **Daniel F. Robinson**, **Danielle Drozdzewski** and **Louise Kiddell** discuss the practice of biopiracy: how multinational companies patent and appropriate genes, breeds and other natural resources whose uses were discovered or known, developed and deployed for centuries by Indigenous communities. Those communities carefully held, nurtured and transferred these scientific (medical, nutrition, ecological management) knowledges between people and generations as common resources. Yet the intellectual property regime turns such knowledge into commodities that are enclosed and exploited – in other words, sold for profit. This exemplifies how piracy can be conceptualized as a counter discourse that, in this case, aims to expose how multinational industries use intellectual property rights to pirate resources that were traditionally communal.

The ontology section ends with a text that takes us back to the origins of piracy, highlighting the consistencies in the discourse about high-sea pirates of the past with contemporary digital piracy. In *Piratical Community and the Digital Age: The Structural Racialization of Piracy in European Law and Culture*, **Sonja Schillings** discusses how the definition of maritime piracy in early modern legal history is deeply integrated with the construction of European colonialism. This is further linked with the racialization of piracy throughout European and American history. Highlighting how piracy presents new ways of understanding modernity, Schillings discusses how discourses on digital piracy continue to be structured along conceptions from the colonial past. In this chapter, we see how leakages from modernity were never tolerated.

Part 2. Politics

Shillings' text also points to the fundamentally political aspects of piracy. In this picture, piracy is not an incidental interference in contemporary information politics. Piracy engages with the basic social and political structures of modern society. **Sean Johnson Andrews** echoes this approach in his chapter *Modernity, Law and the Violence of Piracy, Property and the State.* Andrews places piracy within the global political economy in general, and the neoliberal agenda more specifically. He discusses piracy as a phenomenon that exposes the contradictions within contemporary capitalism and highlights neoliberalism as a failed project of modernity. Like Shillings, Andrews draws our attention to an aspect that is often overlooked in discussions of digital piracy: violence. Violence is inherent to the history of maritime piracy. Monopolized, state sanctioned violence is the ultimate force underpinning the private property regime, the regime that contemporary piracy challenges. As with law-and-order ramp-ups (or 'crack-downs') the world over, this state-sanctioned violence is a response to leaks that destabilize the established political economy.

In his compelling chapter, Andrews also makes the bold gesture to envision the end of capitalism – reminding us that no system lasts forever. This utopian position demands that we keep the door open for alternative ways of imagining the world. The fact that none of us can give a comprehensive outline of a political and economic system to succeed capitalism is no reason to imagine that the current state of organizing resources is perpetual. No one came up with capitalism in a single stroke – it evolved over a long period of time through the practices of people and institutions beginning to do things differently, in most cases without a thought of changing the world. In the same way the multitude of heterogeneous practices called 'piracy' that we discuss in this book might very well form a small part in the great scheme of change that is just under way.

The crisis of capitalism and leakages of intellectual property are also themes in **Yannis Mylona's** chapter *'Pirates' in EU's (Semi) Peripheries.* Drawing on critical literature on new media, Mylonas empirically examines the practices that hegemonic mainstream political and economic discourses frame as 'piracy'. While this description is used for many practices, Mylonas finds that few Internet or digital technology users identify themselves as 'pirates'. The exception is Pirate Party members – though the terms are very different. Mylonas challenges the hegemonic construction of copyright piracy by looking at the concrete realities of people using new media and digital technologies in local contexts where different national histories of social and economic transformations are reflected in shifting attitudes to file-sharing.

Lucas Logan's chapter, *The IPR GPR,* also uses a political economy framework. Logan's work highlights the abovementioned interplay between modernity and piracy by discussing the emerging global prohibition regime (GPR) over intellectual property rights (IPR). GPRs are made up of legal, economic, social and political regimes that attempt to regulate prohibited practices – and in so doing, establish and enforce international standards. As we witness piracy destabilize the institutions of modernity, Logan highlights how it also gives rise to social interaction and communication between and within modern nation-states and global markets.

Ekin Gündüz Özdemirci's chapter *BitTorrent: Stealing or Sharing Culture* reflects on the countercultural discourse that has emerged around the concept of piracy: where file-sharing is seen as a technology of democracy and enlightenment, fully comparable to the birth of the printing press. Özdeirci's work highlights the complexity of piracy: it does not undermine the institutions of modernity like democracy, but potentially strengthens them. Özdeirci shows how new political meanings and potentials are attributed to piracy when new media technologies turn culture and information from a 'private good', underscored by scarcity thinking, into a potentially public good that can be infinitely shared and distributed. This reminds us how the challenges to the contemporary copyright regime sit within a wider reconfiguration of the demarcations between private and public. Özdemirci's text indicates that the supporters of The Pirate Bay tend to regard piracy and file-sharing as a defense of the commons against imposed scarcity and enclosure.

Özdemirci highlights that the utopian vision of the Internet as a tool for civic empowerment forms one basis for an emerging political mobilization around issues of free speech, access to knowledge and respect for privacy in a digital world. In her chapter *The Internet between Politics and the Political*, **Mariachristina Sciannamblo** further explores this politicisation of piracy in the guise of the Pirate Party movement, which has made digital rights and freedom of information on the Internet its core issue. Sciannamblo argues that the emergence of pirate parties is a direct political expression of a radically different social order representing the changing distribution constellations described earlier. Far from being a mere technical innovation, peer-to-peer networks represent the political conflict between two economic models of knowledge and social organization: 'open' and 'closed' approaches. Sciannamblo sees this conflict emerge through the 'open' social practices of the Internet – such as content and information sharing which threatens established 'closed' power relationships based on ownership, property rights and monetary exchange: here the contestation continues.

These new forms of distribution of culture and knowledge level a critique at the dominance of the copyright industry. We can discern echoes of the criticisms made by the members of the Frankfurt school towards the culture industries here (Adorno and Horkheimer 1968/1994). It is indeed an inspiring thought to envision the BitTorrent protocol as the fulfillment of the age of technological reproduction. In so doing, however, we must not forget that the very technologies Walter Benjamin envisioned as potentially transmogrifying art from a sacrosanct privilege of the few to a collaborative act of the masses also formed the basis for the media economy that he railed against. One can imagine that Benjamin would be at the forefront of the challenges created by digital piracy against the established media industry interests. Yet we may also ask if those new digital technologies are not as likely to be co-opted and commodified by the culture industry as the film medium of the 1930s. It is here we can situate the chapter by **You Jie**, *Cultural Resistance or Corporate Assistance: Disenchanting the Anti-Capitalist Myth of Digital Piracy*. You Jie directly questions the radical, anti-capitalist potentials of file-sharing networks. In so doing, he highlights – as we have – that nothing about this complex phenomenon should be taken for granted or simply categorized.

Part 3. Practices

You Jie's questions point to the need for more in-depth analysis of what piracy practices actually mean to those involved. **Stefan Larsson** and **Jonas Andersson's** chapter, *The Justification of Piracy*, introduces us to a deeper understanding of the practices of piracy. Larsson and Andersson build on a large-scale study of attitudes among thousands of Pirate Bay users that challenge the often homogenous yet polarized image of file-sharers as either indifferent thieves or ideologically coherent activists. They expose diverse and contradictory attitudes among file-sharers that might point to 'a revival of a norm pluralistic conception of law in a digital society'.

Balázs Bodó's chapter, *Set the Fox to Watch the Geese: Voluntary IP Regimes in Piratical File-Sharing Communities*, also discusses the heterogeneity of piracy practices. Bodó examines the diversity of file-sharing groups by looking at a wide range of closed and often very specialized file-sharing networks that exist beyond mainstream platforms like The Pirate Bay. Bodó's conclusions are challenging: he argues that such alternative networks also impose strict rules of exchange that often reflect those of conventional IP-regimes, but tend to be more efficient. Again, in these practices we find a challenge to mainstream practices as Bodó argues that insiders who respect the artists provide a better regime of managing IP than externally imposed, heavy-handed enforcement mechanisms.

File-sharing is thus not necessarily free from norms and gatekeepers, nor is it always free of charge. In closed file-sharing networks, the users often get a ratio of downloads partly based on how much uploaded material s/he contributes to the community. As Bodó points out, copyright holders can sometimes be rewarded with extra credits for allowing their works to be available.

Pavlos Hatzopoulos and **Nelli Kambouri's** chapter, *Pirate Economies and the Production of Smooth Spaces,* brings to life the Bertolt Brecht play, *Mother Courage and Her Children.* In this fascinating case study the authors track the life of illegal immigrants in Greece selling pirated goods across the protest lines on Syntagma Square in Athens: supplying water, Greek flags, torches and other necessities to both the left wing, human rights inspired protestors and the right wing anti-immigration groups. Again we witness the practices of piracy refusing to recognize established boundaries – political, social, physical or otherwise.

In her chapter, *After Piracy*, **Yi-Chieh Jessica Lin** looks at piracy from the perspective of industrial designers in Taiwan. The article focuses on the design exhibition, "Copycat," where a number of Taiwanese industrial designers elaborate on the theme of originality, copying and counterfeits. Taking their work as an example, Lin explores how western brands are remixed and reconfigured to articulate certain aesthetic and political meanings against the backdrop of China's long *Shenzai* tradition of churning and counterfeiting. We can see how the work of these designers epitomizes the creative dimensions of copying and challenges established dichotomies between innovation and reproduction that are also tied to a (post)colonial polarization between West and East.

Vanessa Mendes Moreira de Sa's chapter, *The Collaborative Production of Amateur Subtitles for Pirated TV shows in Brazil,* acknowledges the extensive creative work invested in voluntary labor such as 'fansubbing' (or the production of subtitles for foreign language television programs). Unlike in professional sub-titling, no money is exchanged. Rather, recognition and appreciation from the wide community of file-sharing 'fans' replaces financial gratification as the incentive and reward for unpaid work. However, Moreira de Sa also challenges the wide spread conception of collective, networked labor as an intrinsically un-hierarchical activity. Like You Jie, Moreira de Sa acknowledges that what appears to be a collaborative act of free sharing of culture might, in some cases, also serve the purpose of the media industry in the sense that fansubbing can be seen as unpaid labor that promotes American TV-shows in foreign markets.

The final chapter, *Piracy is Normal, Piracy is Boring: Systemic Disruption as Everyday Life,* is written by **Francesca da Rimini** and **Jonathan Marshall**. As the title indicates, the chapter discusses how piracy has become a commonplace, mundane and everyday activity. The authors describe piracy as 'a commonplace disorder' which emerges within 'the order of information capitalism'. It is a process, as we discussed above, that is 'created by the ubiquitous orders of information capitalism and suppressed by those orders' – and by the dynamic relationships between the two. Piracy is not radical, according to da Rimini and Marshall, but the end product of a consumer society that is trained to seek instant gratification with the availability of endless credit.

It might appear somewhat strange to end this book, which itself claims piracy can redefine the way we understand modernity, with a text that declares piracy to be boring. This is, however, exactly what makes it so interesting and relevant:

piracy is not separate from the processes of modernity, just another expression of them. The fact that a practice that is still so legally and politically controversial has become so quotidian and integrated in everyday practices says something about the inconsistencies of contemporary society. Above all else, this book attests to the inconsistencies surrounding piracy by highlighting how the (same) practice can be a crime, a rebellious act, a technological, aesthetic or commercial innovation, a source for constructing community and identity, and a marketing tool for the very cultural industries that it attempts to challenge. This returns us to our starting point:

> What do we mean when we say piracy and why do we insist on using a term that has become so infested with prejudices, preconceptions and rigid dichotomizations?

The many inherited preconceptions that accompany the concept are what make piracy such an interesting phenomenon, because of the processes involved, and what we can learn about the society that created yet spurned them. This book offers no consistent position on piracy, for it is an ambiguous concept. Nor is there a grand unifying conclusion or theory that explains piracy, because one of the inherent aspects of piracy is that it morphs and mutates, and rejects all such attempts.

Our final point is that while each of the chapters embodies much labor, sometimes representing the culmination of years of research, this book is in itself not the end but the beginning of greater learning and exploration. We have just begun to see the outlines of a sphere of knowledge that will grow and contribute greatly to our understanding of contemporary society over the coming decades. We are looking forward to this with excitement and hope to follow and engage more with these debates about what piracy is, can be and should be. One forum for this will be an online presence including 'Piracy Lab' (http://piracylab.com) – we hope to interact with you there.

Martin Fredriksson and James Arvanitakis
Berlin, July 2013

References

Adorno, Theodor W. and Max Horkheimer (1969/1994). *Dialectic of Enlightenment.* (John Cumming, Trans.). New York: The Continuum Publishing Company.

Arvanitakis, James (2007). *The Cultural Commons of Hope.* Berlin: VDM.

Drahos, Peter and John Braithwaite (2003). *Information Feudalism: Who Owns the Knowledge Economy*?. New York: The New Press.

Karaganis, Joe (ed.) (2011). *Media Piracy in Emerging Economies.* New York: Social Science Research Council.

Liang, Lawrence (2005). "Porous Legalities and Avenues of Participation". *Sarai Reader.* 2005, 6-17.

Sundaram, Ravi (2010). *Pirate Modernity: Dehli's Media Urbanism.* London & New York: Routledge.

Uricchio, William (2004). "Cultural Citizenship in the Age of P2P Networks". In Ib Bondebjerg and Peter Golding (eds). *Media Cultures in a Changing Europe.* Bristol: Intellect Press, Ltd, 139-164.

List of Acronyms

Agreement on Trade-Related Aspects of Intellectual Property Rights (TRIPS)
Anti-Counterfeiting Trade Agreement (ACTA)
Australian Federation Against Copyright Theft (AFACT)
Cyber Intelligence Sharing and Protection Act (CISPA)
Digital Rights Management (DRM)
Department of Professional Employees (DPE)
Erosion Technology and Concentration (ETC) Group
European Commission (EC)
Federation Against Copyright Theft (FACT)
General Agreement on Trade and Tariffs (GATT)
Global prohibition regime (GPR)
Information and Communication Technology (ICT)
International Association for the protection of Intellectual Property (AIPPI)
International Federation of the Phonographic Industry (IFPI)
International Intellectual Property Alliance (IIPA)
Internet Service Providers (ISP)
Intellectual Property (IP)
Intellectual Property Rights (IPR)
Internet Relay Chat (IRC)
Motion Picture Association of America (MPAA)
Motion Pictures Association (MPA)
Non-government organizations (NGOs)
PATRIOT Act
Peer-to-peer (P2P)
Plant Genetic Resources (PGRs)
Protect Intellectual Property Act (PIPA)
Record Industry Association of America (RIAA)
Research Works Act (RWA)
Stop Online Piracy Act (SOPA)
The Pirate Bay (TPB)
United Nations Convention on Biological Diversity (CBD)
United Nations Declaration on the Rights of Indigenous Peoples (UNDRIP)
United States Trade Representative (USTR),
UPOV Convention, (the International Union for the Protection of New Varieties of Plants)
US Patent and Trademark Office (USPTO)
US Trade Representative (USTR)
World Intellectual Property Organization (WIPO)
World Trade Organization (WTO)
Associacao Antipirataria de Cinema e Musica – The Brazilian Phonographic Industry and Cinema and Music Anti-Piracy Association

Part I – Ontology

The Pirate Imaginary and the Potential of the Authorial Pirate

James Meese

Introduction

The figure of the pirate and acts of piracy themselves are most frequently defined by their opposition and exception to the legal framework of copyright law. However, the term 'pirate', used to describe those who have been seen breaching such a legal framework, does not just evoke images of rows of computer towers in a back room, adjacent to a pile of blank discs ready for commercial reproduction and distribution, or the ubiquitous footage of the youthful and impressionable 'movie downloader' found on the beginning of DVDs (see Loughan 2008). It also carries a deeper cultural resonance, reminding us of bands of renegades, hijacking European ships returning from colonial outposts, or in the contemporary era, of the two most evocative pirate imaginaries which exist concurrently: The machine-gun wielding Somalian pirate – a martyr-rebel and a refugee of globalization – or more humorously, Johnny Depp's, Keith Richards inspired, Captain Jack Sparrow, the debonair star of the successful Walt Disney franchise *Pirates of the Caribbean* (Ali and Murad 2009).

While Captain Sparrow originally appears as a scheming pirate, in subsequent films he slowly reveals an ethical side, which belies his rough exterior. This character's development becomes even more interesting, considering the franchise owner Walt Disney has exhibited a fierce determination to protect their intellectual property rights from pirates (and also the entirely legal public domain) over the years (see Lessig 2004). The Walt Disney Company seems to refuse the possibility of a piracy, which is good-hearted unless that piracy involves Jack Sparrow or another such fictional pirate, and so can contribute to their extensive intellectual property holdings and profits. However, this writer is much more hopeful, and the following chapter will reveal how 'the pirate' has been structured discursively and materially by intellectual property law itself, as well as the interested parties surrounding this discussion, and will go some way to explaining how piracy manages to operate productively through and beyond these constraints.

The past decade has seen content industries and a collection of academics, lawyers and librarians engage in an increasingly public battle around copyright's transition to a digital landscape. These 'copyright wars' (Hunter 2005) have led to some productive discussions around the future of information management and knowledge curation, however, both sides have a tendency to continually focus on specific forms of piracy. The content industries regularly frame the figure of the pirate as a criminal, with the famous campaign – 'Piracy, it's a crime' – which features on the start of most commercial DVDs clearly stating that downloading is both an ethical wrong and illegal. This is a claim, which manages to educate the consumer, while also justifying the industry's broader public and legal campaign against the pirate (Grimmelmann 2009, 20–21). Conversely, the aforementioned advocates for 'free culture' qualify their support for piracy, often viewing certain piratical practices as a form of free speech, while ignoring the constitutional specificity of such a political programme.

When certain kinds of piracy are normalised and idealised in public debate, alternative discourses of piracy, and other piratical practices, are pushed out of view. The chapter will compare and contrast three imaginaries of piracy, in order to explore the ramifications of this process. The pirate as criminal and the pirate as revolutionary will be explored through a discussion of the recent debate around the Stop Online Piracy Act (SOPA) and the Protect Intellectual Property Act (PIPA), and the recent shutdown of digital locker website Megaupload. Following on from this discussion, a subsequent examination of *Roadshow Films Pty Ltd & Ors v iiNet Ltd* will instead position the pirate as a neutral media consumer, establishing piracy as a banal form of media practice.

In so doing, this chapter will draw on work by Lawrence Liang (2005, 2009), Kavita Philip (2005), Rosemary Coombe (1998) and Rebecca Tushnet (2004), in order to outline the residual authorial capacity that can be inherent within the neutral pirate. Imaginaries that populate the public sphere regularly fail to acknowledge both the productive and creative capacities of the pirate figure as a liminal subject and the 'dialogic' nature of cultural production and consumption (Coombe 1998). The chapter views the neutral pirate as the imaginary best able to illuminate these capacities, but also raises the possibility of abandoning the term 'piracy' completely, as the word fails to capture these nuances and too often falls victim to an unproductive criminal/hero dichotomy.

The relationship between authorship and piracy

In order to seriously engage with the pirate, this essay will move beyond the pirate's traditional position at the edges of legality, and instead undertake a positive analysis of piracy, treating the pirate as a productive and heterogeneous figure. This is a substantial shift away from how most scholars have approached piracy, and a brief examination of the scholarly record reveals a deep ambivalence about the pirate, most clearly seen in the often arbitrary distinctions that are made between commercial and non-commercial piracy. When discussing commercial piracy, scholars usually refer to large-scale operations that occur in street markets throughout the global South (for examples see Sundaram 2010; Athique 2008). It can also refer to services like Kazaa!, where businesses are built off the back of widespread digital piracy (Rimmer 2007). Conversely, non-commercial piracy such as bootlegging, particular file-sharing practices or transformative amateur media creation, that may or may not fall under particular copyright exceptions such as fair use or fair dealing provisions, are generally viewed in a positive light by many scholars (Benkler 2006; Jenkins 2006), who see this sort of copying as inherently 'creative'. These differences lead to unequal mobilisations of the pirate and piracy, and so these terms are often imbued with a questionable ideology.

Such trends are particularly noticeable when looking at the work of scholars who focus on contemporary issues surrounding digital media. While they eagerly critique the hegemonic tendencies of copyright law, the majority are happy to either distance or seriously qualify their support for 'piracy'. Noted copyright reform campaigner and scholar Lawrence Lessig, for example, argues that large-scale, commercial piracy "is not just a moral wrong, but a legal wrong" (2004, 63). Further, while Lucas Hilderbrand (2010) is willing to recover bootlegging from its 'negative' or 'criminal' connotations, he still refuses to acknowledge other acts of piracy as a productive force. In Hilderbrand's eyes, while bootlegging is concerned with the egalitarian or productive redistribution of culture and information, pirates steal for profit, and are simply involved in the commercial duplication and the sale of knockoffs. He is willing to acknowledge the "grey areas and contradictions" (2010, 23), which remain in his differentiation, but stops short of providing a detailed argument for maintaining it.

Lawrence Liang (2005) and Kavita Philip (2005) have come closest to clearly outlining the issues that these predominantly Western scholars have with commercial piracy. Liang (2005, 10) notes that their opposition generally can be classified as either 'strategic or ethical'. Many might have little opposition to commercial piracy, but are wary of supporting such a problematic practice as part of their advocacy against stricter IP regimes. Of greater concern to these scholars however, are the ethical distinctions that 'free culture' advocates such as Richard Stallman and Lawrence Lessig make between commercial and non-commercial piracy. In comparison to media practices such as remix culture and sampling, which have creative potential, these writers view non-transformative commercial piracy as a practice with few redeeming features, and in particular position Asian piracy as a "limit point of difference from bourgeois law" (Philip 2005, 212). But, as Liang goes on to argue, this is an intellectual position that is not only rooted in privilege, but also one that refuses to acknowledge alternative ways of looking at piracy. Conversely, Liang, through a postcolonial reading of citizenship, convincingly situates non-transformative piracy as a form of cultural infrastructure that provides disenfranchised citizens from the global south with access to cultural goods (2005; 2009). He offers a pathway through the vague assumptions that surround the spectre of piracy and the pirate, suggesting that any such future analysis must shift from looking at what piracy is, but rather at what it does (2005, 15).

In addition to this work, a group of legal scholars have recently turned their attention towards the communicative potential of non-transformative copying, echoing the attempt to frame piracy as productive. This scholarship is another useful way of extending our perceptions of the pirate, as it frees us from only being able to think about piracy as a positive strategy when available to culturally disenfranchised subjects. Rebecca Tushnet (2004), for example, makes a convincing case for the free speech capacities of non-transformative copying and in a similar fashion; additionally, John Tehranian (2011) explores the ways in which copyrighted works can still shape and form personal identity. These works suggest that use, consumption and even pure non-transformative copying can serve a vital social purpose (Tushnet 2004, 566), raising questions around exactly what constitutes 'piracy'. This work represents a worthy attempt to understand non-transformative copying and commercial piracy as a potentially progressive social practice, rather than a practice that can only exist and be understood in relation to the broader legal framework of copyright law.

The chapter contributes to this emerging space of scholarly interest by conducting a holistic investigation of the figure of the pirate, one that allows commercial piracy and non-transformative copying to be viewed as an activity which can be analysed and understood, not just as an extant problem or as an issue of taxonomy, but as a practice and object of analysis worthwhile in and of itself. The following section will examine various imaginaries of the pirate, outlining the limited scope available to the pirate in contemporary discourse, before drawing on evidence from a recent court case to outline the mundane realities of piracy. Over the course of this analysis, the true figure of the pirate slowly emerges – as a subject in copyright law but also as a political agent and a potential creative force – and a case is made for viewing the pirate as a productive site that requires serious analysis.

Imagining the Pirate: The 'activist' pirate and the SOPA and PIPA protests

The standard limited imaginaries of the pirate figure become particularly apparent when looking at the debate that raged over the potential enactment of SOPA and its Senate sister bill PIPA, two anti-piracy bills which were due to be enacted by the United States legislature in 2011. Despite emerging public concern around the scope of the legislation, the bills themselves were introduced to the House and the Senate respectively with strong bipartisan support (Carter and Grim 2011), and the Motion Picture Association of America, the Recording Industry Association of America and the U.S. Chamber of Commerce also publicly backed the bill (McCullagh 2012). The text of the legislation itself was concerned with offshore websites who are infringing the copyright of United States businesses and creative artists. Whereas PIPA was a comparatively measured bill, only targeting "domain name system providers, financial companies, and ad networks" that supported or dealt with the offending website (McCullagh 2012). SOPA was seen to be much more draconian, giving the U.S. Attorney General the power to remove entirely potentially infringing foreign websites from the Internet with little to no oversight, as well as carrying a host of potentially actionable monitoring and blocking privileges.

In a sense, this legislative trajectory should not be a surprise. It echoes the existing narrative of copyright reform in the United States, which has regularly seen the heavy influence of industry in the creation of new legislation in the U.S Congress, leading to the exclusion of the public from the copyright legislative process (Litman 2001). This proposed legislation attempted to marginalize piracy and frame it as a wholly negative crime in a similar fashion to previous copyright reforms, outlining the consistency of this legislative approach and its direct connection to the content industries view of piracy. Rather than situating piracy as generative or even as a passive form of consumption, content industries have historically tended to see piracy as opposed to these two modes of engagement, and the legislative text generally echoes this framing

These proposed bills were consistent with this history, and legislators sought to position this reform as only of concern to 'pirates'. However, it was clear from the emerging public disquiet, that the scope of these bills was broader than intended. This was evidenced by the growing coalition of like-minded technology companies, public interest groups and free speech advocates started to publicly voice their concerns with the bill. It wasn't until Wikipedia announced plans for a twenty-four hour blackout beginning on 18 January 2012 (blocking access to their site and linking visitors to SOPA and PIPA related information and petitions), that a formal day of protest became a reality. Outlining their reasons for the blackout, Wikimedia Foundation Executive Director Sue Gardener (quoting a Wikipedia public statement), referred to the proposed legislation as "devastating" to the "free and open" web, and voiced her support for "everyone's right to freedom of thought and freedom of expression," noting that the response to a call for a protest, saw the largest participation in a community discussion ever seen on Wikipedia. The action publicised the issue of SOPA and PIPA to the general public, with an estimated 90 million people visiting Wikipedia during the blackout, only to be redirected to information about SOPA and PIPA (Cohen 2012). Even establishment media stalwarts like the *New York Times* welcomed the ensuing "collapse...of two flawed bills to prevent online piracy" (Editorial 2012).

Yet this engaged political protest, which also saw people taking to the streets in New York, San Francisco and Seattle (Wortham 2012), barely explored the potential agencies and capacities of piracy. The protest was largely about the problematic means of enforcement rather than questioning whether or not piracy itself was an issue. There was a general critique of the legislative framing of piracy, however even this account was limited due to the protesters own tendency toward hyperbole. The debate was largely positioned around political issues of democracy, first amendment rights and censorship (Tsukayama 2012), and despite Wikipedia's attempt to globalise these issues, this was a discussion that largely concerned affluent consumers who were on the right side of the information economy. The broader protest was able to elide a full engagement with the pirate figure, and ten days after the event, the *New York Times* saw no problem in separating the righteous anger of SOPA protesters, from the "piracy by Web sites in countries like Russia and China," which were still "a real problem for the nation's creative industries" (Editorial 2012).

The criminal pirate: Megaupload and Kim Dotcom

A day after the SOPA protests, U.S. authorities shut down Hong-Kong based website Megaupload, one of the world's largest file-sharing sites, and arrested and charged seven people residing in New Zealand with copyright crimes. A statement released by the Federal Bureau of Investigations (FBI) and the U.S Department of Justice explains that the individuals were charged with "engaging in a racketeering conspiracy, conspiring to commit copyright infringement, conspiring to commit money laundering, and two substantive counts of criminal copyright infringement" (FBI 2012). The statement goes on to accuse the Megaupload consortium of causing in excess of 500 million dollars harm to 'copyright holders', and earning more than 175 million dollars "through advertising revenue and selling premium memberships" (FBI 2012). Although Megaupload was promoted as a digital locker site, ostensibly for long-term and personal digital storage, the statement alleges that particular activities, such as paying regular uploaders of popular infringing content prove that Megaupload made its money on the back of substantial copyright infringement. These were unprecedented charges, and the arrests represent the start of one of the largest criminal copyright cases in United States history.

The case would appear to be of immediate interest, namely due to the fact that an international anti-piracy operation was successfully conducted within twenty-four hours of worldwide protests against a set of controversial proposed copyright reforms, which aimed to better facilitate such enforcement activities. However, a significant amount of attention was solely focused on Megaupload founder and owner Kim Schmitz (also know as Kim Dotcom). Within hours of his arrest, lurid stories about this well-proportioned, German ex-hacker, who had made millions off the back of his latest venture, emerged. Kim Dotcom commandeered a fleet of luxury cars with suggestive personal numberplates such as 'GOD', 'WANTED' and 'GUILTY', he lived in a New Zealand mansion worth over US 20 million dollars (TorrentFreak 2010), and for added novelty value, for a period of time he also was the world's number one player on popular online multiplayer game *Call of Duty: Modern Warfare 3* (MW3) (Kim Dotcom aka MEGARACER is #1 in MW3, 2011). To add to this intriguing portrait, in the initial raid, he was arrested in a panic room, which he retired to, following "a prearranged plan formulated by his bodyguard" (TorrentFreak 2010).

At the time of writing, the case has not yet been adjudicated, nor the accused extradited; however, no matter the result, what is of particular interest is how Kim Dotcom conveniently fit into an established narrative around criminality, as he engaged in the expected activities of a high-flying criminal entrepreneur. This positioning of Kim Dotcom as a 'criminal pirate', is not so much a comment on his guilt or innocence, but rather a comment on how the pirate figure can be so easily positioned as one of excess. Indeed, whereas the SOPA and PIPA protests aimed to position their 'use' and any accusation of piracy as excessively virtuous, in comparison, Kim Dotcom was framed as excessively criminal, and indeed a master of excess in all of its forms, be it bodily, or in terms of his 'geekiness' (as noted in his ridiculously high MW3 ranking).

Despite Megaupload being the 13th most visited Internet site at one point (Superseding indictment 2012, 2), the discourse around Dotcom echoed the awkward discursive positioning of the *New York Times.* Piracy was something that foreigners did, and in particular eccentric foreign criminals. Although everyday users regularly accessed Megaupload, the ensuing narrative was able to differentiate these activities, from the clearly criminal 'piracy' of Kim Dotcom. However, as the following detailed examination of the ongoing case *Roadshow Films Pty Ltd & Ors v iiNet Ltd* shows, piracy itself functions in opposition to these previous examples. Rather than the pirate being a figure of democratic or indeed criminal excess, a more productive way of understanding the pirate figure is to view it as a terribly mundane figure.

The 'ordinary' pirate: Roadshow Films Pty Ltd & Ors v iiNet

Roadshow Films Pty Ltd & Ors v iiNet Ltd offers a valuable space from which to explore the practice of piracy and the pirate figure. The legal framing of the case is relatively narrow, with the majority of the case centred on questions of authorisation and reasonable steps. Robert Burrell and Kimberlee Weatherall offer a succinct summary of the case, which the full bench of the High Court of Australia found in favour of iiNet:

> The High Court [was] being asked to determine whether an Australian ISP, iiNet, which refused to implement a graduated response policy, [could] be held liable for having authorised the copyright infringement of its subscribers (2012, 725)

Despite appearing to be a relatively limited legal brief, the case is a touchstone for a number of pressing issues around digital regulation, and as David Lindsay (2012, 53.1) notes:

> ...[t]he decision is significant, both domestically and internationally, as it is the first time that a court at the apex of a national legal system has considered the liability of an ISP for infringements committed by its subscribers.

Therefore, as will become apparent throughout this discussion, the case cannot avoid engaging with the broader policy debate around digital piracy and the resulting judgment carries a wider impact than just the issues of infringement and authoriation at hand.

The case itself has had a problematic trajectory, with the applicants appealing every step of the way. After an initial appeal to the full bench of the Federal Court of Australia was dismissed, the subsequent appeal to the full bench of the High Court was heard in late 2011 and a judgment was handed down on 20 April 2012. While this drawn out legal to and fro provides a wealth of information to analyse, this essay will focus predominantly on the initial Federal Court case, rather than the judgement of the Full Court of the Federal Court or the High Court, as the substantive facts of the case are clearly outlined in the lower court, with only the specific aspects of the appeal dealt with in the High Court judgement. The setting of a court case provides a valuable space from which to assess the figure of the pirate, as unlike the rhetorical flourishes, which often inform public debate and the process of legislative reform, in the arena of a courtroom, statements and facts do not go unchallenged and specificity becomes all important when identifying and locating both acts of piracy and the pirate figure proper.

The applicants in the case were "34 film and television production companies that own copyright in an extensive catalogue of popular movies and television series, [and] the litigation [was] co-ordinated by the Australian Federation Against Copyright Theft (AFACT)," who accused one of Australia's largest Internet service providers of authorising infringement committed by its customers via BitTorrent (Burrell and Weatherall 2012, 726). However, this case has an extensive history and the initial charge was constructed strategically, it being merely the final stage in AFACT's sustained effort to establish and ultimately win a landmark online piracy case. They began testing the waters in September 2007, when they hired web security firm DtectNet to investigate "190 Australian ISPs in relation to four different types of file-sharing protocols" (Roadshow Films Pty Ltd v iiNet Limited 2010). They then narrowed their investigations to the BitTorrent protocol and targeted four Australian ISPs: Optus, Internode, Exetel and iiNet.

AFACT then went on to assist in the general collection of evidence for the applicants. Aaron Guy Herps, Manager of Digital Affairs for AFACT signed up to iiNet, and on 27 June 2008, went to and used uTorrent to download popular films and television programs of the applicants. A few months later, between 11 to 20 February 2009, Herps repeated this process, but employed an IP address filter, which allowed uTorrent to only connect to iiNet users. AFACT Operations Manager Greg Fraser also assisted in this process, and collectively their efforts, ably assisted by the Dtectnet software, allowed AFACT to prove clear evidence of copyright infringement (Roadshow Films Pty Ltd v iiNet Limited 2010). They were allowed to select twenty of these accounts (herein referred to as RC-20) that would stand in as a representative sample of infringers during the court case.

The authorization charge levelled at iiNet stemmed from their apparent refusal to take action following allegations against their infringing users. From 2 June 2008 to 9 August 2009, AFACT sent weekly emails to Michael Malone, Managing Director of iiNet, alleging that particular iiNet users had infringed copyright. A spreadsheet was attached to the email detailing the date and time of infringement, the IP address of the customer, the particular films and television shows downloaded and the studio to which the particular piece of intellectual property was attached. AFACT alleged that as per the terms and conditions of iiNet's Customer Relationship Agreement, iiNet should have disconnected these users rather than continuing to serve the infringing users, despite allegedly 'knowing' that they were consistently infringing copyright. The applicants also intimated that the structure of iiNet's data plans and their actions (or rather lack of) regarding users who pirated, suggested that the company had a direct financial interest in continuing to ignore this sort of activity (Roadshow Films Pty Ltd v iiNet Limited 2010).

Conversely, iiNet argued that the AFACT notices carried no legal weight. While AFACT viewed their weekly notices as clear cut evidence, iiNet contended that any legal issues should be passed on to the relevant authorities, and that "iiNet will not take the responsibility of judge and jury in order to impose arbitrary and disproportionate penalties purely on the allegations of AFACT" (Roadshow Films Pty Ltd v iiNet Limited 2010). Michael Malone and Steven Dalby also argued that the actual spreadsheets were not self-evident, and that they had difficulty understanding exactly what AFACT was alleging, or what they expected iiNet to do. The second plank of iiNet's argument was that mere provision of the Internet could not be seen to be inducing or even authorising copyright infringement, and noted that the infringements took place exclusively through the BitTorrent system, which is not an illegal protocol, and not under iiNet's control. Furthermore, by cutting off a user's access to the Internet, they wouldn't just be cutting off the means of infringement, but would also be cutting off their access to a host of other services such as access to Internet banking, news and email, and that this would represent a disproportionate punishment, especially when based on such limited evidence.

Federal Court Judge Justice Cowdroy found in iiNet's favour and drawing on precedent set by landmark authorization case *University of NSW v Moorhouse*, decided "that the respondent did not provide the 'means' of infringement' in the sense that the phrase was used by Gibbs J, 'in that it did not extend an invitation to the iiNet users to use its facilities to do acts comprised in the copyright of the Copyright Owners" (Roadshow Films Pty Ltd v iiNet Limited 2010). His judgement continued, noting that the respondent did not stand in the way of copyright holders pursuing people who had "directly infringed their copyright" or "constituent parts of the BitTorrent system for authorisation," that iiNet had "adopted and reasonably implemented a repeat infringer policy". Further, he noted that the infringement notices supplied by AFACT were in no way self-evident, and that AFACTs own name "blurs the distinction between tortuous copyright infringement and criminal acts involving copyright".

Undeterred by this decision, the collection of production companies marshalled by AFACT appealed to the full bench of the Federal Court, and subsequently took their case to the High Court, who dismissed the appeal. The final judgment was unequivocal, noting that "the concept and the principles of the statutory tort of authorisation of copyright infringement are not readily suited to enforcing the rights of copyright owners," and that AFACT's demands of disconnection, presented ISPs with an 'uncertain legal standard'. However, rather than providing closure to this long-running saga, the High Court instead gestured to Government, sagely noting that "pressures for change…are best resolved by legislative processes rather than by any extreme exercise in statutory interpretation by judicial decisions" (Roadshow Films Pty Ltd v iiNet Ltd 2012).

The RC-20 and the banal realities of piracy

The arguments and evidence advanced by both iiNet and the collective of production companies in the Federal Court case provide a compelling picture of modern day practices of piracy. The Internet usage and downloading practices of the RC-20 accounts, which feature throughout the case, are analysed intensely and from this evidentiary base, we can start to draw out a clearer picture of the pirate figure as it operates under copyright law. A number of particular aspects of this case demand attention, and a close reading reveals that piracy is better understood as a discrete media practice, and one that is not particularly profitable, rather than as an epidemic or indeed a revolutionary practice. Instead of being viewed as outlaw consumers or revolutionary protestors, the pirate can instead be viewed as a mainstream digital citizen, more interested in questions of infrastructure and access than opposition and exclusion.

In the initial hearing the applicants attempted to argue that one of the reasons that iiNet ignored the AFACT warning notices, was because it was more commercially advantageous for them to allow users to keep infringing copyright. However, as Justice Cowdroy made clear in his judgement, this claim would only be substantiated if subscribers to iiNet used up ever-increasing amounts of bandwidth and then upgraded to a more expensive plan. Of the selected RC-20 accounts, only ten subscribers actually did this, and one that did so actually reverted back to a cheaper plan. In addition to this, fifteen of the twenty subscribers "used up their full monthly quota regularly," meaning that these 'pirates' were in commercial terms, some of iiNet's least profitable subscribers. This activity stood in stark contrast to the appellants attempt to frame the RC-20 as voracious consumers of pirate media, who needed more and more bandwidth to maintain their downloading habits. In a series of exchanges during his cross-examination, iiNet CEO Matthew Malone explained how many of these users were not necessarily solely engaged in illegal copyright infringement, but instead were most likely balancing these practices with the legal consumption of numerous other forms of media (Roadshow Films Pty Ltd v iiNet Limited 2010).

This position was supported by a further finding of the court, which again questioned the incessant framings of piratical excess outlined by the appellants. The RC-20 were selected as a representative example of copyright infringers, and it was never in doubt that many of these Internet users pirated regularly. However, as Malone suggested earlier, the court found that copyright infringement was "not a primary or even significant usage of quota on th[e]se accounts," even when looking at the "worst examples" of infringement (Roadshow Films Pty Ltd v iiNet Limited 2010). This was a challenging finding as it suddenly brought the figure of the pirate forward and approached it holistically. The pirate wasn't an ideological revolutionary storming the barricades of the content industries, or a criminal opportunistically stealing from artists. Instead, pirates were revealed to be simply engaging in a form of media practice, one that existed alongside a number of other mundane activities.

This sense of piratical banality was explored further when Justice Cowdroy productively drew on *Universal Music Australia Pty Ltd v Sharman License Holdings Ltd* in order to establish the difference between the activities of iiNet and its users in relation to the structural operation of file sharing networks in the early 2000s (Roadshow Films Pty Ltd v iiNet Limited 2010). Sharman Networks owned Kazaa, an early P2P client, and their system was shaped around and used solely for the infringement of copyright. Executives actively sought to promote file sharing and frame it as a positive action, with the most obvious example being their 'Join the revolution' advertising campaign, positioning piracy as a political tool:

> THE
> KAZAA
> REVOLUTION
> 30 years of buying the music of [sic] they think you should listen to.
> 30 years of watching the movies they want you to see.
> 30 years of paying the prices they demand.
> 30 years of swallowing what they're shovelling.
> 30 years of buying crap you don't want.
> 30 years of being a sheep.
> Over. With one a single click.
> Peer 2 peer, we're sharing files.
>
> .
>
> 1 by 1, we're changing the world.
> Kazaa is the technology.
> You are the warrior.
> 60 million strong. And rising.

Join the revolution
KAZAA
Share the revolution

This language stands in stark contrast to the activities of the RC-20, who clearly did not access media solely through oppositional or revolutionary infrastructure. This doesn't empty out the politics from the act of piracy, but it does mean that one can start to think of piracy in a more nuanced manner, rather than as something that simply inhabits a marginal and counter-hegemonic site of production and circulation.

Indeed, perhaps the most useful element of iiNet, is that it refuses to remove the pirate figure from the broader legitimate political environment, in which this form of consumption operates. Whereas AFACT were seeking the disconnection of users following allegations of piracy, the Court took time to note the political necessity of the Internet as a technology. The Constitutional Council of France's characterisation of access to the Internet as akin to a 'human right' was mentioned, and the Court took "judicial notice of the fact that the Internet is increasingly the means by which the news is disseminated and created" (Roadshow Films Pty Ltd v iiNet Limited 2010). While the court was predominantly following this line of argument in order to demonstrate the neutrality of iiNet as a service provider, this argument also established the citizenship demands and human rights of alleged pirates and their households. In acknowledging that pirates are citizens, the Court opened up a space for potentially understanding piracy as a legitimate and democratic (as opposed to revolutionary or oppositional) political activity, one that formed part of a genuine attempt to actively engage with questions around general cultural critique (Coombe 1998) and the formation and maintenance of types of cultural infrastructure (Liang 2009).

Towards a new understanding of the pirate

Once the banal nature of piracy is established, the aura of hyperbole around the pirate dissipates and a neutral assessment of the agencies and capacities of this problematic figure can take place. The pirate is too often positioned in opposition to creativity, transformation and all that the author can feasibly represent and a neutral assessment suggests that there is an authorial capacity, which resides within the pirate: one which significantly challenges the hegemonic structure of copyright law. The work of Rosemary Coombe (1998), Kavita Philip (2005) and Rebecca Tushnet (2004) is useful in developing Lawrence Liang's (2009) framing of piracy as a form of cultural 'infrastructure', and helps to outline how non-transformative copying can form part of a progressive social practice, further clarifying and contextualising the piratical activities of the RC-20, and the legal and social arena in which these practices are assessed and debated.

Coombe (1998, 253) explains the historical and institutional background of this separation between author and pirate, noting that the category of the author "reinforced exclusions elsewhere enacted to restrict membership in the public sphere". The "institutionalisation and legitimation of certain modalities of production, circulation, and consumption" helped to "limit the number of cultural producers who might claim authorial privilege" (1998, 253). However, as she argues elsewhere, this very institutionalisation ignores the 'dialogic' nature of culture, and the political and material ways in which such a dialogue is instantiated (1998, 86). She explains how the "overzealous application and continuous expansion of intellectual property protections" limits the "quintessentially human" need to "make meaning, challenge meaning, and transform meaning" (1998, 84), and suggests that the struggle to fix meanings of cultural property through the use of intellectual property rights, limits this ability to "respond to a sign with signs" (1998, 85). This limitation is not just democratically dangerous, Coombe notes, but also calls forth the "simultaneously prohibitive and productive" power of law, invoking the signifying power of the law itself (1998, 87).

Conclusion

Coombe's work helps to situate the practice of copying within a postmodern society, where signs and semiotic inference form a part of daily life, and also explains the quotidian effects of law, where certain forms of authorship and copying are allowed and others marginalised, shaping particular legal subjectivities. These examples, which echo the mundane, daily activities of the RC-20, allow us to reframe copying as a form of cultural communication, existing in a culture where the "repressive function of the law of copyright" is always present, continually policing "transgressive authorial acts" (Philip 2005, 217). This communication can take place in overt displays of cultural critique, such as the transformative practices of parody and satire, but even non-transformative copying can be viewed as a form of authorial agency, with the use and consumption of cultural signs and goods adding to greater cultural literacy, communication and connection, as users engage with the contemporary cultural milieu. This stance is supported by Tushnet (2004, 565-71), who outlines how copying can establish distributive infrastructures of access in developing nations, contribute to the development of self-expression through the shared consumption of cultural material, and can require the exercise of judgement and creativity. All of these practices are materially generative activities, which are supported and sustained by non-transformative copying and in many cases by what the law would otherwise term piracy.

This chapter has established the pirate as a constituent subject with its own productive and creative capacities. Rather than seeking to only highlight 'acceptable' forms of piracy, the pirate has been approached holistically, with the essay weighing up the ramifications of this repositioning. Such a theoretical trajectory has allowed a number of different elements of piracy to come to the fore. The iiNet case outlined the mundane and many times limited nature of what is too often termed excessive piracy, and the subsequent discussion of the generative capacities of piracy have helped to problematize traditional understandings of the pirate figure. This is not to say that the author and pirate are essentially the same, but in explaining the authorial capacities of piracy, this chapter has sought to highlight the porousness between these subjects, a porousness that subverts the artificial barrier that copyright law maintains between them.

Looking ahead, this theoretical repositioning raises serious questions about the validity of the term 'pirate', especially considering the ways scholarship, media and the law itself have consistently positioned it as a figure of revolutionary or criminal transgression. Acknowledging this relational connection between subjects of copyright law seriously challenges the dominant positioning of the author in law, but more importantly brings the pirate back from the margins, and allows it to take up a central role in discussions around copyright law. However, the communicative potential of cultural artefacts, suggests that non-transformative copying will continue to move beyond the discursive constraints placed around it by law. Considering the similar agencies and capacities available to both the author and the pirate, it becomes increasingly clear that terms like 'piracy' simply reinforce unequal institutional structures, at the expense of a fully realised understanding of how we all engage with, create and reproduce cultural artefacts.

References

Ali, Muna and Zhara Murad (2009). "Unravelling narratives of piracy: Discourses of Somali pirates". *darkmatter journal*, 5. Retrieved 10 July 2013, from http://www.darkmatter101.org/site/2009/12/20/unravelling-narratives-of-piracy-discourses-of-somali-pirates/

Athique, Adrian (2008). "The global dynamics of Indian media piracy: export markets, playback media and the informal economy". *Media, Culture and Society*, 30:5, 699-717.

Benkler, Yochai (2006). *The wealth of networks: How social networks transform markets and freedom*. Hartford, CT: Yale University Press.

Burrell, Robert and Kimberlee Weatherall (2012). "Before the High Court: Providing services to copyright infringers: *Roadshow Films Pty Ltd v. iiNet Ltd*". *Sydney Law Review*, 33, 723-753.

Carter, Zach and Ryan Grim (2011). "SOPA, Internet censorship bill, lauded by both parties in key house hearing". *The Huffington Post*, 17 November 2011, Retrieved 14 March 2012, from http://www.huffingtonpost.com/2011/11/16/sopa-Internet-censorship-online-piracy-house-hearing_n_1098255.html

Choi, Bryan (2006). "The Grokster dead-end". *Harvard Journal of Law and Technology*, 19:2, 394-411.

Cohen, Noam (2012). "Wikipedia absence is noted, but as a brief inconvenience". *New York Times*, 18 January 2012. Retrieved 14 March 2012, from http://www.nytimes.com/2012/01/19/business/media/wikipedia-protest-noticed-but-some-yawn.html?_r=0

Coombe, Rosemary (1998). *The cultural life of intellectual properties: Authorship, appropriation and the law*. Durham: Duke University Press.

Editorial (2012). "Beyond SOPA". *New York Times*, 28 January 2012, Retrieved 14 March 2012, from http://www.nytimes.com/2012/01/29/opinion/sunday/beyond-sopa.html

FBI (2012). "Justice Department charges leaders of Megaupload with widespread online copyright infringement". *Federal Bureau of Investigation*, 19 January 2012. Retrieved 14 March 2012, from http://www.fbi.gov/news/pressrel/press-releases/justice-department-charges-leaders-of-megaupload-with-widespread-online-copyright-infringement

Grimmelmann, James (2009). "The ethical visions of copyright law". *Fordham Law Review*, 77:5, 2005-2037.

Hilderbrand, Lucas (2009). *Inherent vice: Bootleg histories of videotape and copyright*. Durham: Duke University Press.

Hunter, Dan (2005). "Culture War". *Texas Law Review*, 83, 1105-1136.

Jenkins, Henry (2006). *Convergence culture: Where old and new media collide*. New York: NYU Press.

"Kim Dotcom aka MEGARACER is #1 in MW3" (2011). *YouTube*. Retrieved 10 July 2013, from http://www.youtube.com/watch?v=l-ltcCF_cAQ

Lessig, Lawrence (2004). *Free culture: How big media uses technology and the law to lock down culture and control creativity.* New York: Penguin.
Lessig, Lawrence (2006). *Code 2.0.* New York: Basic Books.
Liang, Lawrence (2005). "Porous legalities and avenues of participation". *Sarai Reader*, 5, 6-17. Retrieved 10 July 2013, from http://www.sarai.net/journal/05_pdf/01/02_lawrence.pdf
Liang, Lawrence (2009). "Piracy, creativity and infrastructure: Rethinking access to culture". Working paper. Retrieved 10 July 2013, from http://ssrn.com/abstract=1436229
Lindsay, David (2012). "ISP liability for end-user copyright infringements: the High Court decision in Roadshow Films v iiNet". *Telecommunications Journal of Australia*, 62:4, 1- 53.
Litman, Jessica (2001). *Digital copyright.* Prometheus Books. New York.
Loughlan, Patricia (2008). "'You wouldn't steal a car…' Intellectual Property and the language of theft". *Legal Studies Research Paper*, 08:35 (2008). Retrieved 10 July 2013, from http://ssrn.com/abstract=1120585
McCullagh, Declan (2012). "How SOPA would affect you: FAQ," *CNET*, 18 January 2012. Retrieved 14 March 2012, from http://news.cnet.com/8301-31921_3-57329001-281/how-sopa-would-affect-you-faq/?tag=TOCmoreStories.0
Philip, Kavita (2005). "What is a technological author? The pirate function and intellectual property". *Postcolonial Studies*, 8:2, 199-218.
Rimmer, Matthew (2007). *Digital Copyright and the Consumer Revolution: Hands off my iPod.* Cheltenham: Edward Elgar.
Superseding indictment (2012). United States District Court for the Eastern District of Virginia – Alexandria Division.
Sundaram, Ravi (2010). "Pirate Modernity: Delhi's media urbanism". New York: Routledge.
Tehranian, John (2011). "Parchment, pixels and personhood: User rights and the IP (Identity Politics) of IP (Intellectual Property)". *Colorado Law Review*, 82:1, 1 – 84.
"The mega-money world of MegaUpload" (2010). *TorrentFreak* 6 June 2010. Retrieved 14 March 2012, from http://torrentfreak.com/the-mega-money-world-of-megaupload-100606/
Tsukayama, Hayley (2012). "Google to state anti-SOPA stance on home page," *The Washington Post*, 17 January 2012. Retrieved 14 March 2012, from http://articles.washingtonpost.com/2012-01-17/business/35441414_1_wikipedia-blackout-piracy-bills-foreign-rogue-websites
Tushnet, Rebecca (2004). "Copy this essay: How fair use doctrine harms free speech and how copying serves it". *Yale Law Journal*, 144, 534-590.
Wortham, Jenna (2012). "With Twitter, blackouts and demonstrations, web flexes its muscle". *New York Times*, 18 January 2012. Retrieved 14 March 2012, from http://www.nytimes.com/2012/01/19/technology/protests-of-antipiracy-bills-unite-web.html?pagewanted=all

Cases cited

Roadshow Films Pty Ltd & Ors v iiNet Limited [2010]
Roadshow Films Pty Ltd v iiNet Ltd [2012]
Universal Music Australia Pty Ltd v Sharman License Holdings Ltd [2005]
University of NSW v Moorhouse [1975]
Thanks to Esther Milne, Ramon Lobato and Jock Given for their comments on earlier drafts of this essay.

To Name a Thief: Constructing the Deviant Pirate

Virginia Crisp

The term "piracy" is accompanied by considerable amounts of ethical, moral and legal baggage. Indeed, it is often discussed as "nothing but robbery," a heinous act that offends "the most precious aspects of our capitalist system, which protect individuals' property, creativity, and investment" (Pang 2004, 19). Within popular and much academic discourse it is hard to escape the understanding that pirates are nothing more than deviant thieves. On the rare occasions that pirates can escape this categorization, there is still little space to be seen as anything other than subversive radicals or potential consumers. This chapter focuses on a particular form of digital piracy, the circulation of East Asian films within file sharing forums, and asks how the file sharers within this context perceive themselves and to what extent these perceptions are shaped by external discourses on the nature of piracy. By drawing on ethnographic research conducted from 2006-11, I consider how the individuals within these communities understand and negotiate the moral and ethical ramifications of their actions. In doing so, I argue that file sharers within these groups see themselves as distinct from the "real" pirates because their form of copyright infringement does not involve monetary reward.

Piracy is a broad term to describe any instance of "the unauthorized copying, distribution and/or sale of copyrighted content" (Yar 2008, 607). Digital piracy describes a specific form of piracy most commonly associated with the unauthorized distribution of software, music and movie files through the Internet. Within this definition there exists a subcategory of digital piracy: file sharing. File sharing is used to refer to the process of sharing files directly with others through peer-to-peer technology such as BitTorrent.

File sharing is by no means the only form of digital piracy but the terms are often used interchangeably, glossing over the subtle differences between them. For instance, the act of file sharing implies that the user both downloads and uploads digital files through the Internet. On the other hand, while forms of digital piracy may include file sharing, it is possible to engage in digital piracy without ever sharing the downloaded files with others. Such a distinction may be subtle, but it does highlight that the terms are not transposable and that digital piracy takes a variety of forms, of which file sharing is only one.

The academic literature on these various forms of digital piracy is extensive, but within such literature there is often an overriding concern with examining a few key issues: to what extent are the cultural industries damaged/assisted by digital piracy (Liebowitz 2006; Oberholzer-Gee and Stumpf 2007; Zentner 2006); how might 'pirates' be translated into consumers (Bounie, Bourreau and Waelbroek 2007); what factors influence the propensity to engage in digital piracy (Podoshen 2008; Taylor, Ishida and Wallace 2009); and, how effective are the current technological and legal deterrents to digital piracy (Sinha 2010; Waterman 2007)? In many respects these preoccupations could be tentatively linked to any variety of academic disciplines with specialists in economics, psychology, marketing and law all, rather unsurprisingly, prioritizing certain approaches within their research.

As noted above, within this broad and interdisciplinary area of interest, the figure of the digital pirate has been constructed in a number of ways: as deviant thieves, subversive radicals or inquisitive (potential) consumers. These categorizations by no means represent the *only* ways digital pirates are constructed, but I would suggest that certain, rather narrow, constructions are dominant and linked to the priorities and interests of certain groups within both academia and public discourse. The first section of this chapter will examine these constructions in detail, allowing the second half to consider how these constructions have been negotiated and internalized by the file sharers themselves.

The constructed pirate – a deviant thief

Undoubtedly, the most ubiquitous pirate is the figure of the 'deviant thief': instantly recognizable from the anti-piracy rhetoric cultivated and circulated by the copyright owners within the music and movie industries. Overall, this deviant is constructed as someone who only wishes to obtain something for nothing and threatens the very existence of the cultural industries. The deviant thief is often described as young, unconcerned about the rights of creators, lacking in self-control and unaccustomed to paying for digital content. Indeed, the attempt to associate youth with piracy can be seen as part and parcel of the historical tendency to draw links between youth, crime and delinquency (Yar 2008, 609).

This caricature of the deviant pirate has been developed and fostered by the anti-piracy campaigns from the Motion Picture Association of American (MPAA) in the USA and the Federation Against Copyright Theft (FACT) in the UK. Through high profile public awareness campaigns, such organizations have attempted to convince audiences that digital piracy is no different from any other form of property theft. However, in criticizing these attempts, Yar argues that we should see such campaigns as "rhetorical performances"; that is, "...attempts to establish effectively the legitimacy of a given point of view, set of claims or assertions of rights, entitlements and responsibilities" (2008, 210).

Arguably, associating piracy with traditional notions of deviance and theft is problematic on a number of levels. Firstly, associating digital piracy with the theft of goods such as handbags and cars tries to convince audiences of the "equivalence of tangibles and intangibles" (Yar 2008, 610). However, one obvious issue with this equivalence is that digital copies are 'non-rivalrous' goods: thus through obtaining a copy of the latest Hollywood blockbuster, by legal or illegal means, I am not denying that opportunity to anyone else (Condry 2004, 349). Secondly, it has been argued that associating piracy with deviance is a deliberate strategy to control the activities of others by attempting to dictate the boundaries of normality (Denegri-Knott 2004). Indeed, naming piracy as 'theft' supports a deliberate ideological agenda and "labeling unauthorized copying as 'piracy' suggests an undue rhetorical certainty about the property conceptions underlying copyright" (Kretschmer, Klimis and Wallis 2001, 434).

Furthermore, these 'property conceptions' are invariably Western in nature. As such, associating piracy with theft within anti-piracy discourse serves to reinforce the claim that Western notions of copyright and intellectual property (IP) are somehow universal and enduring. Whereas, a historical examination of copyright "shows that copyright laws are the outcome of a political bargaining process and do not necessarily reflect any unwavering norms or values" (Nill and Giepel 2010, 34). With this in mind, the project of an institution such as the World Intellectual Property Organization (WIPO) to produce an international IP system will undoubtedly produce rules and regulations that are devised through such political bargaining. Inevitably, the Western nations who have more power and influence within such an organization, and upon the global stage more generally, will be best placed to mould the global IP regime in their own image and to their own ends.

Furthermore, there are mixed results when it comes to actually *proving* the losses that the cultural industries claim to have sustained as a result of piracy (Krishnan, Smith, Tang and Telang 2007, 205). In fact, some even suggest that "rather than seeing these statistics as facts, one should view them as discursive strategies for attempting to construct a political and public consensus about the immorality of piracy" (Yar 2008, 608). Indeed, many have argued that despite the loud complaints about the threat of illegal circulation of their cultural products, Hollywood is actually making record profits (Lewis 2007; Lobato 2009). So, while profits are undoubtedly decreasing in some areas (for example, the rental market), DVD and cinema ticket sales are actually increasing (van Eijk, Joost Poort and Rutten 2010, 37). Even when evidence has been found to prove that Hollywood is incurring some loss due to piracy, it has also been suggested that those losses have been significantly exaggerated by the film industry (Hennig-Thurau, Henning and Sattler 2007, 14). Indeed, while it is indubitable that the development of the Internet and digital technologies are having far reaching effects on the cultural industries, it is a gross oversimplification to suggest that piracy is chiefly to blame for the state of the industry when other factors such as increasing competition from computer games and mobile phones are undoubtedly also at play (Hennig-Thurau, Henning and Sattler 2007, 14).

The focus within anti-piracy campaigns on the economic losses incurred by the industry reinforce the idea that pirates are nothing but thieves whose activities threaten the continued existence of the cultural industries, and thus cultural production. However, in reality, artistic creation is not dependent on the existence of the cultural industries, those industries exist in order to harness the economic potential of artists and provide a framework for cultural production but they are not *de facto* necessary. Indeed, individuals and collectives create artworks, music and films outside of the associated industries and without economic reward. Whilst many might seek remuneration, economic recompense might not be desirable or achievable for all who create cultural works. However, the anti-piracy rhetoric would have us believe that artists need industries and that those industries are invaluable because they provide economic rewards for the artists who create within them. However, "authors and artists seldom retain control over copyright, but routinely assign those rights to corporate entities who then have virtual *carte blanche* over decisions as to the work's commercial exploitation" (Yar 2008, 616).

Therefore, the industry is not in a war against piracy solely because copyright infringement damages artists and jeopardizes future artistic production, but partly because piracy allows individuals to attain cultural products without the mediation of the cultural industries. Thus, the protection afforded by copyright is jeopardized by individuals who are able to circumvent the control that large corporations have over traditional channels of distribution. Thus, while piracy can be understood as outright theft, it can also be interpreted as a political statement against the commodification of artistic works and/or a wish to challenge the control that a few major corporations hold over most of the cultural industries.

From deviance to subversion

Aside from the oft-criticized figure of the deviant thief, another construction of the 'pirate' is as a 'subversive radical' engaged in a power struggle with the cultural industries. This conception of the digital pirate sees the pirate as liberator, as someone who deliberately challenges the current corporately owned structure of the cultural industries. Such individuals not only have opposing views about current IP and copyright regimes, but also wish to destabilize the pre-existing monopolistic models for the distribution of music, films, software and games.

One of the reasons that such a figure can exist is because the image of the music and film businesses is often far from favourable. According to Bishop, "with such a history of unfairness and one-sided contract negotiations with artists, greed, the lust for power, price gouging, and price fixing, the industry has worked hard to earn its unfavorable reputation" (2004, 101). Indeed, it has been suggested that some music file sharers "are likely to justify their behavior with reference to the perceived egregiousness of record companies" (Huang 2005, 40). Furthermore, it has also been claimed that the motivation to share files online might be linked to a wish to distance oneself from the taint of the commercially orientated music industry or in some circumstances as a means of actively challenging the control wielded over the music industry by a few large companies (Giesler and Pohlmann 2003, 273).

That is not to say that all pirates and file sharers view the industry negatively. I have discussed elsewhere that my own file sharer subjects are surprisingly supportive towards certain sectors of the industry (Crisp 2012b). Marshall also suggests in his study of bootleggers that while "their actions seem to critique it," bootleggers and tape traders actually "offer strong ideological support for the legitimate industry" (2003, 57). Indeed, the romantic "ideas about art and creativity which form the bedrock of the legitimate industry" are equally important for traders and bootleggers who distribute content precisely because it brings them closer to the revered 'artist' (Marshall 2003, 69). Marshall suggests that while academic scholars would readily identify bootlegging and trading as an anti-industry political statement, the individuals concerned are unlikely to view themselves in such terms (Marshall 2003, 64–65). Thus, while it may be true that some individuals view their participation in the illicit circulation of goods as a means of destabilizing the current media landscape, this is by no means the only interpretation. Indeed, even though it may be tempting to assign to file sharing behaviour a political motivation, it may be that the file sharers themselves do not view their activities as particularly politically motivated.

Pirate as consumer

Moving on from the subversive pirate, the potential consumer conception of the digital pirate is a picture of an individual who is probably not doing as much damage to the creative industries as is often claimed, and furthermore can be seen as an *explorer*: a voracious consumer who uses file sharing as a form of sampling so they might investigate products before they buy (Bounie, Bourreau and Waelbroek 2007, 168). Indeed, these authors are not alone in their suggestion that users may in some instances use file sharing as a form of sampling content before purchasing it, rather than instead of it (Cenite et al. 2009, 208). In such a context the downloaded copy is not seen as equivalent or equal in value to the purchased product and so sampling online encourages the individual to seek out the 'superior' version through legitimate channels (Peitz and Waelbroeck 2006, 908). Thus, while it may seem like the availability of free copies would cause sales to fall, this need not necessarily be the case if the copy was not seen as equivalent to the 'original'. When a film airs on television, there is a growth in both illegal downloads and legitimate sales (Smith and Telang 2009, 321). This is because a "television broadcast of a movie is sufficiently differentiated from the DVD version (in terms of convenience, usability, and content)" (Smith and Telang 2009, 322). However, it is important to note that while there is some support for the sampling argument, unauthorized copying takes various forms, meaning that this argument is not applicable to all forms of digital piracy (Holt and Morris 2009, 382) and is not the only way that pirates are seen as potential consumers.

According to van Eijk, Poort and Rutten, "when it comes to attending concerts, and expenses on DVDs and games, file sharers are the industry's largest customers" (2010, 44). However, the authors do not claim that there is a causal relationship between downloading and purchasing behaviour, they rather recognize that file sharers are often early adopters of technology and enthusiasts who are likely to voraciously seek out content using legal and illegal methods. Consequently, while piracy may be still understood as both immoral and illegal within such discussions, these criticisms might be accompanied by the suggestion that piracy has nonetheless, "directly and indirectly spurred the creation of legitimate and innovative business models" (Choi and Perez 2007, 169).

Do file sharers dream of virtual pirates?

The following section of this chapter considers how certain communities of file sharers have internalized, interpreted, rationalized and appropriated these varying understandings of pirates as deviants, radicals or consumers. The communities in question consisted of two file sharing forums, referred to within this chapter by the pseudonyms *Chinaphiles* and *Eastern Legends*. Both forums provide links to downloadable copies of East Asian films. They might also provide links to tangentially connected materials such as anime, soundtracks, music or *manga*, but the main focus of each forum is the discussion and circulation of East Asian films. The research concerning these communities was part of a wider research project conducted from 2006-11 into formal and informal distribution networks for East Asian film that has also been discussed elsewhere (see Crisp 2012a; 2012b).

As will be seen, the discussion below illustrates how the file sharers attempt to distance themselves from the notion of piracy, defining and labeling others as the 'real' pirates. Indeed, we can see within these forums that the label 'piracy' is not appropriated as a badge of honour but is viewed in distinctly negative terms. The 'pirate' label is used by the file sharers to label others as deviant: reinforcing their own moral credentials by juxtaposing their not-for-profit 'sharing' activities against the circulation of tangible goods in exchange for monetary reward. The file sharers align themselves with a moral code that constructs their activities as a form of sharing that facilitates the 'sampling' of film texts. They imagine their own activities as ultimately promotional thus distinguishing themselves from the immoral, illegal and indefensible actions of the for-profit pirates. By constructing others as encompassing all the negative traits of piracy they leave themselves free to align their own activities with the more palatable notions of sharing, sampling and reciprocity.

Such distinctions can be seen to mirror those observed by Marshall in relation to tape traders and bootleggers, where tape traders see their "activities as vastly different from those of commercial bootleggers": practices that might appear indistinguishable to the untrained eye (Marshall 2003, 66). Of particular importance is the role that money has to play in the equation. For the file sharers discussed here, and the tape traders examined by Marshall, it is important for their sense of authenticity that each group defines themselves against the more commercial concerns of those that profit from the illegal distribution of goods. Thus, understanding themselves as different from the real pirates is not just about accepting the anti-piracy rhetoric and demonizing the 'deviants', it is arguably about distancing oneself from the taint of commercialization so as to maintain the authenticity of one's fan practices.

Within discussions on both forums, an emphasis was often put on the fact that file sharing activities *should* be used as a form of sampling. Forum members would argue that they owned vast DVD collections, the contents of which would have been brought to their attention through downloading (Garfeld, BBC News Article Discussion, 2009).[1] Indeed, there is evidence that file sharers often suggest their activities are a form of sampling and thus not harmful to content creators (Levin, Conway and Rhee 2004, 48; Bounie, Bourreau, and Waelbroeck 2007, 168).

Another reason that forum members saw file sharing as sampling was that the files they downloaded were generally of low quality (Quill, Thanks Discussion, 2004) and thus were not seen to be equivalent to legitimate purchased DVDs (Murb, Thanks Discussion, 2004). According to one forum member, Restel, downloads, regardless of their quality, were no substitute for the 'real thing' (Thanks Discussion, 2004). Such assertions mirror the ideas from earlier that the availability of free copies might not negatively affect sales as long as the copies were not considered equivalent (Peitz and Waelbroeck 2006). Indeed, as well as being concerned about the inferior quality of the downloaded files, forum members also complained that the virtual files lacked the 'shelf impact' of bought DVDs (Helo, Best Movie Discussion, 2003). Thus, in a similar way to the tape traders and bootleggers discussed by Marshall, while the activities of file sharers

1 Due to the illegal nature of the activities on the forums under discussion it was decided to provide pseudonyms for both the overall forums and their individual members. Furthermore, since any direct quotations would be searchable in Google, no direct quotations from forum discussions have been used within the chapter. Instead, user comments have been paraphrased accompanied by an intext reference indicating the forum member's pseudonym, the discussion thread that is being paraphrased and the year in which the discussion thread began.

appear on the surface to go against the industry, they actually reinforce its position. Through fetishizing the official physical DVDs produced by the industry, they legitimize and reinforce the dominant position that the cultural industries have as gatekeepers to culture.

Not only were downloads perceived as inferior, certain methods were employed to encourage members to view the materials on the forum as 'samples' and to encourage users to purchase films that they particularly enjoyed. As a result, an understanding that files were inferior copies and thus could only be samples was not organically present within the forums but was instead actively promoted by certain forum members. This might be through a general plea to support East Asian cinema (Helo, Thanks Discussion, 2004) or by encouraging individuals to purchase specific DVDs (Kolmon, Thanks Discussion, 2004). In other cases, particular companies were referred to as specifically in need or worthy of support (Fishtank, BBC News Article Discussion, 2005). Thus, as in other work on file sharing, individuals are more likely to view their activities as sampling, and feel prompted to purchase legal copies at a later date if they feel an emotional connection with a particular artist or industry (Condry 2004, 353).

However, we cannot assume that just because file sharers perceive their activities to be a form of sampling that it actually is. Although users claim to have extensive DVD collections (and some undoubtedly have) it does not mean that there is a causal relationship between their online sampling and their legal consumption of DVDs. Indeed, it may be that the file sharer's claim that their activities are not harming anyone is a way of justifying their participation in some ethically dubious behaviour. For example, Hinduja argues that, "individuals are largely allegiant (rather than oppositional) to a normative belief system, and must therefore employ justifications to engage in deviant behavior" (2007, 190-91). If we were to accept that piracy is a form of deviance, then would we not expect file sharers to justify their own actions to make them less morally reprehensible?

This is a question worth considering, though I would argue it is rather patronizing to suggest that file sharers need to exist in a constant state of denial because they cannot face up to the moral realities of their own behaviour. Indeed, it has been posited that file sharers are more than capable of making their own distinctions between different forms of piracy and their own decisions about the ethical nature of each activity (Coyle, Gould, Gupta and Gupta 2009, 1034). Furthermore, there is also some question concerning whether individuals are as concerned with conforming to norms as is often suggested (Hinduja 2007, 191). Within both *Chinaphiles* and *Eastern Legends* there was evidence that file sharing was not undertaken in a vacuum and forum members were acutely aware of the wider ethical and legal concerns that surrounded their activities. There was much discussion of, and disagreement concerning, larger questions of ownership, copyright, and the free circulation of information and intellectual property. Interestingly, within such discussions it became clear that forum members perceived their own sharing and sampling activities as something other than piracy. Indeed, they constructed their own identity as file sharers in opposition to the revenue stealing, 'for-profit' pirates.

Overall, it was profit and commercial concerns that were considered problematic. In particular this concern was leveled against the perceived commercial focus within certain sectors of the film industry. Thus, the forum members attempted to establish the morality of their own file sharing activities by denigrating any activity where tangible goods were sold for profit: whether legally or illegally. This was made apparent during discussions related to Hollywood where discussions described DVDs as generally overpriced (Detset, BBC News Article Discussion, 2009) and the film industry as "greedy" (Elegent, BBC News Article Discussion, 2009).

The 'real pirates' were identified as those that sought to gain economically from file sharing. Within both communities, individuals distanced themselves from the illegal and unethical connotations of the more pejorative term 'piracy' by defining it as something other than file sharing: that is, the for-profit distribution of physical goods. Within one particular discussion of the sale of DVD bootlegs on eBay it became clear exactly how for-profit piracy was viewed within the forums. The discussion concerned the fact that 'custom rips' made by members of the *Eastern Legends* community had been used by a third party to create bootleg DVDs available for sale on eBay (eBay Discussion, 2009). One particular forum member, Gouy, described the activities on *Eastern Legends* as individuals sharing their collections of bought DVDs, and so he/she saw their actions as very different from bootleggers or 'The Scene' (eBay Discussion, 2009). Thus, when it was discovered that a forum member was *profiting* from the 'custom rips' circulated within the forum that individual was instantly labeled a pirate by members of the community (Solon, eBay Discussion, 2009). A reward was even offered by one of the administrators for information that could identify the culprit and so that they might be dealt with appropriately (eBay Discussion, 2009).

Again, parallels can be drawn with Marshall's work as one group engaged in illegal distribution (file sharers/tape traders) show contempt for those who *profit* from circulating the very same materials (Marshall 2003, 66). Indeed, within the *Eastern Legends* community there was some discussion of how the transgression should be dealt with. This debate mainly centered on how the forum member selling the bootlegs should be punished, with one member suggesting that the individual be reported to eBay (Maloi, eBay Discussion, 2009). In addition, there was also some discussion of how to protect the forum members from future unauthorized distribution of their 'custom rips'. Indeed, there was some concern that measures be taken to prevent a similar situation arising in the future with one person arguing that forum rips be watermarked to avoid future "pirating" (Xirit, eBay Discussion, 2009).

The suggestion of watermarking again highlights how the forum members perceive their own activities as very different from the eBay bootlegger. The fact that watermarking is commonly used by the film industry as an anti-piracy measure highlights how the appropriation of such a strategy confirms the distinction drawn between file sharing and piracy. The suggestion of watermarking was made in order to protect what the forum members perceived as, in some respects, their own intellectual property. Through the laborious encoding process and the addition of elements such as 'fansubs', the file sharers saw their activities as 'adding value' to the files they circulated (Crisp 2012a). Thus, they would not align their own activities with pirates who simply redistributed the work of others.

In addition to the concern that the eBay seller was violating their own rights, community members were also particularly concerned that his or her actions might draw unwanted attention to their community (Usef, eBay Discussion, 2009). The communities in question are password protected and members are particularly concerned about keeping their communities hidden due to the possible repercussions of being discovered by the authorities. Thus, when other file sharing websites and forums were shut down due to anti-piracy crackdowns, this was obviously of some interest to the members of the forums and would be discussed at length. Interestingly, within such discussions, forum members would suggest that other sites were targeted precisely because they asked for donations or subscriptions from members (Newzbin Discussion, 2010). Again, this represents the perception that somehow being associated with profit or commercialization was what earmarked the 'real' pirates.

While I have made the claim that some forum members discussed their activities as somehow distinct from the for-profit pirates, there was by no means a consensus within the community. Indeed, some forum members thought it hypocritical that others were complaining about the actions of the eBay seller (Mellos, eBay Discussion, 2009) while others suggested that bootlegs bought on eBay formed an important part of their collection (Avves, eBay discussion, 2009). Indeed, the differing opinions expressed within this particular discussion thread suggest that there was not a universally ethical understanding of piracy within the forum. Nevertheless, it is clear that some forum members see their activities as sampling, and thus perceive a significant distinction between their own sharing practices and other forms of piracy.

Conclusion

This chapter has examined the dominant construction of digital pirates as deviant thieves, subversive radicals or potential consumers. In doing so, I have discussed that the labels of theft and deviance most commonly attributed to piracy serve to support a particular ideological agenda and maintain the status of the cultural industries as the primary gatekeepers of cultural content. By considering how these common constructions of piracy have been received within file sharing communities, we find that the pirates themselves have neither entirely embraced nor rejected the construction of the deviant thief. Instead they have adopted parts of the anti-piracy rhetoric to pour scorn on those that they perceive to be the real pirates: that is, both those who engage in the unauthorized circulation of physical goods for economic reward as well as some of the major owners of copyright.

On some occasions file sharing might be seen as a political act to subvert the shackles of the creative industries over the artistic output of musicians and filmmakers. Indeed, within the work of Giesler and Pohlmann (2003) there emerges the suggestion that file sharers might be motivated by a wish to either avoid the taint of the industry or try to topple the balance of power. However, among the file sharers discussed here we see very little evidence of individuals who wish to subvert the industry. Indeed, rather than wear piracy as a badge of honour, individuals on these forums see piracy as a resolutely negative categorization, one they wish to avoid being associated with. In order to establish their own 'ethical' credentials in opposition to others, members of both forums are more likely to cast themselves in the mould of the potential consumer and dedicated fan: understanding their file sharing practices as a method of product sampling rather than theft.

References

BBC News Article Discussion (July, 2005). *Chinaphiles Forum.* Retrieved September 4, 2009.

Best Movie Discussion Thread (August, 2003). *Chinaphiles Forum.* Retrieved September 9, 2009.

Bounie, David, Marc Bourreau and Patrick Waelbroek (2007). "Pirates or Explorers? Analysis of Music Consumption in French Graduate Schools". *Brussels Economic Review*, 50:2, 167-192.

Bishop, Jack (2004). "Who are the Pirates? The Politics of Piracy, Poverty, and Greed in a Globalized Music Market". *Popular Music and Society*, 27:1, 101-106. doi: 10.1080/0300776042000166639

Cenite, Mark, Michelle Wanzheng Wang, Chong Peiwen and Germaine Shimin Chan (2009). "More Than Just Free Content: Motivations of Peer-to-Peer File Sharers". *Journal of Communication Inquiry* 33:3, 206-221. doi: 10.1177/0196859909333697

Condry, Ian (2004). "Cultures of Music Piracy: An Ethnographic Comparison of the US and Japan". *International Journal of Cultural Studies,* 7:3, 343-363. doi: 10.1177/1367877904046412

Coyle, James R., Stephen J. Gould, Pola Gupta and Reetika Gupta (2009). "'To Buy or to Pirate': The Matrix of Music Consumers' Acquisition-Mode Decision-Making". *Journal of Business Research,* 62, 1031-1037. doi: 10.1016/j.jbusres.2008.05.002

Crisp, Virginia (2012a). "'BLOODY PIRATES!!! *shakes fist*': Reimagining East Asian film distribution and reception through online filesharing networks". *Journal of Japanese and Korean Cinema,* 3:1, 65-72.

Crisp, Virginia (2012b). "Pirates and Professionals: How Filesharers Perceive Film Distribution Companies". Paper Presented at the *Chinese Film Forum Symposium.* March 28-29, Cornerhouse, Manchester, UK.

Denegri-Knott, Janice (2004). "Sinking the Online 'Music Pirates': Foucault, Power and Deviance on the Web". *Journal of Computer-Mediated Communication,* 9:4, Retrieved 10 July, 2013, from http://jcmc.indiana.edu/vol9/issue4/denegri_knott.html

eBay Discussion Thread (June 2009). *Eastern Legends Forum.* Retrieved December 3, 2009.

van Eijk, Nico, Joost Poort and Paul Rutten (2010). "Legal, Economic and Cultural Aspects of File Sharing". *Communications and Strategies,* 77:1, 35-54.

Giesler, Markus and Mali Pohlmann (2003). "The Anthropology of File Sharing;

Consuming Napster as a Gift". *Advances in Consumer Research*, 30 (2003): 273-279.

Hennig-Thurau, Thorsten, Victor Henning and Henrik Sattler (2007). "Consumer File Sharing of Motion Pictures". *Journal of Marketing,* 71:4, 1-18. doi: 10.1509/jmkg.71.4.1

Hinduja, Sameer (2007). "Neutralization Theory and Online Software Piracy: An Empirical Analysis". *Ethics and Information Technology,* 9:3, 187-204. doi: 10.1007/s10676-007-9143-5

Holt, Thomas J. and Robert G. Morris (2009). "An Exploration of the Relationship between MP3 Player Ownership and Digital Piracy". *Criminal Justice Studies,* 22:4, 381-392.

Huang, Chun-Yao (2005). "File Sharing as a Form of Music Consumption". *International Journal of Electronic Commerce,* 9:4, 37-55.

Klinger, Barbara (2010). "Contraband Cinema: Piracy, Titanic, and Central Asia". *Cinema Journal,* 49:2, 106-124.

Kretschmer, Martin, George M. Klimis and Roger Wallis (2001). "Music in Electronic Markets: An Empirical Study!". *New Media and Society,* 3:4, 417-441. doi: 10.1177/14614440122226164

Krishnan, Ramayya, Michael D. Smith, Zhulei Tang and Rahul Telang (2007). "Digital Business Models for Peer-to-Peer Networks: Analysis and Economic Issues". *Review of Network Economics,* 6:2, 194-213. doi: 10.2202/1446-9022.1117

Langenderfer, Jeff and Steven W. Kopp (2004). "The Digital Technology Revolution and Its Effect on the Market for Copyrighted Works: Is History Repeating Itself?". *Journal of Macromarketing,* 24:1, 17-30. doi: 10.1177/0276146704263813

Lessig, Lawrence (2004). *Free Culture: The Nature and Future of Creativity.* London: Penguin.

Levin, Aron M., Mary Conway and Kenneth Rhee (2004). "Money for Nothing and Hits For Free: The Ethics of Downloading Music from Peer-to-Peer Web Sites". *Journal of Marketing Theory and Practice,* 12:1, 48-60.

Lewis, Jon (2007). "'If You Can't Protect What You Own, You Don't Own Anything': Piracy, Privacy, and Public Relations in 21st Century Hollywood". *Cinema Journal,* 46:2, 145-150. doi: 10.1353/cj.2007.0015

Liebowitz, Stan J. (2006). "File Sharing: Creative Destruction or Just Plain Destruction?". *Journal of Law and Economics,* 49:1, 1-28. doi: 10.1086/503518

Lobato, Ramon (2009). "Six Faces of Piracy: Global Media Distribution from Below". In Richard C. Sickels (ed.) *The Business of Entertainment (Vol. 1): Movies.* Westport, Connecticut: Greenwood Publishing Group.

Marshall, Lee (2003). "For and against the Record Industry: An Introduction to Bootleg Collectors and Tape Traders". *Popular Music,* 22:1, 57-72. Retrieved 10 July 2013, from http://www.jstor.org/stable/853556

Newzbin Discussion Thread (March 2010). *Eastern Legends Forum.* Retrieved May 4, 2010.

Nill, Alexander and Andreas Geipel (2010). "Sharing and Owning of Musical Works: Copyright Protection from a Societal Perspective". *Journal of Macro-*

marketing, 30:1, 33-49. doi: 10.1177/0276146709352217
Oberholzer-Gee, Felix and Koleman Stumpf (2007). "The Effect of File Sharing on Record Sales: An Empirical Analysis". *Journal of Political Economy,* 115:1, 1-42. Retrieved 10 July 2013, from http://www.jstor.org/stable/10.1086/511995
Pang, Laikwan (2006). *Cultural Control and Globalization in Asia: Copyright, Piracy and Cinema.* London: Routledge.
Peitz, Martin, and Patrick Waelbroeck (2006). "Why the Music Industry May Gain from Free Downloading: The Role of Sampling". *International Journal of Industrial Organization,* 24:5, 907-913. doi: http://dx.doi.org/10.1016/j.ijindorg.2005.10.006
Podoshen, Jeffrey S. (2008). "Why Take Tunes? An Exploratory Multinational Look at Student Downloading". *Journal of Internet Commerce,* 7:2, 180-202. doi: 10.1080/15332860802067664
Rodman, Gilbert B. and Cheyanne Vanderdonckt (2006). "Music for Nothing or, I Want My MP3". *Cultural Studies,* 20:2, 245-261. doi: 10.1080/09502380500495734
Sinha, Rajiv, Fernando Machado and Collin Sellman (2010). "Don't Think Twice, It's All Right: Music Piracy and Pricing in a DRM-Free Environment". *Journal of Marketing,* 74:2, 40-54. doi: 10.1509/jmkg.74.2.40
Taylor, Steven, Chiharu A. Ishida and David W. Wallace (2009). "Intention to Engage in Digital Piracy: A Conceptual Model and Empirical Test". *Journal of Service Research,* 11:3, 246-262. doi: 10.1177/1094670508328924
Thanks Discussion (June 2004). *Chinaphiles Forum.* Retrieved September 9, 2009.
Waterman, David, Sung Wook Ji and Laura R. Rochet (2007). "Enforcement and Control of Piracy, Copying and Sharing in the Movie Industry". *Review of Industrial Organisation,* 30:4, 255-289. doi: 10.1007/s11151-007-9136-x
Yar, Majid (2005). "The Global 'Epidemic' of Movie 'Piracy': Crime-Wave or Social Construction?". *Media, Culture and Society,* 27:5, 677-696. doi: 10.1177/0163443705055723
Zentner, Alejandro (2006). "Measuring the Effect of Music Downloads in Music Purchases". *Journal of Law and Economics,* 49:1, 1-49. Retrieved 10 July, 2013 from http://www.jstor.org/stable/10.1086/501082

"You Can't Change our Ancestors Without our Permission": Cultural Perspectives on Biopiracy

Daniel F. Robinson, Danielle Drozdzewski and Louise Kiddell

Introduction: The emergence of biopiracy as a counter discourse

Congress intended statutory subject matter to
"include anything under the sun that is made by man."
Diamond v. Chakrabarty, 447 U.S. 303 (1980)

The above quote summarises the famous United State's (US) Supreme Court finding that a genetically engineered micro-organism could be patented. This finding is often referred to as a landmark case because it clarified that altered 'non-naturally occurring' organisms could be patented in the US. What began as far back as 1873, when Louis Pasteur obtained a US patent (No. 141,072) on a purified yeast, has continued over the next 100 years with parallel advances in technology. By 1988, the US Patent and Trademark Office (USPTO) granted the first patent for a transgenic animal: the 'Harvard Mouse' (US Patent No. 4,736,866). The Harvard Mouse was subsequently patented in Europe and Japan. For various reasons, however, most countries were not willing to follow the US lead in allowing patents on higher life forms (Robinson and Medlock 2005).

The US has permitted patents on newly invented or discovered asexually reproduced plant varieties since 1930. More recently, countries such as Australia have allowed patents on new plant varieties and components provided the invention meets standard patentability criterion: that is, new, inventive, useful, and not already existing in nature.

In contrast, across the world more generally, few countries allow patents relating to plant and animal species or varieties, whether naturally occurring or transgenic. Even in advanced economies, such as in Europe, where biotechnology industries are prevalent, considerable public debate and concern over the patentability of higher organisms continues. European countries do permit some inventions relating to plants and animals to be patented, however the scope of their patent laws and jurisprudence does not allow for this with relation to plant and animal varieties (European Commission (EC) 2002).

There is, however, increasing pressure on countries to accept patentability of organisms arising through bilateral or regional agreements, as well as through membership of the World Trade Organization (WTO). This later membership demands compliance with the Agreement on Trade-Related Aspects of Intellectual Property Rights (TRIPS) – the implications of this are discussed in more detail below.

One of the main responses against patenting and intellectual property protection over plants and animals (as species or varieties) and their parts, has been the employment of the 'biopiracy' discourse. Usually wielded by Indigenous groups, as well as both Southern and Northern non-government organizations (NGOs) such as the Erosion Technology and Concentration (ETC) Group, the term has been used to brand researchers, companies and others as behaving unethically and even on occasion, illegally. Biopiracy is a counter-discourse that emerged in the early 1990s, and can likely be first attributed to Pat Roy Mooney of the ETC Group. It has been exerted as a powerful rhetoric, counter to the idea of intellectual property 'piracy' constructed by US industry lobby groups with vested interests in copyright protection.

Notably, anti-piracy sentiment has built in recent decades amongst various civil society groups because of the formation of monopolies and cartels in largely US-headquartered transnational companies from industries such as computers, software, entertainment, seeds and pharmaceuticals. This anti-piracy and anti-cartel sentiment spread internationally in reaction to the impacts of at least two major political actions of unilateral and bi/multilateral coercion. The first was the highly hypocritical position adopted by the US Government with respect to copyright protection. This was highlighted by the US decision to only ratify the Berne Convention on the Protection of Literary and Artistic works in 1989 while holding highly restrictive terms for the grant of foreign copyright protection. This approach allowed the US publishing industry to rapidly expand at the expense of foreign authors (Dutfield and Suthersanen 2005). What was most hypocritical was the application of trade sanctions (through US Trade Representative [USTR] 'Special 301' trade powers) on other countries where copying of US copyrighted works (including software, movies and other trade interests) was prevalent.

The 'Special 301' is a process under the US Trade Act 1974 (as amended in 1984 and 1988) whereby the USTR identifies and monitors countries that are deemed not to be providing sufficient protection for US intellectual property rights (largely copyrights and trademarks). Those countries with bad records are listed on a 'watch list' and 'priority watch list', with the worst records listed as 'priority foreign countries' subject to further investigation of their laws and practices on intellectual property. If priority foreign countries continued to allow or encourage breaches of intellectual property rights they would receive trade sanctions under the power (see Drahos and Braithwaite 2002, 88-90).

The second political action was the way that the USTR extraterritorially coerced many countries into compliance with their high standards of copyright and patent protection through bilateral trade agreements during the 1980s and 1990s whilst these countries were often under threat of sanctions on the Special 301 watch list. This move led to an enrolment of countries towards the concept of the TRIPS Agreement during the Uruguay Round of Trade Negotiations that led to the establishment of the WTO and TRIPS in 1994.

Biopiracy was thus a response to the perceived rapid global expansion of private property control over previously public goods such as plants and animals (patentable), or smells and colours (trade-markable). It was also an expression of concern that Indigenous knowledge was being appropriated towards discoveries or inventions relating to plants and animals that would then be held as monopolies. Indian activist, Vandana Shiva, is commonly associated with activism to prevent biopiracy and provides a description of the term:

> Biopiracy refers to the use of intellectual property systems to legitimize the exclusive ownership and control over biological resources and biological products and processes that have been used over centuries in non-industrialized cultures. 2001, 49

Thus, biopiracy was concerned with the capacity for companies to utilize intellectual property systems (especially patents, but also plant variety protection) to claim exclusive rights over an easily replicable or reproducible public good, such as a plant, which might have historically been domesticated, bred or utilized by a community as a crop, medicine or otherwise (also see Robinson 2010a for a more comprehensive definition of biopiracy). For meeting the criteria of 'new', 'inventive' and 'useful' – which have been shown to be a particularly low bar in the US – the inventors or discoverers could be granted a monopoly of 20 years to exploit the scope of their claimed invention (Newman and Cragg 2007).

The concerns around biopiracy were also a response to the outcome of a parallel international negotiation from which the outcome was the United Nations Convention on Biological Diversity (CBD 1992) – which was negotiated then signed, and ratified by most countries in the world (except the US, which is only a signatory). The late 1980s and early 1990s saw a growing interest in the discovery of natural products for industrial use including pharmaceuticals, foodstuffs, biotechnological products, cosmetics, nutraceuticals and industrial enzymes (see Eisner 1990). In an influential book, Reid *et al.* (1993, 2-3) have described biodiversity prospecting (bioprospecting or biodiscovery) as "the exploration of biodiversity for commercially valuable genetic and biochemical resources". For these authors, when conducted appropriately bioprospecting can:

> ...contribute greatly to environmentally sound development and return benefits to the custodians of genetic resources – the national public at large, the staff of conservation units, the farmers, the forest dwellers, and the Indigenous people who maintain or tolerate the resources involved.
> Reid *et al.* 1993, 2-3

The CBD has been described by some as the "grand bargain" because its language and objectives included not just elements that conservationists deemed important, but also "facilitated access to genetic resources" for utilisation in biotechnological and biochemical discovery and subsequent commercialisation (Article 1, which provides the underpinning for the idea of 'access and benefit-sharing' or ABS; Jeffery 2004). The term, 'genetic resources', was seen by many to reflect both the scientific and economic reductionism of organisms to commodifiable genes and extracts. Commentators have noted that the Uruguay Round of Negotiations were going on at the same time and some have suggested that the CBD content on access to genetic resources was being pushed by the same countries seeking to establish an agreement like TRIPS in the soon-to-be established WTO. Many saw a potential boon for society through environmentally benign activities of plant, microbe and animal collection (in relatively small quantities), research and development, and resultant product development of beneficial pharmaceuticals, medicines, crops, fibres and other useful goods. The CBD encourages the sharing of benefits arising from the utilisation of genetic resources, such that provider countries, which have sovereignty over their biodiversity, would gain something from the transaction. Others were more sceptical of the proposed benefits due to the vagaries of the text of the CBD. For example, what exactly does 'utilisation of genetic resources' entail? What about the sharing of benefits relating to traditional knowledge associated with plants and animals?[1]

Out of this disquiet, many biopiracy cases have emerged where concerns have been expressed about the lack of prior informed consent for collection of 'genetic resources', plants, animals and microbes, and in cases where there is a lack of benefit-sharing and/or where spurious patents have been obtained (see Robinson 2010a and Blakeney 2005, for a number of detailed cases). Even in cases where patents appear to be valid and there is a clearly definable 'inventive step', there may be other concerns from 'provider' groups that the subject matter (the plant or animal) should not be patented.

It is this last point that we intend to focus on most closely in this chapter. While many have focused on the legal, scientific, economic and equity implications of biodiscovery benefit-sharing and biopiracy cases (see for example, ten Kate and Laird 1999; McManis 2007; Bhatti et al. 2009), here we detail a less travelled path and point out that there are significant moral and cultural implications of plant (and animal) patents.

What TRIPS requires of member countries

To undertake further analysis of concerns surrounding biopiracy, some discussion of the specific Articles of the CBD and the TRIPS Agreement is required. The 153 Member Countries of the WTO (as of February 2012), are required to have patent systems that allow for patentable subject matter as per the following:

> ...patents shall be available for any inventions, whether products or processes, in all fields of technology, provided that they are new, involve an inventive step and are capable of industrial application... TRIPS Article 27.1

However, Members are allowed some exclusions from patentability. For our interests here, the following exclusions are pertinent:

> Members may exclude from patentability inventions, the prevention within their territory of the commercial exploitation of which is necessary to protect public order or morality, including to protect human, animal or plant life or health or to avoid serious prejudice to the environment, provided that such exclusion is not made merely because the exploitation is prohibited by their law. TRIPS Article 27.2

1 Many of these questions have been hopefully resolved with the development of the Nagoya Protocol to the CBD in 2010 (discussed in the chapter conclusion).

Also, Members may exclude from patentability:

> ...plants and animals other than micro-organisms, and essentially biological processes for the production of plants or animals other than non-biological and microbiological processes. However, Members shall provide for the protection of plant varieties either by patents or by an effective sui generis system or by any combination thereof... TRIPS Article 27.3(b)

From a bioethical perspective, these are important exceptions such that a patent and its exploitation do not disrupt public order and morality. From the perspective of biopiracy, there are still several problems with these exclusions. One major issue is that restrictions in one country do not apply extraterritorially: that is, patents relating to or on plants and/or animals may be granted in a country that allows them, when the plants and/or animals have been obtained from another country. Another major issue is the requirement for effective *sui generis* (unique) systems for plant variety protection.

In practice there are few alternatives to the formal system of plant variety protection established by the UPOV Convention, (the International Union for the Protection of New Varieties of Plants) which provides a similar monopoly to a patent (usually 20 years) for a new plant variety. Thus most WTO Member countries are now forced to allow plant variety protection for new plant varieties. Mooney (2000) has suggested that international law perpetuates biopiracy, and provides little in terms of viable alternative forms of 'protection' than what exists in formal intellectual property law. Mooney (2000: 37) notes that 'in the absence of intergovernmental regulatory mechanisms and agreements, the possibility of equitable benefit-sharing is remote.'

In the following sections we demonstrate that these laws can create a problematic division of culture from nature using science as its medium. Patent law requires examiners to grant patents on the bare 'facts' of 'new, inventive and useful', and plant variety protection provides a similar division (plant varieties must be new, distinct, uniform and stable). We point out that many non-Euro-American cultures have serious concerns about this social construction: the right of culture (humans) to access nature (plants) through a monopoly-based ownership of nature. From certain worldviews, and concerning certain plants, a patent over a plant variety cannot only be offensive but potentially leads to a disregard for alternate – and often Indigenous – systems of belief and knowledge.

Nature/Culture divide in relation to PGR and indigenous worldview

This section discusses how Plant Genetic Resources (PGRs), and the international and national legal mechanisms associated with them, have been developed within the Western conceptualisation of the nature/culture divide. This divide positions the human realm as separate and distinct from the natural realm. In so doing, it positions humans (and state subsidiaries) as the possessors of agency and power over the natural world. Sundberg and Dempsey (2009: 458) have argued that like most modalities central to modernity, the nature/culture dualism "is connected to making and sustaining hierarchies, thus is a technology of power". The manifestation of such power relationships of culture (humans) over nature (and here we refer to plants as their reproducible and divisible parts – PGRs) are evident in the legal mechanisms and dialogues that have in the past posited PGRs as "a heritage of mankind... available [to humans] without restriction" (International Undertaking on Plant Genetic Resources for Food and Agriculture 1983, Article 1).[2]

These technologies of power have further evolved to posit state sovereignty over nature as biological resources (under the CBD) and individual monopoly ownership over dividable units or varieties of plants, animals or microbes (under TRIPS). We argue that the formulation of legal frameworks around a Western conceptualisation of nature/culture opens up pathways of misappropriation and misunderstandings of the importance of some PGRs to alternate and Indigenous worldviews, which position the natural world (and elements such as plants or PGRs within it) and the cultural realm as part of a much more closely bound symbiosis.

The problematic of nature/culture divide is exposed when we consider the positioning of Indigenous worldviews and their traditional knowledges within this dominant paradigm. The Western conceptual divide of splitting culture and nature, and of arguing about their epistemological primacy, "has profound

---

2 In the late 1970s and early 1980s, references to plant genetic resources as the common heritage of mankind were a dominant discourse and this was reflected in text of the non-binding International Undertaking on Plant Genetic Resources for Food and Agriculture (IUPGRFA) which was later superseded by the International Treaty on Plant Genetic Resources for Food and Agriculture (ITPGRFA). See Report of the Conference of FAO, 22nd Sess. FAO (Agenda Item 6) para. 285 (art. I), U.N. Doc. C/83/REP (1983), http://www.fao.org/ag//CGRFA/iu.htm (Acc. 9/10/12).

implications for not only how we understand the world but also for how we act in and upon it" (Jones 2009, 309). In the context of PGRs, there appears a clear distinction between how Indigenous and non-Indigenous communities 'act in' the world, and indeed see the ramifications of their relations 'upon' the world. Humans often equate acting in and upon nature in terms of accessing biodiversity with the 'use' of the environment. Indigenous communities and groups have long traditions of breeding plant varieties, but it is important to note how they view their use of the environment, and how the use of certain plants (and animals) is tied into conceptions of cultural identity. Such conceptions form a significant point of departure from the predominately-utilitarian Western conceptions of 'using' nature as a 'resource', trading it as a commodity, and patenting an object from nature for a monopoly. This chapter highlights some of these Indigenous cultural associations and constructions that bridge the nature/culture divide. Our examples provide fodder for Jones' (2009: 311) argument that by attempting to dissolve the nature/culture divide we may "better understand our relationships with and within biophysical systems". We seek to widen the lens through which we think about the functioning of existing legal mechanisms that are premised on Western understandings of nature/culture.

Indigenous worldviews often pit culture as intimately and inextricably wrapped up with nature, rather than divisively divorced by way of a common punctuation mark. Howitt *et al.* (2009: 361) have asserted that Indigenous peoples' geographies include "multiple and fluid ways of knowing" what we from a Western perspective otherwise categorise as "time and space, nature and the environment." Moreover, the Indigenous perceptions of culture within a Western understanding of the 'culture' in the nature/culture relationship are also different. Taking a post-structuralist approach to understanding the multiplicity of meanings associated with the word 'culture', an Indigenous worldview and/or conception of culture and nature is multifarious and contingent on connections between systems of belief, spirituality, land and family. To this effect, Coombe (2001: 277) reminds us that 'no single position on... [culture] ... can be called an Indigenous one'. Rather, each conceptualisation of a community's relationship between their cultural practices and understandings is contextual and place-specific.

This contextual understanding is displaced with global trade agreements that require a homogenised approach. With global agreements such as TRIPS, countries have essentially been forced to allow for the detachment of PGRs and

Indigenous knowledge from their local contexts for extraterritorial patenting and exploitation in foreign countries.

Moral and cultural objections to life patents

In this section we highlight where Indigenous communities have objected to the patenting of life forms by stating that it is against their moral and cultural norms. Traditional belief systems often encompass strong spiritual and place-specific connections with nature (Mataatua Declaration on Cultural and Intellectual Property Rights of Indigenous Peoples 1993; Schlais 2007; Tauli-Corpuz 2003; Waitangi Tribunal 2011). Through linkages with their cultural heritages, genealogies or customary laws, some Indigenous peoples maintain reciprocal relationships with their natural environment. They may view themselves as custodians or caretakers of the traditional knowledge, natural resources and territories they have inherited, and have assumed the responsibility for guardianship over (Tauli-Corpuz 2003).

Rather than making dangerous assumptions about the many Indigenous peoples of the world (or assuming that anything other than the orthodox view is an Indigenous one), we highlight a number of specific comments or cases whereby the patenting of plants has been viewed as culturally inappropriate, morally offensive or similar. We will employ five primary examples, amongst others, as case studies to explore some of the cultural objections to the WTO TRIPS Agreement and patenting of plants.

Communication from Bolivia

A delegation representing the Government of Bolivia has claimed the "patenting of life forms is unethical as it is against the moral and cultural norms of many societies and [I]ndigenous peoples, of members in the WTO including that of Bolivia" (Bolivian Government 2010, 4). Their communication states that the proliferation of patents that has occurred subsequent to the adoption of the TRIPS Agreement has "serious social, economic and ethical implications," which are likely to have disproportionate and adverse affects for developing countries. In arguing for an accelerated and in-depth review of Article 27.3(b), the communication alludes to the new constitution of Bolivia (adopted in January 2009), which states:

> Negotiation, signature and ratification of treaties will be governed by.....

> Respect for the rights of Indigenous peoples.... Harmony with nature, protection of biodiversity and prohibition of private appropriation of plants, animals, micro-organisms and any living matter for exclusive use and exploitation. Bolivian Government 2010, 2

It also refers to the United Nations Declaration on the Rights of Indigenous Peoples (UNDRIP) (2007). The UNDRIP requires states to "provide redress through effective mechanisms, which may include restitution, developed in conjunction with [I]ndigenous peoples, with respect to their cultural, intellectual, religious and spiritual property taken without their free, prior and informed consent or in violation of their laws, traditions and customs" (Bolivian Government 2010, 2).

In the Indigenous Andean worldview, the deity Pachamama, or 'Mother Earth' is respected and viewed as a living being, inherently connected to people and the environment (Vidal 2011). Following the Bolivian constitutional change, a new law – Law of the Rights of Mother Earth – was passed in December 2010. With reference to Pachamama, the law states:

> She is sacred, fertile and the source of life that feeds and cares for all living beings in her womb. She is in permanent balance, harmony and communication with the cosmos. She is comprised of all ecosystems and living beings, and their self-organisation. Vidal 2011

Since Indigenous Bolivians view the natural world with such reverence and feel such a profound connection to 'Mother Earth', it follows that perceived misuse of natural resources or traditional knowledge relating to those resources/nature, would be deeply offensive. The Bolivian objection to the TRIPS Agreement claims that many patented biological resources "originate in developing countries and are obtained without prior knowledge or consent and in violation of their laws, thus resulting in 'misappropriation' and biopiracy" (Bolivian Government 2010, 3). It also argues that TRIPS "does not explicitly recognise the collective rights of Indigenous peoples and local communities over their biological resources and traditional knowledge" (Bolivian Government 2010, 3).

Maori traditional knowledge and the Wai 262 claim

The Wai 262 claim is a formal expression of the collective concerns of six tribes throughout New Zealand about the collection and use of Indigenous plants for scientific and commercial purposes, occurring without Maori consent. The claim to the Waitangi Tribunal is for recognition and protection of Maori traditional knowledge (*Maātauranga Māori*) in relation to Indigenous flora and fauna, as well as for the species themselves (Solomon 2001; Waitangi Tribunal 2011).

Maori culture is highly integrated with the natural world as the *whakapapa*, or genealogy, of the Maori people links them to all elements of creation (Solomon 2000). In *te ao Māori* (translated as "the Māori world"), all plants, animals, animate and inanimate natural objects, are infused with *mauri* (living essence or spirit) and are seen as alive and interrelated. All plants are believed to be descendents of Tāne-mahuta, the deity of man and forests, who also formed and breathed life into the first woman. The Māori people are thus related to the natural world around them and regard plants and animals in personal terms (Waitangi Tribunal 2011).

Maori values are underpinned by the principle of *whanaungatanga*, or kinship, and *kaitiakitanga*, the obligation arising from the kin relationship, to nurture and care for a person or thing, and protect and look after a person or (part of) the natural environment. *Kaitiakitanga* responsibility is not only understood as a cultural principle, but as a system of law (Waitangi Tribunal 2011). In te ao Maori, humankind have *kaitiakitanga* responsibility to nurture the physical and *mauri* well-being of plants, as *whakapapa* tells that they are all part of the same family tree (Waitangi Tribunal 2011; Solomon 2001). There exist *kaitiaki* (guardian) obligations towards *taonga* (treasured) species such as tuatara, harakeke, kererū, and kūmara (Waitangi Tribunal 2011). Some details of these obligations and their implications are explained in Box 1.

Western legal interpretations of the word 'property' (encompassing rights to control and exclusion) are at odds with the principle of *kaitiakitanga*. Thus, the acquisition and exploitation of intellectual property rights can conflict with the traditional cultural values underpinning *kaitiaki* relationships with *taonga* species (Waitangi Tribunal 2011). Maui Solomon, a respected Maori attorney from *Aotearoa* (New Zealand), explains that "there can be a fundamental clash between the ideological underpinnings of the Intellectual Property Rights system and the philosophical underpinnings of … Indigenous peoples rights and obligations" (Solomon 2000). The Wai 262 claimants believe that IP exploitation can damage *kaitiaki* relationships and are upset that the *kaitiaki* relationship is never seen as strong enough to prevent or restrict the patenting of *taonga* species (Waitangi Tribunal 2011).

Native Hawai'ian resistance to the patenting of Taro (Kalo)

Native Hawai'ian genealogy similarly describes how all-living things are interconnected and dependent on one another (Paoakalani Declaration 2005). For example, the taro plant has particular cultural significance for Native Hawai'ians. According to the *Kumulipo* – the main genealogical creation chant for Native Hawai'ians – the first taro plant, *Haloa*, was the stillborn son of the gods *Wakea*, sky father, and *Hoohokukalani*, star mother (Ritte and Kanehe 2007). Their second born was a man, whose *Kuleana* (responsibility) was to care for *Haloa*, the elder brother. Taro is a staple food crop for Native Hawai'ians, who feel obligated to '*malama* (take care of and protect) their eldest brother' so he will sustain them (Beckwith 1949, 1970; Ritte and Kanehe 2007; Robinson 2010a).

Native Hawai'ians have cultivated taro for centuries and bred nearly three hundred different varieties for culinary, medicinal, cultural and ceremonial purposes. Patents were granted to University of Hawai'i researchers in 2002 (US Patents PP12361, PP12342, PP12772) who developed hybrid varieties resistant to a fungal leaf disease by cross-breeding two different varieties. However the patents were ultimately relinquished due to resistance from Hawai'ian activists who claimed the patented varieties were 'invalidated by considerations of prior art' (that is, they were not sufficiently different from traditional taro varieties) amongst other expressions of cultural concern linked to the Hawai'ian *Kumulipo* (Robinson 2010a; Schlais 2007). In light of the cultural relationship to taro, it is easy to understand why activists promptly contested the attempted patenting of taro varieties. Walter Ritte Jr., a long time native Hawai'ian activist, has been quoted by Schlais (2007, 601) as saying, "owning a patent on Hawai'ian taro is like owning a patent on one's older sibling, one's ancestry".[3]

Thai, Hmong and Karen traditional medicine

To give a final example, a customary law 'injury' such as the unauthorised appropriation of plants may cause the embodiment of physical injury according to certain beliefs in Thailand. In some cases, the theft of resources and knowledge from specific 'chosen' healers who may embody and internalise any wrongdoing, may have the potential for detrimental spiritual and health effects for the healer. Interviews with Hmong healers in Thailand revealed the physical internalisation of 'injury' according to their belief systems:

3 The title quote for this paper is attributed to Walter Ritte Jr (cited in ICTSD, 2006).

> It is fine to be treated and to learn about the herbal medicines. But many herbs require *kha khruu* [a ritual donation] to respect the spirits that protect them. If someone steals the herbs I will get sick because a *kha khruu* donation wasn't paid – it is taboo. Mee Leng, Hmong healer, interview (Baan Khun Khlang 13 February 2006)

In subsequent interviews with local Thai and Karen healers, similar sentiments were expressed, suggesting that between different ethnic groups in Northern Thailand there are linked beliefs drawn particularly from Animism and Buddhism. The customary norms surrounding these rituals (and the shrines mentioned in Box 1) are linked to beliefs such as karma and reincarnation, which cannot easily be reconciled in legal terms. Thus, when a transaction of plants (or other biological resources) and traditional knowledge occurs, a metaphysical transformation takes place, that may manifest in the spiritual or physical injury of a traditional healer if relevant customs or rituals are not followed (Robinson 2010a; Robinson and Kuanpoth 2009; Robinson 2013). The equivalent effect seems likely in cases of biopiracy.

Cultural objections to the patenting of traditional and sacred plants

Harakeke (New Zealand)
Regarded with reverence by traditional weavers, Harakeke is now commercially exploited as an ingredient in skincare products and as a popular garden plant. Patents have been granted in the United States and New Zealand. Māori weavers fear their plants will be misused by non-kaitiaki who do not understand their significance and special properties (Waitangi Tribunal 2011).

Mānuka (New Zealand)
Traditionally used for its physical and medicinal properties, mānuka is increasingly exploited commercially. Patents have been granted internationally for its use in cosmetics, medicinal treatments and mānuka honey. Māori claimants to the Waitangi Tribunal say it is unfair that companies with no prior relationship with mānuka are able to obtain private property rights over the plant, while there is no recognition of the Māori relationship with it or prior knowledge of its properties (Waitangi Tribunal 2011).

Ayahuasca (South American Amazon)
Ayahuasca is a native vine of the Amazon Basin that has been traditionally cultivated by Indigenous communities. It has been used by healers and

religious and tribal leaders for generations and is considered sacred. A US patent was granted to an American scientist in 1986 and revoked in 1999 due to overwhelming opposition from Indigenous communities and public interest groups, who perceived the patenting of the vine as theft and as immoral (Facteau 2001).

Jasmine rice (Thailand)

There have been a number of concerns in Thailand expressed around a US-based jasmine rice research project, the trademarking of 'Jasmati' rice, a patent linked to the company holding this trademark on a rice preparation method, and even surrounding some defensive Thai patents over isolated genes responsible for the aromatic smell of jasmine rice (although the latter was acclaimed by the King of Thailand for defending national heritage over jasmine rice). One concern that has been regularly raised is the close cultural association that Thai people have with not only Jasmine rice, but also its progenitors, going back centuries. There are very strong cultural and spiritual views about guardian spirits in many communities in Thailand (and adjoining countries) that derive from rituals, beliefs and folklore and are evident in shrines dedicated to *Phra-phuum* (spirit lord of the place/village) or *Phïi-baan* (the spirit protector of the house), or to *Mae Phoesop* (mother spirit of rice).

Kakadu Plum

The cosmetics company Mary Kay Inc. has applied for WIPO PCT patent application number WO/2007/084998 on 'Compositions comprising Kakadu plum extract or açaí berry extract' on January 19, 2007. A number of media reports have raised Australian Indigenous concerns about the patent application, including some which have cited cultural concerns related to the fact that Kakadu plum features in some 'Dreaming stories' about the creation of the land by their spiritual ancestors, where people, animals and plants had a common origin (Robinson 2010b; Clarke 2007). In its national phase in Australia this application has been withdrawn after an examiners report rejected numerous claims.

'Awa (Kava) (Hawai'i)

'Awa is a sacred plant of great significance in Hawai'i. Ceremonial offerings were used to communicate with and honour one's ancestors. Traditional stories told of the travels of the gods Kane and Kanaloa around the Hawai'ian islands, during which they created springs with Kane's magical staff because of Kanaloa's desire to drink 'Awa. The plant was also used in sacramental feasts, house blessings and by traditional healers for medicinal purposes (Winter 2004). The U.S. Patent and Trademark Office has awarded several patents relating to 'Awa to non-native corporations, which has generated significant concern from Indigenous people in Hawai'i and also countries such as Vanuatu and Samoa.

Objections from the African Group in TRIPS

Various official and NGO groups from Africa have made objections to the patenting of life allowed under the TRIPS Agreement. In a communication to the WTO, the African Group (representing all African WTO Members) has written:

> Patents on life forms are unethical and the TRIPS Agreement should prohibit them…. Such patents are contrary to the moral and cultural norms of many societies in Members of the WTO... (African Group 2003, 2)

Various African community groups have affirmed their rejection of the patenting of life. With reference to the TRIPS agreement, one such group, the South African Freeze Alliance on Genetic Engineering, claims that the proliferation of patenting is biopiracy, akin to stealing millennia of cultural knowledge and ignoring the collective ownership of resources (SAFeAGE 2012).

Conclusion and discussion

In his work on the Hawai'ian Taro case, Schlais (2007, 586) has sought to unsettle the western orthodoxy of nature/culture by stating that the knowledges and cultural heritages (political, cultural and economic) bestowed on Indigenous people emanate both "from their ancestors *and* their natural environment". This viewpoint is similar to the Maori examples, and alternatively, through the Animist embodiment of plant use through the lens of Animism, karma and reincarnation in the Northern Thailand examples. Crucially, from this viewpoint, conceptions of traditional cultural knowledge and the environment are inseparable, to the extent that one cannot be conceived of without the other. It also then follows that one cannot be determined as pre-existing the other, or at least it can only be traced as far as a belief system's genealogy or karmic understanding of the world allows. Here lies the potential for traditional and Indigenous understandings of the culture and nature relationship to lie outside the ambit of Haraway's (1992, 296) influential argument: "nature cannot pre-exist its construction". That is, as Schlais has suggested of Hawai'ian beliefs:

> ...the tangible and intangible aspects of their culture, the physical materials of their culture as well as the traditions, histories, customs, traditional knowledge, and spiritual beliefs are all intertwined with the environment in which they live. 2007, 590

The crux of this argument is to encourage non-Indigenous policy makers and State actors to recognise Castree and Braun's (2006, 161) contention that "there is no generic social constructionist position [on nature/culture], only specific modalities of social construction".

The Indigenous examples presented here demonstrate the need to look past the generic, and Western-dominated orthodoxy of constructions of nature, and at the very least consider the nature/culture dualism from Whatmore's (2002) perspective of hybridity, where there is 'no state of nature'. Rather, there are only richly inhabited ecologies, through which the "precious metal of bio-diversity is intimately bound up with the diversities of cultural practices" (Whatmore 2002, 115-116). Our examples in this chapter highlight how a more nuanced reading of biodiversity-human relationships, has been important in terms of seeing, accepting or contesting forms of ownership and governance. For example, the Maori have a *Kaitiakitanga* (the kinship relationship to nature), which entails obligations and responsibilities towards their natural environments (plant and animal species). Such relationships are not routinely considered under existing legal frameworks, and claimants of the Wai 262 have challenged the potential misappropriation of Maori knowledge, and the subsequent damage to their existing nature/culture relationship. Drawing from Jones (2009, 322), the different cultural lenses through which nature is named and seen (ancestor, embodied spirit, plants and animals, biodiversity, plant genetic resources) makes a difference to who can own, control, or shape it as it is continually being 'made and re-made'.

Here then, through our examples, we have a range of Indigenous belief systems providing for an unassailable human-nature linkage, where plants may indeed contain spirits, be revered, or have genealogical significance. Yet modern society has constructed 'distinct (and dominant) ontological domains' and dichotomies – for example, nature/culture, humans/non-humans – which are played out, for example, in legal literalism, scientific rationalism, and political secularism. The effectiveness of these established domains means that we often have an "impoverished understanding of the integrated networks in which humans and non-humans are entangled" (Braun 2004, 169). Further, Braun (2004) draws from Latour's (1993) concept of the modern constitution to better elucidate how entrenched these established ontology's are, especially, in our case, in their potential to blind us to alternate ways of viewing PGRs (or anything outside its own conventional domain). Rather than conceptualising humans and non-humans as inherently separate, science as free from the interventions of politics and power, and the gradual retreat of religion from the modern world, Latour's argument is premised on exposing the inherent actants and networks that operate between and within these domains. While our belief and use of established knowledge paradigms ensures certainty, and unproblematic replication – especially within legal instruments – their ability to ensconce a steadfast and uncritical adherence to them means that we accept established norms without considering alternate, and in our case Indigenous, viewpoints. As Braun (2004, 169) argued, our reliance on established binaries "leaves us...unable to consider the way that people and things, science and politics, the world and morality, are all the while mixed together".

The problematic lies with 'who' (state or governing body), within an international regulatory framework is responsible for the governance of PGRs, *and* most importantly how this power is exerted and from what viewpoint. This is at least one of the reasons why we often see Indigenous groups describing patents on a plant variety or extract as biopiracy (other reasons may include a lack of respect/authorisation and inequity/compensation).

On a positive note for Indigenous peoples, there have been significant recent developments that suggest that at least some of the many viewpoints and major concerns of these peoples are being heard. First, the United Nations Declaration on the Rights of Indigenous Peoples (UNDRIP) 2007 has been finalised and provides an important statement on Indigenous rights. UNDRIP includes elements on indigenous cultural property, including Article 31, which recognizes the right of Indigenous peoples to "maintain, control, protect and develop their cultural heritage, traditional knowledge and traditional cultural expressions, as well as the manifestations of their sciences ...including human and genetic resources, seeds, medicines, knowledge of the properties of fauna and flora, oral traditions". Although not legally binding on signatory states, UNDRIP demonstrates movement towards a gradual acknowledgement of Indigenous perceptions of the natural environment and perhaps a re-articulation of the established understandings of the nature/culture divide.

Also evidence of this movement is the Nagoya Protocol on Access to Genetic Resources and the Fair and Equitable Sharing of Benefits arising from their Utilization (2010). This protocol is now being signed and ratified by many countries to support the objectives of the CBD. The Nagoya Protocol was heavily lobbied by Indigenous groups such as the International Indigenous Forum on Biodiversity

(IIFB) and was also influenced by the UNDRIP (see Bavikatte and Robinson 2010). Importantly, in the context of this chapter, the Protocol requires country Parties to implement national systems for the fair and equitable sharing of benefits arising from the utilisation (research and development) of 'genetic resources' and associated 'traditional' knowledge. These stipulations include requirements for prior informed consent from 'providers' of these resources and knowledge, including Indigenous peoples and local communities. While it is not a panacea for biopiracy, nor for reconciling cultural concerns about life patents, it does provide an opportunity for providers to allow or refuse access, or place terms on use (for example, allowing use of a plant for research and development but prohibiting patents on it). The Protocol provides a greater degree of empowerment to Indigenous peoples and provides a better opportunity for their worldviews to be acknowledged and respected (albeit within a framework that recognises sovereign/national rights over biological resources).

References

African Group (2003). "Taking Forward the Review of Article 27.3(b) of the TRIPS Agreement". IP/C/W/404, 26 June. Retrieved 25 March 2012, from http://www.wto.org/english/tratop_e/trips_e/art27_3b_e.htm

Bavikatte, Kabir and Daniel.F. Robinson (2010). "Towards a People's History of the Law: Biocultural Jurisprudence and the Nagoya Protocol on Access and Benefit Sharing". *Law, Environment and Development Journal*, 7, 35. Retrieved 10 July 2013, from http://www.lead-journal.org/content/11035.pdf

Beckwith, Martha (1949). "Function and Meaning of the Kumulipo Birth Chant in Ancient Hawai'i". *Journal of American Folklore*, 62:245, 290-3.

Beckwith, Martha (1970). *Hawai'ian Mythology*. University of Hawaii Press, Honolulu, HI.

Bhatti, Shakeel, Santiago Carrizosa, Patrick McGuire and Tomme Young (eds). *Contracting for ABS: The Legal and Scientific Implications of Bioprospecting Contracts.* IUCN Environmental Policy and Law Paper No. 67/4, Gland.

Blakeney, Michael (2005). "Bioprospecting and Biopiracy". In Burton Ong (ed). *Intellectual Property and Biological Resources.* Singapore: Marshall-Cavendish, 393-424.

Bolivian Government (2010). "Review of Article 27.3(b) of TRIPS Agreement, IP/C/W/545," 26 February 2010. Retrieved 24 March 2012, from http://www.wto.org/english/tratop_e/trips_e/art27_3b_e.htm

Braun, Bruce (2004). "Nature and Culture: On the Career of a False Problem". In James Duncan, Nuala C. Johnson and Richard H. Schein (eds). *A Companion to Cultural Geography.* Singapore: Blackwell Publishing, 151-179.

Castree, Noel and Bruce Braun (2006). "Constructing rural natures". In Paul Cloke, Terry Marsden and Patrick Mooney (eds). *Handbook Rural Studies.* London: Sage, 161-170.

Coombe, Rosemary (2001). "The Recognition of Indigenous People's and Community Traditional Knowledge in International Law". *St. Thomas Law Review*, 14, 275-285.

Craig, Donna (2004). "Biological Resources, Intellectual Property Rights and International Human Rights: Impacts on Indigenous and Local Communities". Burton Ong (ed.). *Intellectual Property and Biological Resources.* Singapore: Marshall-Cavendish, 352.

Drahos, Peter with John Braithwaite (2002). *Information Feudalism: Who Owns the Knowledge Economy?.* New Press, New York.

Dutfield, Graham and Uma Suthersanen (2005). "Harmonisation or differentiation in intellectual property protection? The lessons of history". *Prometheus*, 23:2, 131-147.

EC (2002). *Patent Law in the Field of Biotechnology and Genetic Engineering: Implementation Report. Summary.* Retrieved 4 April 2012, from http://europa.eu/legislation_summaries/internal_market/single_market_for_goods/pharmaceutical_and_cosmetic_products/l26026a_en.htm

Eisner, Thomas (1990). "Prospecting for Nature's Chemical Riches". *Issues in Science & Technology*, 6, 31-34.

Facteau, Leanne M. (2001). "The Ayahuasca Patent Revocation: Raising Questions about Current U.S. Patent Policy". *Boston College Third World Law Journal*, 21, 69-104.

Food and Agriculture Organisation (1983) International Undertaking on Plant Genetic Resources for Food and Agriculture (IUPGRFA). See Report of the Conference of FAO, 22nd Sess. FAO (Agenda Item 6), U.N. Doc. C/83/REP (1983). Retrieved 10 September 2012, from http://www.fao.org/ag//CGRFA/iu.htm

Haraway, Donna (1992). "The Promises of Monsters: A Regenerative Politics for Inappropriate/d Others". In Lawrence Grossberg, Cary Nelson and Paula A. Treichler (eds) *Cultural Studies.* New York: Routledge, 295-337.

Howitt, Richie, Samantha Muller and Sandie Suchet-Pearson (2009). "Indigenous Geographies". In Rob Kitchen and Nigel Thrift (eds). *International Encyclopaedia of Human Geography.* Amsterdam: Elsevier Ltd, 358-364,

International Centre for Trade and Sustainable Development (ICTSD) (2006). "Taro Patents to be Given Back to Hawai'i's Indigenous People". *Bridges Trade BioRes*, 6:1, 16 June.

Jeffery, Michael, I. (2004). "Intellectual Property Rights and Biodiversity Conservation: Reconciling Incompatibilities Between the TRIPS Agreement and the Convention on Biological Diversity". In Burton Ong (ed) *Intellectual Property and Biological Resources.* Singapore: Marshall Cavendish Academic, 185-225.

Jones, Owain (2009). "Nature-Culture". In Rob Kitchen and Nigel Thrift (eds.). *International Encyclopaedia of Human Geography*, Amsterdam: Elsevier Ltd, 309-323.

Kate, Kerry and Sarah Laird (1999). *The Commercial Use of Biodiversity: Access to Genetic Resources and Benefit Sharing*. London: Earthscan.

Latour, Bruno (1993). *We Have Never Been Modern*. Cambridge, MA: Harvard University Press.

Mataatua Declaration on Cultural and Intellectual Property Rights of Indigenous Peoples, Whakatane, New Zealand, 18 June 1993.

McManis, Charles (ed) (2007). *Biodiversity and the Law: Intellectual Property, Biotechnology and Traditional Knowledge*. Earthscan, London.

Mooney, Pat Roy (2000). "Why We Call It Biopiracy". In Hanne Svarstad and Shivcharn S. Dhillion (eds). *Bioprospecting: From Biodiversity in the South to Medicines in the North*. Oslo: Spartacus Forlag AS, 37-44.

Newman, David J. and Gordon Cragg (2007). "Natural Products as Sources of New Drugs over the Last 2 5 Years". *Journal of Natural Products*, 70:3, 461–477.

Paoakalani Declaration (2003). Native Hawai'ian Intellectual Property Rights Conference, Waikiki, Hawai'i, October 2003, reprinted in R. Hokulei Lindsay, (2005) "Responsibility with Accountability: The Birth of a Strategy to Protect Kanaka Maoli Traditional Knowledge". *Howard Law Journal*, 48, 763, 778-79.

Reid, Walter V., Sarah A. Laird, Carrie A. Meyer, R. Gamez, A. Sittenfeld, Daniel H. Janzen, M.A. Gollin and Calestous Juma (1993). *Biodiversity Prospecting: Using Genetic Resources for Sustainable Development*. World Resources Institute, Washington DC.

Ritte, Walter and Le'a Kanehe (2007). Kuleana No Haloa (Responsibility for Taro). "Protecting the Sacred Ancestor for Ownership and Genetic Modification," In Aroha T.P Mead and Steven Ratuva (eds) *Pacific Genes and Life Patents*, Call of the Earth Llamado de la Tierra & United Nations University Institute of Advanced Studies.

Robinson, Daniel F. (2013). "Legal Geographies of Intellectual Property, 'Traditional' Knowledge and Biodiversity: Experiencing Conventions, Laws, Customary Law and Karma in Thailand". *Geographical Research*. Issue pending. DOI: 10.1111/1745-5871.12022

Robinson, Daniel.F. (2010a). *Confronting Biopiracy: Challenges, Cases and International Debates*. London: Earthscan.

Robinson, Daniel.F. (2010b). "Traditional Knowledge and Biological Product Derivative Patents: Benefit-Sharing and Patent Issues Relating to Camu Camu, Kakadu Plum and Açaí Plant Extracts". Discussion paper, UNU Traditional Knowledge Initiative, Darwin. Retrieved 24 April 2012, from http://www.unutki.org/news.php?doc_id=174

Robinson, Douglas and Nina Medlock (2005). "Diamond V. Chakrabarty: A Retrospective on 25 years of Biotech Patents". *Intellectual Property and Technology Law Journal*. 17:10, 12-15.

Robinson, Daniel and Jakkrit Kuanpoth (2009). "The Traditional Medicines Predicament: A Case Study of Thailand". *Journal of World Intellectual Property*, 11, 375-403.

SAFeAGE, Patents & corporate control, ownership of living organisms, Retrieved 23 March 2012, from http://www.safeage.org/index.php?option=com_content&view=article&id=56&Itemid=63

Schlais, Gregory.K. (2007). "Patenting of Sacred Biological Resources, the Taro Patent Controversy in Hawaii: A Soft Law Proposal, The Recent Developments". *University of Hawaii Law Review*, 29, 581-618.

Shiva, Vandana (2001). *Protect or Plunder: Understanding Intellectual Property Rights.* London and New York: Zed Books.

Solomon, Maui (2000). *Intellectual Property Rights and Indigenous Peoples Rights and Obligations*, paper presented to the Global Diversity Forum 15, UNEP Headquarters, Nairobi, Kenya, 12–14 May. Retrieved 25 March 2012, from www.inmotionmagazine.com/ra01/ms2.html

Solomon, Maui (2001). What is Wai 262? From an interview with Maui Solomon conducted by Inmotion Magazine. Retrieved 25 March 2012, from http://wai262.weebly.com/what-is-wai-262.html

Sunberg, Juanita and Jessica Dempsey (2009). "Cultures/Nature". In Rob Kitchen and Nigel Thrift (eds) *International Encyclopaedia of Human Geography.* Amsterdam: Elsevier Ltd, 458-463.

Tauli-Corpuz, Victoria (2003). *Bodiversity, Traditional Knowledge and Rights of Indigenous Peoples.* Malaysia: Third World Network. Retrieved 30 March 2012, from http://www.twnside.org.sg/title2/IPR/pdf/ipr05.pdf

Waitangi Tribunal (2011). *Wai 262, Ko Aotearoa Tenei: A Report into Claims Concerning New Zealand Law and Policy Affecting Maori Culture and Identity: Te Taumata Tuatahi.* Retrieved 12 March 2012, from www.waitangitribunal.govt.nz

Whatmore, Sarah (2002). *Hybrid Geographies.* Great Britain: Sage Publications.

Winter, Kawika (2004). *HAWAIIAN`AWA, Piper methysticum, A Study in Ethnobotany.* Thesis submitted to University of Hawaii. Retrieved 26 April 2012, from http://awadevelopment.org/kavaresearch/kw%20awa%20thesis.pdf

Vidal, John (2011). "Bolivia Enshrines Natural World's Rights with Equal Status for Mother Earth". *The Guardian*, 10 April 2012. Retrieved 26 April 2012, from http://www.guardian.co.uk/environment/2011/apr/10/bolivia-enshrines-natural-worlds-rights

Piratical Community and the Digital Age: The Structural Racialization of Piracy in European Law and Culture[1]

Sonja Schillings

Introduction

The term 'piracy' can be used to characterize a variety of communities that do not share any apparent organizational characteristics with each other. For example, corporations committing 'biopiracy', filesharers committing 'digital piracy' and Somali warlords committing 'maritime piracy' can all be merged under the same heading of piracy despite their diverse structural properties. This chapter argues, however, that some deeply rooted cultural assumptions about the nature of pirate communities exist which continue to shape Western discourses of certain specific communities as piratical.

More specifically, this chapter will argue that the notion of 'race' is decisive to differentiate piratical communities in Western discourse – that indeed, the pirate cannot be thought outside of 'his' race because the race attributed to a given pirate community directly relates to assumptions about its specific form of organization. This chapter will not only focus on race, but will also draw on the related field of 'critical whiteness studies' (see Roediger 1991). Piratical whiteness, in this context, is associated with communities that are strategic partnerships for the economic betterment of each individual member even at the potential cost of other Westerners; piratical non-whiteness is associated with collective and inherently hostile Otherness that seeks to overcome the West at large. These two piratical forms of community, which I will distinguish as piratae (white pirates) and praedones (non-white pirates), are not merely co-existing, but discursively complementary. They appear together and are defined by each other as much as by either relationship to the cultural lump entity of 'the West'. Importantly, a steep hierarchy is imagined between them: the praedo tends to be characterized as a supreme threat that the pirata is structurally derived from.

1 This chapter is a strongly revised and extended version of a paper presented at the "1st Global Conference: Images of Whiteness. Exploring Critical Issues" organized by Inter-Disciplinary.Net at Oxford University in 2011. I thank Prof. Sabine Schülting, Gina Marie Caison, Elisabeth Engel and Ida Jahr for their feedback at earlier stages of this paper. I also thank the editors, James Arvanitakis and Martin Fredriksson, for their valuable suggestions.

The chapter focuses on the questions of why, and how, the notion of pirates' community organization came to be racialized in Western discourse. Further I investigate how the notion of race is of central political importance especially for the digital rights movement today.

The digital rights movement in the West has achieved a characterization of the digital 'pirate' both as a legitimate political voice and as the representative of the structure of 'the Internet' at large. While this is in itself an impressive political achievement, the racialized undercurrents of the pirate discourse become extremely obvious in such a context. After all, the racialization of the pirate is directly derived from the pirate's internal organizational structure. The organization of digital communities has naturally been foregrounded by digital pirates in order to mobilize these communities for political causes; therefore, this chapter argues, the discursive racialization of pirate community has become acutely relevant for the legitimate political representation of 'digital natives' and 'the Internet'.

Interestingly, the racialization of the pirate community is not typical for the racializations usually encountered in Western discourse. The dominant twin properties of racialized discourse in the West are the binary characterization of white and non-white as mutually exclusive, coupled with the normalization of whiteness and the characterization of non-whiteness as deviant. It is especially the latter aspect that tends to make whiteness appear inherently superior in Western discourse, and which underlies structural white privilege. The pirate 'as such' is subjected to both. As I have argued elsewhere, the term 'pirate' itself is part of a language that works to preserve Western positions as privileged and normative. While a critical perspective must often rely on argument alone, sometimes including the establishment of an entire new vocabulary, advocates of the normalizing position of Western privilege can rely on an established, accessible and familiar cluster of narratives that they merely need to *evoke* in order to support their argument (Schillings 2011, 301-306). In their use of such narratives, normalizing positions all too often rely on the implication that they represent 'common sense' – whereas their opponents are, in contrast, hysterical and unrealistic.

On the level of conceptualizing the *internal* structures of pirate communities, however, the pirate discourse assumes a structurally different premise than white superiority. In fact, for most of the pirate's discursive history, a structural superiority and direct domination of non-white pirate communities over white pirate communities have been firmly presupposed. This has important consequences for the digital rights movement today.

The first part of this chapter focuses on early modern legal history, which I consider the origin of pirate communities' racialized distinction. It is sometimes overlooked that piracy is, by definition, a collective crime, and that a legal system based on individual guilt is presented with very specific difficulties by this fact. Western law requires a fairly elaborate idea of how to imagine an illegitimate piratical community in order to determine both the individual pirate's relationship to the community as well as the community's relationship to a legitimate sovereign, as both relationships are integral to the establishment of an individual pirate's guilt. This aspect is not explicit in most historical piracy law, yet it has been addressed by Hugo Grotius (2006) who made an effort to distinguish the various forms of pirate community that were only implicitly presupposed by his contemporaries. His differentiations underlie my use of the terms praedo and pirata that have, in fact, been coined by him (ibid. 2006, 447-448). Using his terminology, I will specify the properties of the two main forms of pirate community that are recognized by race-based differentiation.

Second, I will consider the introduction of the pirate terminology into debates internal to the West, and the increasing use of these terms in order to conceptualize copyright debates in the nineteenth century. I will show that the use of the pirate figure in the context of copyright is traditionally associated with white piracy, and that it goes hand in hand with a racialization of the economic sphere in general.

Finally, I will return to the contemporary debate on copyright piracy, and speculate on the pirate tradition's implications for today's context. Even though I will consider 'traditional' racialization that is based on the assumption of white supremacy, my central point will be a structural one that discusses the implications of the pirate communities' reverse discursive construction: a domination of white pirates by non-white pirates. I will suggest that this discursive tradition of specifically piratical racialization, as it is embedded into a discourse that is biased against 'the pirate' from the start, is able to explain much about the increasing criminalization of digital activity and activism as quasi-terrorist.

Throughout this chapter, I will use the generic 'he' when I refer to pirates, not out of preference but in order to indicate that both forms of pirate discourse are almost exclusively masculinity discourses, particularly explicitly since modernity (Brown 1995, 166-196; Turley 1999, 40-43). Though a fascinating area to pursue, the gender dimension is beyond this chapter's focus, and will be largely disregarded.

White Piratae and non-white Praedones

Definitions of piracy in law are generally based on constellations rather than on discernible acts. The pirate is a fundamentally relational political and legal entity, so all pirate definitions must be considered in the context of larger questions of legitimate political organization. I emphasize the inherently shifting, complex and ambiguous set of criteria and oppositions that pirate definitions rest upon because it helps explain how race could insert itself so deeply and decisively into a legal structure that tends not to explicitly mention it at all.

The pirate is an entity without any coherent positively defined qualities, except that he always appears in a construction of binary antagonism. Unstable legal fictions like this depend on extra-legal (that is, cultural) references to convincingly establish someone as a pirate. However, it takes more than the assumption of naturalized difference to incorporate race into a discourse. The notion of race requires a *complementary* structure: one which is going to be constructed as same and other, as white and non-white, must *exclude* as well as *produce and determine* each other. Especially due to the history of Barbary conflicts in the Mediterranean, piracy law indeed features an elaborate complementary constellation in fictions of pirate communities. The Mediterranean was characterized by continuous maritime violence represented especially by the Muslim Barbary states of Tripoli, Tunis, Algiers and Sallee and the Christian knights of Malta. Rather than a full-scale war, the Barbary conflicts created a century-long atmosphere of threat and violence in the entire region.

The multinational cluster of European pirate law as we know it today was largely established in the early modern period of the sixteenth and seventeenth centuries, when the vastly different confrontations with maritime Others of the Americas and of the Mediterranean had to be harmonized into universal legal categories. In the Mediterranean specifically, pirate law addressed the phenomenon of raids and abductions carried out by privately equipped men-of-war in the name of the Barbary states (Earle 1970, 3-19). In this context, legal application distinguished between corsairs who were native Africans and Muslims, and European corsairs who had adopted Barbary employment and had often converted from Christianity to Islam. The African and the European Barbary corsairs would become the godfathers of the inherently racialized pirate figure.

During the Middle Ages, the difference between African and European Barbary corsairs in the Mediterranean had been established by a whole cluster of properties. Origin, religion, skin color, cultural and political background were all included and typically not differentiated from each other. The early modern period changed that, as the American colonial sphere gained importance for conceptualizing political and legal encounters. Intertwined and increasingly overlapping notions of religion and race came to be the core means to define inherent difference from an increasingly normalized image of white, male, European supremacy. In this vein, a variety of 'non-civilized' nations were increasingly collapsed into one 'non-white' race (Loomba 2002; Haselstein 2000).

The Mediterranean was an especially contested and contradictory space in the early modern struggle for meaning (Greene 2002, 71). The legal discourse of piracy therefore tended to rule on the basis of the smallest common denominator, and followed a largely positivist understanding of what constituted piracy: which meant that the pirate status was determined by a person's relationship to European states. Legal distinctions were loosely set between nationally attached privateers who legitimately attacked foreign traders, and non-nationally attached pirates who were discredited as predatory. Importantly, the privilege of national attachment, and therefore the legitimacy of the maritime aggressor, was directly dependent on European acknowledgement of the commissioning sovereign. The Barbary states were either only grudgingly, or not at all, acknowledged as legitimate sovereigns by early modern legal commentators.

The notion of race came to be significant because the Barbary states frequently employed Europeans, and European pirate law reacted to this practice (Earle 1970, 35). Europeans who aggressively turned against their home countries were persecuted with a total antagonism that European states could not quite exhibit towards the Barbary states themselves. The European renegades, however, were unambiguously charged with piracy and treason. The conviction of such a treacherous renegade as a pirate was the only consensus in legal opinion concerning the definition of piracy (Tindal 1694, 26). Treason therefore became central in defining piracy.

This legal conceptualization had some implications that fostered the racialization of piracy. European renegades who accepted Barbary employment and citizenship, and even converted to Islam, were still legally conceptualized as

Christian Europeans (Rubin 1998, 72-74). Christianity as well as Europeanness – the two central categories which, according to Loomba, would eventually distill into the notion of whiteness (2002, 39-44) – were defined as unchangeable characteristics of a person in treason-based pirate law, even if that person had become a Barbary Muslim in practice. Origin and first religion were treated as essentialized features that continued to define a person despite all of his contrary practices. In this sense, the conviction of European Barbary corsairs as traitors can thus be called the first racializing act of Western pirate law.

In terms of piratical communities, this basic claim of essentialized alliance was translated into specific differentiations of illegitimate collective action. In his long unpublished work *De Iure Praedae Commentarius* (1604), Hugo Grotius differentiated two forms of illegitimate maritime violence that attacked from outside of the national realm itself (Grotius 2006).[2] The *pirata,* according to Grotius, is a private actor who attacks and plunders for his own personal benefit, and does not represent anyone but himself. In contrast, the *praedo* is the representative of a sovereign that benefits from raids, and therefore of a public interest. Praedones are only illegitimate because the sovereigns they represent are unrecognized by 'legitimate' sovereigns.

These separate categories of pirata and praedo became complementary through their association with Islam in the historical Mediterranean context. As was previously mentioned, European and African Barbary corsairs were exchangeable in practice: they operated in the same waters and attacked the same ships in the name of the same sovereign and the same God – but it *meant* something different in European pirate law. African Barbary corsairs were deemed the offspring of a culture that was predatory not least because it was *collectively* Muslim. Such characterization of the Barbary corsairs was especially pronounced in the works of Alberico Gentili (Benton 2010, 279). European Barbary corsairs, on the other hand, were the result of *individual* treason and cultural abandonment – every European corsair delivered his own, and only his own, soul to the Other God. The common reference to Islam made the religious-racial differentiation within pirate law tangible. A converted traitor could, at most, gang up with a brigade of other deviants; he could never merge with the Other community.

In short, praedo and pirata became directly and necessarily related to each

2 In the translation of Grotius' work used here, 'pirata' is translated as 'pirate' and 'praedo' as 'freebooter'. I have chosen to maintain the original terms in order to be able to apply the definitions more clearly.

other as well as hermetically sealed from each other in European discourse on Barbary corsairs. This discourse also established a hierarchy of threat. While the European Barbary corsair's employment by the Barbary states and his acceptance of Islam was condemned in Europe, he was still conceptualized as one who opportunistically supported the real agent of moral bankruptcy and the actual taster of forbidden fruit. The treacherous renegade was a mere sideshow to the central, gruesome antagonist of European civilization: the African Barbary corsair, the 'king of evil' (Crowley 2009, 45).

In summary, the complementary construction of pirata and praedo depended on a shared cultural 'field' of Otherness, in this case religion. Once such a field was established, two separate forms of community were distinguished that helped explain each other. The praedo represented a collectivist outside threat that was not only complemented, but also legally evoked and specified by the pirata's individual abandonment of European civilization. On the other hand, the praedo's religion, Islam, helped explain the fundamental nature of the pirata's transgression to Westerners by characterizing it as a general conversion to Otherness.

The racialization of piracy

With the colonial context, the shared field for praedo and pirata ceased to be the 'predatory' religion of Islam; it came to be a predatory *economy.* This change in the field was rooted in an idea of the pirate that was increasingly derived from colonial rather than the Mediterranean context. The pirates of the early eighteenth century, the so-called pirates of the Golden Age of Piracy (1690-1730), shaped a discourse of pirata communities as economic regimes that were organizationally decentralized yet culturally homogenous (Rediker 2004). At the same time, the praedo was increasingly subsumed in a discourse of more explicitly racialized Otherness that notably included the characterization of colonial spaces themselves.

During the Golden Age of Piracy, the colonial pirata – the European, Christian pirate who plundered for personal gain – was fleshed out as the 'typical' pirate: an ambitious, vengeful, colorful figure that was derived from the maritime tradition of privateering in general rather than the Barbary corsair specifically. Their ability to live by an alternative system was derived from their location in an extra-Western colonial space that was itself personified and racialized, and thus took up some of the praedo's properties that enabled the pirata to function within the requirements of the constellation that originally defined him in Western discourse. For instance, Frederick Jackson Turner attributed aggressive resistance and transformative powers to the colonial wilderness (1964, 39), a characterization that echoed central features of the praedo community in relationship to the pirata.

Importantly, these piratae abandoned European civilization for something other than Islam: they abandoned it for a different regime of distributive justice. Golden Age pirates were primarily characterized by their refusal of the rising economic regime of merchant deep-sea sailing. This trading regime, which established in parallel to the still-significant privateering regime, constituted nothing less than a paradigm shift for the seafaring trade. The two regimes of privateer and merchantman did not so much embody a violent versus a peaceful representation of the nation, but rather specific forms of distributive justice on board, epitomized by the difference in sailors' payment: by shares on the privateer, and by wages on the merchantman. The system of shares had always been an important attraction of privateering for sailors. They received a fixed percentage of any prizes the privateer took, which means their profits varied depending on the richness of rewards. The system of shares gave sailors a significant voice aboard, because they all risked their profits in an unsuccessful enterprise. Both a decisive say on board and the chance to make a considerable profit from his work were practices abolished aboard a merchantman. The merchant sailor received a fixed wage for a fixed journey; his signature on the contract was the only decision he was expected to make. The merchant system was generally characterized by the attempt to cut costs, which resulted in a structural exploitation of sailors, who in turn became the primary pool of pirate recruits.

Rather than being defined by a political antagonist such as the Barbary states, the pirata was now defined by the rivaling practices and priorities of two economic regimes that still existed in parallel. Because the pirata did not 'convert' but merely 'returned' to privateering instead of accepting merchant shipping as a source of employment, the white pirata's 'treason' slowly transformed into 'systemic criticism' – at least it was widely acknowledged that his acts could be read as such. In the eighteenth century, the widespread lament about the loss of the pirata's skills for the nation was often peppered with suspicions that he had originally been pushed into despair by heartless economic exploiters at home (Anonymous 1980, 5). Another famous maxim of the Golden Age was that the merchant was as good a pirate on land as any arch pirate was at sea (Defoe 1724/1999, 57). Together with the transformative space of the wilderness, the capitalist merchant became an entity to characterize the pirata by.

The capitalist was Christian and European like the pirata, and he also represented an economically strategic coalition of individuals rather than a collectivist clan. The reference to the capitalist did not undo the original complementary constellation of racialized difference that had created the pirata as the representative of a specific form of community, but it emphasized the pirata's 'white' properties in a way that rendered his own properties the properties of capitalism itself, and the properties of the praedo the properties of colonial space itself. In the process, the colonial pirata transformed into the epitomization of an individualist, roaming economic man: he organized unstable, egalitarian, exclusively profit-oriented communities, and came to represent an early version of the colonial rogue pioneer.

While piratae were increasingly reclaimed by Western discourse as the epitomizations of pioneering rogue capitalism, the idea of praedones remained that of an inherently threatening and illegitimate bloc from outside. However, praedones were increasingly subsumed into a general discourse of hostile non-white Otherness (Rouleau 2010). The increasing replacement of the term 'Turk' with the terms 'Moor' or 'Black' in the eighteenth and nineteenth centuries is indicative of this process, as these terms were not only used in the Mediterranean context, but increasingly used to describe Amerindians, Indians and Africans in general. The change in terminology indicates a shift in perception that replaces Islam with Blackness as the primary shorthand to describe inherent Otherness (Loomba 2002, 45).

Regarding the construction of collectivity, especially the term 'Moor' transports a certain ambivalence concerning the ways Other communities were to be conceptualized. This racialized term served as a flexible shorthand for political entities that were undoubtedly endowed with culture, religion and political organization, but whose apparently inherent Otherness remained their most striking property in European eyes. This is why very differently organized communities, from small local tribes to the Indian empire or the feared Barbary states themselves, came to be conflated in such discourses. The collective thus evoked by praedones became too large to represent any specific sovereignty; instead, the confrontation with a praedo became constitutive of a more abstract battle between civilization and wilderness, progress and nature, the advanced and the primitive. As prototypical as such a construction is, however, the praedo retained a special role in the discourse of racialized Otherness. Derived from the specific legacy of the Barbary states, he represents the specific case of a racialized Other who is able to *win* and to *prevail* in a confrontation.

The link of the pirata and the rogue capitalist, as well as the merging of the praedo into a racialized lump of Otherness, reinforced the original complementary construction of piratical communities: the pirata as a strategic community of self-interested parasites who can never dis-attach from their original civilizational belonging; and the praedo as the representative of a unified cultural collective that is an inherently different, unknowable, lurking threat. These distinctions were established in the early eighteen hundreds and conserved throughout later centuries, even when the West faced new pirate waves that otherwise might have changed their characterizations (Earle 2006, 222).

By the nineteenth century, the capitalist pirata and the evil, racialized lump praedo had become stock figures in Western discourse. The structural properties of each were stabilized so thoroughly that the common root and the structural dependence of pirata and praedo community characterizations were rendered almost completely invisible. Nevertheless, the structural dependency endured precisely because the stereotype continued to preserve the original constellation's core assumptions. In a recent essay, Sean Grass (2011) has shown how the fraudulent, speculating pirate banker at the heart of the British empire and the racialized Asian pirate thugs of the colonial wilderness were portrayed as inversions of each other in a Victorian novel that is not renowned for its particularly innovative use of existing cultural categories. '*Hard Cash*,' Grass writes, '[...] makes Dodd's voyage from the colonial margins back to England read paradoxically as a return to the heart of darkness, a dangerous approach to the epicenter of the piratical and insatiable Victorian commercial sphere' (2011, 191). This example may demonstrate that it did not require much to unleash the discursive force of the complementary structure of pirate communities, even at a time that did not explicitly problematize such a connection; it also indicates that the colonial backdrop of nineteenth century English discourse, and its general assumption of a lurking lump Other somewhere out there at the fringes of the empire, did much to absorb the praedo requirement in discursive uses of the pirata within the West.

In his essay, Grass also argues that copyright infringement is firmly included in the set of dangerous commercial practices represented by the piratical capitalist by the late nineteenth century (2011, 186), indicating a longer discursive preoccupation with the link throughout the century. The Barbary states' final banishment from Western collective memory after the sacking of Algiers in 1830, and thus the finalization of the Mediterranean praedo's consumption under the heading of a lump Other, indeed coincided with the rise of the white pirate not only as a hyperbole of the capitalist merchant, but also as a discursive representative of more abstract inter-Western piracy debates: most notably, the copyright debate. English and American publishing businesses were at the forefront of a systemic reuse of pirate terminology throughout the century (Knighton 2011; Mattacks 2011).

For the first time, a detached, virtual and paradox notion of property was directly explained by the spatial and economic paradoxes of the disconnected, individualist, roaming white pirate figure (Knighton 2011, 86). The nineteenth century use of the pirata as a discursive representative of the paradoxes of intellectual property and copyright was inviting because apart from representing criminality, this romanticized individualist figure also stood to represent core values of modern Western societies while at the same time transgressing the limitations of prevailing political and economic tradition. Furthermore, the question of copyright addressed a conflict of regimes of redistribution – which was an issue traditionally addressed by the colonial pirata who had been shaped by the conflict of privateer and merchantmen. The pirata was a figure that could be accepted as a discursive representative of the debate on many levels and by both sides.

The link between the pirata and the copyright debate was thus established, but the question arises how the praedo can be fitted into this altered use of the pirata. The Golden Age pirate could be linked to a racialized *space* that replaced the political entity of the Barbary states in decisive aspects, and the requirements of the complementary constellation could be met. But what of a pirata that referred to a virtual and abstract notion of property such as intellectual property – where could the collective hostile bloc of praedones lurk here? There was no hostile Other set on crushing the Western publishing business or the notion of property as a whole.

In the copyright debate, Other spaces could partly retain their role as praedo-replacement, as copyright violators strategically exploited differences in national legal realms. However, as the concerned spaces here were usually inner-Western: Great Britain vs. United States in the nineteenth century debates on reprint literature; the United States, Great Britain and others vs. Sweden in the twenty-first century Pirate Bay debates. As such, the core property of the pirata-praedo structure was no longer met, namely that there had to be an inherently Other, unknowable, extra-Western hostile bloc which informed the pirata activity in some decisive way. This fundamental discursive gap that threatened to destabilize the pirate reference in the copyright context was largely forgotten with the increasing harmonization of copyright laws in the Western world and the general dismissal of the pirate figure from these issues. This gap is, however, the key condition for central discursive developments we witness in the digital piracy debate today. The Internet is able to take the role of the sea and wilderness in earlier discursive constellations, where the warning that 'here be praedones' makes discursive sense even in the abstract context of intellectual property.

Implications for digital piracy – some concluding comments

As was indicated in the introduction to this chapter, the digital piracy discourse is special in the discursive history of piracy. This is because it has replaced the provocative and never fully consistent claim to a legitimate piratical *cause* with an actual serious claim to represent a legitimate piratical *voice* in Western discourse. For the first time since the last generation of the Golden Age Pirates, there is a comparatively big community to consciously consider ways in which piratical community can be organized. In the digital piracy movement, the formation of parties as well as on the organization of grassroot activism are emphasized. This constant evocation of piratical community leads to an acute actualization of the racialized distinction between piratae and praedones.

Politically organized file sharers in the West frequently tend to characterize themselves as piratae specifically, often referring to the Golden Age directly. Examples are the sloop in the Pirate Bay logo and the symbol of the Jolly Roger with a cassette for a skull. Germany is the country with the most successful Pirate Party; its central slogan is a word play changing the swashbuckling 'Make ready to board' into the slogan 'Make ready to change.' Digital rights activists explain their self-characterization as 'pirates' as a direct response to their vilification by the content-owning industries such as the Motion Picture Association of America (MPAA). For example, the Swedish pirate party's founder Rickard Falkvinge speaks of a conscious refusal to "feel shame" for being called a pirate, and characterizes the name of the Swedish pirate party as a "way of reclaiming a word" (2006).

The fact that originally, economic rather than political entities had antagonized file sharers does suggest discourses of Golden Age piracy as a persuasive analogy. File sharers were therefore able to celebrate themselves as pioneering individualists who, by virtue of the very practices that were condemned by their opponents, raised the all-important question of the information age: who legitimately defines property?

In direct reference to Golden Age piratae who had been able to shed off the notion of the renegade, file sharers were discursively able to make this conflict not about cultural treason and economic anarchy, but about a righteous opposition against laws "…which rich Men have made for their own Security, for the cowardly Whelps have not the Courage otherwise to defend what they get by their Knavery" (Defoe 1999, 587). The virtue of digital pirates is based on two pillars of self-characterization: the concept of the postmodern artist who remixes prevailing knowledge and art into something new, and the concept of the republican distributer who demolishes walls of privilege and makes previously restricted expert knowledge available to those underprivileged eager to grow into educated maturity. These discourses characterize digital piracy as a reaction to the needs of prototypical individualists such as the artistic genius or the self-taught social riser. In this sense, 'good' piratical acts are not the result of an impulse to *destroy*, but to *affirm* central Western models of desirable ways of thinking. File sharers were thus able to turn the tables on the corporations without changing the terminology of the discourse.

Next to the pirate parties, the political discourse on digital piracy is represented by organizations such as Anonymous and Wikileaks that also continuously evoke questions of 'who may legitimately own and control information?' All organizations and actors associated with digital rights as a whole tend to be identified as an interconnected community. It is relevant to emphasize this because such a discursive situation feeds into associations of digital rights activists as piratae: a community of persons who, despite their loose and scattered occurrence and the frequency of bitter internal conflicts, represent something like a distinct 'culture' reminiscent of popular conceptualization of Golden Age piracy. As Marcus Rediker notes:

> The transmission of [Golden Age] pirate culture through space and time was linked closely to their success in attracting new recruits and to their democratic – one might say anarchic – form of self-organization. As more and more volunteers joined the pirates, and as the ship became more

> crowded, the moment inevitably arrived when the crew would split. [...] The social organization constructed by pirates was flexible, but it could not accommodate severe, sustained conflict. Those who had experienced the claustrophobic and authoritarian world of the merchantman cherished the freedom to separate. The pirates' democratic exercise of authority [...] produced chronic instability [but] it also guaranteed continuity; the very process by which new crews were established helped to ensure cultural continuity among the pirates. (2004, 80-81)

White piracy is a discursive foil to characterize, first, a diverse digital community as being unified with a common interest. Second, it has implications for the organized political forms that can be chosen in representation of this community. The explicitly interest-bound, recruitment-based character of the pirata was indeed helpful to evoke the grass root potential of digital-rights organizations and parties: the notion of decentralization is directly taken up in pirate party experiments of quasi-autonomous local 'crews' and general notions of liquid democracy. In this way, the pirata reference organizes political activity in representation of the digital sphere, and thus helps characterize 'the Internet' as a sphere from within which political mobilization can occur on a substantial scale.

It is the criminal and terrorist use of 'the Internet' that therefore characterizes the praedo. The characterization of digital praedones can be illustrated, for instance, by the Nigeria email scams. African scammers operated by e-mail and exploited Western ideas about unstable and corrupt third world governments in order to defraud persons in the West of money. The example of Nigeria scammers especially indicates that in the realm of technology, the identification of praedones is directly and primarily based on racialized Western discourses that re-inscribe the nineteenth century's non-white lump Other. The organizational properties of a scamming organization are not inherently non-white. In fact, the Nigeria scam specifically is a technologically advanced version of the nineteenth century Spanish prisoner scam that exploited postal services in much the same way within the West (Jarman 1952). Nevertheless, the firm association of this scam with Nigeria indicates a Western discourse suggesting that predatory digital practices are enabled by their conspicuous embeddedness in a racialized distant elsewhere. These environments are ruthless and lawless, and they are shockingly able to reach right into the privacy of Western living rooms via the Internet.

Kavita Philip (2005) has drawn attention to the fact that digital rights activists themselves are extremely conscious of such racialized criminalizations of the

Internet itself, and have addressed it in rather questionable ways. Philip shows how digital rights activists have sought to differentiate between good white piracy – which is undertaken in the name of creativity and liberty – and bad 'Asian piracy' which is economically predatory. These activists characterize this non-white pirate as a mutual enemy, an outside threat both to the West's economic stability and the white pirate's struggle for political recognition (Philip 2005, 215).

However, I suggest that the digital piratae's attempt to shield themselves from a discursive re-integration with the illegitimacy of the praedo must fail. The elaboration of the digital rights community as an essentially non-hierarchical, rhizomorph network unified by a shared cultural objective has already evoked the pirata in a structural rather than a merely referential way: the praedo only needed to be actualized by a more substantial threat than a Nigerian scam to unfold its deeply rooted discursive force.

This moment came with 9/11 when terror cells claimed to be the violent spearhead of Islam itself. These attacks were overwhelmingly read as the attacks of an extra-Western, extra-modern, racialized Other: Western political and economic institutions were subsequently preoccupied with matters of 'security' throughout their realms of influence. In anti-terrorism and security debates, a general re-characterization of 'networks' as dangerous seats of terrorist infection rather than a pool for democratic grassroots activity has long been obvious. In this context, Eva Horn has shown that in debates such as those on 'Cyberwars,' 'Netwars', 'Sleeper Cells' and 'terror networks', it is the Other *structure* rather than the Other *actor* that is constructed as constitutive in identifying dangerous antagonists to Western civilization (2007, 481). Furthermore, the general proximity of legal and discursive conceptualizations of piracy and post-9/11 terrorism (Engels 2007) have reinforced the reading of Islamic terrorists as praedones who complement the Western digital pirata on the Internet. Indicative of their praedo function in this context, security experts tend to emphasize terrorists' use of the Internet for recruitment: that is, the conversion and transformation of Westerners.

Reminiscent of the praedo and the pirata in the early modern legal assessment of Barbary corsairdom, the terrorist explains to Westerners what the constitutive threat *is* while the digital pirate explains how the agents of constitutive threat *operate.* In this vein, the pirata as the figurehead of the digital rights movement has come to be the foil for imagining the organizational structure of predatory terrorist threats. I see both the increasingly pointed racist undertones in the digital rights debate identified by Philip as well as debates on the appropriateness of the pirate reference for the digital rights movement (Liang 2010, 356-359) as indicators that digital rights activists are aware of this discursive conflation. As such, they attempt to disassociate themselves from the implications of their potential association with 'terrorist' or generally 'predatory' activities on the Internet.

However, the deeply rooted complementary characterization of white and non-white pirates in the West, along with its structural tendency to require a hierarchy of threats that renders the praedo superior to and constitutive of the pirata, makes the digital right movement's disassociation from terrorist 'security threats' difficult. The use of the term 'terrorism' in documents such as the Clean IT project, which is the successor of the publicly heavily opposed and therefore abandoned ACTA (Anti-Counterfeiting Trade Agreement) treaty in the European Union, is a case in point. Clean IT fails to define terrorism via any properties or even the motivation of agents, but only identifies potentially dangerous structures of the Internet. This strategy is accompanied by the open acknowledgement that a distinction between terrorists and legitimate Internet users cannot be made in any convincing way (EDRI 2012; CleanIT 2012, in particular # 4).

The field of digital technology has re-evoked a structural aspect of piracy that had been rendered comparatively invisible in the nineteenth century, and had therefore been largely overlooked in histories of piracy and copyright. Western as well as non-Western digital rights activists will have to face the strong discursive link beween themselves and a vague lump notion of terrorism. These developments can no longer be deflated by an abandonment of the pirate name, and especially not by a racialized disassociation from alleged praedones. Institutional suspicions against grassroots political mobilization are themselves a consequence of the inherently racialized image of piratical community in the West. If the pattern is to be broken, taking the same line of racializing predatory Others will not help the cause of digital pirates but, as this chapter has argued, will rather reinforce the pattern and work against them in the end.

References

Anonymous (1980). *The Life and Adventures of Capt. John Avery*. Los Angeles: University of California, Augustian Reprint Society.

Benton, Lauren (2010). "Legalities of the Sea in Gentili's *Hispanica Advocatio*". In Benedict Kingsbury and Benjamin Straumann (eds). *The Roman Foundations of the Law of Nations. Alberico Gentili and the Justice of Empire*. Oxford: Oxford

Univ. Press, 269-282.
Brown, Wendy (1995). *States of Injury: Power and Freedom in Late Modernity.* Princeton: Princeton Univ. Press.
Clean IT Project - Draft Document (August 2012). Retrieved 20 September 2012, from http://www.cleanitproject.eu/
Crowley, Roger (2008). *Empires of the Sea: The Final Battle for the Mediterranean, 1521-1580.* London: Faber and Faber.
Defoe, Daniel (1724 & 1728/1999). *The General History of the Pyrates.* Manuel Schonhorn (ed.). Dover: Mineola.
Earle, Peter (1970). *Corsairs of Malta and Barbary.* London: Sidgwick & Jackson.
Earle, Peter (2006). *The Pirate Wars.* St. Martin's Griffin: Thomas Dunne Books.
Engels, Jeremy (2007). "Floating Bombs Encircling Our Shores: Post-9/11 Rhetorics of Piracy and Terrorism". *Cultural Studies <=> Critical Methodologies*, 7, 326-349.
European Digital Rights (EDRI) (2012). *Clean It – Leak Shows Plans For Large-Scale, Undemocratic Surveillance Of All Communications*, 21 September 2012. http://www.edri.org/fcleanIT
Falkvinge, Rickard (2006). "'Avast ye scurvy file sharers!': Interview with Swedish Pirate Party Leader Rickard Falkvinge". *Wikinews.* Retrieved 6 September 2012, from https://en.wikinews.org/wiki/%22Avast_ye_scurvy_file_sharers!%22:_Interview_with_ Swedish_Pirate_Party_leader_Rickard_Falkvinge
Grass, Sean (2011). "Piracy, Race and Domestic Peril in Hard Cash". In Grace Moore (ed.). *Pirates and Mutineers of the Nineteenth Century. Swashbucklers and Swindlers.* Farnham: Ashgate Publishing Ltd. 181-196.
Greene, Molly (2002). "Beyond the Northern Invasion: The Mediterranean in the Seventeenth Century". *Past and Present*, 174:1, 42-71.
Grotius, Hugo (2006). *Commentary on the Law of Prize and Booty.* Martine Julia van Ittersum (ed.). Indianapolis: Liberty Fund.
Haselstein, Ulla (2000). *Die Gabe der Zivilisation. Kultureller Austausch und literarische Textpraxis in Amerika, 1682-1861.* München: Wilhelm Fink Verlag.
Horn, Eva (2007). *Der geheime Krieg. Verrat, Spionage und moderne Fiktion.* Frankfurt: Fischer.
Jarman, Rufus (1952). "How the Spanish-Prisoner Swindle Works". In *The Saturday Evening Post,* 8 November 1952, 29 & 151-154.
Knighton, Andrew Lyndon (2011). "The Wreck of the *Corsair*: Piracy, Political Economy and American Publishing". In Grace Moore (ed.). *Pirates and Mutineers of the Nineteenth Century. Swashbucklers and Swindlers.* Farnham: Ashgate Publishing Ltd., 79-94.
Liang, Lawrence (2010). "Beyond Representation. The Figure of the Pirate". In Gaëlle Krikorian and Amy Kapczynski. (eds). *Access to Knowledge in the Age of Intellectual Property.* New York: Zone Books, 353-375.
Loomba, Ania (2002). *Shakespeare, Race, and Colonialism.* Oxford: Oxford University Press.

Mattacks, Kate (2011). "Acts of Piracy: *Black Ey'd Susan*, Theatrical Publishing and the Victorian Stage". In Grace Moore (ed.). *Pirates and Mutineers of the Nineteenth Century. Swashbucklers and Swindlers.* Farnham: Ashgate Publishing Ltd., 133-148.

Philip, Kavita (2005). "What is a Technological Author? The Pirate Function and Intellectual Property". *Postcolonial Studies*, 8:2. 199-218.

Rediker, Marcus (2004). *Villains of All Nations. Atlantic Pirates in the Golden Age.* London: Verso.

Roediger, David R. (1991). *The Wages of Whiteness: Race and the Making of the American Working Class.* New York and London, Verso.

Rouleau, Brian (2010). "Maritime Destiny as Manifest Destiny. American Commercial Expansionism and the Idea of the Indian". *Journal of the Early Republic*, 30:3, 377-411.

Rubin, Alfred P. (1997). *The Law of Piracy.* New York: Transnational Publishers.

Schillings, Sonja (2011). "The Concept of Hostis Humani Generis in Cultural Translation: Somali Piracy, Discursive Containment, and the Creation of an Extralegal Space". In Winfried Fluck, Katharina Motyl, Donald E. Pease and Christoph Raetzsch (eds). *States of Emergency: States of Crisis.* Tübingen: Narr, 295–316.

Tindal, Matthew (1694). *An Essay concerning the Law of Nations, and the Rights of Soveraigns.* London: Richard Baldwin.

Turley, Hans (1999). *Rum, Sodomy and the Lash. Piracy, Sexuality, and Masculine Identity.* New York: New York University Press.

Turner, Frederick Jackson (1964). "The Significance of the Frontier in American History". In Ray Allen Billington (ed.). *Frontier and Section. Selected Essays of Frederick Jackson Turner.* Englewood Cliffs: Prentice-Hall Inc., 37-62.

Information that directly relates to European pirate parties was primarily collected from the websites http://www.piratenpartei.de/, http://wiki.piratenpartei.de/ and http://www.pp-international.net/, all of which were last viewed on 20 September 2012.

Part II – Politics

Modernity, Law and the Violence of Piracy, Property and the State

Sean Johnson Andrews

Preface/context

The proliferation of books and popular interest in pirates and piracy – both of the seagoing and high school hacker variety – appears a mere fancy and fashion. The practice itself, however, is on the rise: Somali pirates now regularly patrol the Gulf of Arden – soon to be aided by weapons smuggled out of post-Kaddafi Lybia; though largely a misnomer, 'pirates' of intellectual property continue to be prosecuted for said crimes. Over 2011-12, we witnessed the takedown of www.library.nu, the prosecution of Pirate Bay's founders, and criminal proceedings brought against the nearly legitimate operator of Megaupload. In addition, we saw a series of US legislative debacles ("PIPA" 2011; "RWA" 2011; "SOPA" 2011) supposedly targeting piracy and other Intellectual Property crimes. Alongside these policies, maritime laws are being changed to allow for international policing of Somalia's coast, attempting to extend the crumbling infrastructure of the nation state into the very global, digital realms designed to undermine the capabilities of those states in delivering on the promises of modernity and modernization.

In other words, whether or not we see every instance of piracy as a conscious rebellion against neoliberal capitalism, this order provides context for an important question: Why are we suddenly seeing a rise in both the concern about and practice of piracy? Proponents of neoliberal globalization promised a new route to modernization and economic development: perhaps it is marked with the Jolly Roger?

In the case of media 'piracy,' the practices in question have a long, if recent history. Before there were Magnet files, Limewire, Bittorrent, or Napster, there was the dreaded 'home taping' of vinyl albums and the scourge of the VCR. US lobbyists for the content industries have been escalating the rhetoric for several decades, demanding legislative efforts to protect their dying business model. Ironically, it is the very technologies facilitating these organisations' global aspirations that now threaten their newly acquired profit base.

On the other hand, the more public nature of this piracy – which now takes place on open networks and in the rec rooms of suburban teenagers instead of shady stalls in Southern markets – amplifies the moral panic around intellectual property rights (IPR) theft: if all this theft is happening, how many lost sales does this create? If a culture of 'theft' is tacitly permitted, what will this mean for the bottom line in the future? After little more than a half-century of carefully inculcating Western youth in the practices of commodified culture, the trends point to a new era where they may be more likely to steal what mainstream culture they desire – and/or remake it into something altogether new.

Below this immaterial level, most of the struggle over IPR regards counterfeit trademarked goods and patent infringements. Anxieties over (and practices of) these forms of IPR infringement and the renewed maritime piracy partially stem from the four decades of deep transformations in the global political economy and the uneven distribution of resources these changes have produced and rely upon. This uneven distribution – and the failure of both modernity and modernization it represents – thereby threatens the legitimacy of the fragile states decimated and then propped up by proponents of neoliberal economic policies: these proponents insist states (and the law) play what James Mittelman calls a "courtesan role:" providing services "to clients, especially wealthy or upper class ones," functioning as the sole defense against violent anarchy and unabashed theft – or at least any theft that might come from below, possibly interrupting these processes (Mittelman 2000, 25).

Though neoliberalism is just another name for capitalism, it is useful as a term because of its historical provenance. It contrasts the current order of capitalism with that of the mid-century. In political, ideological, and material terms, the post-war order of embedded liberalism was the closest capitalism has come to producing the kind of enlightened modernization that western civilization has long promised. The state became a powerful instrument of post-colonial sovereignty, national economic development, and democratic self-determination. It was by no means perfect. For radical leftists the welfare state sapped the energies of the anti-capitalist movement; for social movements of the global South it represented a disciplinary instrument in need of further popular determination. But most importantly, for global capital the mid-century welfare state represented an institution corrupted from its primary role: the defense of property and the economic power of property owners through whatever means necessary.

The dramatic U-turn of neoliberalism brought about, as David Harvey has termed it, "the restoration of class power" (2006, 7-68). Whatever its inefficiencies and corruptions, the developmental state was legitimized internally by its middling efforts to materialize the promises of modernity in actual modernization (McNally 2010; Peet 2007): as Harvey discusses in much of his recent work, neoliberalism not only reverses the previous priorities of the state, but undermines the gains made by development states in that previous era. Debt and finance, the instruments and beneficiaries of the neoliberal order, are used as levers to privatize public assets.

Harvey calls this process "accumulation by dispossession" (2003, 137-181). For instance, Mexico's telecommunications infrastructure was privatized then purchased at fire sale prices by Fortune 500 businessmen like Carlos Slim, who is now the richest man in the world (Harvey 2005, 98-104). As Schiller and McChesney (2003) point out, a similar trend continues across the world, with formerly nationalized media industries privatized by and for global owners of capital. Up until now this has primarily happened in the global South; but the economic crisis from 2007 onwards has brought it home to the wealthiest nations. As of early 2012, both Britain's National Health Service and higher education system began to feel the weight of neoliberal austerity. Similar trends show up in the privatization of American education, health care, and even in what Chalmers Johnson has characterized as a "long established system of state socialism:" the US military (Johnson 2004, 99).

In each case, sovereign debt provides an excuse to reduce the public sector in the interest of privatization. This privatization, in turn, is used as a bludgeon to discipline labor and social movements of various kinds. What this means in practice – particularly for resources that can actually be carried away or stolen at gun point – is that the state is called upon to violently enforce the property rights of owners, often at the expense of the vast majority of the population, facing down protesters and facilitating the easy movement of capital. For the early years of this assault, the pious exhortations of market liberals were largely accepted as dogma. Increasingly, however, the transparent imbalance in the interests served by the neoliberal state creates a contradiction no amount of propaganda can set right. Still, the proponents of this order persist, leading to a generalized crisis of legitimacy around law, the state, violence, and private property.

In what follows I would like to frame piracy – both as a practice and a discursive object – as a particular kind of precipitate of this context. In piracy we can see this crisis in all its plenitude. I am especially interested in how it highlights neoliberalism as a failed project of modernity, whose failures necessitate informal, illegal, and even violent forms of self-sustenance and determination. Far from romanticizing these, I would like to consider how similar they are to the neoliberal project itself – its violence and narrow, destructive political economic effects – and posit the conclusion that the lesson of piracy is actually that we need to re-found the project of modernity on a broader basis.

Violence, modernity, and the state

In March of 2012, as Bashir al-Assad's army unleashed a fresh wave of attacks on the rebel stronghold of Homs, opposition groups passed along a cache of over 3,000 pages of emails they had secretly collected from the private accounts of the dictator and his wife over the course of the past year (Beaumont 2012; Booth and Mahmood 2012; Booth, Mahmood and Harding 2012). Though the communications revealed little relevant intelligence, one set of facts stood out for western media commentators: In defiance of U.S. sanctions, Assad went out of his way to legally purchase music, games, and movies on Apple's iTunes platform (Max Fisher 2012). While activists were sickened by the revelation that, "He was downloading iTunes songs while his army was shelling us," comedian and *The Daily Show* host Jon Stewart offered a different insight: "This guy massacres his own people with impunity, but makes sure he purchases his music legally?!" (quoted in O'Neil 2012). This satirical observation works because of the multiple layers of truth it contains and contests.

In the spirit of Slavoj Žižek, we can parse the possible interpretations of this joke, delivered to a sincere burst of audience laughter. Though it is in itself insignificant, by peeling the layers of meaning, and offering several interpretations, we can examine the deep cultural arguments taking place at the site it inhabits. The media interest in this story and Stewart's summation of its apparent irony indicate a disturbance in the reified surface of the hegemonic order. A close examination illuminates, I argue, the cultural and political stakes of the debate over piracy – a hegemonic struggle that piracy has almost by definition played a role in both unsettling and constituting.

In the first, most basic, interpretation, the joke is based on the supposed irony of the moral equivocation between the mass slaughter of civilians and the illicit pilfering of corporate intellectual property. Both fall on the 'naughty' end of the ethical continuum, but the former is seen as objectively worse than the latter. Yet in recent US public policy debates, the scourge of piracy and intellectual property infringement rate more mention than state violence against civilians (though the Arab Spring and Occupy Movement have provided many opportunities to discuss reactionary repression). The joke is both a reflection of this rhetorical prioritization, and a reflection on its rather skewed set of ideals: why are we worried about piracy when, somewhere else, people are being killed in the streets? And, the reverse: isn't it great that we are so far up the path of civilization that we have the luxury to worry about the legalities of leaking war footage rather than concerning ourselves with staying out of it? 'Barbaric' places like Syria still worry themselves with overthrowing autocrats – in contrast, 'our' major public policy challenge during the time was staging an Internet blackout to keep SOPA from passing.

We could also read it far less charitably: absent Stewart's comic inflection, we could read it as a sincere statement of our real ordering of that equivalency. From the perspective of the US national interest, having a strong-armed dictator in the Middle East murdering his (br)own people is far less of a concern than his allowing that country to become a haven for terrorism or piracy. An Arab country's democracy, in US eyes, has long been only as good as its assurance to stay attuned to US/Israeli interests. Syria's Assad, an ophthalmologist trained in Europe, can see this with Western-augmented vision, predictably defending the actions of his police as part of a struggle against 'terrorists.' Faced only with ineffective sanctions, his life is not the least interrupted by this bloody conflict.

The anecdote of his simultaneously legal (from iTunes) and illegal (violating sanctions) Internet purchases therefore makes Assad a profile in the global defense of neoliberalism. When we view the contemporary attempt to increase punishment for piracy as the latest step in a long series of interventions in the broader world for the purposes of imperial economic development, it is clear that the very best rulers are those who would murder their own citizens for the sake of international capital – perhaps flaunting UN mandates on human rights, but never violating the terms of WIPO or the TRIPS agreements to the WTO. While critics like Max Fisher found Assad's purchase to be evidence that the US sanctions were toothless, US Treasury Department officials likely found it heartening (Max Fisher 2012). Only a month before, the Treasury Department had filed an exception to the broad economic sanctions imposed by the UN (Szubin

2012). This exception, the only one of 15 that was focused on an actual economic activity, would allow Syrian businesses to collect IPR fees, file trademarks and patents, and, perhaps more importantly, allow the US government to collect IPR fees from Syrian businesses and government. There are some things, in other words, that must be maintained even in an atmosphere of brutal repression: honoring global Intellectual Property Rights, it seems, was the single economic activity that the Treasury department felt should continue. That the president of Syria was so willing to honor these rights – by going around sanctions in order to buy music legally – shows him to be a team player.

Informing each of these interpretations is the dialectic of modernity versus modernization: the tension between the enlightenment ideals of democracy, freedom, and the just rule of law and the reality of modernization, which often necessitates both a violent, authoritarian destruction of entire ways of life and expensive, committed development of infrastructure on which those enlightenment ideals can finally be obtained. Without the ideals, we would have nothing to work towards; but without a struggle the authoritarian control (or, what often comes next, total failure) of the state could not be crafted into even a shell of its enlightenment promise.

In the first interpretation, which we might call naïve modernism, modernity is the cultural vision as old as the Orientalism that frames any story about the former Levant. In its most charitable version, the people of this (and every Southern) region merely suffer a time lag: the North is so far advanced that we now know the horrors of autocratic brutality well enough to have banished it from our societies. Violence is now limited to a 'necessary' level; leaders are governed by democratic processes and the rule of law. It is incidental that these sentiments are oxygenated in the heart of the largest military in history and the home to the largest prison population in the world. Protesting overly restrictive IPR is seen as a minor inconvenience compared to Syria's bloodshed – but one with which they'll soon be responsibly concerning themselves, if this Whiggish fantasy of history is any guide. The punchline lies in the fact that Assad is acting like a modern ruler (honoring IPR) but still clearly has some things to work on in that department.

In the second, which we could term Realist Modernization, we see a more brutal truth: that whatever level of enlightenment we've managed to reach, it is based upon an economic and political process of modernization that often –

if not always – stood in sharp contrast to the glowing democratic promises of its enthusiasts. The fortunes of Western Europe were built on a bloody siege against nearly all existing civilizations. Remaking the world was, indeed, a great deal of hard, creative work – but it usually required the absolutist hand of some enlightened dictator to bring it into existence. To prepare the idealized omelets of modernity through the modernization of society, absolutists had to break a few eggs. With the proper drift of history, Assad's wife's interest in the *Harry Potter* franchise could be the stuff of *People* magazine profiles – much like Hitler was profiled in home and garden magazines of the 1930s (Phayre 1938; Waldman 2003).

Running parallel to these concerns over modernization, therefore, is a certain understanding of violence. In everyday discussion, it makes sense to contrast the spectacular violence of Assad's regime with his personal observance of mundane laws regarding intellectual property rights – or property rights in general. Yet this ignores the massive infrastructure of everyday violence necessitated to enforce the Anglo American property rights regime. Following Žižek, in his extended meditation on violence, we can see the violence of the Assad regime – and therefore the supposed barbarity of its leader – as "directly visible 'subjective' violence, violence performed by a clearly identified agent." (2008, 1) Žižek contrasts this subjective violence with the 'objective' systemic violence that permeates 'civilized' societies:

> Subjective and objective violence cannot be perceived from the same standpoint: subjective violence is experienced as such against a background of a non-violent zero level. It is seen as a perturbation of the 'normal,' peaceful state of things. However, objective violence is precisely the violence inherent in this 'normal' state of things. Objective violence is invisible since it sustains the very zero-level standard against which we perceive something as subjectively violent. (2)

Assad's violence appears far more subjective, but all of the invisible objective violence of our society is the outcome of previous impositions of such subjective violence. We are now so thoroughly trained that we fail to recognize objective violence as such, sitting as most believers do outside of the walls of the prison, but on the other side of the wall Jack Nicholson prided himself on doing anything (including the extrajudicial murder of a Marine) to protect in *A Few Good Men* – the wall, ironically, surrounding the Guantanamo Bay Naval Base in Cuba.

At the time of that film, this wall represented one of the few remaining contact zones between the capitalist imperialism of the US and the threat of communism. The latter threat still remains, if only ideologically; since then, the Guantanamo Bay Naval Base has come to stand for a different kind of extrajudicial punishment. However, as with the unconstitutional actions of COINTELPRO, the extrajudicial detention and torture at Guantanamo, illegal wiretapping, and other 'perturbations,' spiked an initial furor, then largely faded into the atmosphere of objective, systemic violence (Saito 2002).

This violence is legitimate because it is performed by the state, which, in its most recent iteration, is supposed to have a monopoly on coercion. This monopoly on the instruments of coercion is simultaneously threatened and constituted by extralegal activities like piracy or terrorism.

It makes sense to say these activities threaten the legitimacy of the state: although it is unlikely that the government could truly protect against all such activities, if it appears incapable then its monopoly on violence is questioned in a more widespread fashion. Yet there is the counterintuitive argument that these activities – or the threat of them – help to symbolically secure the legitimacy of the state. Were it not for the state, for its military and police institutions, we would be more threatened by these activities. On the other hand, according to Janice Thompson (1994), much of the actual demand for control of these activities came from other states – and much of that pressure was generated by states being forced to reel in what she calls, "state-authorized non-state practices": mercenaries, privateers, and pirates previously empowered to do the work of the state. As with the CIA-trained forces of the Taliban, Thomson argues that:

> Not only was the state unable to control those it authorized, but the authorized forms gave rise to unauthorized forms. Most importantly, non-state violence was often turned against the state itself. (6)

Yet simply affirming or noting that the modern nation state maintains a monopoly on violence does not explain what that violence is used for, or why it disappears into the zero-level of systemic, objective violence described by Žižek above. If Assad's brutalization of civilians provides an example of subjective violence, his adherence to US standards of Intellectual Property Rights gives a clue to the objective violence. Here we have grounds for a third interpretation of Stewart's alignment of state repression and anti-piracy. In this interpretation, the moral equivalency should be read as a darker statement on our own society: that battling against piracy has a similar social impact – perhaps an invisible or only nascent one – as brutal repression of the public in the protection of entrenched private interests. This is an exaggeration, but one that relies on a healthy dose of unmediated truth.

Violence, economic power, and contemporary primitive accumulation

It is these everyday forms of violence that Marx discusses as primitive accumulation (Marx 1977, 873; Perelman 2000). Primitive accumulation is a two-sided process. On the one side, certain members of society accumulate resources. In Marx's original example, it was the accumulation of ever-larger pieces of land on the part of the aristocratic and bourgeois landholders in England. But the key to its function is not in the accumulation alone. It is that this accumulation – and the state power that facilitates it – is ultimately one of the key levers of control exercised over free labor – labor made free through the privatization of the means of production. Workers freed from the land were forced into a cash economy of rising rents, eventually leading many of them to industrial factories that benefited from their desperate condition by being able to hire them at rock bottom wages.

In the case of the already predominant wage labor most of us face today, primitive accumulation still works on a different level – through the privatization of the materials and institutional frameworks which valorize the highly developed skill sets workers' possess at this very moment, skills that can be sold to employers in exchange for the cash s/he will need to survive. The current flux in the production of digital knowledge is – or could be – only temporary. One of the dilemmas of the contemporary capitalist system is how to capture (and then reward) this value and how to force people to continue producing it for you. IPR appears to help it do both of these things: all the value produced runs back to the owner, and all the materials with which that value CAN be produced are the owner's intellectual property, thus owners force people to answer to them for its use (Boyle 2003, 2008; Coombe 1998; Lessig 2004)

Whether this means a particular owner can actually force people to work for them or that they merely extract rents from others' creative work makes little difference in the end. Either way, they extract some form of surplus value from this extended labor process. The benefit in the latter case is that owners can be flexible about how this surplus value is extracted – without the responsibility of labor relations implied by the former: that is, they don't have to become 'the boss' and carry all the responsibilities associated with this. Moreover, they can occasionally bankrupt or ruin these producers – just as they would a competitor – with little concern for how those producers will reproduce themselves: there is a veritable army of unemployed culture-industry aspirants producing new content, much of which inadvertently valorizes the old. That is, with the diversified portfolios of the six multinational media conglomerates, their talented legal staff, and their powerful lobbying firms, they are bound to own some profitable culture.

In other words, primitive accumulation and the privatization of productive property establishes a concentration of economic power in society, forcing laborers to work for the owners of this property in some capacity in order to survive. But this only functions in so far as laborers honor the property rights of capital owners – and the state steps in to ensure that they do through potentially violent physical force. When reified into a natural – rather than historical and cultural – phenomenon the inherent violence of this system fades from view. Ellen Mieksins Woods calls this model the "pristine culture of capitalism" (1991). It is characterized by the apparent separation of the political from the economic. By this, she means to say that the economic no longer appears as if it was constructed or operates through some political process, therefore it seems as if it cannot be challenged – or even that it doesn't exist except as a natural force (Wood 1981, 2002).

The separation of the political from the economic is an analytical, rhetorical, and ultimately cultural construction. As in the discourse of neoliberal globalization, it implies that the economy is an apolitical realm: the power of the state operates only in what Isaiah Berlin called a negative capacity, securing natural rights to property and assuring the sanctity of contracts (2002). This characterization of the liberal state exnominates economic power as such, yet insists that democratic authority is only valid in so far as it retains these limits – creating what Chantel Mouffe calls the democratic paradox (2000, 2005). The state, in this ideal, is a neutral party merely enforcing the laws it is asked to by the democratic process. But the democratic process is hindered from ever undermining the capitalist model of property as such. If any social force threatens this model, be it electoral or more demotic, state violence must be used to defend it. The definition and defense against piracy, terrorism, and other words for resistance to this order are constituted as evil in order to legitimate this defense and the abrogation of previously secured rights it often entails, as highlighted by Harvey's process of "accumulation by dispossession" discussed above.

Law, legitimacy, and social crime

It would be cavalier to claim that all acts of extra-legal coercion (or in the case of mere media piracy, theft) are somehow valiant forms of resistance. However, in the conflicted relationship between the narrative of modernism, the realism of modernization, and the paradox of capitalist democracy, there is plenty of room to see any or all of these acts emerging as forms of what Hay, et. al. refer to as 'social crime' (2011, xvi). This concept emerges from a collective historical study of 18th century England – a period that is notable for enclosure of the commons and creating surplus labor. As Hay, et. al. explain, social crimes are those which, while technically illegal, largely receive support and leniency from their local communities. Smugglers, poachers and other 'criminals' defied unpopular authorities and received moral support from those who saw them defending their customary rights and privileges.

They draw this concept from Hobsbawm who was one of the first great radical historians in the present age. He distinguishes what he calls 'social bandits' by the legitimacy and distinction given to these kinds of bandits as opposed to others (Anton 1972; Hobsbawm 1959, 1972, 1981). The good bandits are good because they defy the unjust order of the law in order to protect what were once customary privileges or emergent practices making use of new technologies.

In other words, they were seen as defending the realm or practices of the primitive commons that allowed for basic existence outside of wage labor and commodity exchange. Their defense was against an authoritarian imposition of private property rights which abrogated customary rights to the forest – rights which allowed for peasants to satisfy their needs through hunting, gathering wood, and foraging for food. Once these rights were removed, poor forest inhabitants had little choice but enter the labor force on terms set by nascent industrialists – or to break the law and poach for food. If SOPA, PIPA and the PATRIOT Act appear draconian, the punishment for these social crimes was far higher. As Hay and others recount, poachers (or even suspected poachers) acted in mortal defiance of the law – the death penalty being the punishment for poaching in the newly regulated lands. Rebelling against this nascent authority, with their attempt to enclose what was so obviously a commons, seemed uniquely understood by the culture of their time as a valid, if desperate, form of social protest – even if or especially because that authority defined it as a crime.

Increasingly, piracy (along with activities like the production and sale of 'counterfeit' goods) appears as a social crime. Or, to put it another way, it is difficult to discern the activities of criminals from those of legitimate business people. Counterfeit Wrangler jeans produced by Bolivian cooperatives rely on skills and supply chains developed by workers in their capacity as legitimate laborers of subcontracted firms (Brown 2003; Frazier, Bruss, and Johnson 2004). Aside from what locals view as improvements, the only distinction between licit and illicit is the consecration of the law. Likewise, the coders and programmers who designed and built online platforms for movies and books – such as Ninja Video and the www.library.nu – were responding to down-market demand being unmet by legitimate content providers (Andrews 2012; Ficher 2011; Kelty 2012).

Ninja Video facilitated international TV viewing, disregarding the nationally segmented markets of television that make it impossible to view all broadcasts across the world. Owners of this content limit international broadcasts so that they can sell them later in highly-profitable redistribution and syndication arrangements: meanwhile, consumers interested in this programming and the discussions it creates in that global community have no legitimate outlet through which to view it. In the case of www.library.nu, which became an outlet for a variety of works, but primarily expensive textbooks, great care was taken to produce user-friendly files and a catalog including reviews and extensive metadata. In each case, the distribution service was far better at meeting the needs of the global community than any other on offer – and each entailed a significant amount of work and ingenuity. More importantly, they accord with the Social Science Research Council/World Bank study on Media Piracy in Emerging Economies, which finds that lower priced or lower quality fakes are often the only thing locals can afford – and sometimes the only version of the product distributed widely in the global South (Karaganis 2011).

On the flipside, legitimate corporations engage in theft and destruction on a regular basis. The oil tankers that form one of the key targets for the 'violent' maritime piracy recounted by John Burnett tote the product of companies that regularly engage or turn a blind eye to various human rights abuses and environmental destruction that impacts directly the lives of everyday people around the world: from toxic oil spills impacting the health and safety of indigenous communities in Ecuador to families in rural Pennsylvania who are denied medical care for illnesses resulting from unregulated hydraulic fracturing (Burnett 2002; Business Staff 2012; Sawyer 2004). We could also add the practice of 'biopiracy' through which Pfizer and other pharmaceutical corporations have appropriated long held traditional medicinal practices. The difference between these forms of violence is that one has both the de facto enforcement and de jure legitimation of the nation state (see Robinson et al from this volume).

"Crime" and the stateless state of the neoliberal utopia

In a very practical manner, all of these forms of crime, whether officially sanctioned by the state or not, are made possible by the technological and material changes of globalization and digitization. Maritime piracy would hardly be rewarding on the scale it is were it not for the innovations in port logistics and the invention of the shipping container making it possible to capture an enormously valuable vessel with a miniscule crew (Bonacich and Wilson 2008; Levinson 2006). The ballooning production of counterfeit products cannot be separated from the shift from branded manufacturing to branded marketing – where the bulk of the monetary reward for the production of our clothes and technical objects goes not to the hard labor of Southern factory workers, but to the immaterial work of lawyers, designers, and marketers in the North (Collins 2003; Klein 2002). Media piracy and serious cyber-crime like bank fraud are the inevitable result of the digital revolution that aided the expansion of both of these industries throughout the world (Glenny 2011; Miller, Govil, McMurria, Maxwell and Wang 2005).

This regime uncertainty should give us pause, allowing us consider the kind of world we'd like to live in: instead, we see politicians doubling down in the interest of powerful incumbents.

In this sense, the increasingly organized forms of piracy are homologous to other forms of crime becoming especially prominent in areas of the world newly introduced to the economic pressures of neoliberalism. In his survey of mostly Eastern European and Post-Soviet crime syndicates Misha Glenny gives his assessment of its causes:

> The collapse of the Soviet Union is the single most important cause of the exponential growth in organized crime that we have seen around the world in the last two decades. Almost overnight, it provoked a chaotic

> scramble for riches and survival. From the bitter wars of the Caucasus to the lethal shoot-outs in towns and cities, this was a deadly environment as a new class of capitalist exploited the vacuum of power by seizing whole industries and raiding state coffers. Accompanied by an orgy of consumption and decadent behaviour, the like of which was last witnessed a century ago under Tsar Nicholas, it sucked every citizen into its vortex of violence [...] Russia's economy became a giant Petri-dish of Chicago-school market economics, but among the cultures they were busy cultivating was a Frankenstein that slipped out through the door of their laboratory almost unnoticed. (2009, 66-67, 71)

This environment was not just an accidental product of a rapid transition: it was designed by International Monetary Fund (IMF) bureaucrats and US Treasury Department officials like Lawrence Summers and Jeffrey Sachs who presumed that the neoliberal paradise they preached is the baseline of human nature, requiring little to no functioning state. In a sense they were correct: the state could no longer guarantee safety and, according to Glenny:

> The police and even the KGB were clueless as to how one might enforce contract law. The protection rackets and mafiosi (*sic*) were not so clueless – their central role in the new Russia was to ensure that contracts entered into were honored. They were the new law-enforcement agencies, and the oligarchs needed their services. Between them, the oligarchs and the mafia groups defined the justice system of the new Russia. Between 1991 and 1996, the Russian state effectively absented itself from the policing of society, and the distinction between legality and illegality, morality and immorality barely existed. (73)

It is in this context of the neoliberal dissolution of the state that piracy and crime become such a major concern. For while Russian crime syndicates may watch out for the needs and interests of their paymaster oligarchs, they are unlikely to concern themselves with protecting international contracts or foreign intellectual property rights. 'Crime' in this context becomes a site of contestation; many things that would be off limits in a different setting become permissible, if not necessary.

I highlight this not just to muddle permissive relativism with regard to criminality and the law. Instead it is to point to the process through which the legitimacy of the law is constructed and the role that 'illegal' actions and actors often play in its constitution. The liminal space occupied by contemporary piracy is evidence of the lack of legitimate jurisdiction on the part of the state. This gap is opened by the political disintegration of the imperial North, on one side, and the uncertain regime of neo-imperial control those formerly hegemonic nations have imposed via treaties of trade and mechanisms of international finance.

The fantasy of a purely neoliberal law overlooks the imperative that its coercive political instruments must be secured by the consent of the governed. Ultimately, the force that will compel adherence to the law is not tighter restrictions or highly technical monitoring mechanisms: it is the feeling that the law and the dominant order has something to offer other than, as the old man said, 'chains' (Marx 1988, 86). Here, the violence of the state coerces the population to jump at the command of transnational capital.

Conclusion

In his book *Remix*, Lawrence Lessig looks at the technological capabilities available to the children of the global North – and the attempts to make posting a Youtube video punishable to the same extent as opening a bootleg video store. This prompts him to ask what it means to raise a generation of criminals. In the US context, youth are the main victims of the "'war' on 'piracy'" we're staging: "Criminalizing an entire generation is too high a price to pay for almost any end. It is certainly too high a price to pay for a copyright system crafted more than a generation ago" (2008, xviii).

While the stakes appear high in the domestic struggles over intellectual property rights, the real controversy is not the criminalization per se, but the interests the law seems to serve. Thus we have (at least) two further alternative interpretations of Jon Stewart's long forgotten joke – though by now it has morphed from throwaway basic-cable humor to a rallying cry. On the one hand, politically, it points out that these equivalent forms of violence are perpetrated on us all at some level – either literally or potentially – and the appropriate response to both should be massive civil disobedience. Social crime should win the day precisely because it challenges the often corrupt, nay criminal, enforcement of the law. We are a class in ourselves and should therefore support all actions that advance our interests – such that we become a class for ourselves.

The key objection here is a reification of capitalism: if there is no copyright, if there is no property, how will we make a living? How will we support ourselves if we cannot rely on the sale of our labor or the sale of the fruits of our labor? I am sympathetic to this objection, not because it is true, but because I feel sorry for those who expect that it will always be true. We are living through a tiny blip in historical existence called capitalism: it will end and something else will emerge in its place. Will we be the ones to shape it or will someone else? This is both a reversal of the realist understanding and its hopeful revision.

It's rather surprising that this limited horizon of imagination still exists for so many. It has been twenty years since Francis Fukuyama famously pronounced the "End of History" – where the Hegelian dialectic of history reached its final synthesis with liberal (i.e. neoliberal) capitalist democracies (Fukuyama 1992). Yet since that time we've witnessed a range of system-wide failures, capped off by what Alex Callinicos calls "The Twin Crises of the Liberal World:" the catastrophe of the US war on Iraq (which Fukuyama eventually denounced) and the 2007-08 financial collapse, which, like the war in Iraq, was only the most recent and most colossal of the series of failures we've been treated to as careful adherents of the key tenants of neoliberalism (Callinicos 2010; Fukuyama 2006). Why then is his and his comrades' vision still the defining discourse of our age? Why is it ,"Easier to imagine the end of the world than it is to imagine the end of capitalism," as Mark Fisher paraphrases Slajov Žižek paraphrasing Frederic Jameson (2009, 2).

It is possible that we just didn't understand neoliberal boosters like Fukuyama. In his dismissal of the Bush Doctrine in Iraq, and neo-conservatism in general, he distanced himself from the interpretation that his book declared liberal (capitalist) democracy inevitable. Evidently he never intended this as his argument. Instead, he writes:

> *The End of History* is in the end an argument about modernization. What is initially universal is not the desire for liberal democracy but rather the desire to live in a modern – that is, technologically advanced and prosperous – society, which, if satisfied, tends to drive demands for political participation. Liberal democracy is one of the byproducts of this modernization process, something that becomes a universal aspiration only in the course of historical time. (2006)

In other words, the only thing that makes people interested in his liberal utopia is modernization and prosperity – or a proportional share of them. He may have a point, but he still seems naïve about this process: since the imperial powers took the reins, the modernization process has tended towards the maintenance of an international division of labor and power. The only route to modernization for an increasing swath of the world is to rise up in anger against those preventing it, be it the British Empire, the local courtesan potentate, or the transnational corporations that now rule over both.

This leads to the final interpretation, which is really just the complete reversal of the dominant moral inequivalence fundamental to this chapter's framing joke. In this, the resistance against both autocratic dictators and the economic power secured by the current hoarders of intellectual property rights are not just common elements of our collective struggle – they are necessary to the advancement of civilization and modernity as such. We must push past both in order to truly achieve the promises of modernity.

This hearkens to the early modern days of seafaring pirates and pirate publishers, both of whom were challenging the dominant order, both of whom presented an alternative to the current order, an alternative we could and should continue to explore. In addition to the cultural memory of those 17th century bandits, pamphleteers, and Levellers, we have four centuries of social and technological advancement. We should be using both to our advantage rather than settling for a system of wage labor and private property that was conceived of as innovative when long range communication was conducted by semaphore telegraph – or allow the reification of an intellectual property rights regime that insists we progress no further. With the eclipse of the welfare state and the generalized condition of precarity, we should finally realize that we really all are in this thing together.

References

Andrews, Sean Johnson (2012). "Library.Nu: Modern era's 'destruction of the library of Alexandria". *Breaking Culture.* Retrieved 10 July 2013, from http://breakingculture.tumblr.com/post/17697325088/gigapedia-rip

Anton, Blok (1972). "The peasant and the brigand: Social banditry reconsidered". *Comparative Studies in Society and History*, 14:4, 494-503.

Beaumont, Peter (2012). "Syria in turmoil: Assad launches fresh shelling of civilian houses". *guardian.co.uk*, 10 March 2012. Retrieved 10 July 2013, from http://www.guardian.co.uk/world/2012/mar/10/kofi-annan-peace-mission-falters?newsfeed=true

Berlin, Isaiah (2002). "Two concepts of liberty". In Henry Hardy (ed.), *Liberty: Incorporating four essays on liberty.* Oxford: Oxford University Press, 166-217.

Bonacich, Edna and Jake B. Wilson (2008). *Getting the goods: Ports, labor, and the logistics revolution.* Ithaca, N.Y.: Cornell University Press.

Booth, Robert and Mona Mahmood (2012). "How the Assad emails came to light". *guardian.co.uk*, 14 March 2012. Retrieved 10 July 2013, from http://www.

guardian.co.uk/world/2012/mar/14/how-Assad-emails-came-light
Booth, Robert, Mona Mahmood and Luke Harding (2012). "Secret Assad emails lift lid on life of leader's inner circle". *guardian.co.uk*, 14 March 2012. Retrieved 10 July 2012, from http://www.guardian.co.uk/world/2012/mar/14/Assad-emails-lift-lid-inner-circle

Boyle, James (2003). "The second enclosure movement and the construction of the public domain". *Law and Contemporary Problems*, 66:33, 33-75.

Boyle, James (2008). *The public domain: Enclosing the commons of the mind.* New Haven: Yale University Press.

Brown, Paul (2003, Sept. 4). "World's poor prefer fake designer gear". *Guardian.co.uk*, 3 September 2003. Retrieved 22 January 2009, from http://www.guardian.co.uk/uk/2003/sep/04/clothes.lifeandhealth

Burnett, John S. (2002). *Dangerous waters: Modern piracy and terror on the high seas.* New York, N.Y.: Plume.

Business Staff, Associated Press (2012). "Doctors say drilling law hurts public health". *Cleveland.com*, 11 April 2012. Retrieved 10 July 2013, from http://www.cleveland.com/business/index.ssf/2012/04/doctors_say_drilling_law_hurts.html

Callinicos, Alex (2010). *Bonfire of illusions: The twin crises of the liberal world.* Cambridge: Polity.

Collins, Jane L. (2003). *Threads: Gender, labor, and power in the global apparel industry.* Chicago: University of Chicago Press.

Coombe, Rosemary J. (1998). *The cultural life of intellectual properties: Authorship, appropriation, and the law.* Durham: Duke University Press.

Ficher, Rob (2011). "A ninja in our sites". *prospect.org*, 15 December 2011. Retrieved 10 July 2013, from http://prospect.org/article/ninja-our-sites

Fisher, Mark (2009). *Capitalist realism: Is there no alternative?.* Washington: Zero Books.

Fisher, Max (2012). "Sanctions hurt Syrians, but they can't even keep Bashar Al-Assad off iTunes". *theatlantic.com*, 15 March 2012. Retrieved 10 July 2013 from http://www.theatlantic.com/international/archive/2012/03/sanctions-hurt-Syrians-but-they-cant-even-keep-bashar-al-Assad-off-iTunes/254567/

Frazier, Barbara J, Mozhdeh Bruss and Lynn Johnson (2004). "Barriers to Bolivian participation in the global apparel industry". *Journal of Fashion Marketing and Management*, 8:4, 437-451.

Fukuyama, Francis (1992). *The end of history and the last man.* New York: Free Press.

Fukuyama, Francis (2006). "After neoconservatism". *New York Times,* 19 february 2006, 62. Retrieved 10 July 2013, from http://www.nytimes.com/2006/02/19/magazine/neo.html?pagewanted=all&_r=0

Glenny, Misha (2009). *Mcmafia: Seriously organised crime.* London: Vintage.

Glenny, Misha (2011). *Darkmarket: Cyberthieves, cybercops, and you.* New York, NY: Alfred A. Knopf.

Harvey, David (2003). *The new imperialism.* Oxford ; New York: Oxford University Press.

Harvey, David (2005). *A brief history of neoliberalism.* Oxford ; New York: Oxford University Press.

Harvey, David (2006). *Spaces of global capitalism: Towards a theory of uneven geographical development.* London ; New York, NY: Verso.

Hay, Douglas, Peter Linebaugh, John G. Rule, E. P. Thompson and Cal Winslow (2011). *Albion's fatal tree: Crime and society in eighteenth-century England* (2nd ed.). London: Verso.

Hobsbawm, Eric (1959). *Social bandits and primitive rebels; studies in archaic forms of social movement in the 19th and 20th centuries.* Glencoe, Ill.,: Free Press.

Hobsbawm, Eric (1972). "Social bandits: Reply". *Comparative Studies in Society and History*, 14:4, 503-505.

Hobsbawm, Eric (1981). *Bandits* (Rev. ed.). New York: Pantheon Books.

Johnson, Chalmers A. (2004). *The sorrows of empire: Militarism, secrecy, and the end of the republic* (1st ed.). New York: Metropolitan Books.

Karaganis, Joe (ed.) (2011). *Media piracy in emerging economies.* New York, NY: SSRC.

Kelty, Christopher M. (2012). "The disappearing virtual library". *aljazeera.com*, 1 March 2012. Retrieved 10 July 2013, from http://www.aljazeera.com/indepth/opinion/2012/02/2012227143813304790.html

Klein, Naomi (2002). *No space, no choice, no jobs, no logo.* New York, New York: Picador.

Lessig, Lawrence (2004). *Free culture: How big media uses technology and the law to lock down culture and control creativity.* New York: Penguin Press.

Lessig, Lawrence (2008). *Remix: Making art and commerce thrive in the hybrid economy* (1st UK paperback ed.). London: Bloomsbury Academic.

Levinson, Marc (2006). *The box: How the shipping container made the world smaller and the world economy bigger.* Princeton, N.J.: Princeton University Press.

Marx, Karl (1977). *Capital: A critique of political economy* (Ben Fowkes, Trans. Vol. I). New York: Vintage Books.

Marx, Karl (1988). "The communist manifesto: Annotated text". In Frederic L. Bender (ed.). *The communist manifesto: A Norton critical edition.* New York: W.W. Norton.

McChesney, Robert Waterman and Dan Schiller (2003). "The political economy of international communications: Foundations for the emerging global debate about media ownership and regulation" (1-43). Geneva, Switzerland: United Nations Research Institute for Social Development.

McNally, David (2010). *Global slump: The economics and politics of crisis and resistance.* Oakland, CA: PM Press.

Miller, Toby, Nitin Govil, John McMurria, Richard Maxwell and Ting Wang (2005). *Global Hollywood 2.* London: British Film Institute.

Mittelman, James H. (2000). *The globalization syndrome: Transformation and resistance.* Princeton, N.J.: Princeton University Press.

Mouffe, Chantal (2000). *The democratic paradox.* London ; New York: Verso.

Mouffe, Chantal (2005). *The return of the political.* London ; New York: Verso.

O'Neil, Chuck (Writer) (2012). "'Homs despot'". In Jon Stewart (Producer), *The Daily Show with Jon Stewart, #17075*. USA: Viacom.

Peet, Richard (2007). *Geography of power: The making of global economic policy*. London, UK ; New York, NY: Zed Books Ltd.

Perelman, Michael (2000). *The invention of capitalism: Classical political economy and the secret history of primitive accumulation*. Durham, N.C.: Duke University Press.

Phayre, Ignatius (1938). "Hitler's mountain home: A visit to 'haus wachenfeld' in the bavarian alps". *Homes and Gardens*, November, 193-195.

PIPA - preventing real online threats to economic creativity and theft of intellectual property act of 2011, S.968, United States Senate (2011).

Research Works Act (RWA), H.R. 3699, U.S. House of Representatives (2011).

Saito, Natsu Taylor (2002). "Whose liberty? Whose security? The USA patriot act in the context of Cointelpro and the unlawful repression of political dissent". *Oregon Law Review*, 81:4, 1051-1132.

Sawyer, Suzana (2004). *Crude chronicles: Indigenous politics, multinational oil, and neoliberalism in Ecuador*. Durham: Duke University Press.

SOPA - stop online piracy act, H.R. 3261, U.S. House of Representatives (2011).

General license no. 15 certain transactions related to patents, trademarks, and copyrights authorized, Executive Order 13582 of August 17, 2011 Blocking Property of the Government of Syria and Prohibiting Certain Transactions With Respect to Syria C.F.R. (2012).

Thomson, Janice E. (1994). *Mercenaries, pirates, and sovereigns: State-building and extraterritorial violence in early modern Europe*. Princeton, NJ: Princeton UP.

Waldman, Simon (2003). "At home with the führer". *The Guardian*, 2 November 2003. Retrieved 10 July 2012, from http://www.guardian.co.uk/world/2003/nov/03/secondworldwar.blogging

Wood, Ellen Meiksins (1981). "The separation of the economic and the political in capitalism". *New Left Review*, 127(May/June), 66-95.

Wood, Ellen Meiksins (1991). *The pristine culture of capitalism: A historical essay on old regimes and modern states*. London: Verso.

Wood, Ellen Meiksins (2002). *The origin of capitalism: A longer view*. New York, NY: Verso.

Žižek, Slavoj (2008). *Violence: Six sideways reflections* (1st Picador ed.). New York: Picador.

'Pirates' in EU's (Semi)Peripheries
A Comparative Case Study on the Perceptions of Poles and Greeks on Digital File-sharing

Yiannis Mylonas

Introduction: Copyrights, piracy and informal media practices

Drawing on critical literature on new media uses, this chapter examines the practices that hegemonic politico-economic discourses frame as "piracy". Empirical research on people's media practices, challenges the hegemonic construction of copyright piracy. Few Internet or digital technology users, identify themselves as "pirates" – with the possible exception of Pirate Party members or the administrators of The Pirate Bay website, who in every case articulate their pirate identity in very different terms than the copyright industries do. By looking at the concrete realities of people using new media and digital technologies in local contexts, defined by diverse socio-historical, political and economic characteristics, we gain important insights into the complex nature of piracy that directly challenges this hegemonic frame.

"Piracy" concerns informal media and communication technology practices, involving unauthorized uses of intellectual property. Digital "piracy" is made possible by the advances of digital technology and access to new media. Main social developments connected to the development of "piracy cultures" (Castells and Cardoso 2012, 1) across the globe concern both the development of the speed and the spread of the Internet, and the popularization of affordable software and hardware devices of new Information and Communication Technologies (ICT). Such developments allow creative practices to emerge that enable the flourishing of a Do-It-Yourself (DIY) "free culture" (Lessig 2004), among different new media and ICT users across the globe. Such practices expand the use of technology into domains either not covered by the law or into legal "grey areas".

Digital technology innovations and new media/ICT uses are connected to late modern social changes that informalize social practices, institutions, norms, and social relations (Slavnic 2009). Informal media practices occur in precarious and "fluid" social spaces – characterized by a somehow permanent state of crisis –

defined by commercial imperatives (Bauman 2005a; 2005b). This occurs with minimal opportunities for public representation or political participation, and growing precarious economic conditions related to deepening social inequalities. To return to the question of piracy, the advance of universal intellectual property regimes, emphasize the deep commodification of the social, including intimate spheres of the lifeworld (Virno 2004). In such contexts, the informal aspect of everyday life practices and contexts is a space optimized for life tactics and strategies (DeCerteau 2008/1990) for survival and for the pursuing of the "good life" (however the latter is defined).

While intellectual property rights regimes (IPR) have very much been a dimension of life since the emergence of modernity, we have consistently seen these organizational systems slowly expand and commodify the immaterial lifeworld (Arvanitakis 2007; Virno 2004). This has occurred as we have seen IPR protection policies intensify on a global scale over the last three decades and brought into the governing mechanisms of international trade (May 2009, 76), including the emergence of Trade Related Aspects of Intellectual Property Rights (TRIPs). As this has occurred, we have seen intellectual, cultural or informational entities become reified as commodities, economically exploited by the actors that formally own them.

A key issue that has emerged in the development of IPRs is the crisis that the capitalist economy has found itself in over the last thirty years (Harvey 2012, 30). This is a permanent state of crisis due to the impossibility of maintaining adequate levels of economic growth on capital's terms. The situation of crisis is connected to the contradictions inherent in the processes of capitalist valorization and accumulation, related to global antagonisms, the exhaustion of natural resources, or subjective issues related to resistances towards the exploitation of labor and the commodification of human activity (Harvey 2005, 2012; Hardt and Negri 2009). Capital's as well as policy makers' response to this crisis has been increasing levels of economic deregulation, the flexibilization of labor, the expansion of unconstrained financial activity, neoliberal politics and ideology and fundamentally, capital's increasing investment in "immaterial" capital such as finance, but also creativity, innovation and intellectual property rights. The latter aspect is connected to the commodification and reification of a variety of aspects characterizing the "lifeworld": that is, the private and intimate aspects of life. Capital responds to this crisis by intensifying economic activity and labor processes; promoting material scarcities and an affective work ethos; making labor progressively colonize the realms of leisure and to disguise itself as leisure; as well as requiring constant innovation connected to market objectives that are related to commodification and the creation of limitless consumerist needs.

Before moving on to present the empirical work, I will briefly discuss how we can understand "piracy" in this context.

How to understand "piracy"?

The discourse of piracy is central in the rationales underlining contemporary IPR policies. Copyright enclosures advance through the negative discourses of piracy, aiming to criminalize the advance of illegitimate uses of intellectual and cultural goods (David 2010, 43). "Piracy" discourse attempts to vilify practices that new media and new ICT users across the world develop, often involving unauthorized uses of intellectual property. The control and monopolization of information, culture and creativity, aim at sustaining the monopolistic advantages of particular cultural industries usually based in specific countries (May 2009; McChesney 2009).

Tight IPR regimes with a simultaneous emphasis on the need of freedom and innovation for growth may seem contradictory. Copyright regimes though, often express internal tensions and antinomies of interest between different economic objectives and different industrial sectors. As I will demonstrate bellow, the industries attempt to capture, regulate and exploit both the outcomes of creative processes (such as products of intellect), and the creativity of individuals and multitudes. In order to do that, policy, laws and norms are required to ensure the proprietization of such reified entities.

It is from this perspective that we can understand why the frame of piracy and deviance is so readily applied to those who break out of this model of strict IPR enforcement.

Context: Empirical realities of new media/ICT usages in Greece and Poland

In this manner, piracy is formulated as a negative discourse used in two main ways: to criminalize cultural habits that occur with the use of media, and to normalize the imperatives of neoliberal economics. It is necessary to decontextualize "piracy" from its hegemonic and negative frame, and to view it as something related to how people use media, ICT and culture, as well as how they communicate and consume culture. Here I am not attempting to romanticize piracy, for there is nothing intrinsically emancipatory, progressive or political in piracy (Hall 2009, 2). Indeed, the prospects of copyright freedom is very complex in a "free market" oriented social terrain, where markets seek their infinite reproduction and expansion through the commodification of potentially anything.

It is therefore important to see the social, historical, economic and political contexts of any such cultural practices (Curran 2012, 21). In this regard Greece and Poland, two (semi) peripheral members of the complex European Union (EU) constellation, are approached empirically. New media/ICT users were asked to discuss socio-political and cultural aspects of their own informal media practices. The research questions were organized according to Dahlgren's (2009) civic circuit model, which is used reflexively in order to anchor the interview questions on specific key ideas that can help to gather information on informal new media/ICT usages and the meanings people develop. The civic circuit model includes six "moments" relating to key ideas to evaluate the civic and political potential of lifeworld practices: these concern the variants of values, knowledge, trust, space, practice and identities. The importance of political questions regarding new media uses which may not be political as such, concerns the possibilities of broader social change that can derive from informal spheres of everyday life.

The local context is crucial to understand the diversity and the ways different everyday life practices develop (Davis 2006; Lobato et al. 2011; Lule 2011; Miegel and Olsson 2011; Ong 2006; Shaefer 2009). This is because popular uses of media and the development of ICT rely on issues related to identity, ideology, structures or particular events that unfold in distinct ways in different localities. These are two countries that are understudied in the uses of new media. The term semi-periphery is reflexively used to describe the internal power asymmetries, antinomies and political and economic differences inscribed in the transnational political constellation of the EU (McGiffen 2005, 43).

Despite important politico-historical differences, parallel political trajectories can also be identified between the two countries. These include what Carpentier (2011, 69) described as a "minimalistic" form of democratic polity, characterized by limited forms of citizens' participation in formal politics, political corruption, as well as limited rights and social provisions. The collapse of "socialism" in Poland was followed by harsh "shock doctrine" policies, introduced by neoliberal actors (Klein 2006, 179). Greece is experiencing an ongoing neoliberal and undemocratic restructuring – which can also be described as "shock" policies, since early 2010 (Kouvelakis 2010, 303). Finally, nationalism enjoys a great deal of popularity in both these countries.

Simultaneously though, different ideological and social trajectories characterize the historical experiences of the two countries. Ideological disillusionment from the "socialist" experience of Poland accompanied by the hegemonic "end of history" narrative, are by no means characteristic of the social context of Greece. Ideologically laden debates and social movements are strong in Greece, driven by different historical trajectories related to the hegemony of right wing ideology, dictatorial regimes and economically capitalist politics. Also, strong narratives critical to Western culture and to consumerism co-exist with consumerist and individualist perspectives common to the rest of the world. The prosperity of the middle class in contemporary Poland meets the fall of the middle class in contemporary Greece.

The Internet penetration is 47 percent for Greece and 56 percent for Poland (Internetworldstats 2010a, 2010b.). International Intellectual Property Alliance's (IIPA 2011) research classified counterfeiting as the main threat to copyrights in both countries. "Street piracy" is identified as the main source of copyright infringement in Greece: such practices are often the survival tactics of immigrants in Greece which sell copies of blockbuster films and popular music albums mass copied by different black market networks as they experience formal and informal exclusion from the possibilities of making a living within the realm of law. The mass production and distribution of copies of films and popular music, by networks expanding throughout many eastern European, post-socialist countries, is the main threat to copyrights in Poland (IIPA 2005). "Internet piracy" is a secondary threat to copyrights, according to IIPA's reports. Both countries have seen anti-piracy advertising campaigns and educational programs supported by the EU (Mylonas 2011) in order to create "piracy awareness". In Poland in particular, as several interviewees stated, lectures against downloading of copyrighted goods from the Internet, are regularly held in schools.

As part of the freedom of exchange that characterizes culture throughout time (Lessig 2004), different legacies of "piracy" developed in both countries. Pirate radio flourished in Greece from 1960s to date, mainly due to people's discontent with the state monopoly on radio frequencies. Pirate radio developed for both communicating music and politics (Theodosianou 2010). Do-it-yourself (DIY) culture also had an important presence in the country from the 1970s, relating to far left and anti-authoritarian politics and to avant garde arts. The development of tape recorders and VCR systems further advanced home taping, along with a variety of innovative practices of users.

Samizdat press from counter hegemonic political groups was common in the "socialist" era of Poland, articulating the voice of different clandestine political groups operating both within and outside the country's borders (Jakubowicz 1992, 159). Avant garde arts, often critical of official policy lines of the Polish state but also related to identity issues, developed during the socialist era in a clandestine way. Black markets for Western cultural goods flourished in the country particularly during the 1980s. There was also the political turbulence that followed the development of the Solidarity (Solidarnosk) movement. Counterfeiting of Western goods was encouraged by Western political and industrial sectors, because it was seen as beneficial for the country's transition to a free market economy, from a state controlled one. The black market was seen as a way to develop an entrepreneurial culture among people and would indoctrinate the general public to free market principles and practices (Filiciak and Toczyski 2011) – something that May (2009) argues is often encouraged by multinational corporations in order to open future markets. The regime change of 1989 did not see the elimination of black market activities, rather the black market still exists in the country due to the different forms of exclusion that capitalism advanced in Poland. The official discourses on black market activities however changed and obtained a demeaning content: instead of examples of entrepreneurialism, they were later seen as "remnants of socialism," signs of "socialist mentality" and "Polish backwardness" (Filiciak and Toczyski 2011).

The study that this chapter draws on attempted to answer some important questions: what is the context of the concrete experiences of everyday uses of new media/ICT unfolding in Poland and Greece? How are issues of economic, social or political inequality and exclusion in realities of peripheral EU countries, reflected in the freedom of use offered by new media/ICT affordances? Are there civic and subversive potentials in informal new media/ICT practices? The questions aimed at disclosing the contextual aspects that challenge the monolithic official discrediting of "piracy," as well as informal, everyday life practices that are part of the ways people use their media and cultural goods for self-expression, creativity, identity, connection, cooperation, public participation, education and communication.

In total, 54 respondents from both countries were contacted through private interviews, focus groups, email and questionnaires: 29 from Greece and 25 from Poland. The respondent's age ranged from 17 to 46 years, but most of them were between 25-30 years. All respondents lived in urban centers in both countries (Thessaloniki in Greece, Warsaw and Lublin in Poland). The majority of respondents, 39, were males and 15 were females. Targeted respondents were people actively engaged with new media production/usage informally such as artists, activists, and website administrators (like blogs, torrent trackers and so on).

The political categories of the analysis: Values, trust, knowledge

The first analytical category is "values," and is concerned with substantial and procedural principles that organize social life (Dahlgren 2009, 111). Tolerance and equality are substantial values for the development of social relations beneficial to all. Procedural values concern a minimal consensus on rules defining particular forms of order.

Respondents from Greece demonstrated a rich background of substantial values while discussing file-sharing or other "informal" new media/ICT practices:

> Chloe (Greece): The whole issue of intellectual property foregrounds a clash between the law of market and knowledge in its broader sense; the main issue is what… in the end prevails in a society?

Information, knowledge and culture were seen as important social goods and resources that should be available to all regardless of economic background. Respondents were aware that copyright enclosures occurred on the basis of economic interests and economic exclusion was prioritized in discussions relating to equality. Simultaneously, that universal equality on culture and knowledge transgressed national borders through examples of publicly known cases of copyright infringement persecutions. The particular values were also underlined by critical – yet fragmented – hints against commercialism and industrial expansion into all fields of the social. The majority of the Greek respondents were critical of political lobbying for universal copyright regimes and violations of privacy.

Polish respondents also expressed similar concerns over the importance of free access to culture and knowledge irrespective of economic background. Yet, values were positioned in a more "realist" way, attempting to balance different kinds of interests: an example here is that the respondents acknowledge a need for a compromise between corporate interests and the public and individual interests of Internet users. Bartek (Lublin, Poland), noted:

> I believe that file-sharing should not be prohibited… The simplest solution is to introduce a flat fee for Internet users, no matter how much one who downloads.

Excerpts such as this explicitly express a desire toward legality. Regressive values, related to the hegemonic "piracy" discourses that see free sharing in terms of theft and as a threat to the "free market," were also expressed by very few respondents who, interestingly, simultaneously admitted to downloading certain material online.

> Wojtek (Lublin, Poland): Downloading destroys the works and also destroys the market. People doing it know what they do is theft but they think they can get away with it… I only download old films that are played on the television, because nobody profits from them.

Regarding procedural values, a more complex context related to the category of "trust" emerged. Dahlgren (2009, 110) notes that respect for laws is connected to the development of civic virtue, but he also states that laws should derive from a legitimate locus of authority. The responses of Greek and Polish interviewees indicate a "legitimacy crisis" of political authority and formal policy that possibly exceeds the narrow context of "piracy". This seems to reflect broader civic tensions and contradictions in the particular. This echoes Habermas's (1975) concern that a legitimacy crisis of liberal democracies emerges due to the infiltration of private economic interests into public policy and the unequal development of economic institutions. As Giorgos (Greece) notes:

> Even artists, the sole ones morally deserving protection from law, come out and say they are defenseless against corporate interests… It all comes down to the protection of the big industry distributing and reproducing audiovisual material and technologies. The companies are the only ones benefiting from the existing laws today. They are the ones waging a war on a global scale, not only against any kind of change, but also to further strengthen their position and interests.

Political authority in Poland was resented due to the collective experiences of abuses of power, authoritative bureaucracy and social inequality. Polish respondents demonstrated a similar distrust to political elites on both a national and global scale including towards transnational institutions like the EU and NATO. Issues related to Polish identity constructions, connected to Catholicism, a "Socialist" past, and Europeanism also emerged.

> Kuba (Lublin, Poland): The EU is a tricky thing. They want to control everything. I don't like the EU in general. When I see all this bureaucracy and these logics that they try to spread in order to unify (different member states) I find it stupid… maybe they have some good intentions, but it is making things harder for a common person. So I am against restricting laws, such as the copyrights. It should be convenient for the people... Big companies can lobby and do whatever they want. So I think it is pointless and against people.

This legitimacy crisis often related to the disrespect of formal laws that were seen as upholding both conservative and class-biased values. The explanations of the respondents, however, often entailed both neoliberal and anti-capitalist values. This can be understood by drawing on the position of Boltanski and Chiapello (2006) that late or "new" capitalism reproduces itself through resistance: neoliberal politics and rhetoric seem to colonize public discontent that is often connected to frameworks of exclusion and exploitation through the use of post-political and individualist narratives that are hegemonic in Western societies. Furthermore, the emphasis by most Polish respondents on the political as "problematic" per se, concerns a post-political shift in contemporary liberal societies, in favor of neoliberal forms of polity (Crouch 2011, 47).

> Kryzstyna (Warsaw, Poland): People can try to do things politically, but they will always use the system to make their own rules for their personal benefit.

There is frequently a lack of critique of contemporary economy as a form of political institution. Instead, the state and formal political institutions assume the responsibility for distorting people's "natural" tendencies to be greedy, economically rational and selfish. In an uncritical context of demotion of formal political institutions, the market advances its position as a superior social institution that is supposedly able to tackle social problems (Crouch 2011, 144). Greek respondents, however, emphasized the connection of the political to the economic to express corruption and inequality though not a full eradication of politics per se. As Odysseas (Greece) noted:

> I do not think that file-sharing is a political action per se. I think that it can become political when persecuted and when a series of laws are introduced that attempt to control people's online activities.

Respondents also showed distrust towards the "general public," at both a national and international level, echoing Curran's (2012, 10) position that the general public is not trusted due to the invisibility and cacophony of global digital networks.

> Giotis (Greece): I only use few private torrent trackers where I can find specific material that I am interested in. One has to contribute to the community to be a member. Furthermore, one can find out about a variety of things, just by checking the activity of members and the recommendations they make. I am not interested in public trackers because viruses can often be hidden in torrents.

There is also a certain expression of elitism in the responses here, affiliated to particular subcultures and niche communities that dislike the mainstream and banal cultural tastes of this "general public". Users of P2P structures showed high levels of trust among their peers. Trust is accomplished through the rules attached to P2P structures – usually "private" ones – specializing in niche interests such as "world cinema," which organize membership requirements as well as the formal obligations and modes of conduct required by members. Such collectives were not only uninterested in market developments but actually hostile to the commercial exploitation of art in general. More intimate (although mediated) social relations were noted to occur this way.

A general lack of critique towards niche establishments and the commercial element entailed in sub-cultures was observed in respondents' accounts. Markets move swiftly toward niche consumption and the Internet is an effective channel to attract niche communities (Freedman 2012, 73). Respondents, particularly from Poland, showed enthusiasm for market developments improving niche supply services. As we will see, commodity fetishism was also apparent in different responses by people from both countries.

The category of "knowledge" concerns the general understanding of issues of political interest, such as laws, rights, or social events (Dahlgren 2009, 108). Knowledge here depended on a combination of both the respondent and issues being discussed. Explicit and tacit forms of knowledge (DeCerteau 2008/1990) were demonstrated as respondents from both countries exhibited explicit understanding on issues of technology, popular culture and specialized niche interests.

The category of "tacit knowledge" is worth stressing further, as it highlights the immediate aspects of knowledge obtained from experience. The account of such knowledge, as narrated by respondents, further demonstrates the importance of meaning making and context behind the articulation of experience and action, as well as the function of master frames and hegemonic discourses in meaning making of everyday life contexts. In asking the respondents the question, "Who is the 'pirate', in your opinion?," the following answers were received:

> Alek (Warsaw, Poland): Most likely websites like X (gives name of a website illegally selling films in Poland), but I am not sure who is the pirate. It is a business, not an idea of sharing, but a business.
> Monica (Lublin, Poland): My first contact with Western economy was through the black markets selling all kinds of illegal goods. I thought that this was capitalism.

The depth of knowledge in the excerpts above reveals systemic contradictions that are not explicitly elaborated by respondents which challenge inequalities of power structures and discourses.

Knowledge related to political rights and issues were expressed in greater detail by the Greek respondents with direct references to the ongoing political turmoil within the country. Polish respondents were more likely to express disinterest in political issues, yet they did demonstrate interest in social affairs. They were also quite knowledgeable regarding copyright infringement laws and many Polish respondents had attended educational seminars organized by EU programs and copyright industries on copyright and "piracy awareness" issues. Polish participants were also familiar with Creative Commons (CC) licenses due to public campaigns held by the local CC foundation. Tacit knowledge, related to the experience of media and technology use, the experience of law application and broader everyday social relations, was demonstrated by all respondents from both countries.

The cultural categories of the analysis: Space, practice and identity

The category of "space" concerns the symbolic and material terrain where practices and social relations unfold. Dahlgren (2009, 115) emphasizes the communicative aspect of public space for democratic development. Others, such as

Gauntlett (2011), underline the importance of cooperative and creative spaces for broader processes of progressive change. Informal, everyday life activities create spaces for the expression and the materialization of given processes that cannot appear in different loci. New media/ICT users produce space through the creative, customized appropriation of media and the access to affordable technology. Spaces are created according to particular interests and specific tactical or strategic targets individuals or groups set.

New technologies and media are appropriated according to different subjective motives, practices and values that may relate to lifestyle, politics and business issues. In that sense, spaces are created (such as in the form of certain websites) where particular interests (including political, niche and social) can be expressed through creativity, connection and communication. Spaces are also created through material conditions relating to different forms of scarcities promoted by economic and political structures. People thus create online exchange networks from clothes, to furniture, electric appliances, or food. Social context and events, ideology and material conditions play an important role in the ways that informal and new spaces will be produced.

> Argyris, (Greece): Many people exploit the freedom of the Internet to fill their consumerist lust. Nevertheless the potential of freedom entailed online has also attracted people with different reflexes, like creators that want to hack things and to give them away for free. The whole issue is mainly economical. We save money. The (economic) crisis may thus contribute in the further development of such networks.

The scarcity of basic everyday goods in Greece due to austerity policies has led to the development of different forms of social organization based on exchange of goods that often bypass commercial intermediates (Mylonas 2012a). New, post-capitalist forms of economic models are created, based on online infrastructure, and new social imaginaries: as "post" these should not be seen as a "return" to barter economies (Graeber 2011, 28).

The Polish context is underlined by different events and discourses dominating the public space. The material life conditions may not be substantially different (for the moment) for the majority of Polish people from their Greek counterparts; the difference is in the emergency context of the Greek state of affairs. Informal spaces emerge and are produced by subcultural interests as well as entrepreneurial and artistic aspirations.

> Marek (Lublin, Poland): There is no audience here in Poland for me, that is why I am moving out. Poland has four cities and that's it: Krakow, Warsaw, Gdansk, Wroclaw … (as an artist) you can't do much without the Internet nowadays. As we talk about it right now, there may be 50 people who understand that.

In such examples, access to new media and ICTs offer potential for entrepreneurialism, as well as for the acquisition of economic, social and cultural capital. In the case of free-sharing of digital materials, Polish respondents noted the use of such materials as "free" entrepreneurial resources, used by amateur artists to pursue mainstream artistic fantasies of fame and riches (Mylonas 2012b, 9). Furthermore, Polish respondents noted that digital cultural goods were also appropriated and sold illegally by local, private online platforms.

NGOs working with "information society" issues, ranging from educational to online privacy protection oriented organizations also create spaces for people to engage in through such mechanisms as the development of free online databases for e-books or other resources. Though these spaces are informal, these organizations are strategically attempting to formalize them. By so doing they are creating a contingent aspect of new media/ICT to "officially" make interventions into the online economy.

> Michal (Warsaw, Poland): … we try to get funding and work with the ministry because they agreed to fund it but it takes months, the project which will benchmark the levels of media literacy in Poland, and then we will work out the media literacy education resources based on benchmarks.

Neoliberal discourses relating to the cultivation of entrepreneurial culture, often underlined the logics of user "empowerment" through the liberalization of IPR laws, and popularization of ICT uses. The development of "competitive individuals" seemed to tacitly underline the type of arguments that are necessary for the economic-political establishment's policy reforms.

Practices unfold in spaces, and are susceptible to the values, motives or identities of people performing them. "Practice" concerns the actual uses of new media/ICT, relating to performances as well as the learning of new competencies that can lead towards the opening of new ways of communicating, thinking or living (Dahlgren 2009, 117). According to the respondents, practice is highly reflexive, individualized and further connected to broader socio-cultural identities.

People's engagement in various online practices concerns individual motivations or aspirations and may relate to personal solutions for different issues, including a lack of money to purchase cultural goods. The material element is therefore a crucial denominator behind what is described as "piracy": that is, practices related to needs developed by consumer culture. Many respondents used free sharing to accumulate different materials simply because they were "free" and because they needed to be "up to date" with international trends. Market scarcities and insufficient supply of cultural goods, and the convenience of downloading are also reasons stated by respondents. As Janek (Warsaw, Poland) noted:

> First it is economic reasons, second it is easy. In Poland you need 5 minutes to download. It is convenient.

It is also important to note that many respondents admitted that they were not contributing anything to free cultural online spaces or participating in any creative individual or P2P activity. In such cases, the consumerist reflexes guided the way they used new media/ICT, and the communal and free potentials provided by new media did not transform their views and habits on the production and usage of cultural goods. Cultural needs that are triggered by market mechanisms continue to produce constant desires for commodities and permanent deference of gratification (Bauman 2005, 80). The online access to different sorts of niche cultures from all over the world triggers the fantasy, the curiosity and the consumerist desire for different sorts of cultural goods. The nature of the Internet in particular is seen as flexible and free – and this "free" nature of informal media/ICT activity legitimizes the very nature of new media.

Finally, identities played a crucial part in the ways that different practices developed. Identities today are plural, expressing diverse social roles and contexts (Dahlgren 2009, 119). Articulations of locality and tensions in the configurations of the nation, particularly in relation to the "international" were evident in the way the respondents' accounted for their use of new media and ICTs. Christos (Greece) noted that:

> To name a whole generation as thieves is an extreme, in so far as its sole crime is to use the available technologies in order to learn, to communicate and to have fun, in a time where due to the economic impoverishing of the most, the Internet has become one of the few solutions to a number of things.

The use of new media and ICTs reflect a transnational generational identity of people growing up with the Internet. This creates subcultural traits and interests as well as a desire for a commodity culture (Olsson and Miegel 2011). Fan identities dominated many people's creative use of new media and ICT and further shape media practices related to free online culture. The re-shaping of both individual and collective identities is also linked to professionalism in both the cultural industries and beyond. These changes are challenging established social identities related to professionalism, particularly through the advent and recognition of amateur production and user generated content.

Simultaneously, the development of introvert and narcissist subjectivities is enveloped by fantasies generated by the neoliberal and commercial aspects of the Internet. This is particularly related to the hype of connectivity, spectacles of banal cosmopolitanism, the praising of novelty, the illusion of possibilities, promises of individual consumption and the development of innumerable individualist desires. Subject positions, related to the norms of niche subcultures in the case of amateur producers are performed and articulated (Carpentier 2011, 178) in terms antagonistic to national identity. Individualist social identities concerning the "cool," reflexive individual, related to the identity of the "flaneur," the connoisseur or the collector, were also expressed. After asking the question, "Do you buy any CDs or DVDs?" Kryzstof (Lublin, Poland) responded as follows:

> Sometimes; it depends on where I am, and it depends on my moods. If I am at the mall, I mainly buy music DVDs and compilations.

While the hybridity and openness of identity are potentially democratizing, they are also subject to exploitation and manipulation by late capitalist processes. National identity is the hegemonic identity frame for the respondents even when it is contested by late capitalist meta-narratives such as consumerism and entrepreneurialism. Counter-cultural subject positions are also challenging national identity and consumerist/entrepreneurial identities. In every case, identity is a contingent entity, escaping full determination (Carpentier 2011, 176).

Conclusions

The reflexive uses of Dahlgren's (2009) analytical categories intersect in the above analysis. Identity is connected to values, while practice is determining and determined by values and identities. The analysis comparatively demonstrates that consumerism, class, identity, citizenship, resistance as well as entrepreneurship, are entailed in free file-sharing practices of ICT users. Though as Tolentino (2011) has identified, "free culture" often conceals class inequalities and sustains middle class fantasies for those from the lower class, in an era of diminished social mobility.

The social context of informal new media/ICT uses marks the political bias of IP regulations, which is strictly guided by monopolistic economic interests. Lifeworld practices, "the general intellect" and popular technological/communicational tools are important areas for the development of a new political culture. Simultaneously, contextual and subjective issues, as well as particular events, are important denominators related to the course that particular practices can take, whether or not they can be connected to political projects or advance democratic culture by supporting a collective egalitarian ethos in everyday life. The very different political cultures of the two countries reveal differences in the ways interviewees understand the potential of new media for social change and social change itself. Greek respondents would politicize "piracy" easier than their Polish counterparts, by stressing the exploitatory aspect of copyright restrictions and crude political economy issues. Greek respondents would also be able to imagine the development of alternative distribution networks through digital media, and were also keen with the gift economy culture emerging online, as something liberating. Polish respondents show more entrepreneurial opportunities in digital culture that could advance their position in the market as laborers or as consumers.

File-sharing often emerges as a resistant tactic towards mainstream, popular culture. P2P structures entail a particular ideological frame. Sometimes, free sharing within a gift economy is a form of resistance towards degrading living conditions and a social strategy for survival. Simultaneously, in a different context, free sharing online is a resource to be utilized for entrepreneurial aspirations. The common denominator of both possibilities is material scarcity. The difference lies in the ideological frames organizing reality, identities and practices.

A space of commons is created through people's informal uses of new media/ICT tools. The element of "free" in informal practices destroys "free market" rules (Freedman 2012, 73). Market pressures to control and commoditize this space are relatively successful through the construction of alternative equivalents that promise efficiency and offer consumerist fantasies. "Offline" scarcity seems to determine new media/ICT uses. Simultaneously, the creative utilization of digital technology and networks provide possibilities for the transgression of socially imposed scarcities. Neoliberal rationales, practices and policies, attempt to curb such possibilities through ideology, law and logics of scarcity and efficiency. Disciplinary acts, such as copyright indoctrination seminars, seem to have an ideological effect, although practices are not compromised since market rules cannot compete with free access. Simultaneously different contradictions rise, proving the contingency of the social and the impossibility of its full closure by hegemonic and dominant forces.

References

Bauman, Zygmunt (2005a). *Liquid life.* London: Polity.

Bauman, Zygmunt (2005b). *Work, consumerism and the new poor.* Maidenhead: Open University Press.

Brown, Wendy (2003). "Neo-liberalism and the end of liberal democracy". *Theory and Event,* 7:1, 1-43. Retrieved 10 December 2013, from http://muse.jhu.edu/login?uri=/journals/theory_and_event/v007/7.1brown.html

Bruno, Isabelle, Sophie Jacquot and Lou Mandin (2006). "Europeanization through its instrumentation: benchmarking, mainstreaming and the open method of co-ordination... toolbox or Pandora's box?". *Journal of European Public Policy,* 13: 4, 519-536.

Bryman, Alan (2010). *Social research methods.* Oxford, UK: Oxford University Press.

Carpentier, Nico (2011). *Media and participation: A site of ideological-democratic struggle.* London: Intellect.

Castells, Manuel (2001). *The Internet galaxy.* Oxford: Oxford University Press.

Castells, Manuel (2004/1997). *The power of identity, second edition.* Oxford: Blackwell.

Crouch, Colin (2011). *The strange non-death of neoliberalism.* London: Polity.

Curran, James, Natalie Fenton and Des Freedman (2012). *Misunderstanding the Internet.* London: Routledge.

Dahlgren, Peter (2009). *Media and political engagement: Citizens, communication and democracy.* Cambridge: Cambridge University Press.

Daoud, Adel and Johan Söderberg (2012). "Atoms want to be free too! Expanding the critique of intellectual property to physical goods". *tripleC,* 10:1, 66-76. Retrieved 2 April 2012, from http://www.triple-c.at

David, Matthew (2010). *Peer to peer and the music industry: The criminalization of sharing.* London: Sage Publications.

Davis, Mike (2006). *Planet of slums.* London: Verso.

Dean, Kathryn (2003). *Capitalism and citizenship: The impossible partnership.* London: Routledge.

De Certeau, Michel (1990/ 2008). *The practice of everyday life.* Athens: Smili. (In Greek).

Deuze, Mark (2007). *Media work.* London: Polity.

Filiciak, Mirosław and Piotr Toczyski (2011). "Peer re-production and extended culture industry: Case of TV content and redistribution in Europeanizing and globalizing Poland". (Unpublished work, cited after kind permission of the authors).

Flew, Terry (2007). *Understanding global media.* New York: Palgrave McMillan.

Fuchs, Christian (2012). "Google capitalism". *tripleC,* 10:1, 42-48. Retrieved 2 April 2012, from http://www.triple-c.at

Garnham, Nicholas (2004). "Class analysis and the information society as a mode of production". *The public,* 11:3, 93-104.

Gauntlett, David (2011). *Making is connecting, the social meaning of creativity from DIY and knitting to YouTube and Web 2.0.* London: Polity.

Graeber, David (2011). *Debt, the first 5000 years.* New York. Melville House.

Habermas, Jürgen (1975). *Legitimation crisis.* Boston: Beacon Press.

Hall, Gary (2009). "Introduction: Pirate Philosophy". *Culture Machine,* 10 (2009), 1-4. Retrieved 2 April 2012, from http://www.culturemachine.net/index.php/cm/issue/view/21

Hardt, Michael and Antonio Negri (2009). *Commonwealth.* London: The Belknap Press of Harvard University Press.

Harvey, David (2005). *A brief history of neoliberalism.* Oxford: Oxford University Press.

Harvey, David (2010). *The enigma of capital and the crises of capitalism.* London: Profile.

Harvey, David (2012). *Rebel cities: from the right to the city to urban revolution.* London: Verso.

IIPA Report (2011). Greece: Special 301 report on copyright protection and enforcement. Retrieved 15 June 2011, from http://www.iipa.com/rbc/2011/2011SPEC301GREECE.pdf

Internet World Stats (2010a). Greece: Internet usage and marketing report. Retrieved 10 January 2011, from http://www.Internetworldstats.com/europa.htm#gr

Internet Usage Stats and Market Report (2010b). Poland. Retrieved 23 November 2011, from http://www.Internetworldstats.com/eu/pl.htm#links

Jakobsson, Peter and Fredrik Stiernstedt (2012). "Reinforcing property by strengthening the commons: a new media policy paradigm?". *tripleC,* 10:1, 49-55. Retrieved 2 April 2012, from http://www.triple-c.at

Jakubowicz Karol (1992). "Musical chairs? The three public spheres in Poland". Dahlgren Peter and Colin Sparks (eds). *Communication and citizenship, journalism and the public sphere.* London: Routledge.

Klein, Naomi (2007). *The shock doctrine: the rise of disaster capitalism.* New York: Metropolitan books.

Kompatsiaris, Panos (2012). "Novelty and the politicization of the creative field: creative labour and the 'open work'". *Critical Contemporary Culture (CCC): Novelty,* I. Retrieved 5 April 2012, from http://www.criticalcontemporaryculture.org/

panos-kompatsiaris-novelty-and-the-politicization-of-the-creative-field-creative-labour-and-the-%E2%80%98open-work%E2%80%99/
Lapavitsas, Costas, Peter Bratsis, Stathis Kouvelakis and Etienne Balibar (2010). "The Greek crisis: politics, economics, ethics". *Journal of Modern Greek Studies*, 28, 293-309. The John Hopkins University Press.
Lessig, Laurence (2004). *Free culture*. New York: Penguin Press.
Lister, Martin, Jon Dovey and Seth Giddings (2008). *New media, a critical introduction* (2nd ed). Milton Park: Routledge.
Lobato, Ramon, Julian Thomas and Dan Hunter (2011). "Histories of user-generated content: between formal and informal media economies". *International Journal of Communication*, 5, 899-914. Retrieved 10 June 2011, from http://ijoc.org/ojs/index.php/ijoc
Lule, Jack (2011). *Globalization and media*. New York: Rowman & Littlefield Publishers.
May, Christopher (2009). *The global political economy of intellectual property rights: The new enclosures*. London: Routledge.
McGiffin, Steve (2005). *The European Union, a critical guide: new edition*. London: Pluto Press.
Mylonas, Yiannis (2011). "Accumulation, control and contingency: A critical review of intellectual property rights' 'piracy'". *First Monday*, 16:12, 5 December 2011.
Mylonas, Yiannis (2012a). "Piracy culture in Greece: local realities and civic potentials". *Piracy Cultures, Special Issue, International Journal of Communication*, 6:1, 710–734. Retrieved 25 October 2012, from http://ijoc.org/
Mylonas, Yiannis (2012b). "Amateur creation and entrepreneurialism: a critical study of artistic production in post-Fordist structures". *tripleC*, 10:1, 1-11. Retrieved 2 April 2012, from http://triple-c.at/index.php/tripleC
Olsson, Tobias and Friedrik Miegel (2010). "A generational thing? The Internet and new forms of social intercourse". [Manuscript submitted for publication.]
Ong, Aihwa (2006). *Neoliberalism as exception: Mutations in citizenship and sovereignty*. London: Duke University Press.
Sassen, Saskia (1994). "The informal economy: Between new developments and old regulations". *Yale Law Journal*, 103:8, 2289–2304.
Slavnic, Zoran (2010). "The political economy of informalization". *European Societies*, 12:1. 3-23.
Stallman, Richard (2004). "Why 'Free Software' is better than 'Open Source'". Retrieved 30 October 2012, from http://www.gnu.org/philosophy/free-software-for-freedom.html
Theodosiadou, Sophia (2010). "Pirate radio in the 1980's: A case study of Thessaloniki's pirate radio". *The Radio Journal–International Studies in Broadcast and Audio Media*, 8:1, 37–48.
Tolentino, Rolando (2011). "Media piracy and Philippine cosmopolitanisms". *Special issue: Piracy as activism; Re-public, re-imagining democracy*. Retrieved 21 March

2011, from http://www.re-public.gr/en/?p=3884
Virno, Paolo (2004). *A grammar of the multitude.* Los Angeles: Semiotext(e).
Wesolowski, Wlodzimierz (1995). "The nature of social ties and the future of post-communist society: Poland after Solidarity". John Hall (ed.). *Civil society, theory, history, comparison.* Cambridge: Polity Press.
Žižek, Slavoj (2010). "A Permanent Economic Emergency". *New Left Review*, 64, 85-95.

Acknowledgments

The author wishes to warmly thank Ms. Teresa Klimowicz (PhD scholar at Philosophy Department, Marie Curie University, Lublin) for her help in informing him of the Polish socio-political-historical context, and in establishing local contacts with people interviewed and in translation. The author also wishes to warmly thank Dr. Kuba Nowak (Lecturer from the Political Science Department, Marie Curie University, Lublin) for providing valuable information on the Polish context of new media uses and copyright history, as well as for distributing questionnaires of the research to respondents.

The IPR GPR: The Emergence of a Global Prohibition Regime to Regulate Intellectual Property Infringement

Lucas Logan

Introduction

In 2007, *Roja Directa*, a Spanish web site that specializes in the online streaming of broadcasts of sports matches, was taken to court for alleged copyright infringement (McSherry 2011). Spanish courts found that, since the web site only acted as a directory for users to stream broadcasts and did not stream any of the broadcasts itself, *Roja Directa* was not in violation of the national copyright law (McSherry). In 2011, however, several of *Roja Directa's* Internet domain names, http://rojadirecta.com and http://rojadirecta.org, were seized by the US government for copyright infringement (*Puerto 80 Projects, S.L.U. v. United States of America, Department of Homeland Security and Immigration and Customs [Puerto 80 v. U.S.] 2011).* Additionally, the US government was found to be working closely in secret with the Spanish government to adopt new copyright laws so that sites like *Roja Directa* would be criminalized in Spain. In the eyes of the many Spanish citizens that took to the streets of Madrid and protested their government's hidden dealings with the US, the real infringement was not that of Internet users over copyright, but of the US over Spanish sovereignty (Slattery 2011).

In this research, I argue that cases including *Roja Directa*'s are evidence of an emerging global prohibition regime (GPR) over intellectual property. GPRs, a concept presented by Nadelmann (1990) and Andreas and Nadelmann (2006), are made up of legal, economic, social and political regimes that regulate prohibited norms. My research highlights how an emerging GPR is concerned with the enforcement of international standards of intellectual property rights (IPR), and I explain how this affects systems of social interaction and communication between and within states. Consequently, this study is guided by the following question:

> Do current and emerging global regulations and police enforcement regarding IPR fit into a working model of a GPR, and if so, how do these laws and regulations affect communicative and social interactions in the global political economy?

In this research, I am specifically examining online production, reproduction and dissemination of digital knowledge-based goods. This builds on literature regarding the political economy of communication and information policy by analyzing the social power relations between states, markets and society in regard to intellectual property rights. First, I briefly describe the place of IPR in an information economy. I then evaluate descriptions of the global political economy as defined by Mosco (2009), Fuchs (2008, 2011) and Schiller (1999) in order to define a political economic critique of the global communication infrastructure and explain how this critique encapsulates the current place of IPR. After examining larger theoretical explanations of the global political economy, I discuss literature addressing the policy mechanisms and communication technologies related to IPR. Specifically, I review Braman's (2007) work on information policy as the mechanisms by which IPR are enforced and review Benkler's (2006) discussion of the nature of information and communication technologies. After establishing this theoretical framework, I turn to discuss Nadelmann's (1990) and Andreas and Nadelmann's (2006) model of global prohibition regimes. After presenting the case study regarding Spain's experience with the IPR GPR, I conclude the chapter by discussing the way that the GPR disrupts the political economy of the state and causes social conflicts that may undermine efforts at prohibiting acts associated with intellectual property infringement.

Defining IPR in an information economy

Following the direction established by Fuchs (2011, 130), I use the term 'information economy' to describe only the parts of the economy that deal in information-based goods, services, trading and commerce. Both intellectual property and IPR are an important layer of the information economy, but are only part of a larger global communication infrastructure also based on services and investment (Thussu 2006, 68-70). Intellectual property underpins the areas of the information economy that rely on e-commerce and cultural goods (Thussu 2006, 156; 223).

Intellectual property policy is generally construed in a manner that protects the most powerful economies and multinational corporations. Thussu, for instance, noted that the Motion Picture Association of America (MPAA) is known as a "little state department" (2006, 156-162). The organization not only promotes and lobbies certain policies, but also is even known to write policy that has resulted in the liberalization of cultural industries (ibid.) This liberalization has been identified as sparking the demise of national film industries and cultural identity (ibid.).

This chapter is critical of the IPR policy system and skeptical of the specific mechanisms that it uses to create a global information economy. This is because it is built on the perspective that the expansion, acceleration and consolidation of the US and, increasingly, EU-led global political economy, through trade agreements, international organizations and transnational police forces potentially weaken or endanger the well-being of other states and civil society. In the next section, I address literature that engages with the global political economy that is responsible for the current IPR regime.

The political economy of communication and information policy

Mosco (2009), Fuchs (2008) and Schiller (1999) all provide analysis of how information and communication technologies operate in the global political economy. Mosco defines the political economy of communication as the study of social power relations that mutually constitute the production, distribution and consumption of communication, or the social process of exchange of social relationships (2009, 67-68). In the author's critical perspective, the post-industrial, information-driven form of capitalism that envelops the global economy is based on the manipulation of communication technologies by multinational corporations. This is because communication technologies allow multinationals to accumulate capital by outsourcing labor and management functions worldwide (Mosco 2009, 69-71). Once the multinationals have a large enough presence within the global economy, they are able to overcome the authority of some states and integrate with the regulatory systems of others in order to protect elite economic interests. The global capitalist agenda of these corporations is also reflected in international governmental organizations such as the European Union and World Trade Organization, and through bi- and multi-lateral trade agreements (Mosco 2009, 177).

Likewise, Schiller (1999) proposes that the global capitalist agenda of multinationals is reflected in the regulatory regimes and economic foreign policy of hegemonic actors in the global political economy, especially the United States. A clear example of the state promoting the agenda of the private sector is the United States Trade Representative (USTR), which, with research directly provided by the International Intellectual Property Association (IIPA), issues scathing reports and threatens trade sanctions against states it perceives as out of compliance with intellectual property rights (Drahos 2002). Here, the agenda of the state and the market essentially become inseparable, and powerful states are able to assert authority over, and force legal, regulatory and economic regimes, on weaker states.

Fuchs (2008) offers a similar description of the global political economy as Mosco (2009) and Schiller (1999). Fuchs defined the state as a unit of political self-organization whose procedures and institutions are responsible for economic regulation; controlling and legitimizing the means of violence; surveillance of society; distribution of rights to citizens; control over the membership of society; fostering national identity; and creating population policy (2008, 75-81). When the state supports a liberalized economic agenda that empowers the ability of multinationals to accumulate capital, then, the state has significant power in influencing norms and policing activities within its borders and, in the case of the US and EU, around the globe. As certain communication technologies – including Internet-enabled technologies such as peer-to-peer technology and social networks – can pose a threat to the established economic order, they are then opposed by the dominant market actors (Fuchs 2008, 129-134). As such, states that encourage global information capitalism, such as the US, will place barriers around the use of such communication technologies within their borders and will exert pressure toward other states to do the same.

As the policies of the most powerful states and multinational media industries become increasingly intertwined, we see regimes crafted that control access to communication technologies (Fuchs 2011). This is driven by claims controlling access to information is essential to exploiting cultural goods and creative works for profit (Fuchs 2011, 5). E-commerce is steadily growing worldwide and accounted for $145 billion in sales among US retailers in 2009 (US Census Bureau, 2012), and the European Commission has detailed plans to double e-commerce sales in the EU by 2015 (European Commission [E.C.], 2011).

The struggle to control the flow of content makes the Internet what Fuchs refers to as the "field of conflict" between the media industries and actors that support the notion of the Internet as a cultural commons wherein regulation should be cautionary of civil liberties and open communication (2011, 5). The result is that most Internet regulation reflects a capitalist worldview that privileges the accumulation of capital over the cultural commons or democratic ideals of open communication. Market growth and profits fundamentally drive the direction of Internet policy and laws are mechanisms for protecting the private property of corporations (Fuchs 2011, 38; 225-229). Resistance emerges through leftist alternative media and politicized civil society organizations such as Wikipedia's stand against the US's Stop Online Piracy Act (SOPA).

Each of the above authors offers a series of arguments that communication technologies are the fuel for the 21st century global economy and are regulated by capitalist market forces and states that further entrench established power relations. While not part of the conversation on the global political economy, Braman (2007) builds upon the theoretical basis for the regulation of communication technologies. Braman (2007) argues that in an information-based economy, states weld information policy as a mechanism for structural power in society. For instance, information policy is used to identify which communication technologies and what cultural content are commodities; which are public goods; which are restricted for use by governments; and which are inaccessible to individuals. Information policy, then, controls the flow of communication and social interaction in global society.

In the US and EU, Braman notes that intellectual property rights are governed by policies that are most often built to regulate knowledge-based goods as strict commodities instead of public goods (2007, 177-179). Emerging global information policy is especially restrictive of open access to intellectual property because IPR underpins a large portion of the information economy.

Communication technologies also make it easy for individuals to create, disseminate and manipulate information-based goods, so there is a push by policy makers to be especially restrictive on how individuals are allowed to handle intellectual property (Braman 2007, 177). While copyright policy makers attempt to maintain control, copying, distribution and sharing knowledge-based goods is easier than ever before (Braman 2007, 162). Such individual distribution of knowledge-based goods and resources leads to what Braman referred to as the "deprofessionalization of policy issues," resulting in policymakers crafting laws that regulate individual behavior in addition to industrial-scale intellectual property infringement (2007, 62). Traditional approaches to media policy that emphasize the economic relationship between professional organizations should be reconsidered when making policy to regulate electronic communication tools.

This reconsideration often fails to materialize since the reproduction of content by individuals is taken as a threat to traditional corporate manufacturers and gatekeepers of media, and these corporations use their capital and governmental influence to pressure policymakers to lock down intellectual property through policy that tightly controls the distribution and reproduction of creative goods (Benkler 2006; Braman 2007). I argue that the manner in which states and markets have taken to controlling the distribution and reproduction of knowledge based goods is in that of a global prohibition regime, which is defined in the next section.

Global prohibition regimes

Global prohibition regimes (GPRs) are made up of legal, economic, social and political regimes that regulate prohibited norms (Andreas and Nadelmann 2006; Nadelmann 1990). GPRs encompass a diverse range of activities, including but not limited to counterfeiting, high seas piracy, money laundering, terrorism, the killing of endangered species and the trade of drugs, prostitution, ivory, and weapons (Andreas and Nadelmann 2006). As diverse as GPRs are, there are certain commonalities that link these different regimes. Primarily, GPRs are socially constructed; that is, they are based on social norms that are developed by elite states, economic actors and civil society (Nadelmann 1990, 480). GPRs take shape for a number of reasons including the need of states to protect the wellbeing of its citizenry, the need to protect markets, through the moral outcry of non-state actors such as civil society groups and religious organizations, or any combination of these (Nadelmann 1990, 480). Andreas and Nadelmann (2006) describe most GPRs as developing through a five-stage model, as follows:

1. The proscribed activity is legitimate under certain conditions: that is, there is state support for the activity and any constraints have more to do with treaties and "political prudence" than with moral notions or international norms;
2. Scholars, religious groups and other 'moral entrepreneurs' begin to label the proscribed activity as problematic or even 'evil': As such, state involvement in the practice is gradually delegitimized and support for the activity begins to wane, although states may still sponsor private groups and non-state actors that engage in the activity;
3. Prohibition proponents begin to actively agitate "for the suppression and criminalization of the activity by all states and the formation of international conventions" (ibid., 21): Enough hegemonic influence is exerted that leads

to a push for international prohibitions through methods ranging from the formation of intergovernmental organizations, diplomatic pressures, economic inducements, military interventions and propaganda campaigns;

4. International institutions and intergovernmental organizations launch criminal sanctions and police action regarding the activity: Intense pressure emerges on all states to adopt the legal regimes that enforce prohibition, and states that refuse are labeled as illegitimate actors in global society. Challenges to instituting the GPR include dissident states, states that institute prohibition standards but do not enforce them, dissident individuals and criminal organizations; and,
5. The prohibited activity is nearly eliminated and only persists in isolated areas.
6. Achievement of the fifth stage is exceptionally rare, and only applies to prohibitions that can be successfully tackled through criminal sanctions and law enforcement (Andreas and Nadelmann 2006, 22). In fact, GPRs for which resources are readily available, where expertise is required, and for which demand is consistent and resilient are unlikely to ever reach the fifth stage. Additionally, the international harmonization of regulation is difficult to achieve, and harmonization does not guarantee implementation (Drezner 2008, 11). As such, in the rare case that a GPR makes it to the fourth stage, it is unlikely to ever overcome the dissenting factors.

An example of a regime that reached the fifth stage was that of high seas piracy and privateering (Andreas and Nadelmann 2006, 22-26). In the first stage of this prohibition, prior to the 18th century, the practice of piracy and privateering was generally accepted during wartime and even in times of peace by European states. Privateering was considered crucial to the economic survival of the state, and was generally off-limits only when bilateral treaties and diplomatic agreements between individual states had restricted the practice. After the rise of the British Navy and the ascension of Turkish pirates, the practice began to enter the second stage of a prohibition regime. Moral arguments were made that privateering by infidels (the Turks) was wholly immoral, and should not be replicated by Europeans. The power of the British fleet to enhance colonization and build empire also eliminated the need for the British to engage in privateering and made the practice somewhat of a nuisance for the colonial power. The third stage of the GPR involved multilateral treaties and conventions to end piracy among the European states, and military alliances to destroy pirate bases in China, Oman, Algiers and elsewhere. The fourth stage was reached when the United States, long a defender of its right to privateer in order to establish its economy, finally gained the naval strength in the late 1800s to become independent of the practice and signed on to European treaties and conventions declaring piracy a crime. With the US on board, the GPR on privateering was eventually completed and high seas piracy was nearly eliminated for several decades by the turn of the 20th century.

In contrast to high seas piracy, the war on drugs is an example of a global prohibition regime that will never move beyond the fourth stage of development (see Andreas and Nadelmann 2006, 44-45 for a more detailed analysis). The failure of this drug war is one of the more dramatic cases of a GPR's inability to reach the fifth stage, and is not indicative of all GPRs stuck in the fourth stage. As Drezner (2008, 13) notes, the success of international regulatory regimes may be incremental. For instance, if international regulations on a chemical pollutant are designed to eliminate that pollutant but only succeed in significantly reducing the pollutant, the regulation may still be considered a partial success and superior to alternative measures. When analyzing the emerging GPR toward IPR, it is important to understand if the GPR can reach the fifth stage, but also whether or not the legal regimes put in place will be significantly efficient in reducing intellectual property infringement, or if the regimes will be over-reaching, dangerous and ineffectual, as is the case in the drug war.

Andreas and Nadelmann (2006, 54-58) detail the emerging GPR toward intellectual property. GPRs on IPR are part of the post-World War II international legal regimes pursued primarily by the US and EU. The legal regimes include regulatory harmonization, bi- and multi-lateral trade agreements, international governmental bodies and systems of international police and judicial cooperation that allow cross-border arrests, freezing monetary assets and extradition programs. The most prominent example that Andreas and Nadelmann (2006) give in regard to the culmination of the GPR on intellectual property is Operation Fastlink: which was described by the US Department of Justice in 2004 as "the most far-reaching and aggressive enforcement action ever undertaken against organizations involved in illegal intellectual property piracy over the Internet" and included cooperation between Belgium, Denmark, France, Germany, Hungary, Israel, the Netherlands, Singapore, Sweden and the U.K. (Department of Justice 2004). The operation involved police search and seizures of the computer servers of hundreds of websites and arrests of dozens of individuals across the globe, and primarily targeted 'warez' sites hosting illicit copies of copyrighted software (Department of Justice 2004, 2006). Web sites hosting copies of movies and music were also targeted, and the Justice Department claimed that the FBI and trade associations including the Business Software Alliance, Recording Industry Association of America, and Motion Picture Association of America all assisted in the investigations (Department of Justice 2004, 2006).

The creation of TRIPS and the various seizures and arrests relating to IPR and the Internet point directly to a GPR in the latter part of the third stage. Like other GPRs, prohibitions on intellectual property are socially constructed and reflect the hegemonic interests of the most powerful global economic actors, namely the US and the EU. Unlike some other GPRs, the regulation of media content largely intersects with the construction of information capitalism in the global political economy. In the next section, I consult literature on the evolution of prohibitions over intellectual property infringement to illustrate the manner that the IPR GPR came into existence.

The emergence of the IPR GPR

Drahos (2002) and Johns (2009) both describe the early history of cross-border intellectual property theft as an issue taken seriously by European states but largely dismissed by the US before the 20th century. US enforcement of intellectual property rights rapidly accelerated after the Second World War, when emerging economic realities made evident the fact that the control of IP would be a key driver of the emerging global economy (Drahos 2002, 39). The dominant force in persuading policymakers how to regulate intellectual property has been the multinational corporation, which promotes a legal regime that favors complete market control over knowledge-based goods (Drahos 2002). Cartels made up of multinational corporations representing the software, entertainment, pharmaceutical and publishing industries, among others, act as the primary outlets for the IPR industries to create and promote policy preferences.

The largest regulatory success for the multinationals to date is TRIPS, which, as part of the Uruguay Round of the General Agreement on Trade and Tariffs (GATT) in 1994, created an international regulatory regime based on the intellectual property standards of the US and EU (Drahos 2002, 5). TRIPS affected all levels of IPR, from biotechnology to counterfeit DVDs, and pressured the developing world to import the intellectual property norms of the US and Europe. In addition to TRIPS, both the US and EU have engaged in establishing bilateral and multilateral agreements with other states that invariably favor the economic interests of the two hegemonic powers. Those states that have refused to harmonize to the standards demanded have been labeled 'pirates' and accused of harboring counterfeiting and theft (Drahos 2002, 73-74). For states that signed on to TRIPS, violations can result in a WTO court hearing as well as enforced trade sanctions. The primary weapon that the US uses to enforce IPR standards is the USTR's Special 301 list, which is primarily informed by suggestions from the IIPA and is used to threaten trade sanctions on other states (Drahos 2002, 96).

The regulatory mechanisms for enforcing IPR are only half of the story for Drahos (2002), as a key element of the US and EU's export of IP regimes is in asserting moral authority. For instance, the entertainment industry declares that through supporting strict copyright laws, it is defending the integrity of artists and ensuring the future of the arts and cultural industries (Drahos 2002, 177). The entertainment industry also supports 're-education campaigns' in which states are obliged by treaties to use resources to educate law enforcement officials and students of the importance of protecting copyrights (Drahos 2002, 27). Additionally, the very label of what is or is not piracy is consistently shifting as new laws and regulations are instituted. For instance, once the US and EU developed regulations preventing the circumvention of digital locks placed on media like DVDs and MP3s that prevent that media from being copied, the definition of piracy and intellectual property theft expanded to include breaking the digital locks (Drahos 2002, 184). The very notion of the figure of the intellectual property pirate has been expanded from organizations to individuals when communication technologies began to make home taping, recording, remixing and copying easily accessible to individuals (Johns 2009). So not only is the counterfeiter or the owner of the peer-to-peer enabled web site a pirate, but so are the users of the technology.

Furthermore, Drahos (2002, 184) argues that the moral prohibitions on individual copying and sharing are doomed to fail and will require the entertainment industry to push for more draconian copyright laws and protections. Included here is the increasing effort of the multinational intellectual property industry to demonize the act of piracy and intellectual property infringement. In the next section, I turn to discussing the issue of piracy in terms of the political economy of communication, information policy and global prohibition regimes.

Elements of the IPR GPR

An analysis of the literature supports the argument that there is a GPR emerging regarding IPR. From the arguments discussed regarding the political economy of communication, information policy, global prohibition regimes and historical trends in IPR regulation, I conclude that there are five elements that are most important to the discussion of the emerging IPR GPR. First, while the IPR GPR moved toward a third stage during the Cold War era as communication technologies became essential to an increasingly globalized economy, this stage was achieved in the last decade of the 20th century. Evidence of a fully articulated third stage materialized with the combination of what Drahos (2002) describes as bi, multi, and unilateral pressures from the US and EU on other states to both adopt established IPR regimes and the ascension of intergovernmental organizations like the World Trade Organization to enforce trade policies across borders. Additionally, the use of the judicial and police system to make arrests, extradite individuals accused of copyright infringement, freeze the assets of alleged pirates, and seize the computers of individuals is evidence of an international criminal justice system that is rapidly enabling the IPR GPR to enter a fourth stage of prohibition enforcement.

Secondly, the actions of the US and EU in prohibiting intellectual property infringement take place largely because of statistics, research and other information provided by IPR industries: fusing together the interests of the multinational organizations and these hegemonic states. Coalitions of multinationals assist in the international enforcement of IPR and provide the statistics, economic analysis and research that guide policymakers in the craft of regulations, policies and diplomatic pressures.

Thirdly, the moral element that decries social norms and strengthens the state's commitment to GPRs is evident in prohibitions on intellectual property infringement. An example of moral condemnation in copyright enforcement includes the labeling of individual infringers as 'pirates' and equating the infringement of copyright to physical and violent crimes such as bag snatching. Further, we have seen the continual expansion of the figure of the pirate to include individuals that violate new laws such as cracking digital locks on DVDs and MP3s (Johns 2009, 184). Additionally, the entertainment industry insists that draconian copyright policies are integral to the flow of cultural production and the integrity of the arts, and that states not up to the task of using resources to increase IPR protections are creating a "crisis of international copyright" (Drahos 2002, 75).

The fourth element of the IPR GPR is that it is comprised of information policy: that is, the regulatory mechanism that controls the flow of communication and social interaction in global society (Braman 2007). Thus, the IPR GPR regulates prohibitions on communicative interactions and technologies. This GPR is regulating and enforcing the way that humans communicate and share information. A GPR based on information policy differs from prohibitions on, for instance, counterfeiting money or hunting endangered species in that it seeks to regulate the production and exchange of knowledge. In the case of the IPR GPR, policymakers and multinationals as a purely economic, as opposed to cultural, transaction, present the exchange of knowledge.

The final element of the IPR GPR is directly related to the use of information policy as a tool for prohibiting IPR violations. The policy mechanisms for regulating knowledge-based goods are rooted in international trade regimes, criminal justice systems and the reassignment of moral norms regarding IPR. For physical infringement – such as counterfeit pharmaceuticals or DVD factories – police enforcement is relatively straight-forward. For digital infringement, enforcement is more complex due to the ease of copying and altering media content on computers and the Internet and the lack of established cultural norms against digital violations of IPR. Without norms against infringement, it becomes less likely that violations will be reported to authorities. Also, enforcement mechanisms such as digital locks are easily overcome (Johns 2009, 506), and while the physical computer servers of alleged pirates can be seized by police, the resources required to create and share media content online are minimal. This is not to say that a fifth stage of the IPR GPR is impossible, but rather to note that the act of IPR infringement on the Internet as it currently stands partially parallels Andreas and Nadelmann's (2006) requirements for prohibitions that legal regimes are unable to eliminate.

Roja Directa and digital infringement in Spain

Recently, Spain has been accused by both the intellectual property industry and the USTR of having one of the highest piracy rates in the world (USTR 2011; IIPA 2011). The reason for Spain's out-of-control piracy problem, the IIPA contends, is government sponsored "Internet-wide safe harbor for infringing activities" (IIPA 2011, 1). IIPA's estimates accuse the Spanish of losing up to

$6 billion due to piracy, with roughly half of that number coming from digital copyright infringement alone. The IIPA has accused Spain of violating EU directives on e-commerce and IPR enforcement, and described it as having "the worst per capita Internet piracy problem in Europe and one of the worst overall Internet piracy rates in the world" (KARAGANIS 2011, 95). Though Spain has rebutted the IIPA's claims, citing its own data, this has had little effect on the IIPA's ongoing campaign. Additionally, the International Federation of the Phonographic Industry (IFPI) criticized Spain's Internet piracy problem in its 2010 Digital Piracy Report, claiming that the "victims" of Spain's lax copyright laws were "local acts" (2010, 6). The IFPI claimed that Spain's "state-sponsored apathy" toward piracy has lead to the near-death of the Spanish music industry, and cites a drop in sales of local music in Spain (ibid., 19).

Whether or not Spain's piracy problem is as dramatic as has been claimed, the IFPI and IIPA's figures regarding revenue loss and infringement provide the foundation for mounting pressure to alter the country's intellectual property system. Spain particularly aggravated the IIPA and IFPI in 2006 when its courts found that Spanish copyright law does not consider downloading copyrighted media content illegal so long as the downloader only uses the content for personal use (Tremlett 2006).

Additionally, Spain's attorney general, on the heels of the legal decisions regarding digital copyright infringement, announced that web sites that index – as oppose to directly host – copyrighted content are not liable for criminal or civil prosecution (IIPA 2011). The attorney general's comments were not a direct legal statement, but did guide the courts in practice (IIPA 2011). For instance, *Roja Directa*, a website that allows users to upload digital streams of sports matches, was found not to be in violation of copyright in a Spanish court (McSherry 2011). Despite the Spanish court's finding, the US later seized eighteen of the website's domain names (*Puerto 80 v. US* 2011, 2-3). A US lawyer that was influential in *Roja Directa's* seizure later stated that the "fact that a country doesn't protect intellectual property is no excuse to just give them free reign to do whatever they want" (quoted in Anderson 2011). In other words, the legitimacy of the Spanish courts was considered questionable, as it was in violation of the legal regime supported and exported by the US. Despite appeals by the owners of *Roja Directa*, the US refused to relinquish the domain names for 18 months, when the case was dismissed in a California court of law (Bharara 2012).

In addition to the seizures of websites by US agencies, the key element that emerged was the heavy pressure on Spain to dramatically overhaul its copyright system. The IIPA, in its annual letter to the USTR, made the following suggestions: that Spain rebuke its attorney general's statements on digital content infringement; make it easier for IPR holders to sue for damages; force Internet service providers to monitor the Internet use of customers and punish them for alleged content infringements; create provisions that would ban websites featuring 'pirated content'; and, create new branches of the Ministry of Interior, Civil Guard and National Police to administer Internet piracy enforcement (IIPA 2011, 2-3).

In December 2010, when Spain was about to insert a new copyright law, the Sinde law, into significant economic reform legislation, Wikileaks unveiled diplomatic cables revealing that the USTR had secretly been negotiating with the Spanish government to adopt every one of the IIPA's suggestions (Hinze 2010). The Wikileaks' cables caused reactions amongst Spanish Internet users, igniting protests throughout social media and leading to marches through the streets of Madrid (Slattery 2011). The passage of Sinde was delayed, but eventually carried through. The new law enabled the removal of allegedly infringing websites with no judicial oversight and forced Internet service providers to hand over the identifying information of individuals alleged to have infringed copyright – though it did not adopt the full criminal measures demanded by the IIPA and USTR (*Hollywood playing hardball on piracy* 2012). Because the law fell short of US demands, Spain was put back on the USTR's Special 301 list in 2011 (USTR 2011, 37). In the Special 301, the USTR attacked the Spanish attorney general's comments on digital copyright violations and expressed concern that Spain will be too slow in prosecuting infringers (USTR 2011, 40). The USTR also lamented Spain's lack of criminal enforcement procedures, and expressed a desire to continue working with Spain on the implementation of enhanced police efforts to tackle IPR infringement (USTR 2011, 40).

Discussion of the Spanish case

The Spanish case study illustrates how the IPR GPR operates in the global political economy and the role that information policy plays in the diplomatic relations between states. The pressures that the US put on Spain are reflective of the hegemonic state's ability to force weaker states to alter legal regimes. The USTR became an outlet for multinational corporations to exert diplomatic pressure on a state that was accused of not protecting the industry's economic model. Additionally, the IIPA worked to incite the European Commission by accusing Spain of being in violation of EU directives in order to create diplomatic pressure from the primary intergovernmental body to which Spain is liable, the European Union. The IFPI played the role of the moral entrepreneur by backing up its condemnation of Spain's piracy problem with accusations that the Spanish government's apathy toward copyright was destroying Spanish culture and endangering local artists (2010, 19). The IIPA and USTR's push for Spain to adopt criminal enforcement procedures and to use human and economic resources to police Internet piracy are symptomatic of the demands that powerful actors put on weaker states during the third stage of a GPR.

The seizure of *Roja Directa's* domain names and condemnation of the Spanish attorney general is evidence that the IPR GPR is moving from a third to a fourth stage of development. In the fourth stage, states that do not conform to the GPR is increasingly identified as dissident players rather than a sovereign state (Andreas and Nadelmann 2006, 21). We see this through the outright dismissal of the Spanish legal system and the seizure of *Roja Directa's* domains. The USTR's refusal to take Spain off of the Special 301 list even after Spain changed its laws is evidence of the severity of the IPR GPR and of how important controlling the flow of information-based goods is to the most powerful actors in the global economy.

The final point to be noted is that the outrage among Spanish citizens after the Wikileaks cables revealed that Spain was rewriting its copyright laws at the request of the US is evidence of a democratic deficit that may occur during the implementation of a GPR. In the 'war on drugs', for instance, a failure to instill norms in the populace and a general impression by citizens that the policymakers are overstepping their bounds with draconian prohibition laws contribute to the failure of the drug trafficking GPR (Andreas and Nadelmann 2006, 45-46). In the case of the Sinde law, citizens were forced to turn to an outside actor, Wikileaks, to discover how the US was pressuring Spain to change its laws (Puegra 2011). The Wikileaks discovery led to the de-legitimation of the state in the eyes of some Spanish citizens who went on to protest the Sinde law. GPRs become more difficult to institute when distrust in the legitimacy of the state is present, and this distrust is a contributing factor in their failure to reach the fifth stage (Andreas and Nadelmann 2006, 45-46). Distrust of the state could also lead to the legitimization and support of illicit social actors – such as file sharing or streaming websites, or civil society agents such as Wikileaks.

As citizens build relationships of trust with these actors, the state's failure to address the deprofessionalization of policy issues becomes apparent. Individuals who are casually streaming a sporting event as a matter of convenience are suddenly on the wrong side of a legal apparatus originally designed to manage the behaviors of competing firms. In most cases, information policy makers do not properly take cultural and social norms that encourage the sharing or modification of digital texts into consideration. The IPR GPR is designed to prioritize the economic interests of powerful states and established media organizations over competing interests including civil liberties and the public interest. The lack of consideration that policymakers give toward the democratic interests of citizens further erodes the political economic and cultural legitimacy of state and international law.

Conclusion

In this research, I analyzed literature and evidence that a global prohibition regime is emerging around IPR policy that is currently in its third stage and rapidly accelerating toward the fourth. The IPR GPR was crafted and accelerated by the US during the Cold War and was finalized in the late 1980s with a series of bilateral and multilateral treaties as well as unilateral mechanisms that pressure weaker states to comply with international policy, and large-scale attempts by multinationals to create social norms extolling the evils of IPR infringement. I raised questions regarding the way this regulation may be affecting communicative and social interactions, concluding that the framework for the IPR GPR is based on the premise of controlling the flow and structure of information in the global political economy (Braman 2007; Fuchs 2008; Mosco 2009). Hence, any effort to institute prohibitions on IPR alters the flow of knowledge and the means by which individuals communicate.

Additionally, as illustrated with Wikileaks' exposure of the behind-the-scenes ideation of the Sinde law, the overreach of the IPR GPR can lead to the perception of a democratic deficit in the state and promote citizens to becoming indifferent or even supportive toward activities, organizations and individuals engaged in the prohibited activity. Intellectual property law governing creative works and resources online should be considerate of the norms that govern the way that individuals use digital communication technologies. The IPR GPR, as a regime built around the necessity of the state to criminalize and police behaviors without consideration for the legitimate ways that individuals share information across networks, is an inappropriate mechanism for governing intellectual property.

References

Anderson, Nate (2011). "Why the US needs to blacklist, censor pirate web sites". *Ars Technica*, 1 April 2011. Retrieved 10 July 10, 2013, from http://arstechnica.com/tech-policy/news/2011/04/why-the-us-needs-to-censor-pirate-websites.ars/

Andreas, Peter and Ethan Nadelmann (2006). *Policing the globe.* New York: Oxford University Press.

Benkler, Yochai (2006). *The wealth of networks: How social production transforms markets and freedom.* New Haven: Yale University Press.

Bharara, Preet (2012, August 29). "*United States of America v. RojaDirecta.org, et. al* notice of dismissal". Retrieved 10 July 10 2013, from http://www.techdirt.com/articles/20120829/12370820209/oops-after-seizing-censoring-rojadirecta-18-months-feds-give-up-drop-case.shtml/

Braman, Sandra (2007). *Change of state: Information, policy, and power.* Cambridge, MA: MIT Press.

Department of Justice (2004, April 22). "Justice Department announces international piracy sweep." Retrieved 10 July 10, 2013, from http://www.justice.gov/opa/pr/2004/April/04_crm_263.htm/

Department of Justice (2006, February 28). "Justice Department announces four pleas in Internet music piracy crackdown." Retrieved 10 July 2013, from http://www.justice.gov/opa/pr/2006/February/06_crm_103.html/

Drahos, Peter (2002). *Information feudalism: Who owns the knowledge economy?.* New York: The New Press.

Drezner, Daniel W. (2007). *All politics is global : Explaining international regulatory regimes.* Princeton, N.J.: Princeton University Press.

Fuchs, Christian (2008). *Internet and society: Social theory in the information age.* New York: Routledge.

Fuchs, Christian (2011). *Foundations of critical media and information studies.* New York: Routledge.

Grabosky, Peter N. (2001). "Crime in cyberspace". In Phil Williams and Dmitri Vlassis (eds). *Policing the Globe.* Portland, Oregon: Frank Cass Publishers, 195-208.

Hinze, Gwenn (2011, December 17). "Not-so-gentle persuasion: US bullies Spain into proposed website blocking law". *Electronic Frontier Foundation.* Retrieved 10 July 2013, from https://www.eff.org/deeplinks/2010/12/not-so-gentle-persuasion-us-bullies-spain-proposed/

"Hollywood playing hardball on piracy" (2012, January 28). *The New Zealand*

Herald. Retrieved 10 July 2013, from http://www.nzherald.co.nz/technology/news/article.cfm?c_id=5&objectid=10781695640V&csi=257912&hl=t&hv=t&hnsd=f&hns=t&hgn=t&oc=00240&perma=true/

International Federation for the Phonographic Industry [IFPI] (2010). "IFPI Digital Music Report 2010". Retrieved 10 July 2013, from http://www.ifpi.org/content/section_resources/dmr2010.html/

International Intellectual Property Alliance [IIPA] (2011, January 21). "Spain: IIPA 2011 Special 301 Report on copyright protection and enforcement." Retrieved 10 July 10 2013, from www.iipa.com/rbc/2011/2011SPEC301SPAIN.pdf/

Johns, Adrian (2009). *Piracy: The intellectual property wars from Gutenberg to Gates.* Chicago: University of Chicago Press.

Johnson, Bobby and Jemima Kiss (2009). "Internet pirates pledge to fight again after court jails them for copyright theft: Swedish defendants may keep site open and appeal: Entertainment industry welcomes rare victory". *The Guardian (London) - Final Edition*, 18 April 2009, 3.

Karaganis, Joe (ed.) (2011). *Media piracy in emerging economies.* New York: Social Science Research Council. Retrieved 10 July 2013, from http://piracy.ssrc.org/

Kravets, Dan (2012). "Feds seize $50 million in Megaupload assets, Lodge new charges". *Wired*, 17 February 2012. Retrieved 10 July 2013, from http://www.wired.com/threatlevel/2012/02/megaupload-superseding-indictment/

Lessig, Lawrence (2004). *Free culture: The nature and future of creativity.* New York, NY: Penguin.

McSherry, Corrinne (2011). "Court refuses to return seized domain name, claims shutting down speech doesn't cause a substantial hardship". *Electronic Frontier Foundation*, 4 August 2011. Retrieved 10 July 2013, from https://www.eff.org/deeplinks/2011/08/court-refuses-give-seized-domain-name-back-claims/

Mosco, Vincent (2009). *The political economy of communication* (Vol. 2). Thousand Oaks, CA: Sage Publications.

Nadelmann, Ethan (1990). "Global Prohibition Regimes: The Evolution of Norms in International Society". *International Organization.* 4:44, 479-526.

Office of the United States Trade Representative (2011). "2011 Special 301 Report". Retrieved 10 July 2013, from http://www.ustr.gov/about-us/press-office/reports-and-publications/2011/2011-special-301-report/

Prodhan, Georgina (2012). "UK student faces US extradition in copyright case". *Reuters*, 11 January 2012. Retrieved 10 July 2013, from http://www.reuters.com/article/2012/01/13/us-filesharing-extradition-idUSTRE80C15C20120113/

Puerto 80 Projects, S.L.U. v. United States of America, Department of Homeland Security and Immigration and Customs [Puerto 80 v. U.S], 11 Civ. 3983 (PAC), Document 15 (2011).

Schiller, Daniel (1999). *Digital capitalism.* Cambridge: The MIT Press.

Slattery, Laura (2011). "Planet business". *The Irish Times.* 27 May 2011. 6.

Strange, Susan (2007). *States and markets.* New York: Continuum.

Thussu, Daya (2006). *International communication: Continuity and change* (2nd ed.).

London: Hodder Education.
Tremlett, Giles (2006). "Spanish court rules free music downloads are legal for own use". *The Guardian UK*, 3 November 2006. Retrieved 10 July, from http://www.guardian.co.uk/technology/2006/nov/03/news.spain/
"Web music charges" (2008). *The Times (London)*, 13 September 2008, 4.

BitTorrent: Stealing or Sharing Culture? A Discussion of the Pirate Bay Case and the Documentaries "Steal This Film I & II"

Ekin Gündüz Özdemirci

Introduction

Since Plato raised his concerns that "writing will replace the memory and bring the omission" (quoted in Danziger 2008, 34), new developments in the distribution of information have attracted both doubt and caution when first introduced. It appears that Plato's reaction emerged from the prediction that writing would revolutionize ways of both thinking and remembering. Such concerns have emerged repeatedly: when printing brought the information out of the 'glass palace' that trapped it; when cinema brought art to the masses; and, when video carried this art into people's homes. In each instance, those who held a monopoly over information reacted against each innovation. Despite repeated backlashes, evolving innovation has always gained a foothold and information has eventually passed into other hands and gained new owners.

This chapter begins with the premise that (illegal) file-sharing over the Internet, which is a key subject of contemporary debates, should be evaluated in the same way. The Internet has not only generated new forms of production and distribution of information, it also raises questions about 'information ownership' that surpasses the revolution created by the printing press. Mark Getty, owner of the world's largest online photograph and video distributor *Getty Images*, puts his finger on the values at stake when he describes the information economy with the words: "Intellectual Property is the oil of the 21st century" (quoted in Ross & Binghamton 2000, 486).

The peer-to-peer (P2P) protocol 'BitTorrent', that allows free online sharing of video and music files, has become the object of similar reactions as previous technological innovations. This is because 'owners' of cultural artifacts such as films or television series can neither control its structure nor operation.[1] In

1 An analysis of the top 10.000 BitTorrent 'swarms' (as measured by number of active downloaders or leechers) found that pornography (35.8 precent), film (35.2 percent) and television (12.7 percent) were the most popular content types (Price, 2011).

response, the giant film studios of Hollywood have reacted by labeling such practices as 'piracy' because it steals part of their profits. Subsequently, these studios worked with various government and supra-government agencies to develop policies that pursue and prosecute users of torrent protocols. Despite the pursuit of such practices and mass advertising campaigns warning against online 'piracy', many torrent users do not consider file-sharing an unethical act comparable to counterfeiting or stealing. As I will discuss, many see this process as simply the free sharing of cultural products.

Such discussions raise two important issues: firstly, there is a need to re-evaluate the regulation of intellectual property rights as the current approach has repeatedly been proved inadequate; and, secondly, we must consider the sharing of cultural products in this way through the conception of 'artworks'.

In this chapter, I will consider conflicts surrounding piracy by analyzing the two-part documentary *Steal This Film*, produced in support of the popular torrent sharing website The Pirate Bay.

This chapter consists of five sections beginning with the major Hollywood film studios' response toward file sharing. I then move on to discuss the legal case against The Pirate Bay and the discourse of BitTorrent support articulated in the documentaries *Steal This Film I & II.* In the section that follows, I reflect on the issue of file sharing as the final stage of what Walter Benjamin (1936/2008) in the 1930s described as the 'Age of Mechanical Reproduction'. Benjamin described the relationship between the rise of art's social function that emerged in parallel with its 'massification', and the fall of an artwork's 'special atmosphere', or 'aura', as a result of mechanical reproduction. Today, copyright constitutes a legal mechanism meant to maintain an artwork's aura, while the Internet and the torrent system are the technological devices providing the opportunities for its reproduction and massification. In the final section, I review the way the torrent system is positioned against the copyright industry and consider whether it could be effective in creating an alternative copyright regime.

Hollywood's strategy against the BitTorrent threat

As file sharing is difficult to track, it is not possible to confirm Hollywood's claims of having lost billions of dollars as a result of the sharing of cultural products through the activities of P2P networks. Even if the number of films shared was transparent and exact, it can be argued that "it would be even more challenging to quantify and evaluate the economic impact of that activity upon the motion picture industry," because we would never know "how many consumers would have bought the DVD or gone to the cinema had they not downloaded it" (Currah 2004, 24).

The Motion Picture Association of America (MPAA) has presented various figures regarding the financial losses brought on by piracy. In 2005, it was estimated that the American Film Industry lost approximately US$6.1 billion. Of this, 62 percent was said to be the result of pirated DVDs, while 38 percent (or US$2.3 billion) resulted from Internet file sharing (L.E.K. Consulting 2005). Furthermore, the Department of Professional Employees (DPE) estimates that US workers in copyright industries lose US$16.3 billion in earnings annually as a result of piracy (DPE 2010, 4).

Despite such claims, the International Intellectual Property Alliance (IIPA) produced a 2011 report demonstrating that the copyright industries continue to experience significant growth. According to the IIPA, in 2010 the value added for the total copyright industries was US$1.627 trillion (or 11.1 percent of U.S. Gross Domestic Product). Even though there was a notable downturn between 2008 and 2009, the report notes that the core copyright industries fared better than the rest of the U.S. economy during the period 2007–2010, growing at an aggregate annual rate of 1.1 percent. The situation of the copyright industry also looks positive internationally: in 2010 the export of copyrighted materials was ahead of sectors such as aircraft, automobiles, food and pharmaceuticals. The sales of U.S. copyright products in overseas markets amounted to US$134 billion in 2010, and was described as experiencing a "significant increase over previous years" (IIPA 2011, 1).

This contradiction between MPAA claims and the statistics presented again highlights the difficulty of estimating the losses claimed by the copyright industries. Since the copyright industries know that their argumentation suffers from important judicial gaps and lack of material data, they also move to frame the socio-legal dimensions of file sharing: drawing on the social sensibility of piracy and linking it to unemployment, the death of cinema, organized crime and terrorism. For example, the FBI examined assertions that the 1993 bombing of the World Trade Center in New York was financed by sales of counterfeit goods; UK authorities have also claimed that the IRA has financed its paramilitary activities through film piracy – both claims lacked credible evidence (Yar 2005,

688). Another strategy used by copyright organizations is to compare piracy in the entertainment sector with counterfeit production in the pharmaceutical and industrial sectors that threaten human life (The Office of the United States Trade Representative 2010, 5).

The copyright industries regularly draw on international trade agreements that create sanctions against countries accused of not being active enough in the fight against piracy. The 1994 agreement that the Trade-Related Aspects of Intellectual Property Rights (TRIPS) constituted under the auspices of the World Trade Organization (WTO) is just one such example. Accordingly, countries that are placed on WTO's 'priority watch list' are forced to take measures against piracy or risk being exposed to retaliatory actions that will cause commercial losses. In his commentary on the TRIPS Agreement, Carlos M. Correa notes that: "The agreement does not impose constraints on measures that states can take at the border"; yet his following statements point to the possibility of an over control: "but it **deeply interferes** with national discretion in establishing rights that can be claimed by private parties in national jurisdictions" (2007, 10, my emphasis).

The major film studios continue this battle today in their attempts to stop the free online file-sharing through such trade sanctions and legal battles. This is highlighted by the ongoing attempts to introduce new measures to control Internet content. Draft bills such as SOPA (Stop Online Piracy Act) and PIPA (Protect IP Act) were recently submitted – and rejected - in the USA, but their successor CISPA (Cyber Intelligence Sharing and Protection Act) as well as their international version ACTA (Anti-Counterfeiting Trade Agreement) are still pending. These bills moved to prohibit the access to websites containing 'illegal' content. Such bills threaten to impose sanctions on Internet Service Providers (ISPs) who are now expected to cooperate with copyright owners, control any illegal content on websites related to them, and share the IP numbers - all without any additional court decrees.

Such moves have been fiercely rejected by a cross section of the public and have led to protests and a backlash against the copyright industry. The concerns raised about such policy initiatives as SOPA have been twofold: directed both against the surveillance techniques required *and,* the way that the freedom on the Internet is being undermined (Lee 2012). SOPA was also widely criticized by technology companies - both large and small - because it would have penalized websites for illegal content uploaded by users. Leading organizations including

Google, Facebook, EBay and Yahoo published a joint open letter to voice their concerns. Additionally, the ACTA reporter, Kader Arif, publically resigned in protest after making it clear that this bill, which was almost pushed through contrary to public opinion, would negatively impact civil liberties. Such reactions led to these bills being delayed in the US with many European countries stepping back from signing the agreement in Europe ("Acta: Germany delays" 2012; Gaudiosi 2012).

The intense public reactions highlight many Internet users' views about online file sharing. As outlined in various studies - including Cheung (2005) and Harris & Dumas (2009) - the fact that illegal file sharing is not considered a serious crime is an important factor that contributes to the ongoing use and support of BitTorrent. Torrent websites and their supporters criticize the Hollywood studios for making no distinction between illegal production and sale of DVDs and online file sharing without commercial purpose: both are labeled as 'piracy' and are pursued as a material crime.[2]

Steal This Film Parts I & II gives voice to a wide spread feeling that Hollywood's approach is simply about maintaining its dominance over the cultural industries and controlling the emerging technologies that challenge them. As discussed in the opening paragraphs of this chapter, Hollywood is seen as attempting to oppress technological innovation rather than taking the opportunity to re-shape the industry.

The conflict between cultural oligopoly and technology

This suggests that the copyright industries have a problematic attitude toward the Internet: seeing it as an opportunity to market their products while simultaneously feeling threatened by its reproduction potential. The studios insist on using ruthless but ineffective methods to regulate the digital world in order to protect their profits and maintain the status quo. The strategies of holding back innovation is actually placing the industry at a disadvantage as they are unable to provide services that support and respond to consumer habits.

Consequently, the major studios are ignoring the potential of the Internet in order to protect more established though low capacity markets such as DVD sales and rentals. The system that Hollywood protects relies on income sources dispersed over different markets in a way that reflects Adorno and Horkheimer's

2 See the documentary "Steal This Film" Part I and Part II (http://www.stealthisfilm.com).

characterization of the culture industry as structured in "branches of sectors that are economically interwoven" (1969/1994, 123). The inter-relationships created with Hollywood at the center results in an oligopoly that is both reactive and resistant to innovations.

Occasionally, copyright holders indeed attempt to adapt to those innovations by trying to control the spread and use of torrent websites. In 2006 for example, various corporations linked to the Motion Picture Association of America (MPAA) paid more than US$20 million to Bram Cohen, the creator of BitTorrent protocol, to convert the software into a legal structure in an attempt to limit its irrepressible popularity. Even though Cohen attempted to provide a service compliant with the structure requested by the industry, free online file sharing has continued to grow and innovate.

Despite Hollywood's various strategies, users continue to support the torrent community. A key reason for this is that the conception of film as an "artwork" is changing: reflecting the way music changed from content purchased on a CD to mp3 files that are shared digitally. As Nico Meissner states,

> …before the Internet, movies were a scarce product, what economists call a 'private good', but the Internet turned them, like other products that are based on information, into public goods, which are non-rivalrous and non-excludable (2011, 196).

This shift highlights both the demand and the need for developing new methods of production and distribution within the film industry.

This is difficult however, due to the industries' entrenched and profitable oligopoly. Large production companies account for approximately 80 percent of the American film industry's income.[3] The founders and supporters of The Pirate Bay, which has become a key symbol of the torrent movement, argue that their movement is not simply about 'free content', but rather about breaking down this oligopoly structure.

Understanding the motivations behind organizations such as The Pirate Bay that have created an alternative infrastructure without any material income or benefit is as important as analyzing the behaviors of the users who download free content. This is necessary to understand the online social solidarity created around the torrent community. The two-part documentary, *Steal This Film*,

3 See Top-Grossing Distributors 1995-2012 – Retrieved 25 March 2012 from http://www.the-numbers.com/market/Distributors/

which was produced in the process of The Pirate Bay trial, is an important source for understanding the motivations of the website's founders as well as its users. After a brief discussion of The Pirate Bay trial, I will turn to examine the perspective that this documentary gives on the torrent community's attitudes towards Hollywood.

The Pirate Bay case

The Pirate Bay, based in Sweden, is one of the mostly visited torrent websites in the world. The Hollywood studios have long criticized The Pirate Bay for its overt support of 'piracy' and have initiated legal action against it, leading to the Swedish police suddenly raiding the server rooms of The Pirate Bay on 31 May 2006.

The letter sent by the MPAA to the Ministry of Justice of Sweden, dated 17 March 2006, clarifies the process that led to this raid. This letter clearly states that requests to act against The Pirate Bay had been previously communicated via the US Embassy and various warnings had been issued:

> As we discussed during our meeting, it is certainly not in Sweden's best interests to earn a reputation among other nations and trading partners as a place where utter lawlessness with respect to intellectual property rights is tolerated. I would urge you once again to exercise your influence to urge law enforcement authorities in Sweden to take much-needed action against The Pirate Bay.[4]

This letter, which prepared the way for the raid, has been interpreted as proof that even the Swedish Ministry of Justice is open to influence from lobbying related to MPAA.[5] Following the raid, no copyright breach case could be filed directly against the founders of The Pirate Bay as the server did not contain any stolen or illegally accessed material. Rather, what was found was definitive data including links and file names. Consequently, though arrested, the website founders were released after three days, but despite this, the authorities pursued the case until 2012 (see Fiveash 2012).

Following the raid, the website was again online within three days. This was partly due to a massive wave of both international and domestic support, with

4 A copy of the letter can be found at http://torrentfreak.com/mpaa-begged-sweden-to-take-down-the-piratebay/ - accessed March 2013.

5 This is discussed by Sweden's then Secretary of State, Dan Eliasson in *"Steal This Film" Part 1.*

the site quickly doubling its membership. As a result of this support, the Swedish Pirate Party's membership grew to almost 9,000, closing in on the nation's Green Party (9,550), which holds 19 seats in the Parliament (Sarno 2007).

As this was unfolding, plaintiff companies made several efforts to undermine the website including attempts to limit its access throughout Europe. Even more disturbing, there was a number of serious accusations leveled towards the founders including statements that: they were mediating the distribution of child pornography; they had connections to radical far-right groups; and, that they had become millionaires from selling advertisements through The Pirate Bay (Oates 2008a, 2008b). As the accusations made the headlines, it was discovered that a number of MPAA members had made an agreement with an anti-piracy service provider, MediaDefender, to post harmful files on The Pirate Bay server (Leyden 2007). Additional evidence also emerged that key investigator, Jim Keyzer, who was a professional witness for the prosecution, had been hired by the Warner Brothers Company (Graham 2009).

On 31 January 2008 the founders and facilitators of The Pirate Bay, Peter Sunde, Gottfrid Svartholm, Fredrik Neij and Carl Lundström, were put on trial accused of "promoting other people's infringements of copyright laws" ("Pirate Bay file-sharing" 2009). The defendants claimed that they did not store any illegal files on their servers, and that the structure of the Internet allowed the access to 'pirated' content entirely through legal websites such as Google. Defense attorney, Per Samuelson, ironically emphasized the complexity of identifying the website's users and also pointed out the impossibility of holding The Pirate Bay responsible for their acts:

> EU directive 2000/31/EG says that he who provides an information service is not responsible for the information that is being transferred. In order to be responsible, the service provider must initiate the transfer. But the admins of The Pirate Bay don't initiate transfers. It's the users that do and they are physically identifiable people. They call themselves names like King Kong... The prosecutor must show that Carl Lundström[6] personally has interacted with the user King Kong, who may very well be found in the jungles of Cambodia. Quoted in Schofield 2009

On 17 April 2009, the defendants were found guilty of breaking copyright law and sentenced to a year in jail. They were also fined US$ 4.5 million in damages.

6 Owner of the The Pirate Bay's Swiss Internet service provider Rix Telecom AB and one of the defendants of the trial.

Following the decision, one of the defendants Peter Sunde stated:

> Even if I had the money I would rather burn everything I owned, and I wouldn't even give them the ashes... The court said we were organized. I can't get Gottfrid out of bed in the morning. If you're going to convict us, convict us of disorganized crime. Quoted in "Court Jails Pirate Bay" 2009

The defendants appealed in November 2010 and though the verdict was sustained, the prison sentences were reduced due to 'individualized assessment' (Fiveash 2010). The final attempt to appeal was rejected in February 2012 (Fiveash 2012).

While the case was proceeding, there were also legal suits filed against 50,000 torrent users in USA and successful bans of The Pirate Bay website in various countries including Italy, Denmark, Belgium, and the Netherlands. Despite this, users easily circumvented these prohibitions by using several intermediate websites that allowed them to access The Pirate Bay. As the defendants have been claiming; it simply wasn't possible to stop the torrent sharing network.

Steal This Film documentaries

In order to support The Pirate Bay and draw attention to the power of P2P networks and technologies, an organization called The League of Noble Peers produced a two-part documentary series titled *Steal This Film*. These two films are an invaluable source for gaining insights into the way a significant population uses and supports The Pirate Bay.

The first part of the documentary focuses on The Pirate Bay case and the website's founders' broader reflections on the actions of the media industry and the ongoing persecution they are facing. The second part discusses the broader copyright system, presenting the views of academics, film and music sector representatives, activists and torrent users. These documentaries reflect how online file sharing is frequently seen as a struggle against copyright holders who prevent the innovation and development of technology in order to control and limit access to cultural content. This struggle, many underline, is not simply based on the free sharing of cultural products; but is also understood as defending the right to information and freedom of speech.

Reflecting on the way the documentary describes the torrent system, I argue that online file sharing can be understood by drawing on Walter Benjamin's discussion of the "Age of Mechanical Reproduction" (1936 / 2008). Here Benjamin defines the reproduction and massification as a liberating process that can undermine the 'aura' of an artwork – breaking the 'supply-demand verdict'. This mechanism of supply and demand is something that Adorno and Horkheimer (1994, 133) described as a "check in the rulers' favor in the superstructure," based on Marxist theory which argues that the economic substructure determines the cultural superstructure. Accordingly, the "supply-demand verdict" helps the rulers maintain control over the production and distribution of culture and is thus a primary factor in the formation and production of the cultural superstructure, including the artwork.

A critique against the copyright system

As discussed, the two-part documentary, *Steal This Film*, aims to present both an overview of The Pirate Bay trial as well as broader critique of the contemporary copyright system. The entertainment industry in Hollywood is described in the films as the core of the 'supply-demand verdict'. The industry's attitude towards the Internet is seen as one of 'control': that is, much like any monopoly or oligopoly, they attempt to limit access to and use of information. From this perspective, the industry attempts to impose a logic of 'scarcity' in information that is reflective of the 1500's. The documentaries reference the way the newly invented printing press was seen as the unholy work of the 'Devil' and subjected to attempts at control: the film makers argue that Hollywood's attitude toward technology is a perpetuation of this process. As Gottfrid Svartholm, notes in his reflections:

> A lot of what the major media companies do today is so obviously based around the copyright model. I mean, in the US you speak about the tent pole model. You find a space of intellectual property that hasn't yet been claimed and you put your tent pole down and raise a whole tent up around it, like for example, if you make a movie you also sell plastic toys and such, which kind of makes up the tent. And obviously that sort of modus would be impossible with a different intellectual property climate.

There is a clear message that profit and 'excess earnings' is the priority of copyright holders – something emphasized in both the documentary and during The Pirate Bay trial. This includes the belief that the major copyright holders make these huge profits at the expense of smaller producers. As such, a cross section of studies shows that many downloaders reject Hollywood studios' claims of suffering financial damage because they see "publishers earning excess profits" (see Cheung 2005, 14; Harris and Dumas 2009, 387-390).

Consequently, defenders of online file sharing argue that the current copyright system must be changed to improve access and limit control. The documentaries argue that the copyright industry's fight against online file sharing aims to preserve profit and maintain the idea that financial benefit must be the priority in cultural production. In this context, the first documentary highlights the following statement of Dan Glickman, former president of MPAA:

> It's ridiculous to believe that you can give products away for free and be more successful… If they don't make a profit in this world, they're out of business. That's just the laws of human nature.

A second key theme in the film is that, technically, it is basically impossible to stop torrent users sharing files. Any attempt to do so, it is argued, will lead to new innovations that aim to circumvent controls. Thus the documentary argues that "the market is not nature and Hollywood can't outlaw social change."

To emphasize this point, the documentary makers draw on the successful Hollywood franchise, *The Matrix* (Andy and Lana Wachowski 1999). Hollywood is compared to the Matrix: a system in which reality is distorted. The documentary makes Neo, the savior and 'hero' in the film, the embodiment of the Internet and online file sharing. While a challenge against the virtual world is subjected in *The Matrix*, *Steal This Film I* points out that in fact the challenge will take place in a covert way, which means that the evolution will arise from the heart of the virtual world. After the scenes from *The Matrix*, the phrase 'Burn Hollywood Burn' is reflected on the screen.

A third theme in the documentaries is that artworks are more likely to reach their full potential within an open access regime. This approach positions cultural products as information sources rather than income sources. Free online sharing of film and music is something that is reflected in the very structure of the Internet and captured in the essence of information flows. In the first documentary, this is echoed by a torrent defender when discussing the real potential of an artwork:

> I think that the music we see on MTV and these music channels that kind of music will disappear more or less. And we'll have music which is more for the listeners and not just for people to make money on it, you know, 25 million dollars per album, it's absurd.

The social function of the art-work

The documentaries also interpret the online file sharing system as the first step of an (un)avoidable revolution that will demand the current copyright system to radically change. Using revolutionary images of radical and systemic change and pointing to a longing for a "huge and destructive social change," the films state:

> P2P networks unleashed a massive wave of change on the world. Today tens of millions of people use the Internet to share media.

By employing language such as "the piracy of culture" and "the culture of piracy," supporters of The Pirate Bay, including the filmmakers, confirm their position that online file sharing and 'copying' are considered social and cultural acts – and in a way disconnected from the legal dimensions that are the focus of the Hollywood studios.

This is reflective of Walter Benjamin's (1936/2008, 6) argument that mechanical reproduction made it possible for the original artwork to come *closer* to the person 'consuming' it, whether in the form of a photograph or through the use of a gramophone record. Echoing Benjamin, *Steal This Film I & II* define the massification of the artwork through reproduction as restoring the original meaning of its social function. Media theoretician Felix Stalder, who is interviewed in the second documentary, states that:

> The fundamental urge to copy had nothing to do with technology. It's about how culture is created.

Likewise, Sebastian Lütgert, a member of Pirate Cinema, argues that copying mechanisms shape people's habits, giving "people completely new ideas how they could work, how they could work together, how they could share, what they could relate to, what their lives could be."

Benjamin argued that technological reproducibility freed the work of art, for the first time in history, from its existence as a parasite upon ritual (1936/2008, 11-12). This is because mechanical reproduction brought the social function of art in parallel with its massification, instead of glorifying the beauty and aesthetics resulting from its cultic feature. Consequently, this altered the relationship between art and broader society (Benjamin 1936/2008, 26). Writing in the 1930s, Benjamin saw the art of cinema as the most important example of such a transformation as it offered a more direct relation to reality than painting. To make the point, Benjamin stated that:

> The more the social significance of an art diminishes, the greater the extent (as is clearly turning out to be the case with painting) to which the critical and pleasure-seeking stances of the public diverge... In the cinema, the critical and pleasure-seeking stances of the audience coincide (1936/2008, 26).

Such a position sees cinema as an art form which the audience feels closer to, embraced by, and which an individual can directly relate to. With the details it offers, cinema provides us with "a vast, undreamt-of amount of room for maneuver" (Benjamin 1936/2008, 29). Benjamin mentions that cinema satisfies "the claim to mass attention" of artworks because it is an "object of simultaneous reception by large numbers of people" (1936/2008, 27). In Benjamin's words, the movie industry's preservation of the "cultic value" of the film "bars modern man's legitimate claim to be reproduced from being taken into consideration" (1936/2008, 23) – implying that the social potential of cinema was therefore ignored.

Benjamin argued that, despite successful massification, the artwork preserved its cultic value because of the 'human face': that is, faces of movie stars are cults that can be adapted to all forms of popular culture consumption and become a component of the profit seeking 'supply-demand verdict'. Benjamin asserted that the production of cultic values weakened the social functionality that the cinema obtained through technical reproduction, noting that:

> Film's response to the shriveling of aura is an artificial inflation of 'personality' outside the studio. The cult of stardom promoted by film capital preserves the magic of personality that for years has lain solely in the rancid magic of its commodity character. 2008, 21

Adorno and Horkheimer (1969/1994, 121), echo Benjamin when they note that cinema did not have to pretend to be art. Cinema was defined as an industry and as a consequence of this the income it generated was prioritized above the social necessities. That is, the film's potential of being a social good was replaced by the profit motive.

Today, when mechanical reproduction has reached a new level with the Internet, the social potential of cinema once again has the ability to emerge. This concept is captured by supporters of file sharing who consider the film as both an artwork *and* an information source, which can be utilized as a 'public good'.

It is from this perspective that we must understand Hollywood's conflicts surrounding the BitTorrent networks. This is captured in *Steal This Film Part 1* by the statement:

> "Hollywood is a business..." and "the war on piracy is a war to preserve profit."

To Hollywood, the profit expectation is more important than both the films' artistic value and originality. Further, the cultic values that, according to Benjamin (1936/2008, 23), hide the social potential of cinema correspond to the current copyright system. For the documentary makers and the many supporters of file sharing, the BitTorrent technology has the potential to restore this social function of the cinema, and the artwork in general.

BitTorrent in the "age of mechanical reproduction"

Can it be argued that 'freeing reproduction' through which the artwork would gain its social function has found its true equivalent in the age of the Internet? In *Steal This Film I & II*, torrent defenders clearly argue that the current copyright system oppresses the creative potentials in society. In contrast, file sharing brings back the artwork's social function by involving the audience in the reproduction and creative process. This reflects Benjamin's claims that technologies "allowing the reproduction to come closer to whatever situation the person apprehending it is in, actualizes what is reproduced" (1936/2008, 7).

Consequently, both the documentaries expect that file sharing will contribute in a positive way to the production of culture. Free online file sharing contributes to the massification of the artwork by making alternative voices heard and allowing creative works that address different groups available.

The Internet provides opportunities of unlimited massification for the artwork and its structure makes it possible to circumvent ownership calculations that attempt to limit it as a 'reproduction tool'. As Felix Stalder explains:

> I think one of the things that we are seeing coming out is culture where things are produced because people care about it and not necessarily because they hope other people will buy it.

Stalder sees the emergence of a cultural production system where the artwork is shaped by the free command of the creator rather than the demands of capital. In this system, profit expectations are subservient to social goals – rather than disappearing all together - in order to transmit the artwork to broad audiences.

Consequently, artists can produce their works without constraints and on equal conditions with other artists.

This is one of the powerful aspects of P2P networks, which Ron Burnett (2005) claims, are as much of a response to the issues of information management as they are an expression of the need to maintain some control over the flow of information.

In parallel, the documentaries point out that online file sharing satisfies the Internet users' desires to be participants rather than passive audiences and consumers. This leads us back to the discourse of social effect that would be created through the massification of the artwork. As Peter Sunde points out that:

> If everything is user-generated it also means that you have to create something in order to be part of the society.

The torrent system, where users at least partially control both consumption and production, and websites facilitate file sharing, creates a 'communication environment' that operates like a community: that is, there is a desire to exchange beyond financial transactions (Arvanitakis 2009). An invitation to join a torrent site is often a part of this exchange as it requires an agreement to take part in rather than simply to consume the exchange. This creates, as clearly identified in the documentaries, a strong sense of unity and solidarity consistently evident in identity communities. Ron Burnett describes this as the occurrence of "micro-cultures," which he defines as "places where people take control of the means of creation and production in order to make sense of their social and cultural experiences" (2005, 62).

Importantly, this is not a homogenous community – something that the documentaries also highlight. These micro-cultures include people from a cross section of ages, professions and social environments that consider free sharing and reproduction of information on the Internet as a social right. They reject the current copyright system on the grounds that it is a limiting form of cultural administration out of sync with the technological developments. Gottfrid Svartholm describes such a stance as a form of 'civil rebellion': the torrent community, in other words, is more concerned with free culture than saving money.

The oligopoly structure of the American film industry means that only six major companies share a vast majority of the profits: The Walt Disney Co.'s Disney Studio, News Corp.'s Twentieth Century Fox, Viacom Inc.'s Paramount

Pictures, Sony Corp.'s Sony Pictures, General Electric Co.'s Universal and The Time Warner Inc.'s Warner Bros (Young et al. 2008, 28). The film industry's attempt to preserve the 'cultic value' of the artwork and control access to it, places it in open conflict with the decentralized structure of BitTorrent networks. This is particularly the case as the BitTorrent protocol has a structure that offers an alternative production and consumption model that spreads art to the "public" within the process of massification of creative works.

Conclusion

Adorno and Horkheimer (1994, 121) argue that, "the basis on which technology acquires power over society is the power of those whose economic hold over society is the greatest." For what appears to be for the first time in history, the BitTorrent protocol makes it impossible to maintain dominance over technology. This protocol seems to have a potential to free the artwork from the 'control of the capital owners' which Adorno and Horkheimer (1994, 122) called as the "economic mechanism of selection" and replace it with the individual mechanism of selection.

As global corporations attempt to respond to the challenge posed by the torrent system by raising more barriers to the flow of information, file-sharers respond. As control of this system is technically impossible, conflict deepens. While technology enables innovation, improvement and the birth of new cultural forms, Hollywood is looking for a solution based on commercial and legal sanctions, and focusing on the ethical position of piracy and its perceived 'evils' rather than reflecting on the potential of these new technologies.

BitTorrent file sharing can be interpreted as a whole set of activities that challenge and threaten the current intellectual property regime as well as an indicator of this system's self-destruction. International production, distribution and consumption networks created by global capitalism have given birth to illegal businesses along with legal commerce: this is 'piracy', which as the title of this collection indicates, is a leakage from this system, though only one example. This has become a key conflict of the global economy: on one side the consumption of technological innovations are encouraged as a source of profit, and on the other, this creates a threat against producers and copyright owners.

In his writing shortly before the Second World War, Walter Benjamin criticizes the way technology has been surrendered to the war machine rather than serving social causes:

> ...war, which with its destructions affords proof that *society was not sufficiently mature to make technology its organ*, that *technology was not sufficiently developed to cope with society's elemental forces...* Rather than develop rivers into canals, it diverts the human stream to flow into the bed of its trenches; rather than scatter seeds from its airplanes, it drops incendiary bombs on cities... 1936/2008, 37-38

Just like the destructiveness of war limits the constructive use of technology, Hollywood's war against file sharing points to how the intellectual property system limits the social, cultural and artistic contributions offered by the Internet – one of our most advanced technologies. The social movement that The Pirate Bay symbolizes is what Benjamin calls society's desire "to make the technology its organ" (1936/2008, 38). Even though the 'seeds' of BitTorrent seem sufficiently rooted, time will show if technology has developed far enough "to cope with society's elemental forces" (Benjamin 1936/2008, 38).

References

"Acta: Germany delays signing anti-piracy agreement" (2012). *BBC News*, 10 February 2012. Retrieved March 15, 2012, from http://www.bbc.com/news/technology-16980451

Adorno, Theodor W. and Max Horkheimer (1969/1994): *Dialectic of Enlightenment* (John Cumming, trans.). New York: The Continuum Publishing Company.

Arvanitakis James (2009). "Staging Maralinga and Desiring Community: (Or why there is no Such Thing as a 'Natural' Community)". *Community Development Journal*, 44:4, 448-459.

Benjamin, Walter (1936/2008). *The Work of Art in the Age of Mechanical Reproduction.* (J.A. Underwood, trans.). London: Penguin Books.

Burnett, Ron (2005). *How Images Think*, Cambridge: MIT Press.

Cheung, Shelly S.K. (2005). *Illegal Download Attitudes, Leisure Boredom, Sensation Seeking and Value of Honesty.* Master's Thesis, The Chinese University of Hong Kong, School of Journalism & Communication, Hong Kong, China.

Correa, Carlos M. (2007). *Trade Related Aspects of Intellectual Property Rights, A Commentary on the TRIPS Agreement.* New York: Oxford University Press.

"Court jails Pirate Bay founders" (2009). *BBC News*, 17 April 2009. Retrieved February 20, 2012, from http://news.bbc.co.uk/2/hi/8003799.stm

Currah, Andrew (2004). *The Disruptive Impact of Internet Piracy on the Hollywood Studio System.* Paper presented at the "Putting E-Commerce in its Place" Workshop, University of Nottingham.

Danziger, Kurt (2008). *Marking the Mind: A History of Memory.* New York: Cambridge University Press.

Department of Professional Employees (2010). *Intellectual Property Theft: A threat to US Workers, Industries, and Our Economy Fact Sheet.*

Fiveash, Kelly (2010). "The Pirate Bay verdict: Three operators lose appeal". *The Register*, 26 November 2010. Retrieved July 8 2013, from http://www.theregister.co.uk/2010/11/26/pirate_bay_appeal_verdict/

Fiveash, Kelly (2012). "Swedish Supreme Court chucks out Pirate Bay appeal bid". *The Register*, 1 February 2012. Retrieved July 8 2013, from http://www.theregister.co.uk/2012/02/01/pirate_bay_supreme_court_chucks_out_appeal_request/

Gaudiosi, John (2012). *Obama says so long SOPA, killing controversial Internet piracy legislation.* Retrieved July 8 2013, from http://www.forbes.com/sites/johngaudiosi/2012/01/16/obama-says-so-long-sopa-killing-controversial-Internet-piracy-legislation/

Graham, Flora (2009). "How The Pirate Bay sailed into infamy". *BBC News*, 16 February 2009. Retrieved July 8 2013, from http://news.bbc.co.uk/2/hi/7893223.stm

Harris, Lloyd C. and Alexia Dumas (2009). "Online Consumer Misbehavior: An Application of Neutralization Theory". *Marketing Theory*, 9:4, 379-402.

International Intellectual Property Alliance (2011). *Fact Sheet: Copyright Industries in the US Economy: The 2011 Report.*

L.E.K. Consulting (2005). *The Cost of Movie Piracy.* An Analysis prepared for MPAA.

Lee, Dave (2012). "Acta: Europe braced for protests over anti-piracy treaty". *BBC News*, 6 February 2012. Retrieved 25 July 2013, from http://www.bbc.com/news/technology-16906086

Leyden, John (2007). "Pirate Bay sues media giants for 'sabotage'". *The Register*, 24 September 2009. Retrieved from http://www.theregister.co.uk/2007/09/24/pirate_bay_counterstrike/

Meissner, Nico (2011). "Forced Pirates and the Ethics of Digital Film, Journal of Information". *Communication & Ethics in Society*, 9:3, 195-205.

Oates, John (2008a). "Pirate Bay to sue music industry". *The Register*, 16 April 2008. Retrieved July 8 2013, from http://www.theregister.co.uk/2008/04/16/piratebay_sues_music_industry/

Oates, John (2008b). "Pirate Bay evades Italian blockade". *The Register*, 16 August 2008. Retrieved July 8 2013, from http://www.theregister.co.uk/2008/08/11/pirate_bay_italy/

"Pirate Bay file-sharing defended". Retrieved March 10, 2012, from http://news.bbc.co.uk/2/hi/technology/7892073.stm

Price, David (2011). *Technical Report: An Estimate of Infringing Use of the Internet-Summary.* Piracy Intelligence, Envisional Ltd.

Ross, E. Wayne and Binghamton, Suny (2000). "The Promise and Perils of E-Learning". *Theory and Research in Social Education*, 28:4, 482-491.

Sarno, David (2007). "The Internet sure loves its outlaws". *Los Angeles Times*, 29

April, 2009. Retrieved July 8 2013, from http://www.latimes.com/technology/la-ca-webscout29apr29,0,5609754.story

Schofield, Jack (2009). "Pirate Bay Day 3- King Kong and the Beatles". *The Guardian*, 18 February 2009, Retrieved July 8 2013, from http://www.guardian.co.uk/technology/blog/2009/feb/18/pirate-bay-day3-kingkong

The Office of the United States Trade Representative (2010). *Special 301 Report.*

Yar, Majid (2005). "The Global Epidemic of Movie Piracy: Crime-Wave or Social Construction?". *Media Culture Society*, 27:5, 677-696.

Young, S. Mark, James J. Gong and Wim A. Van Der Stede (2008). "The Business of Making Movies". *Strategic Finance.* 89:8, 26-32.

The Internet Between Politics and the Political: The Birth of the Pirate Party

Mariacristina Sciannamblo

"The technical and the political are like the abstract and the concrete,
the foreground and the background, the text and the context,
the subject and the object"

(Donna Haraway 1997)

Introduction

The focus of this chapter is a discussion of the political implications brought on by the development of digital technologies and computer-mediated communication (CMC). I will particularly concentrate on the birth of the Pirate Party as a case of an anti-establishment political organization with no right-left orientation or nationalistic values. It could be regarded as the first political party that sees the Internet not only as a major tool for the "Information Society" (Webster 2006) but also as a central subject for political debates. This is a political group that is deeply rooted in the ongoing conflict between file sharing networks and copyright owners, and raises issues around property rights and freedom of expression that have characterized the history of copyright and piracy (Fredriksson 2012).

To begin with, I argue that the Pirate Party is a direct political expression of a social order based on openness and inclusion that is manifested in the highly democratic technical architecture of the Internet. Theoretically, I argue that online piracy – one of the most controversial issues of the 'digital turn' – can be framed by two different theoretical perspectives on the relationship between innovation and society: diffusionism and the Social Shaping of Technology (SST). Far from being a mere technical innovation, peer-to-peer networks represent the political conflict between two economic models of knowledge and social organization: 'open' and 'closed' approaches. The conflict emerges through the 'open' social practices of the Internet – such as the sharing of contents and information – that have not only enabled individuals to develop their own agency, but also threaten established 'closed' power relationships based on ownership, property rights and monetary exchange.

Secondly, I will discuss the transformation of digital piracy into a specific political phenomenon embodied by the spread of the Pirate Party. I approach this issue through Peter Dahlgren's (2004) concept of "civic cultures" as a new form of citizenship based on social agency. Within this current historical juncture, where many scholars see a general decline in political participation but a growing interest in informal politics (Arvanitakis 2011), the Pirate Party seems to overcome the traditional model of representative democracy by being both engaged and empowered as outlined by the model of "insurgent citizenship" (Holston 2007 cited in Arvanitakis 2011). This is a term used to describe the attempt to bring back citizenship into the realm of politics through various means of participation, to engage with civic institutions and political processes.

The central question that this exposition explores is the changing role of the Internet as it is increasingly becoming a tool that can both support and challenge political institutions. The question that follows is: are cyberspace and its governance influence are gaining a deeper influence in the broader political sphere?

The promise of equality: Peer-to-Peer as a new socio-technical paradigm

An attempt to discuss the social, cultural, economic and political implications of digital piracy can only take shape from the important starting point of establishing a definition of 'media'. The distinction between media and technologies used by Marshall McLuhan (1994) and the Toronto School suggested a definition of 'media' as cognitive artifacts able to shape the perceptual processes through which individuals experience the world and social relations that surround them (McLuhan 1994). The merit of McLuhan is thus that he places the physical tools (or *hardware*) and the codes (or *software*) conveyed by them on the same footing. This definition, however, was formulated to account for a media landscape characterized by uncertainty.

Michele Sorice (2009) also emphasizes that media can be categorized both according to their linguistic and technological features. This distinction is particularly crucial when analyzing the process of media digitization, in which the convergence of linguistic codes coexists with the evolution of the processes of production, distribution and consumption. Sorice refers to Fausto Colombo's definition of media, according to which "the media are socio-technical devices that play a role in mediating the communication between individuals" (2003,

17). Such an interpretation allows us to study media from several perspectives: as socio-technical systems, as instruments of mediation, as cultural technologies and as systems operating in the cultural industries.

The development of information and communications technology (ICT) and CMC has drawn new attention to the process of mediation since the convergence of technologies requires us to reappraise the interaction between individuals, as well between individuals and technologies (Lievrouw and Livingstone 2006). The digitization of media calls for us to consider new information technologies not only as powerful tools to produce messages that influence the behaviors of social bodies, but also as resources that enable individuals to develop their own *agency*. This requires us to focus on the use of media rather than only its effects. In this context, mediation is not only constituted by technical tools in the process of communication, but includes all the aspects of the infrastructure created by the process of technological convergence: that is, devices, practices and social organization.

Lievrouw and Livingstone (2006) argue that the development of the 'network' – that is, the ubiquity and interactive effects that distinguish established (or 'old') mass media from digital media – requires us to look at the process of re-intermediation generated by information and communication technologies. The issue of technology has to be reviewed in the light of the two main theories that have addressed the relationship between innovation and society: diffusionism and the Social Shaping of Technology (SST). Although they belong to different intellectual, theoretical and methodological traditions, both approaches claim that the spread of technology has important social implications that need to be both understood and problematized. They both propose an analysis of the dynamics of progress substantially different from that offered by 'technological determinism' – or the idea that technological outcomes and effects are pre-determined and, therefore, easily defined.

In the case of peer-to-peer networks – which Massimo Comi (2007, 154) defines as "the action of mutual exchange of information and services directly between the maker and the consumer in order to get significant results" – the comparison between the two conceptual formulations above suggests even more interesting social, economic and political interactions (Bauwens 2002; Andersson 2009; Jenkins 2006). As noted, the great value of the social theories of technological innovation was that of imagining technology and society as mutually articulated

– although with different ways of regarding the deployment of this articulation (Murru 2007). Where diffusionism considers innovation as an external event with a different mode of propagation within the social system, SST provides an interpretative model able to imagine technology as embedded in the social world. The contexts of use, the interests of the users and the symbolic codes of communication compose such an interpretation.

Leah A. Lievrouw (2006) notes that the development of a technology touches on various critical points in which contingency and determination are expressed in different forms. The separate theories of diffusion and SST suggest different interpretations regarding the relationship between determination and contingency in technological processes. What I mean by the term 'determination' here is "the effort to specify the conditions and to impose coherence in a situation with the aim to achieve the desired result" (2006, 279); whereas, the term 'contingency' refers to "the existence of many possible conditions in a situation of uncertainty" (ibid.).

For instance, theories of diffusion of innovations tend to consider the imposed aspects of 'determination' in the evaluation of distribution processes, design and involved actors. In contrast, contingency considers the human choices and consequences that are at play. SST thus gives a predominant role to contingency in the different stages of innovations, with different standpoints depending on the field of research.

The last phase of this path of evolutionary development is defined by the consequences: that is, both the planned and unplanned effects an innovation has within the social system in which it flourishes. It is one of the few points where diffusionism intersects with the SST since in both cases the introduction of a new technology is a factor of social change (Murru 2007).

These perspectives of determination and contingency represent important conceptual and methodological tools when studying the history of the Internet and the new role of the audience (Sorice 2009).

Such models of innovation that are based on the relationship between determination and contingency effectively outline the diffusion and evolution of the Internet. In this framework, a diffusionist model of Internet development is convincing only if hybridized with the theory and analysis of network dynamics (Lievrouw 2006). Accordingly, the relationships between social actors are more relevant than individual actions in the diffusion of networks.

The development of an innovation model confronts social relations, economic and political logics as well as cultural patterns. It also avoids the pitfalls of both technological and social determinisms. This echoes Manuel Castells' statement that "technology is society, and society cannot be understood or represented without its technological tools" (1996, 5). Therefore, the social dimension assumes a crucial relevance in the discussion about the cultural production and consumption related to peer-to-peer networks and file-sharing.

Many authors, including Paccagnella (2010) and Lessig (2004), have argued that the negative connotations attributed to file-sharing when it is associated with illegal practices hide the content industry's significant economic interests. In this regard, the diffusion of innovations theory appears inadequate in analyzing a complex phenomenon such as peer-to-peer file-sharing. This is not just simply technological innovation but rather highlights the conflicts that arise from a 'paradigm shift', as two (ideal) models of knowledge, the 'open' and 'closed' clash.

It is here that the key concept of 'agency' becomes central and confronts the weakness of technological and social determinism (Slack and Wise 2007). This relates to the long-lasting issue of causality, which has traditionally characterized the study of technology. Raymond Williams (1981), for example, has proposed an interpretation that overcomes the mere binary assumption that technologies of new media (television in his case) unilaterally stem from social factors such as the "decisive commonality of intentions and creative impulses" (cited in Slack and Wise 2007, 140). Agency is one way to reinterpret the new status of the audience fostered by media convergence such as wikis, peer production and file-sharing (Livingstone 2005). Such an approach considers the capacity in which information technologies give different, individual or collective, actors the opportunity to develop social agency.

Another relevant aspect when analyzing the phenomenon of peer-to-peer is Harold Innis' concept of "media bias" (1951). According to Innis, each medium has both a propensity and characteristics under which they can be classified. The concept of 'bias' is particularly effective when applied to digital media: that is, we can ask whether technologies either facilitate the centralization of power and closed networks, or tend to encourage openness or decentralization. This idea is clearly expressed by Winner (1986, cited in Lievrouw 2007), who argues that each technology has an inherent disposition prior to its particular use that reflects a certain social order. Winner explains how technologies are inherently political and represent ways of building a certain social order: fostering centralization or decentralization, control or freedom, equality or inequality.

Following this interpretation, the social orientation of the Internet has been well explored (see Bauwens 2002; Castells 2001; Jenkins 2007; Lessig 2005; Mason 2008; Paccagnella 2010). The evolution of the Internet has been particularly characterized by debates about social practices aimed at promoting openness and inclusion, such as file-sharing, peer production and free software. It is within this history that we need to frame the so-called 'war on piracy'. From a theoretical point of view, both diffusion of innovation and the SST assist in explaining the different steps in the development of the Internet: the social practices related to the use of the Internet have raised conflicts that threaten established power relationships based on values such as ownership, clear property rights, commercial exchange of goods, hierarchical production and "permission culture" (Lessig 2005: 2).

According to Michel Bauwens (2002), peer-to-peer systems, in addition to offering an alternative to the technological paradigm of the content owners, also represent social networks that provide an alternative ideology to that of informational capitalism. This is an ideology of open knowledge conveyed by open source software and alternative licenses which are shaped by an open architecture based on cooperation, the absence of central nodes, and the inclusiveness of communication protocols (Lessig 2005; Paccagnella 2010). It is a real socio-technical model whose success is hampered by the reluctance of publishers and content industries. Interestingly, Bauwens has compared the conflict to the historical clash between the stable structure of the feudal system and the first stirrings of capitalist production. Nevertheless, supporting simple dichotomous visions such as open *equals* good and closed *equals* bad is a mistake. In fact, although many examples of peer production have restored the idea of human knowledge as a common good, we must not neglect the existence and importance of inequalities that comes with the digital divide and uneven distribution of Internet literacy.

Theft or gift? Towards a cultural framework for online piracy

As discussed, technological innovation needs to be understood in relation to controversial phenomena such as online piracy, hacking, peer-to-peer and free software – all of which have resulted in a "paradigm shift" in the use of media (Verlhust 2007). In doing so, it is possible to employ the idea of "articulation" (Hall 1986 cit. in Slack and Wise 2007 142) proposed by cultural studies and that of "genealogy" (Foucault 1977), as both concepts seek to move the understanding of technology as 'causal', challenging the assumptions of inevitability and progress (Slack and Wise 2007). Reading the development of technology through the concept of 'articulation', allows us to understand the existing, as well as emerging, connections between technology and its social, cultural, political and economic implications.

Taking a genealogical approach, instead, allows us to understand the response to online piracy within a political system imbued with power, analyzing the developments in the Western tradition of intellectual property and the response to the advent of Internet technologies (Lessig 2004). If the concept of 'genealogy' defies the assumption that ideas and practices retain their own logic, we should analyze "the way in which multiple elements advance, collide, invade, fight, loot and play in such a way that complex and changeable organizations define the apparatus in which technology is poured" (Slack and Wise 2007, 146). By historicizing the concept of "piracy," however, Martin Fredriksson (2012) describes the entanglement between copyright and the structures of international trade relations within a postcolonial order of power. Following the hypothesis of "Empire" by Michael Hardt and Antonio Negri (2000), he explains how contemporary international intellectual property rights, codified in international agreements such as GATT (General Agreement on Tariffs and Trade) and TRIPS (Agreement on Trade-Related Aspects of Intellectual Property Rights), have become an example of a new kind of global governance with neither centers of power nor fixed boundaries or barriers.

A compelling articulation of the concept of 'piracy' is offered by Lawrence Lessig (2004) in *Free Culture.* Lessig considers two forms of piracy: one harmful, the other more ambiguous. The former is the simple appropriation of copyrighted content without a transformation of the work or of the market where it competes. It is, according to Lessig, a manifestly unlawful act. The latter, however, relates to peer-to-peer file-sharing and is distinguished from the first kind of piracy for three reasons: it wants to escape the excessive control of the industry; it is simply a new mode of content distribution; and, there is no financial exchange through peer-to-peer services. While being severely critical of current enforcement regimes, Lessig attempts to balance the need to protect copyright for the creative industries with the need to promote information sharing systems.

One fundamental issue that piracy raises is Internet regulation. All the key players – governments, users, industry and artists – simultaneously desire and fear a revision of telecommunication rules. It is particularly complicated to confront regulatory changes in a system where disintermediation has come to dominate, and change is ongoing and dynamic. Here we have seen the rise of new content producers and the ability for users to access information without intermediaries. In such a digital environment, the power moves from the content provider to the user, creating the possibility of developing a communication system described as "many to many" (Castells 2007; Lessig 1999; Mason 2008).

The "war on piracy" (Lessig 2005: 17) has sparked a heated political debate revolving around expanding law enforcement on the one side, and the users' reaction and right to privacy on the other. Accordingly, the clash between governments and corporations against the 'free Net' movements originates from two fundamental issues: the commercialization of the Internet and the consequent tightening of controls. According to Lessig (2005), the need to protect intellectual property rights has led to the development of new software architectures that attempt control communication among users. Furthermore, some authors (Fredriksson 2012; Lobato and Thomas 2011) describe the process of evolution of anti-piracy enforcement into a business through the development of digital rights management (DRM), and other technologies of surveillance and control. For Lessig, governments have a clear choice regarding how to reckon the information society: should it be 'free' or 'feudal'. This distinction lies at the heart of the debate about whether intellectual property rights must be exercised in the most restrictive way or if there should be a balance between proprietary claims and open access.

This is a struggle that has existed since the early years of the Internet. The Internet we recognize today developed through a highly democratic technical architecture, where content was circulated with a minimum of rights reserved. The patterns of Internet development and innovation have changed over time. The phenomenon of piracy, then, can be read not so much as an action (even though it is) of revolt against a system of regulation that is regarded as too oppressive, but rather as an important sign of a need to reconfigure the current legal, political, economic and cultural framework in which the Internet exists. We are very far from the 'Pirate Utopias' prefigured by Hakim Bey or the 'Temporary Autonomous Zone' free from political power and controls (Wilson 1991): rather, several developments involve a participatory ethic that has fostered the rise of cooperative practices, such as peer-to-peer networks and open source software (Barbrook 1998; Jenkins 2006).

An additional element is that the structure of cyberspace is technically arranged to copy and remix information. According to Tim Berbers-Lee, "there is a need for the underlying infrastructure to be able to make copies simply for reasons of efficiency and reliability" (1996). Accordingly, a concept such as intellectual property, central to a market economy, is technically and socially obsolete when applied to the original patterns of the Internet (Barbrook 1998).

A re-occurring argument by the copyright industry is that piracy threatens the creative industries. The clash between rights holders and 'digital pirates' took very harsh forms, often leading to widely recognized lawsuits such as *the Napster* case in 1999. Despite such claims about the evils of piracy, this emerging information economy and the traditional market economy are not necessarily incompatible models. According to Richard Barbrook (1998), it is possible to describe the Internet economy as a "mixed economy" where the market economy (based on commodities) and the hi-tech gift economy (based on gift relations) coexist, influencing each other towards mutual benefit. In fact, the free flow of information not only depends on the industrial production of computers, software and telecommunication infrastructure, but, as Tapscott and Williams (2006) argue, it can even become an important part of the economic system in the form of Wikinomics. It is not surprising, therefore, that the spread of piratical practices keeps pace with the "ongoing commodification and enclosure of the commons" (Arvanitakis 2006, 13).

Pirates go to politics: The rise of the Pirate Party

The phenomenon of digital piracy can be approached from different perspectives. In the previous sections I have underlined that the infringement of intellectual property is a phenomenon that has escalated and taken on new forms with the development of the Internet and its commercial use. However, piracy assumes an essentially political dimension when it changes from a mere legal issue to an individual and collective action to gain free access to culture and becomes a political practice with democratic claims. In this section I discuss how the recent development of piracy has formed the basis for institutional and political actors, which is most evident in the rapid spread of the Pirate Party.

The Pirate Party was born in Sweden in 2006 as a political manifestation of strong popular support for file-sharing among Swedes (Lindgren and Linde 2010). The party, founded by Rick Falkvinge, marks the transition of piracy to institutional politics.

Sweden is possibly the European country where the debate on piracy and copyright infringement has been most active given the presence of organizations committed to both file-sharing and anti-copyright activism such as *Piratbyrån* (the Bureau of Piracy) and The Pirate Bay (Li 2009; Spenders 2009). The latter, founded in 2003, has become one of the largest BitTorrent trackers and, according to *Los Angeles Times*, "the most visible member of a burgeoning international anti-copyright or pro-piracy movement" (Sarno 2007). Following high profile lawsuits launched by the Recording Industry Association of America (RIAA) and Motion Picture Association of America (MPAA) against peer-to-peer application developers in the Unites States, the Pirate Bay received a great deal of media attention when the Swedish police, in May 2006, conducted a massive raid against its web hosting company, seizing over one hundred servers. Rather than having the desired effect of scaring people away from piracy, the raid drew international attention to the issue and resulted in street protests and an increasing number of Pirate Bay users. In addition, the new political party, the Pirate Party, emerged and quickly attracted many members and followers due to the media attention.

According to Rickard Falkvinge (founder and first leader of the Swedish Pirate Party), the issue received wide-scale media coverage and generated large public interest while politicians basically failed to take account of the emerging debate (Li 2009; Miegel and Olsson 2008; Spender 2009). Rather than catering to an uninterested political élite, Falkvinge decided to bypass politicians entirely and focused on their power base. When the website of the Pirate Party went live, the key goals included recruiting volunteers, refining the party's manifesto and gathering enough signatures to get the Pirate Party registered with Sweden's electoral authority. It listed three issues as its primary focus: the fundamental reform of the copyright system, the abolition of the patent system and the respect for personal privacy.[1]

Falkvinge argues that the official aim of the copyright system has always been to find a balance between the interests of the authors and the users, aiming to promote the creation and distribution of culture (Spender 2009). Today that

1 Pirate Party, "Declaration of Principles," retrieved from http://en.wikisource.org/wiki/Pirate_Party_Declaration_of_Principles.

balance has been completely lost as copyright laws severely restrict access to the very thing they are supposed to promote: culture. The Pirate Party is convinced that the copyright holder's monopoly to commercially exploit an intellectual product should be limited to five years after publication: such a copyright term for commercial use is seen to be more than enough because "nobody needs to make money seventy years after he is dead".[2]

In the 2006 Swedish elections, the party received a mere 0.63 percent of the national total with only 34,918 votes. Even though it collected more votes than several established politicians and became the third largest force outside the parliament, Falkvinge and his fellows felt a need to do more and began to work on a strategy for the election to the European Parliament in 2009 as well as prepare for the next domestic election in 2010. The first step was to create a youth section called "Young Pirate" with the aim of developing young political talent to counterbalance the elders (Anderson 2009).

In June 2009 the Pirate Party overcame the 4 percent threshold, gaining 7.1 percent of the votes in the European Parliamentary elections, giving them two representative seats in Brussels. This was due in large part to its youth arm as 19 percent of the voters were less than 30 years of age. However, the Party failed to enter the *Riksdag (the* Swedish Parliament) in the national election of 2010. Despite the electoral defeat in Sweden, the Party has spread around the world: Pirate Parties have been started in 66 countries. They are coordinated by the Pirate Parties International, which is an association of Pirate Parties, formally founded in 2010 with the purpose of helping, supporting and promoting communication and co-operation between 'pirates' around the world.[3] Lately, the party has had significant success in the 2011 Berlin state parliament elections, and has had its first pirate senator elected in the Czech Republic (October 2012) and first mayor in Switzerland (September 2012).

One of the distinctive features of the Pirate Party is its nature as an advocacy movement deeply rooted in the libertarian culture of the Internet. This is highlighted by the Party's choice of name and logo, as well as its relationships with anti-copyright organizations and its decision to host many of Wikileaks' new servers. The Pirate Party's first Minister of the European Parliament, Christian Engström, explains that the party is basically a civil rights movement aiming to

2 Pirate Party, "Reform of copyright law," retrieved from http://p2pfoundation.net/Pirate_Party
3 Pirate Party International, "About," retrieved friom http://www.pp-international.net/about

highlight its own key issues within traditional politics.[4] As Miegel and Olsson (2008) remark, pirates chose to establish a political party and run for general elections but it is hard to define the Pirate Party as a traditional political party inasmuch as its representatives are not traditional politicians and its political platform questions established democratic practices such as the current model of representative democracy, the ownership of knowledge and information, and the protection of freedom of speech and integrity. Its non-hierarchical organization (Spenders 2009) distinguishes it from the traditional system of most political parties with which it must deal, in particular where the pirates hold elective offices. Thus, even though the Pirate Party has become a formal political force, it has its roots in a movement committed to a free Internet and anti-copyright activism. It relies on the fact that young people's growing engagement in file-sharing has evolved into a significant political question. The key features of these kinds of movements are, as Manuel Castells notes (2007), their *informality* and *virtuality*.

Such an organizational structure seems to belong to the dimension of 'political' rather than to that of 'politics'. By observing the unavoidability of conflicts that every democratic society entails, Chantal Mouffe (2000) proposes this distinction between the 'political' and 'politics'. The former indicates "the dimension of antagonism that is inherent in human relations, antagonism that can take many forms and emerge in different types of social relations" (Mouffe 2000, 25). In contrast, the latter is "the ensemble of practices, discourses and institutions which seek to establish a certain order and organize human coexistence in conditions that are always potentially conflictual because they are affected by the dimension of 'the political'" (Mouffe 2000, 25). Her thesis is that 'agonistic pluralism' is the condition for existence of democracy: the antagonism is transformed into *agonism* and passions are included in the public sphere towards democratic objectives. Within this framework, we can see that the Pirate Party has brought the political into politics, contributing to subvert the symbolic representation of the information society with its naturalized patterns.

Politics, sub-politics or in-between

The Pirate Party represents an interesting case study for two main reasons: it is a protest movement that uses the Internet as a tool for recruitment and promotion; and, it is the first political party occupying elective offices that makes the

4 See http://www.theglobeandmail.com/news/technology/all-in-favour-say-yar-har/article1176721/

governance of the Internet a central issue of its political agenda. As for the first point, there are many scholars that study new forms of political participation and civic engagement in order to identify the impact of digital technology and Web culture on political communication.

Peter Dahlgren, for example, explores a new form of political engagement, called 'civic cultures', based on Internet-activism (2003). Dahlgren is interested in discussing the theme of civic engagement as a new notion of citizenship based on social agency. In order to understand what kind of civic culture new media are proposing, the Swedish scholar reworks the concept of citizenship within new analytical frameworks beyond the legal and normative sphere. This multi-dimensional analytic framework highlights the subjective side of citizenship that is strictly linked to the dimension of identity. As Dahlgren states, "civic cultures are cultural patterns in which identities of citizenship, and the foundations for civic action are embedded" (2004, 4). This concerns the process through which people develop into citizens that see themselves as potential participants in societal development. According to Dahlgren, civic cultures are shaped by an array of factors, including traditional mass media as well as newer digital media that directly and routinely contribute to the character of modern public spheres.

It is important to relate this engagement in informal politics (and possibly Mouffe's 'politics') to the concerns raised by many scholars regarding a general decline in popular participation in traditional politics (Arvanitakis 2011). As Emiliana De Blasio and Michele Sorice (2009) point out, this assumption sees tendencies such as the emergence of new political subjects and the growth of networking as a tool to increase social participation as alien to the formal political sphere. Conceptual frameworks like 'civic culture' are built on ideas such as 'life politics' as articulated by Anthony Giddens (1991) and 'sub-politics' by Ulrich Beck (1994). They describe two main trajectories in the contemporary political situation: the increasing weakness of institutional politics in confronting global issues and the emergence of new political actors that are unrelated to the traditional political system such as alter-globalization movements, Indignados, Occupy movement and the Pirate Party. These movements build new areas of participation and are engaged in various forms of knowledge production based on a critique of the current political system. Additionally, they elaborate alternative forms of economic, social, and political organization that challenge neoliberal hegemony.

These new political movements use many strategies and different media to influence various public spheres. In 2001, Manuel Castells speculated whether the Internet played a mere instrumental role in political conflicts or if rules, forms and objectives of political actors have changed within and because of cyberspace. This is an inquiry that, in hindsight, reflects Dahlgren's idea on the power of media in shaping civic cultures. The existence of the Pirate Party raises questions regarding the Internet's role in current political and social life as well as the relation between the use of the Web and the political issues it evokes, such as 'the war on piracy', open access and all the ways in which information technology permits extensive forms of collaboration with the potential to transform the economy and society.

Accordingly, the Pirate Party could be considered a clear political result of a subpolitical movement and, secondly, it appoints the Internet as a specific, and possibly even, defining issue of its identity. Therefore, it tends to retain its informal and virtual character, remaining indeed in the so-called *subpolitic* area (Beck 1994; Sorice 2011).

Conclusion

To conclude, I argue that the Pirate Party highlights some of the irreversible changes in political participation that Pippa Norris (2007) has pointed out, including an increasing distrust in political parties, indicated by rising anti-party sentiment and falling party membership; the loss of power of traditional political agencies as a consequence of the growth of communication networks that encourage direct and individual political actions; and finally, the rise of cause-oriented activism, which focuses attention upon specific issues and policy concerns.

This echoes the crisis of participation in traditional politics noted by Arvanitakis (2011) and the expanding global gap between international networks and national states. In contrast, we are witnessing the emergence of issue-centered parties that often tend to disappear after one or two elections, but sometimes have a great impact in transforming established political coalitions (Demker 2008). A study by Erlingsson and Persson (2011) explains the Pirate Party's sudden and unexpected success in the 2009 Swedish European Parliament election within these terms. The starting point of their research calls into question the general and wide spread assumption that new political parties gain votes by exploiting dissatisfaction with established political coalitions. The aim of Erlingsson and

Persson is not so much to characterize the party's voters in demographic terms, but rather to explain why they support the Pirate Party. The conclusion of their study is worth quoting:

> …voters for the Pirate party were not more dissatisfied with the established Swedish parties than the electorate as a whole. Rather, the Pirate Party's success is best explained with reference to issue voting: the main reason why individuals chose the Pirate Party is the importance they ascribed to the party's main issues. 2011, 122

Its collaborative and 'sharing' practices indicate that the Pirate Party represents a specific 'political moment' (Arvanitakis 2011) striving for an open and diverse information society (Spender 2009) and with wider political implications. It aims at promoting progressive political change and a different kind of everyday politics challenging the media industry and the limitations of the traditional model of representative democracy.

This chapter has analyzed the Pirate Party's social and political significance through a variety of different theoretical perspectives that reflect different aspects of this highly multidimensional movement. By relating piracy to theories of technological innovation, I have tried to show how the Pirate Party can be regarded as a political articulation of the conflicts that grow out of a currently ongoing socio-technological, paradigmatic change. Theories of political participation, such as Peter Dahlgren's work on 'civic cultures' and Chantal Mouffe's distinction between 'politics' and 'the political', have on the other hand shone some light on how this articulation forms into a social movement on the subpolitic area in the expanded political sphere of the 21st century.

The party's socio-technological agenda and its identity as a part of a civic, subpolitical culture mark the cornerstones of the political and social context of belonging that the party relies on in order to formulate a convincing and well-founded agenda. At the moment, it is difficult to predict the future development of the international pirate movement but it will be interesting to see how the party will handle this distinctive and, in some ways, conflicting heritage from a space of contestation as it struggles to make its way into the traditional political arena.

References

Anderson, Nate (2009). "Political pirates: A history of Sweden's Piratpartiet". *Ars Technica*. Retrieved July 8 2013, from http://arstechnica.com/tech-policy/2009/02/

rick-falkvinge-is-the-face/
Andersson, Jonas (2011). "For the good of the net: The Pirate Bay as a strategic sovereign". *Culture Machine*, 10 (2009). Retrieved July 8 2013, from http://www.culturemachine.net/index.php/cm/article/viewArticle/346_
Arvanitakis, James (2006). "The Commons: Opening and enclosing non-commodified space," *PORTAL Journal of Multidisciplinary International Studies*, 3:1, 1-21. Retrieved July 24 2013, from
http://epress.lib.uts.edu.au/journals/index.php/portal/article/view/120/85
Arvanitakis, James (2011). "Redefining the political moment: Or the way Politics hollows out politics and how we should respond". *Cosmopolitan Civil Societies: An Interdisciplinary Journal*, 3:2, 72. Retrieved July 8 2013, from http://epress.lib.uts.edu.au/journals/index.php/mcs/article/view/2184/2363_
Bakardjieva, Maria (2009). "Subactivism: Lifeworld and Politics in the Age of the Internet". *The Information Society*, 25: 91–104.
Bauwens, Michel (2002). Peer to peer: From Technology to Politics to a new Civilisation?. Retrieved July 8 2013, from http://scholar.googleusercontent.com/scholarq=cache:QoXwwooR_kJ:scholar.google.com+Peer+to+peer+From+technology+to+politics+to+a+new+civilization&hl=it&as_sdt=0,5_
Barbrook, Richard (1998). "The Hi-Tech Gift Economy". *First Monday*, 7 December 1998. 3:12.
Beck, Ulrich, Anthony Giddens and Scott Lash (1994). *Reflexive Modernization: Politics, Tradition and Aesthetics in the Modern Social Order.* Cambridge, Polity Press.
Berners-Lee, Tim (1996). "The World Wide Web: Past, Present and Future," Draft response to invitation to publish in *IEEE Computer* special issue of October 1996. Retrieved 8 July 2013, from http://www.w3.org/People/Berners-Lee/1996/ppf
Castells, Manuel (1996). *The Information Age: Economy, Society and Culture,* Vol. 1: *The Rise of the Network Society.* Blackwell, Oxford.
Castells, Manuel (2001). *Internet Galaxy.* Oxford Press.
Colombo, Fausto (2003). *Introduzione allo studio dei media.* Carocci, Roma.
Comi, Massimo (2007). Il P2P come fenomeno sociale. In Fausto Colombo (ed.), *La digitalizzazione dei media.* Carocci, Roma.
Dahlgren, Peter (2003). "Net-activism and the Emergence of Global Civic Cultures". European Doctoral Summer School in Communication and Media, University of Westminster, August 2003. Retrieved 8 July 2013, from http://scholar.googleusercontent.com/scholar q=cache:Q4UaoYvg4fQJ:scholar.google.com+Peter+Dahlgren+Netactivism+and+the+Emergence+of+Global+Civic+Cultures&hl=it&as_sdt=0&as_vis=1
De Blasio, Emiliana and Michele Sorice (2009). *Italian Politics in the Web 2.0.* Roma, CMCS Working Papers LUISS University.
Demker, Marie (2008). *"A New Era of Party Politics in a Globalised World. The Concept of Virtue Parties".* Gothenburg: *QoG Working Paper Series,* 2008:20.
Erlingsson, Gissur Ó. and Mikael Persson (2011). "The Swedish Pirate Party and the 2009 European Parliament Election: Protest or Issue Voting?". *Politics,* 31:3, 121–128. Retrieved 8 July 2013 from http://onlinelibrary.wiley.com/

doi/10.1111/j.1467-9256.2011.01411.x/abstract
Foucault, Michel (1977). *Microfisica del potere. Interventi politici.* Einaudi, Torino.
Fredriksson, Martin (2012). "Piracy, globalisation and the colonisation of the Commons". *Global Media Journal – Australian Edition*, 6:1 2012. Retrieved 24 July 2013, from http://www.commarts.uws.edu.au/gmjau/v6_2012_1/martin_fredriksson_RA.html
Grossberg, Lawrence (1986). "On postmodernism and articulation: An interview with Stuart Hall," *Journal of Communication Inquiry* June, 1986 10: 45-60. doi:10.1177/019685998601000204
Innis, Harold Adams (1964). *The Bias Of Communication.* Toronto University Press.
Jenkins, Henry (2006). *Convergence culture.* New York University.
Lessig, Lawrence (1999). *Code and Other Laws of Cyberspace.* New York, Basic Books.
Lessig, Lawrence (2004). *Free Culture: The Nature and Future of Creativity.* Penguin Press.
Li, Miaoran (2009). "The Pirate Party and the Pirate Bay: How the Pirate Bay Influences Sweden and International Copyright Relations". *Pace International Law Review*, 21:1.
Lievrouw Leah A. and Sonia Livingstone (eds) (2006). *The Handbook of New Media.* Sage, London.
Lievrouw Leah A. (2006). "Progettazione e sviluppo dei new media: diffusione delle innovazioni e modellamento sociale della tecnologia". In Boccia Artieri, Paccagnella, Pasquali, *Capire I new media. Culture, comunicazione, innovazione tecnologica e istituzioni sociali* (eds), Hoepli, Milano 2007.
Lindgren, Simon and Jessica Linde (2010). "The subpolitics of online piracy: A Swedish case study". *Convergence*, 18:2. Retrieved 8 July 2013 from http://con.sagepub.com/content/18/2/143.abstract
Mason, Matt (2008). *The Pirate's Dilemma. How Youth Culture is Reinventing Capitalism.* Free press.
McLuhan, Marshall (1964). *Understanding Media.* Mc Graw-Hill book Company, New York.
McLuhan, Marshall, McLuhan Eric (1992). *The Laws of the Media: The New Science.* University of Toronto Press, Toronto.
Miegel, Fredrik, Olsson, Tobias (2008). "From Pirates to Politicians: The Story of the Swedish File Sharers Who Became a Political Party". In Carpentier, Pruulmann-Vengerfeldt, Nordenstreng, Hartmann, Vihalemm, Cammaerts, Nieminen & Olsson (eds.), *Democracy, Journalism And Technology: New Developments In An Enlarged Europe: The Intellectual Work Of Ecrea's 2008 European Media And Communication Doctoral Summer School.* Tartu University Press, Tartu, pp. 203-215.
Mouffe, Chantal (2000). "Deliberative Democracy or Agonistic Pluralism". *Social Research* 66, 745-758.
Murru, Maria Francesca (2007). "Social shaping of technology e diffusionismo: due prospettive a confront". In Fausto Colombo (ed.), *La digitalizzazione dei media*, Carocci, Roma.

Norris, Pippa (2007). "Political activism: New challenges, new opportunities". In Carles Boix and Susan Stokes (eds). *The Oxford Handbook of Comparative Politics.* Oxford: Oxford University Press. 628-652. doi: 10.1093/oxfordhb/9780199566020.003.0026

Paccagnella, Luciano (2010). *Open access. Conoscenza aperta e società dell'informazione.* Il Mulino, Bologna.

Sarno, David (2007). "The Internet sure loves its outlaws". *Los Angeles Times*, 29 April 2012. Retrieved 8 July 2013, from http://www.latimes.com/technology/la-ca-webscout29apr29,0,5609754.story

Slack, Jennifer Daryl and Macgregor J. Wise (2007). "Cultural studies e tecnologie della comunicazione". In Leah A. Lievrouw and Sonja Livingstone (eds.) (2006/2007). *Capire I new media. Culture, comunicazione, innovazione tecnologica e istituzioni sociali* (trans. Boccia Artieri, Paccagnella, Pasquali), Hoepli, Milano.

Sorice, Michele (2009). *Sociologia dei mass media*, Carocci, Roma.

Sorice, Michele (2011). *La Comunicazione Politica.* Carocci, Roma.

Spender, Lynne (2009). *Digital culture, copyright maximalism, and the challenge to copyright law.* PhD Thesis, University of Western Sydney. Retrieved 8 July 2013, from http://arrow.uws.edu.au:8080/vital/access/manager/Repository/uws:7052

Tossell, Ivor (2009). "All in favour say 'Yar har!'". *The Globe and Mail.* Retrieved 8 July 2013, from http://www.theglobeandmail.com/technology/all-in-favour-say-yar-har/article4355452/

Verhulst, Stefaan G. (2007). "La società dell'informazione rivisitata". In Leah A. Lievrouw and Sonja Livingstone (eds.) (2006/2007). *Capire I new media. Culture, comunicazione, innovazione tecnologica e istituzioni sociali* (Trans. Boccia Artieri, Paccagnella, Pasquali), Hoepli, Milano.

Webster, Frank (2007). "La regolamentazione dei contenuti digitali". In Leah A. Lievrouw and Sonja Livingstone (eds.) (2006/2007). *Capire I new media. Culture, comunicazione, innovazione tecnologica e istituzioni sociali* (trans. Boccia Artieri, Paccagnella, Pasquali), Hoepli, Milano.

Wilson, Peter Lamborn (aka Bey, Hakim) (1991). *TAZ – The Temporary Autonomous Zone, Ontological Anarchy, Poetic Terrorism.* New York, Autonomedia..html
7).

Cultural Resistance or Corporate Assistance: Disenchanting the Anti-Capitalist Myth of Digital Piracy

You Jie

Introduction

Since Shawn Fanning launched Napster.com near the end of the last century, transnational digital piracy[1] of copyrighted products on the Internet has been framed by the copyright industry as a shameless globalized act of intellectual property theft. The following indignant statement by the Record Industry Association of America (RIAA) remains representative of the position of the major copyright holders:

> Today's pirates operate not on the high seas but on the Internet, in illegal CD factories, distribution centers and on the street. The pirate's credo is still the same – why pay for it when it's so easy to steal? The credo is as wrong as it ever was. Stealing is still illegal, unethical, and all too frequent in today's digital age. RIAA 2003

The International Federation of the Phonographic Industry (IFPI) and the Motion Picture Association of America (MPAA) have consistently claimed that digital piracy has cost the industries they represent millions of dollars in lost revenues annually. The IFPI asserted in its *Digital Music Report 2010* that "the growth of illegal file-sharing has been a major factor in the decline in legitimate music sales over the last decade, with global industry revenues down around 30 percent from 2004 to 2009" (2010, 18). In addition, the MPAA attributed US$2.3 billion of lost revenues to global digital piracy in 2005 (L.E.K. 2005).[2]

In sharp contrast, however, digital piracy seems to occupy a moral high ground among ordinary 'netizens' due to its distinctive feature: unlike physical piracy (such as the pirating of CDs and DVDs), digital piracy is 'free'. This enhances piracy's well-recognized capacity to spread cultural enlightenment by

1 Throughout this paper, the term "digital piracy" refers only to the digital reproduction and distribution of original media products without any or only with trivial alterations. Digital appropriation arts like audio or video mashups are not included.

2 L.E.K. is an international strategic consulting firm, which compiled this report for the Motion Picture Association (MPA), the international counterpart of MPAA.

undermining the monopolistic prices charged by the media industry and thus making commercially distributed cultural products more readily available to people who cannot afford them. Furthermore, it makes these products accessible in domestic markets where political censorship limits their availability. Piracy also turns upside down the 'there-is-no-free-lunch' rationality at the base of economic theory, upon which the whole modern capitalist market economy is firmly based. Digital piracy has significantly promoted the value of free information sharing – a concept that is viewed as the fundamental principle by many Internet visionaries. In fact, this concept of 'free access' has been frequently championed by a cross section of advocates – from anarchist commentators, to technological entrepreneurs and leftist artists – as the leading force of cultural resistance in the network age against both the control mania of the major studios and the underlying commodification logic of the global copyright industry (Fairchild 2008; Hesmondhalgh 2007; Reyman 2010; Slater 2000).

This dichotomy between the exploitative corporate capitalism represented by the US-dominated global copyright industry and the transnational grassroots' anti-capitalist dynamic sustained by the digital citizens in wired nations seems to be well recognized both within academia and among ordinary digital pirates (Fairchild 2008, 56; Karaganis 2011, 34; Reyman 2010, 26; Strangelove 2005). On the one hand, by framing the file-sharing phenomenon as blatant piracy, a term originally associated with armed outlaws on the sea, the copyright industry attempted to circumvent the widely spread moral challenge against its intellectual monopoly. This terminology also obscures the uneven power structure embedded in the relationships between media conglomerates and ordinary consumers. But by voluntarily uploading and exchanging digitized media products on the Internet without profit motivation, file-sharers replace the capitalist private property mentality with a commons-based egalitarian vision of knowledge accumulation. Such an action has the potential to emancipate human creativity from the locked chambers of copyright owners.

However, as some researchers have pointed out, this seemingly well-established dichotomy between a controlling copyright industry and subversive pirates is too simplistic (Fairchild 2008, and also Da Rimini and Marshall from this volume). This is because it ignores both the skillful manipulation of strategic promotion efforts by the copyright industry to continuously shape "the acts and spaces of consumption" (Fairchild 2008, 23) and the strong adaptive capacity inherited by the copyright industry through its numerous battles with new copying technologies (Hesmondhalgh 2007; Spar 2001). While these challenges try to undermine that dichotomy, they fail to recognize the possibility that both the rhetoric and the practice of piracy themselves might have been co-opted by the copyright industry to maintain the very productivity of this dichotomy.

The following three case studies suggest that the anti-capitalist grassroots resistance championed by digital pirates might have served more as an accessory myth insidiously working for rather than a righteous revolt against the monopolistic power of the copyright industry. By exposing the illusionary nature of the resistance myth surrounding digital piracy, this chapter aims to unveil the double subjugating structure of the supposed dichotomy between corporate capitalism and digital activism in the arena of copyright. In so doing, I am aiming to inform an alternative intellectual production ethics based on a radical conception of de-propertization or collectivation.

Software piracy in Mainland China: An usher for Microsoft

Even before the advent of massive end-user piracy enabled by peer-to-peer (P2P) file-sharing technologies, one particular sector within the copyright industry had already stumbled upon the tremendous accessory potential of piracy for its long term market strategy: producers of operating systems. In the 1990s and early 2000s, the rampant physical rather than digital piracy of Microsoft's Windows and Office Tools by Chinese consumers constituted the decisive force behind Microsoft's dominant position in Mainland China's operating system market.

The use of software usually exhibits typical traits of network effects: that is, the greater the number of people using a particular type of software, the more utility each of those users can derive from it. This occurs because the resulting network can have a larger communicative and functional capacity (Katz 2005, 164-165). Operating system software presents an especially strong case of such effects. This is because a wider user base establishes the operating system as the de facto platform standard which forces secondary applications and services to be compatible with it. As a result, users of the dominant operating system will face a considerably high switching cost if they decide to adopt an alternative operating system later on, as they have to make necessary efforts to retrain themselves in order to become familiar with the new system and purchase compatible supplementary applications and services. Put in other words, users will simply be locked into the dominant operating system (Karaganis 2011, 51-52; Katz 2005, 171). It is the very existence of network effects that informs software vendors' relentless efforts toward expanding their user base, which in turn situates the indispensable role of software piracy in certain markets.

Ariel Katz (2005) argues that software piracy serves a number of important functions for the pirated manufacturers: it helps them to achieve network monopoly; enables price discrimination; exploits users' lock-in dependence; and deters competitive market entries. Joshua Slive and Dan Bernhardt (1998) even expose a possible two-stage strategy to be adopted by a software manufacturer to make full use of the profitability of software piracy: tolerating piracy in the first stage to achieve market monopoly and lock users in, and deploying various anti-piracy maneuvers in the second stage to transform the pirates into paying customers. Microsoft's road to domination in Mainland China's market clearly demonstrated the practical validity of these academic claims about the utility of software piracy.

Between the time it established its first office in Mainland China in 1992 and the early 2000s, Microsoft adopted a particularly uncompromising position against software piracy: often suing small businesses out of existence for using pirated Windows and Office tools, when at the same time keeping the prices of its products sold in Mainland China in line with those in developed countries (Kirkpatrick 2007; Zheng 2007). While having no perceptible effect in deterring piracy, this strategy did succeed in alienating the Chinese government, which started to promote open source Linux system around the turn of the new century (Shen 2005, 192; Smith 2000a), and arousing widespread anti-Microsoft sentiment among Chinese computer users, one of whom even sued the software giant for unfair pricing (Smith 2000a; Zheng 2007).

Microsoft's then Chief Executive, Bill Gates, quickly realized the enormous benefit of the rampant piracy of Microsoft's products in the emerging market of Mainland China and started to tone down the company's litigant anti-piracy rhetoric. In 1998, when talking to students at the University of Washington, Bill Gates publicly declared:

> And as long as they're going to steal it, we want them to steal ours. They'll get sort of addicted, and then we'll somehow figure out how to collect sometime in the next decade. (Quoted in Piller 2006).

With a street price of just a few US dollars, as opposed to the prohibitively high official prices, pirated Windows and Office software which had the same functionality as the authorized one was widely purchased and installed by ordinary Chinese computer users. This quickly established Windows operating system as the dominant platform throughout the Mainland China. By the middle of 2000s, Windows had been installed on 90 percent of Mainland China-based computers, which matches the estimated piracy rate calculated by the Business Software Alliance: 92 percent in 2003 (BSA 2004). Reports confirm that even the Chinese President Hu Jintao uses Microsoft products every working day in his office (Kirkpatrick 2007). Windows' fast hegemonization of Mainland China's operating system market has automatically rendered competition from other software vendors, including Linux, simply irrelevant (Shen 2005, 194). In fact, Bill Gates himself candidly admitted the formidable market entry barrier set by the pervasive piracy of Microsoft products:[3]

> It's easier for our software to compete with Linux when there's piracy than when there's not. (Quoted in Kirkpatrick 2007)

Piracy not only helped Microsoft achieve market monopoly in Mainland China within a decade, but also did it without compromising the company's global pricing strategy. Microsoft could have adopted an elaborate scheme of price discrimination in Mainland China to achieve the same speed of market monopolization by charging the Chinese computer users roughly the same amount as the street pirate prices. However, such a scheme of country-based price discrimination could create arbitrage of Microsoft products across borders from low-income China into high-income rich countries. In fact, the mere knowledge that Microsoft products could be legally obtained at such a low price in Mainland China might devastate marketing efforts by Microsoft in wealthy countries and even encourage consumers in these countries to look for pirated products. Since revenues from Mainland China has been considerably insignificant compared to revenues from developed countries, especially the US domestic market, maintaining a uniform global price was necessary for Microsoft to ensure the security of its most profitable revenue sources. In light of this, the rampant software piracy in Mainland China has served exactly the same purpose of price discrimination: providing ordinary Chinese computer users with the same products at an affordable price, while avoiding all the potential troubles which might result from an

3 Microsoft also deployed the same strategy in Africa. See May 2010, 136-142.

explicit scheme of price discrimination (Katz 2005, 179-186).[4]

As the Chinese government gradually changes its intellectual property policies and law enforcement to meet its World Trade Organization (WTO) membership obligations, and with Chinese computer users firmly locked in their Windows experiences and skills (Kirkpatrick 2007; Lu and Weber 2008, 81; Shen 2005, 194), Microsoft started to develop a comprehensive and sophisticated two-front anti-piracy strategy to "convert them (previous pirates) into licensing the software" (Mondok 2007). On the much more profitable front of public institutions and IT community, Microsoft has persuaded the Chinese government and some major PC makers to obtain authorized Windows and Office tools offered at discounted prices, taking full advantages of new government regulations requiring all government units to use legal software and all domestically produced computers to preload authorized operating systems before sale (Chinese State Council 2010; Kirkpatrick 2007; Liu 2007; Lu and Weber 2008, 85; Xu 2011). On the corporate and personal markets, especially from late 2000s, Microsoft has combined mass promotional campaign and technological updating harassment towards ordinary end users with litigations against large companies and unauthorized distributors (Xu 2011). As a result of these multi-layered anti-piracy manipulations and coercions, the licensing of authorized Microsoft products has witnessed a noticeable increase in Mainland China (Yang 2011), while the software piracy rate has dropped to 78 percent in 2010 (Bass 2011).

Digital piracy: A pusher for the global music industry

Due to the ease of transforming CD-based music into mp3s and the relative high speed of downloading these files even in the age of dial-up Internet connection, the record industry has been the first branch within the broader copyright industry to feel the allegedly destructive forces of file-sharing. Paralleling the rapid ascendance of online music file swapping since the launch of Napster, the recorded music industry suffered an unprecedented sales decline: Global music sales fell from UD$39.7 billion in 2000 to US$33.6 billion in 2004, representing a 16 percent fall (IFPI 2006).

4 In 2006, revenues from China accounted for less than 1percent of Microsoft's total sales. According to Steve Ballmer, CEO of Microsoft, in 2011, revenues from China accounted for just 5 percent of the revenues from the US domestic market and Microsoft's revenue per personal computer sold in China was only about a sixth of the amount it got in India. See Workman 2006; Fletcher and Dean 2011.

In contrast to the claims of the major copyright holders, a number of researchers have argued that this continuous sales decline might have more to do with the global economic recession, the diverting effect of other entertainment options and the end of the transition from LPs to CDs (Meza 2007; Oberholzer-Gee and Strumpf 2007). Rather than causing a decline, it has also been argued that file-sharing might have increased the demand for complementary music commodities such as live concerts to offset the likely modest negative effects upon the sale of recorded music (Oberholzer-Gee and Strumpf 2010). Despite such evidence, the recorded music industry has been consistently blaming the file-sharing phenomenon as the main culprit for its financial loss (IFPI 2010).

As many observers have aptly pointed out, both the anti-piracy rhetoric and litigation campaigns aimed at file-sharing networks, ISPs and individual sharers deployed by the major labels have been more about protecting their pre-digital distribution infrastructures than preventing potential losses (Cooper 2005; Honigsberg 2002; Yu 2004). These are infrastructures upon which their old business models are based and whose ultimate aim is to maintain their oligopolistic positions in the music market. Digital distribution, wryly initiated by file-sharing networks, means the obliteration of the globalized physical distribution system. In turn, this means a total transformation of the profit-making pattern long established by the recorded music industry. Even more important, digital distribution can marginalize the record companies as the indispensable intermediary between musicians and listeners in the digital age. Now music artists can reach their fan base directly via their own websites or some newly emerged online music aggregate services that are more flexible in terms of contract arrangement. This means that artists can distribute their works without sacrificing their artistic integrity to fit in the marketeering agenda of record companies.

The enormous cost of structural transformation, the fear of unauthorized copying and its uncertain status in the digital environment held back, or considerably slowed down, the record industry's adventure into cyberspace. This was particularly the case with the biggest incumbents. The most telling example of this is the failure of the two earliest legal online music services. In 2002, the recorded music industry hastily launched two online music services – MusicNet (Warner, EMI and BMG) and PressPlay (Sony and Universal) – to materialize its claim made in its lawsuit against Napster that the emergence of illegal file-sharing services tremendously enhanced the market entrance threshold for legal online music services. The two sites provided a very limited repertoire of songs in low quality format for their base subscribers (Spring 2002), set up ridiculously strict Digital Rights Management mechanisms (Mark 2003) and required other online music services who wanted to sell music produced by the then 'big five labels' to enter into restrictive arrangements with them (Honigsberg 2002). Concerned by the anti-competitive implications of these strategies, the US Department of Justice soon launched a 2-year long antitrust investigation against them (Mark 2003).

It is only after the painful (and costly) realization that digital piracy will not decline substantially in the near future, but rather is more likely to gain momentum, that the recorded music industry finally began to engage itself more enthusiastically, aggressively and comprehensively in the digital arena to compete with the free file-sharing practiced by millions of ordinary Internet users around the world. Since 2004, the recorded music industry has become both more ambitious and flexible in licensing music and testing various business models with a plethora of eclectic partners from the computer and communications industries. This has resulted in a nascent but promising legal digital music market worldwide. By the end of 2009, the global music industry had built a US$ 4.2 billion digital business, which represented a 12 percent increase from 2008 and accounted for 27 percent of record company revenues that year (IFPI 2010). This was achieved with an amazing variety of established business models including downloading, ISP and mobile partnering, music subscriptions bundled with device, streaming, ad-supported distribution of professional music videos online and direct-to-consumer sales of music, merchandising and concert tickets (IFPI 2010).

A statistical comparison between the digital market in 2003 and 2009 is particularly revealing in terms of the structural transformation undertaken by the recorded music industry in the first decade of the 21st century – see Table 1.

Table 1:

	2003	2009
Licensed music services	Less than 50	400+
Catalogue available	1 million	11 million
Industry's digital revenues	US$ 20 million	US$ 4.2 billion
Percent of industry revenue from digital channels	Negligible	27 %

Source: IFPI 2010, 6

It is both alarming and interesting to note that digital piracy essentially maintained its momentum along the same time frame as the recorded music industry was witnessing the rapid growth of a digital market (IFPI 2010). This expansion in revenue was occurring within an industry that described itself as desperately threatened by the 'free lunch' offered by file-sharing networks and other non-P2P forms of digital piracy. Each issue of IFPI's annual digital music report since 2004 routinely devotes one-third of its pages to accusing digital piracy of impoverishing the creative capacity of the global recorded music industry, while the labels themselves have been consistently evolving, "purchasing the rebel players…and developing new models of online commerce" (Spar 2001, 366). In fact, relevant data has shown that in the first decade of the 21st century, total expenditures on music have at least been stable and that, as a whole, the music industry has witnessed a quite considerable overall growth rate (Hesmondhalgh 2007; Karaganis 2011; Oberholzer-Gee and Strumpf 2010). This information indicates that the music industry actually possesses a well-functioning self-adaptation mechanism in the face of digitalization.

Using neo-institutional economics terms (Lin 1989), Napster-initiated global, digital music piracy served ironically as a Robin Hood-like agent: that is, it imposed forced institutional change upon the recorded music industry in the digital age when the perceived or, more accurately, imagined high costs of industry-wide digital transformation did not provide much incentive for change. In other words, the oligopoly formed by those powerful incumbents wanted to maintain the status quo but was forced into action by the emerging digital pirates. Shepherding the whole copyright industry, the recorded music industry gradually transplanted the private property regime into cyberspace to consolidate the digital foundation of its future market.

(Digital) movie piracy in Mainland China: A pioneer for Hollywood

Hollywood has been outraged by the rampant movie piracy in mainland China ever since pirated VCDs swept across this enormous developing country in the middle of the 1990s. According to *The Cost of Movie Piracy*, the major US motion picture studios lost US$6.1 billion in 2005 to piracy worldwide, while revenue loss in mainland China was estimated at US$244 million (L.E.K. 2005). This calculation, however, was not only methodologically problematic, since it was based on the now discarded "one-to-one correspondence between pirated goods and lost sales" (Karaganis 2011, 14), but also completely (and probably consciously) ignored the positive externalities of movie piracy: by giving more consumers access to movies, piracy has either taught the audience to appreciate Hollywood cinema or exposed them to advertisement for movie-related products in both symbolic and physical forms.[5]

The distinctive feature of intellectual property rights is that it creates an artificial monopoly on a specific intellectual output, which per se is more like a public good that could otherwise exhibit a high degree of non-rivalry and non-excludability. Monopoly inevitably leads to the deadweight loss of social welfare, because a monopolist can charge a price higher than the marginal cost of the production of an individual unit of products or services. This leads to the exclusion of a certain number of consumers whose marginal benefit of buying a product or service actually exceeds the marginal cost of producing it by the monopolistic producer (Landes and Posner 1989). In view of this monopoly-induced deadweight loss, pirated DVDs and Internet downloading in Mainland China might have provided a cost-efficient opportunity for those excluded to sample the overly charged yet unknown Hollywood content. This, it has been well argued, has ultimately helped Hollywood to cultivate a receptive, if not captive, Chinese fan base for Hollywood products since they constitute the content of the dominant majority of pirated DVDs in mainland China and digital movie files on the Internet (Wang 2006).

This cultivation effect has already been clearly demonstrated by two statistical facts related to Mainland China's imported movie market. The first is that, as a whole and compared to Chinese movies, imported Hollywood movies have

5 Pirated DVDs and online piracy (P2P file-sharing and streaming are the leading forms) have replaced pirated VCDs as the dominant form of movie piracy in urban Mainland China since the early 2000s.

performed very competitively in the box office in Mainland cinemas. From 1994 to 2002, imported revenue-sharing foreign movies dominated the box office in Mainland China (The China Film Association Working Committee for Theory and Criticism 2008, 137). Even from 2003, the first year that Chinese movies as a whole began to gross more box office revenues than imported revenue-sharing movies, the rate of average box office receipts for imported revenue-sharing movies remains much higher than that for Chinese movies (ibid., 140; The China Film Association Research Centre for Film Industry 2008, 16).[6] More than a decade ago, a *New York Times* article asserted that the piracy trade in China has dampened the lure of Hollywood films in movie theatres (Smith 2000b). The box office successes in Chinese movie theatres in the last decade of many products, including *The Matrix*, *Harry Potter*, *Avatar* and *Transformations* franchises, have loudly refuted this dire prediction.

The second fact is that the typical 'pirates' are young people living in the urban areas aged between 15-25 years (L.E.K. 2005). This is the very group which constitutes the lion's share of the movie-going population in Mainland China (The China Film Association Research Centre for Film Industry 2008, 344). Although some of them might become persistent pirates, there is likely to be a change of behavior amongst the majority of this group. That is, when they enter the workforce and become well-paid professionals, they will lose the spare time to search for pirated movies, and are likely to turn to official (legal) products or services. This will not only save them time, but official products can provide unique added values only accessible to legal customers.

Besides this cultivation effect, movie piracy also has a promotional function. One of the most distinctive features of contemporary Hollywood is its reliance upon and strategic marketing of blockbusters. This is particularly the case with franchised blockbusters that hold a huge potential to become sustained media events through an ongoing merchandise strategy (Grainge 2007). Domestic box office receipts usually account for only a quarter of franchised blockbusters' long tail streams of revenues (Allen 2005). In a sense, the theatrical release for a franchise blockbuster serves more like a promotional campaign for ensuing derivative products such as DVDs, games, toys, books, clothes, collectibles, drinks and other derived commodities. In light of this, watching the movie itself is the

6 At least until the end of 2007, almost 90 percent of these revenue-sharing movies have been Hollywood blockbusters. See The China Film Association Working Committee for Theory and Criticism, 2008 *Report on Chinese Film Art* (Beijing: China Film Publishing House, 2008: 135).

decisive moment of consolidating brand loyalty (or brand aversion if the movie turns out to be a failed one) among the movie audience. In fact, some audience members may sublime themselves into lifelong myrmidons, enthusiastically consuming all types of ancillary goods spawned by the movie and actively engaging in the symbolic reproduction and reconstruction of the original cinematic text.

In the context of Mainland China's movie market, piracy's promotional effect on the sale of blockbuster-derived downstream commodities should be acknowledged. Because the sales of blockbuster-derived downstream commodities like books, toys and clothes depend heavily on the audience's emotional identification with the movie as a brand, the enlarged consumer base of the pervasive movie piracy in Mainland China might tremendously contribute to the wide demand for those goods among Chinese movie fans. Once those consumer-pirates of a movie become financially established, their attachment toward the movie will be materialized through the purchase of derived goods.

One particular case that has at least partially indicated this promotional effect of piracy for downstream 'commodities' is the TV drama, *Prison Break. Prison Break*, which averaged 9.2 million viewers per week in its first season in the US, was never legally introduced on the Mainland China TV market due to concerns about its anti-law enforcement theme and explicit violence (China Daily 2007). However, *Prison Break* immediately became the most popular American TV drama in Mainland China, especially among college students and young white collar employees, even though the only way for the Chinese audience to gain timely access to every new episode was through digital piracy.[7] An official Chinese website dedicated to *Prison Break* was established by Chinese fans in 2005 to provide information about the development of the plot, the activity and background of the actors, photos, and ringtones derived from the show. This website also posts advertisements for some items presented in the drama such as the black T-shirt the central character, Michael Scofield, wears, and other personal ornaments, which have generated significant sales (Commercial Times 2009).

When the drama series finally ended in May 2009, more than 2 million posts were added to the "*Prison Break* Forum" on Baidu.com, the most used search engine in mainland China, lamenting "the end of Prison Break as the end of

7 The online audience survey conducted by *Prison Break*'s official Chinese website shows that 88 percent of the audience got access to the drama through the Internet. Various accounts made by fans or cultural observers have also confirmed the critical role played by the Internet. See the fan-created official Chinese website for *Prison Break*: http://www.prisonbreak.cn, last visited on 15 June 2010.

everything" (Cheng 2009). This enthusiasm made Wentworth Miller, the actor who played Michael Scofield, a superstar in Mainland China. When Miller came to Shanghai in October 2008 to do an advertisement for a local fashion brand, he not only took away RMB 5 million (US$700,000), but also created a sensation at every public appearance (Enorth 2008).

While these two positive effects of movie piracy cannot be easily quantified to measure exactly to what extent they have compensated for the revenue loss claimed by Hollywood, MPAA representatives seem to have noticed their existence. As such, they have softened their stance toward piracy, treating piracy more as "a proxy for unmet consumer demand" (Karaganis 2011, 66) rather than outright robbery.

Dismantling the subjugation/resistance dichotomy and beyond

These three case studies are not just isolated accidents but rather quite representative of the overall trajectory. In fact, the copyright industry of the US – music, movie, TV, software, video game – witnessed a "veritable golden age" in the 2000s (Karaganis 2011, 40-41). Apart from this statistically demonstrable phenomenon, digital piracy has facilitated the necessary nirvana of creative destruction for the copyright industry in the age of the Internet, spurring it to be more efficient in introducing the regime of intellectual property rights into cyberspace to build a robust and sustainable digital economy to at least supplement its analog counterpart. Free-of-charge pirated media products have deeply entrenched consumers into a habitual pursuit for more convenient ways to obtain new content, thus situating them in a more susceptible position to accept those more accessible yet paid-for digital services and products touted by the copyright industry 2.0.

This breaks down the conventional dichotomy between the copyright industry's demonizing of piracy as a destructive attack on the livelihood of media producers on the one hand, and the digital citizens' and some authors' idealization of piracy as their moral resistance against capitalist exploitation of human creativity on the other. What we see is the supposedly resistant pole assisting rather than resisting the corporate pole. This then dissolves the dichotomy into a double subjugation. One is imposed by the copyright industry, which has been trying, through anti-piracy rhetoric, to subjugate the susceptible portion of digital pirates into guilty criminals who then subjectively converted themselves into docile consumers.

The digital pirates themselves impose the other subjugation: they have been trying, through anti-capitalist declarations, to subjugate the die-hard digital pirates into self-deceived grassroots heroes. These 'heroes' then righteously continue to upload and exchange digitized media products on the Internet only to increase the fan/user base for industry-produced media artifacts.

A bold hypothesis can be proposed based on Foucault's insight that power "needs to be considered as a productive network which runs through the whole social body, much more than as a negative instance whose function is repression" (1980, 119). Contrary to the Frankfurt School's argument that the culture industry maintains its power by depriving the public of their consciousness of resistance (Horkheimer and Adorno 1944/2006), the industry cunningly cultivates the illusion of resistance among digital pirates by its provocative anti-piracy language to sustain a necessary level of piracy. This not only provides the very pretext for its copyright discourse and worldwide copyright education campaigns, but also helps to ensnare potential pirate-consumers who would otherwise be excluded from the consumption of industry-produced media products. The purportedly resistant pirates are no less productive – or 'consumptive' – than the docile consumers. Both of them are integral parts in the operation of the uneven power relations between the copyright industry and the consuming public.

The copyright industry may contemptuously ridicule this 'cunning cultivation hypothesis', denying any intention of maintaining an ecology of digital piracy to achieve some kind of sustainable development. However, the exercise of power does not always have to be intentional: it can also be non-subjective and strategic (Heller 1996, 87-88). As the three cases demonstrate, the copyright industry initially did try to launch an anti-piracy crusade to eradicate this economic menace, but later on, the industry unintentionally came to notice the positive externality effects of digital piracy. A tacit maneuvering of the (anti-)piracy discourse thus emerged among the industrial players in the blurred intersection of intention and accident, which did not end the subjugation, but changed the way of exercising it.

The anti-capitalist resistance marshaled up by digital piracy is thus doomed to be futile. This is because both the activity and rhetoric of the digital pirates are still entrapped within the very discursive hegemony of intellectual property that they have been seeking to subvert (Harold 2007, 130-132, 137-138). Unless digital pirates start to voluntarily share creative products made by themselves rather than those made by other people without their prior permission, they will not provide an alternative discourse to replace the copyright regime and constitute a formidable force of cultural resistance (Reyman 2010, 145). It must be recognized that taking and sharing other people's creative products without their prior permission is exactly what the capitalist conception of private property was conjured up to illegalize and thus to subjugate with various institutional mechanisms of enforcement such as courts, litigation and police. In view of this, the most, if not the only, effective way for digital citizens to resist capitalist copyright discourse is not to further motivate its subjugation mechanism by indulging and self-subjugating in the anti-capitalist myth of digital piracy, but to de-subjugate themselves by refusing to participate, materially and rhetorically, in the exclusivity-based copyright discourse at all. In other words, rendering irrelevant the copyright discourse, upon which the corporate media's dominant power is based, is the ultimate weapon of destroying its exercise of power.

However, voluntarily sharing cultural products made by digital citizens themselves constitutes only the nascent beginning of marginalizing the copyright regime. The conception of intellectual creation as private property which underlies the whole intellectual property discourse and justifies the owners' final control of the distribution and consumption of their creative products may still haunt us at this stage, as the effort of Creative Commons has indicated (Elkin-Koren 2006, 344).

An alternative disciplinary regime that reconstructs the field of human creativity must be based upon the de-propertization or collectivization of intellectual creations, which centers around the historically accumulative contributions made by individuals as components of a collective human community (Zemer 2007) or on the voluntary mutual respect cultivated among all community members (Carter 1988, 126-141). Wikipedia has already proven the efficiency of this alternative intellectual production and distribution model, which will certainly increase as the costs associated with creative co-operation continue to decrease with the rapid improvement of digital technologies. If digital citizens really want to resist the cultural monopoly held by the copyright industry, then what they should do is not to "steal bits and pieces of property from the kingdom while leaving the monarchy intact" (Harold 2007, 131). Rather, there is a need to make full use of enabling digital technologies and distribution platforms to form a collectively creative community which relies on a shared respect for each member's intellectual contribution to voluntarily produce peer-based cultural artifacts without any constraint of exclusivity.

It is the subjectivity constituted within such a non-property-based discursive regime that holds the revolutionary potential to gradually disintegrate the copyright rhetoric and deliver it to the garbage heap of history.

References

Allen, Robert C. (2005). "Technology, Social Change, and the Transformation of American Cinema," paper presented on the Centennial Anniversary of Chinese Cinema Conference, Shanghai, China.

Bass, Dina (2011). "Software Piracy Losses Jump to $59 Billion in 2010, Report Says." *Bloomberg*, 12 May 2011. Retrieved 1 December 2011, from .http://www.bloomberg.com/news/2011-05-12/software-piracy-losses-jump-to-59-billion-in-2010-report-says.html

Blume, Steven E. (2004). "The Revenue Streams: An Overview." In Jason E. Squire (ed.). *The Movie Business Book* (3rd ed.). New York: Fireside.

Business Software Alliance (2004). "2004 Piracy Study." Retrieved 15 June 2010, from http://www.bsa.or.jp/file/PiracyStudy_E.pdf

Carter, Alan (1988). *The Philosophical Foundations of Property Rights*. Hemel Hempstead: Harvester.

China Daily (2007). "CCTV Won't Introduce the Violence-themed *Prison Break*." China Daily, 31 January 2007. Retrieved 15 June 2010, from http://www.chinadaily.com.cn/hqylss/2007-01/31/content_797398.htm

Chinese State Council (2010). "Furthering the Use of Legal Software Copies in Government Units." Retrieved 1 December 2011, from http://www.gov.cn/zwgk/2010-10/28/content_1732603.htm

Cheng, Xuelian (2009). "From Small Audience to Mass Audience." Retrieved 15 June 2010, from http://chenxuelian.blshe.com/post/11461/440292

Commercial Times (2009). "This Is The Way *Prison Break* Has Been Making Money In China," 19 May 2009. Retrieved 15 June 2010, from http://epaper.lnd.com.cn/sdsb/20090519/index.htm

Cooper, Mark N. (2005). *Time for the Recording Industry to Face the Music: The Political, Social and Economic Benefits of Peer-to-Peer Communications Networks*. Stanford: Stanford Law School Center For Internet And Society.

Enorth (2008). "Miller in Shanghai to be an Advertisement Spokesperson." Retrieved 15 June 2012, from http://ent.enorth.com.cn/system/2008/10/19/003727683.shtml

Kirkpatrick, David (2007). "How Microsoft Conquered China," *CNN Money*, 17 June 2007. Retrieved 1 December 2011, from http://money.cnn.com/magazines/fortune/fortune_archive/2007/07/23/100134488/

Elkin-Koren, Niva (2006). "Exploring Creative Commons: A Skeptical View of a Worthy Pursuit." In Lucie Guibault and P. Bernt Hugenholtz (eds). *The*

Future of the Public Domain: Identifying the Commons in Information Law. Kluwer Law International.
Fairchild, Charles (2008). *Pop Idols and Pirates: Mechanisms of Consumption and the Global Circulation of Popular Music*. Hampshire: Ashgate Publishing Limited.
Fletcher, Owen and Jason Dean (2011). "Ballmer Bares China Travails." *The Wall Street Journal*, 26 May 2011. Retrieved 1 December 2011, from http://online.wsj.com/article/SB10001424052702303654804576347190248544826.html#
Foucault, Michel (1980). *Power/Knowledge*. New York: Pantheon Books.
Grainge, Paul (2007). *Brand Hollywood: Selling Entertainment in a Global Media Age*. London: Routledge.
Harold, Christine (2007). *Our Space: Resisting the Corporate Control of Culture*. Minneapolis: University of Minnesota Press.
Heller, Kevin Jon (1996). "Power, Subjectification and Resistance in Foucault." *SubStance*, 25:1.
Hesmondhalgh, David (2007). "Digitalization, Music and Copyright," *Open University CRESC Working Paper Series*, No. 30. Retrieved 15 June 2010, from http://www.cresc.ac.uk/sites/default/files/wp30.pdf
Honigsberg, Peter Jan (2002). "The Evolution and Revolution of Napster," 36 *U.S.F. L. Rev*. 474.
Horkheimer, Max and Theodor W. Adorno (1944/2006). "The Culture Industry: Enlightenment as Mass Deception." Meenakshi Gigi Durham and Douglas M. Kellner (eds). *Media and Cultural Studies: KeyWorks*. Oxford: Blackwell Publishing.
IFPI (2006). *2006 Digital Music Report*. Retrieved 9 July, 2013, from www.ifpi.org/content/library/digital-music-report-2006.pdf
IFPI (2010). *2010 Digital Music Report*. Retrieved 9 July, 2013, from http://www.ifpi.org/content/library/DMR2010.pdf
Karaganis, Joe (ed.) (2011). *Media Piracy in Emerging Economies*. New York: Social Science Research Council.
Katz, Ariel (2005). "A Network Effects Perspective on Software Piracy." *The University of Toronto Law Journal*. 55, 155.
L.E.K. (2005). *The Cost of Movie Piracy*. Retrieved 9 July, 2013, from http://www.austg.com/include/downloads/PirateProfile.pdf
Landes, William M. and Richard A. Posner (1989). "An Economic Analysis of Copyright Law." *Journal of Legal Studies*, 18, 325.
Lin, Justin Yifu (1989). "A Theory of Institutional Change: Induced and Imposed Change." *Cato Journal*, 9, 1.
Liu Binjie (2007). "Thoroughly Implementing the Spirit of the 17th National Congress of CPC to Further Promote the Use of Authorized Software." *China Press and Publication Journal*, December 17 2007.
Lu, Jia and Ian Weber (2008). "Chinese Government and Software Copyright: Manipulating the Boundaries between Public and private." *International Journal of Communication*, 1, 81.
Mark, Roy (2003). "DOJ Ends Antitrust Probe of Online Music." *Internet News*,

December 24 2003. Retrieved 15 June 2013, from http://www.Internetnews.com/ec-news/article.php/3292801/DOJ-Ends-Antitrust-Probe-of-Online-Music.htm

May, Christopher (2010). *The Global Political Economy of Intellectual Property Rights.* London and New York: Routledge.

Meza, Philip E. (2007). *Coming Attractions? Hollywood, High Tech, and the Future of Entertainment.* Stanford: Stanford University Press.

Microsoft, "Addressing Global Software Piracy," Retrieved 15 June 2013, from http://www.microsoft.com/en-us/news/presskits/antipiracy/docs/piracy10.pdf.

Mondok, Matt (2007). "Microsoft Executive: Pirating Software? Choose Microsoft!" *Ars Technica*, March 12 2007. Retrieved 31 December 2011, from http://arstechnica.com/microsoft/news/2007/03/microsoft-executive-pirating-software-choose-microsoft.ars.

Oberholzer-Gee, Felix, and Koleman Strumpf (2007). "The Effect of File Sharing on Record Sales: An Empirical Analysis," *Journal of Political Economy*, 115, 1.

Oberholzer-Gee, Felix and Koleman Strumpf (2010). "File Sharing and Copyright." In Josh Lerner and Scott Stern (eds). *Innovation Policy and the Economy*, 10, 19-55. Chicago: University of Chicago Press.

Piller, Charles (2006). "How Piracy Opens Doors for Windows," *Los Angeles Times*, April 9 2005. Retrieved 1 December 2011, from http://articles.latimes.com/2006/apr/09/business/fi-micropiracy9

Reyman, Jessica (2010). *The Rhetoric of Intellectual Property: Copyright Law and the Regulation of Digital Culture.* New York: Routledge.

RIAA (2003). "Issues: Anti-Piracy." Retrieved 15 June 2010 from http://www.riaa.com/issues/piracy/default.asp

Slater, Don (2000). "Consumption Without Scarcity: Exchange and Normativity in an Internet Setting." In Peter Jackson, Michelle Lowe, Daniel Miller and Frank Mort (eds). *Commercial Cultures: Economics, Practices, Spaces.* Oxford: Berg.

Slive, Joshua and Dan Bernhardt (1998). "Pirated for Profit," *Canadian Journal of Economics*, 31, 886.

Shen, Xiaobai (2005). "A Dilemma for Developing Countries in Intellectual Property strategy? Lessons from a Case Study of Software Piracy and Microsoft in China." *Science and Public Policy*, 32, 187.

Smith, Craig S. (2000a). "Fearing Control by Microsoft, China Backs the Linux System." *The New York Times*, July 7 2000.

Smith, Craig S. (2000b). "A Tale of Piracy: How the Chinese Stole the Grinch," *The New York Times*, December 12 2000.

Spar, Deborah (2001). *Ruling the Waves: Cycles of Discovery, Chaos, and Wealth from the Compass to the Internet.* New York: Harcourt.

Spring, Tom (2002). "Digital Music: Worth Buying Yet?." *PC World*, January 19 2002. Retrieved 15 June 2010, from http://www.pcworld.com/article/80564/digital_music_worth_buying_yet.html

Strangelove, Michael (2005). *The Empire of Mind: Digital Piracy and the Anti-Capitalist Movement.* Toronto: University of Toronto Press.

The China Film Association Research Centre for Film Industry (2008). *2008 Research Report on Chinese Film Industry.* Beijing: China Film Publishing House.
The China Film Association Working Committee for Theory and Criticism (2008). *2008 Report on Chinese Film Art.* Beijing: China Film Publishing House.
Wang, Shujen (2006). "Breaks, Flows, and Other In-between Spaces: Rethinking Piracy and Copyright Governance." *Policy Futures in Education*, 4, 410.
Workman, Daniel, "Microsoft Global Sales." Retrieved 1 December 2011, from http://daniel-workman.suite101.com/microsoft-global-sales-a8478
Xu, Lun (2011). "A Long Battle," *Global Entrepreneurs*, 5. Retrieved 1 December 2011, from http://www.gemag.com.cn/html/2011/cxyj_0318/23604.html
Yang, Qi (2011). "Authorized Software Fighting Back: Microsoft is Tightening it Control upon End User Market." *Science Times*, May 14 2011.
Yu, Peter K. (2004). "The Escalating Copyright Wars." *Hofstra Law Review*, 32, 907.
Zemer, Lior (2007). *The Idea of Authorship in Copyright.* Hampshire: Ashgate Publishing Limited.
Zheng, Changeng (2007). "Microsoft's Successful Face-Off in China." Retrieved 1 December 2011, from http://www.boraid.com/darticle3/list.asp?id=82195

Part III – Practice

The Justifications of Piracy: Differences in Conceptualization and Argumentation Between Active Uploaders and Other File-sharers

Jonas Andersson Schwarz and Stefan Larsson

It may be that universal history is the history of a handful of metaphors. The purpose of this note will be to sketch a chapter of that history.
(Jorge Luis Borges, 'The Fearful Sphere of Pascal')

Introduction[1]

This chapter is, in part, about law and legal change. Law – especially intellectual property law – is greatly challenged in a digital society where media is distributed in global networks; for example, via BitTorrent sites such as The Pirate Bay. New norms for behavior, set up under new pre-conditions in an online environment, have emerged alongside the legal, emphasizing some sort of norm-pluralism beyond any traditional discourse on deviancy (Larsson and Hydén 2010). This can be seen as a step in a legal development that is bigger than the narrow focus on black letter law. Such developments also force us to see the law's boundaries and constraints, in its metamorphosis and perhaps painful adaptation to the emergence of other types of norms and conceptions of law.

In a highly metaphoric article on legal change, Boaventura de Sousa Santos (1987) uses the Nietzschean three-step metamorphosis of the human spirit to display how law has developed in the modern era. He explains three versions of metamorphosis, in terms of animal metaphors and their respective tales:

> In the first one the spirit becomes a camel; then the camel becomes a lion; and finally the lion becomes a child (1987, 279).

De Sousa Santos is interested in the process of legal change and what these steps mean for legal development. For example, he is concerned with the 'camelization of law,' where it 'allows itself to be loaded with any values or beliefs

1 The work of analyzing the survey results was made possible thanks to funding from Riksbankens Jubileumsfond, The Knowledge Foundation, Lund University Internet Institute (LUii) and the Department for Sociology of Law at Lund University. The authors wish to express their gratitude.

humanity wants to load it with' (1987, 279-280). In the transitional middle-step signified by 'the lion', it is 'the animal in revolt against the values and beliefs it was loaded with before,' which de Sousa Santos explains is 'the spirit of negativity that substitutes "I will" for "thou shalt"'. The lion is stuck in its *state of resistance*, 'incapable of creating new values to replace the old ones,' and in order to take a step further it must undergo a third metamorphosis 'through which the lion becomes a child' – namely, a new beginning, *without resentment*, resulting in the creation of new values.

Online piracy is often described in terms of this state of resistance. Such descriptions somewhat miss the state of innovation that piracy displays (Larsson et al. 2012a; Palmås et al., 2014). In this chapter, we will present empirical data on *the ways the future is envisaged* within a vast, global userbase of file sharers. It categorizes the 'will' and 'would' of two different groups in this community: the core group of high-frequency uploaders and the broader and more common group of non-uploading users. We aim to show the continuities and differences in normative frameworks among these groups, searching for the metamorphosis from the resistance of 'the lion' to the 'new values' of 'the child'.

In April 2011 the Cybernorms research group conducted a global file sharing survey known as the Research Bay study with more than 75,000 respondents (Larsson et al. 2012b; Svensson et al. 2013; 2014). Using previous theoretical findings of the two authors, this chapter analyses the data from the open answers of this survey, in order to understand *modes of justification that different conceptions of file sharing reinforce* and present a model for approaching 'piracy' more systematically than in much of the contemporary literature.

'Piracy' in terms of describing something similar to unauthorized copying of files is, essentially, a metaphor. Cognitive linguists not only teach us that metaphors are of fundamental importance for abstract thought – metaphors also come in clusters, jointly giving meaning to each other (Lakoff and Johnson 1980; 1999). Although hard to detect, this is of great relevance to rhetorical practices and even legal justification (Larsson 2011a; 2011b; 2011c; 2012a; 2012b; 2013a). Many metaphors rely on, or are constructed from *conceptions* of society. It has been argued that much of the conflict connected to the regulation of copyright today can be described in terms of a battle of such conceptions (Larsson 2011b, 119-124; 2013b).

The mutability of the notion of 'piracy' can serve to illustrate how dependent these conceptions are on what framing of social reality they are based upon. Different *regimes of justification* (Andersson 2010; Boltanski and Thévenot 2006) stipulate different ways of assessing piracy and its alleged good or bad repercussions. For example, within a 'civic' order of assessment where concerns are raised for 'the whole of society,' piracy and/or file sharing might be seen to hit some sectors rather badly, while others would benefit from it: on the whole, however, society would be seen to benefit from it (Andersen and Frenz 2007; Huygen et al. 2009; Peitz and Waelbroeck 2006). The global outcome of piracy, all things considered, is likely to be hard to completely assess as there will be various different developments offsetting each other. On the other hand, within certain industrial orders of assessment and depending on sector, the same phenomenon might be perceived to have more clearly detrimental or beneficial effects (Barry and Slater 2005; Callon 1998).

By assessing examples of file-sharer discourse gathered from the abovementioned survey, we will explore the conceptions that much of this discourse hinges upon. Other studies have indicated that specialization and professionalization takes place within the 'ecosystem' of file-sharing communities (Andersson Schwarz 2013c; Balázs 2013; de Kaminski et al. 2013; Larsson et al. 2012a; 2012b; Svensson et al. 2013; 2014). Therefore, it is of clear interest to focus on one of the key groups within the file sharing community, namely the group of uploaders. This is indeed a minority. Of all the respondents in the Research Bay study, the group that alleged to contribute by uploading files 'every day or almost every day' only consisted of slightly more than 5 percent. In our study, we compare this group to the much larger group of respondents that download files and at the same time held that they 'never upload' (which was approximately 60 percent of participants).

The aim of our chapter is to compare *conceptions of reality*, and more specifically the *regimes of justification* contained therein. Here the purpose is to trace potential *differences in norms and viewpoints* between people who simply download the things they want (while, wittingly or unwittingly, passing it on to others) and those who actively upload new material. In the light of this, a number of more explicit questions may be raised:

1. Given the assumed illegality of their actions, how do these uploaders and non-uploaders justify their own behavior?
2. What different modes of justification can empirically be seen, and how are these distributed?

3. How is the future development of 'piracy' and file sharing approached and conceptualized by these respondents?

In sum, we will explore the ways in which file sharers themselves conceive of the future of 'piracy' – which is of course interrelated with the various ways in which 'piracy' is conceived in wider society.

Metaphors and conceptions in a digital context

The understanding of a structural discrepancy inherent to copyright and piracy can be highlighted through taking a norm perspective. Here, the discrepancy is seen as a gap between *legal norms* (copyright) and *social norms* that do not condemn the vernacular sharing of copyright-infringing content (Feldman and Nadler 2006; de Kaminski et al. 2013; Larsson 2011b; Schultz 2007; Svensson and Larsson 2012; Wingrove et al. 2010). The analysis in this chapter is a way to understand how file sharing and its illegality is differently conceptualized – and, hence, justified – by different types of file sharers. Cognitive theory has been argued to be of significance to norm studies (Larsson 2012b; 2013a) and has been particularly effective in the analysis of law (Johnson 2007; Winter 2001; 2008), legal decision-making (Berger 2009), and particularly, for online piracy (Larsson 2011b; 2012a).

The key idea with metaphors is that they are analogies that allow us to map one experience (*the target domain*) in the terminology of another experience (*the source domain*). This allows us to acquire an understanding of complex topics or new situations such as digital phenomena (Larsson 2011b; 2013b). For example, when we speak of piracy in terms of unauthorized sharing of media files, we use a metaphor which might appear clear and figurative in the source domain, yet hides the much more complex social reality that it is mapped upon. That is because unauthorized sharing can occur due to a number of reasons, in a number of contexts, with a number of outcomes, intended or unintended. Without metaphors, we have no means for speaking and thinking of abstract entities (Lakoff and Johnson 1999). The digital environment, having been introduced very late in the socio-lingual context, is in other words marked by being based on abstract concepts and material realities hidden from vision.

The benefit of analyzing metaphors in relation to digital file sharing is that it can reveal its underlying conceptions (Larsson 2011b; Larsson and Hydén 2010). This is concomitant with Andersson Schwarz's (2010, 2013b) approach where arguments and justifications are focused in order to relate how material constraints prescribe behaviors, as well as how justificatory world-views shape behavior and argumentation. To focus the conceptions is to focus the framing structures of thought (Larsson 2011b, 65-70; 130-132; 2012a; 2012b). This can reveal how the different sides in the 'copyfight' are, respectively, framing the debate (as displayed in Andersson 2012; Larsson 2012b; Yar 2008). We want to argue, however, that there are also differences *within* the file-sharing community which can be elicited. How we conceptualize reality is tightly connected to the norms that control our behavior and how we reflect and justify our actions (Larsson 2013a). In turn, these conceptions may bolster – or at least correlate to – regimes of justification.

Justifications in a digital context

In order to classify or categorize the types of justifications for file sharing, we draw on the typology developed by Andersson Schwarz (2010, 2013b). He argues that acts of justification primarily serve as *ex post facto* explanations of what has already happened or what one has already done (ibid., 312). As shown by García-Álvarez et al. (2009) and Cenite et al. (2009), the morality of accessing culture depends on the social, economic and cultural context in which an individual has been raised. Cenite et al. (2009) draw on Lessig's (2004) observation that file sharing can occur due to a number of reasons and only rarely replaces a sale. However, their study makes the problematic presupposition that file sharing is premised on *gifting*. Andersson (2012) presents an alternative to this view, arguing such a position is valid for some file-sharing protocols and applications, but not necessarily for BitTorrent or so-called 'one-click hosting'. BitTorrent might generate an altogether different experience of inter-user reciprocity and gift giving than, as Giesler and Pohlmann (2003) claimed, Napster would do. Despite such a divergence in research findings, Cenite et al. (2009) confirm many of the pragmatic arguments for file sharing and the rhetoric of reciprocity and sharing. Further, file sharing is fraught with strong dichotomous associations, such as the alleged conflict (Thierer and Crews 2002) between consumers (assuming vernacular, non-hierarchical, non-profit, non-professional conceptions) and producers (assuming industrial, hierarchical, for-profit, professional conceptions). Recently, Edwards et al. (2014) have referred to Boltanski's work in order to show how the copyright industry itself is forced to appeal to general justificatory principles that make a broader claim to legitimacy.

García-Álvarez et al. (2009, 245) have shown that the intention to copy tends to be 'related to the perceived equity or fairness of relationships or exchanges with others'. Boltanski and Thévenot (2006, 27) do not write about file sharing or copying *per se*, but have coined the notion of 'regimes of justification,' in order to show how such explanations fall into different categories. They emphasize that reflexivity – imagining oneself as a part of larger systems – is inherent to processes of justification:

> ...persons must be capable of distancing themselves from their own particularities in order to reach agreement about external goods that are enumerated and defined in general terms. (ibid.)

In so doing, Boltanski and Thévenot recognize different types of generalities that both underpin respondents' analytical frameworks for understanding the social world *and* the ways they justify their behavior (2006, 9). Statistical evidence, for example, often lends itself to instances where subjects follow 'a form of industrial generality,' whereas knowledge based on examples (or anecdotes) is instead valued by 'the testimony of trustworthy informants and thus relies on a form of domestic generality' (ibid.).

Boltanski and Thévenot observe six 'orders or economies of worth'; systematic and coherent principles of evaluation that all coexist and overlap, however with their own criteria for assessment: *civic*, *market*, *inspired*, *fame*, *industrial*, and *domestic*. In Boltanski and Chiapello (2007), a seventh such order (or polity) is introduced: that of the *projective*, pertaining to project-oriented network rationality and flexibility. We will see below how a similar notion of progress could be seen to operate as a justificatory regime among our respondents. It is important to emphasize the situational character of justification as individuals shift in a flexible way 'from one mode of adjustment to another, from one measure of worth to another' (Boltanski and Thévenot 2006, 16).

Applying this template to file sharing, the invocation of *technological unstoppability* could, for example, be described as belonging to both a notion of progress and adaptation (*projective*, flexible rationality), and to an 'engineer' or *industrial* style of reasoning. In contrast, the invocation of *privacy and freedom of speech* would belong to a *civic* style of reasoning (also related to journalistic discourse, speaking 'for' the citizens, as if it were). However, no one respondent could be entirely summarized by any one of these styles alone – which is also in concordance with

Boltanski and Thévenot's findings that any account would incorporate several such partially overlapping styles.

Further, each regime makes reference to or requires different kinds of entities. These entities belong to different categories and modes of thinking, each with their own internal normative rationale that can sometimes be incommensurable. Andersson found, in his study of Swedish file-sharers (2010), that their argumentation invokes *various collective processes* that operate on the level of society at large:

I - 'It's unstoppable'

The existing Internet infrastructure ensures that high degrees of freedom, heterogeneity, and low universal oversight cannot be suppressed without severe curtailments of civil liberties. Two related modes of reasoning invoked this global infrastructure: first, the *utilitarian/pragmatic appropriation* of impossibility of stopping the phenomenon; and second, the *civil rights appropriation* that totalitarian measures would be required to effectively stop the phenomenon on a global level, and that such measures would be disproportionate.

II - 'The artists/producers don't suffer' / 'Culture in general doesn't suffer'

A seemingly undiminished audience interest in cultural products can be noted, as consumption (except for audio CD sales) had remained high throughout the surveyed period (2000-2009). There was little acknowledgement that artistic output would suffer – with the exception of the music sector, where economic incentives for production would be biased more towards live performances and licensing than towards record sales. This mode of reasoning, when sympathizing with professional producers, could be said to fall under a *unionist appropriation*, where the potential economic harm to professional cultural producers is the main referent. When *not* sympathizing with producers/artists, it could rather be said to represent an *audience appropriation*, indifferent to the fate of artists but nevertheless dedicated to the quality of output.

III - It's democratic'

The veritable 'body politic' of the aggregated humans and machines in P2P networks – which is unique in that it is simultaneously an aggregate of topographic machine nodes and of vaguely corresponding human beings – forms something which some of the respondents in Andersson (2010) likened to a 'people's movement'. That is, a nebulous mass that has occasional spokespersons and 'strategic sovereigns' (Andersson 2009) in the form of hubs like The Pirate Bay. Among file sharers, a *collectivist appropriation* can be noted; a notion that culture should be accessible to everyone. This perspective sees communication as a 'commons' or shared resource rather than as discrete units of transmissive 'content'. This notion could be connected to the metaphor of a civic 'multitude' (Hardt and Negri 2004; Virno 2003). It also relates to the *civil rights appropriation* listed under entity (I) above. Arguably, the civil rights appropriation pertaining to (III) is more about the 'weight' of the collective whereas entity (I) would be more about the safeguarding of *individual* rights, like the right to privacy.

The macro-economic appropriation of the alleged 'overall good' for society underpins each of these regimes: a value that is arguably particularly strong in Sweden (Andersson 2011) given the country's unusually high levels of civic trust in the national state.

Method and selection

In April 2011 the *Cybernorms* research group conducted a survey, hyperlinked to the front page of The Pirate Bay website. This study is sometimes referred to as the Research Bay study, due to the fact that during its 72 hours of operation it replaced the famous Pirate Bay ship logo into one displaying a magnifier over the ship (Svensson et al. 2013; 2014). Over these 72 hours, the study received over 75,000 responses from across the world. The survey included an open section where the respondents could freely answer the following question:

> Please give us your own comments on the topic of file-sharing, especially how the situation in your home country looks like and what you think will be the next big thing when it comes to the Internet and/or file-sharing.

Out of the 75,901 respondents, 67,838 had answered this question. In order to handle this massive material and analyze the justificatory regimes for piracy, three strategic selections were made. A *first selection* was made, based on the frequency by which the respondents contributed to the community by uploading material. 5.3 percent (3,593 individuals) had professed to actively upload 'every day or almost every day'. We wanted to compare the answers of this minority of uploaders to the answers of the 61.4 percent (41,616 individuals) who 'never' upload but still admitted to occasionally or often download.

Excerpts from these bodies of text had to be made, as the 'non-uploader' answers contained 5,900,000 characters and the smaller corpus of 'uploader' answers contained 386,000 characters. A *second selection* was made: We randomly chose two 200,000-character excerpts. These two excerpts were quantitatively analyzed[2] in order to see what words were the most common. The most commonly occurring word – other than 'file' and various modalities of 'share' (see Table 2) – was 'will' (including its alternative tense, 'would'). This led to a *third selection*, in order to concentrate on the normative character of how the respondents argued that things 'will be,' 'would be,' or 'would become'. Hence, all statements in each 200,000-character corpus containing the words 'will' and 'would' were categorized, coded, and counted by means of a quantitative content analysis, and in accordance with the theoretically substantiated tropes/invocations/'modes of justification' outlined above.

We analyzed the ways in which the answers to the Research Bay open question were formulated and what generalities they invoke, and compared the answers of uploaders to the answers of those who never upload. We did not aim to make a systematic analysis pertaining to representation or ethnography, as we believe this survey was not entirely representative of file sharers in general, and even less so of general Internet users. This is because participation was limited to those who regularly frequent The Pirate Bay's front page, which is a different group than those who use, for example, Google to find particular torrents. Instead, we concentrated on the ways the arguments were constituted, drawing on an analysis where empirical findings were more interesting in their capacity of being *specimens of reasoning*, rather than giving ethnographic or biographic information about the general population of file sharers and/or Internet users.

First selection: uploaders vs. non-uploaders

The data highlights a significant difference in the frequency of downloading between the groups who share the most and the group that does not upload at all (see Table 1). Of those who upload 'every or almost every day' a very large majority of 82.1 percent also download 'every or almost every day'. Meanwhile, the group that allegedly 'never' upload still asserted that they download, but less frequently: a third of them download 'every or almost every day', another third 'more than once a week', yet another third 'more than once a month'. The composition of this group is likely to be very similar to the composition of the

2 For this, VocabGrabber (http://www.visualthesaurus.com/vocabgrabber/) was used; it has a limit of 200,000 characters per corpus.

overall population of Pirate Bay users. Only 8.8 percent of those who never upload stated that they never download either: we cannot be certain how this group of respondants came across the survey but it is likely they came across it through visiting the Pirate Bay website without really using it to actively up- or download. As such, they are not part of the selection of comments that are analyzed below.

How often do you download?	Never	More than once a month	More than once a week	Every day or almost every day	Total
The group that upload "every or almost every day"	3.9% (138)	4.4% (156)	9.7% (346)	82.1% (2,936)	100% (3,576)
The group that never upload	8.8% (4,013)	30.4% (13,903)	30.5% (13,938)	30.3% (13,826)	100% (45,680)

Table 1: *Downloading frequency for those who upload frequently and those who never upload.*

Other parts of the survey consisted of questions regarding *age*, *gender*, *geographical location*, as well as *up/download frequency*. This has been elaborated upon elsewhere (Svensson et al. 2013; 2014), including issues of anonymity and file sharing (Larsson et al. 2012b; cf. de Kaminski et al. 2013; Larsson et al. 2012a).

Second selection: open answers

The text from the Research Bay answers is extremely large even when only selecting those who are the most frequent uploaders. The answers differed significantly: some had used ASCII coding to make figures with the letters; some answers were pure nonsense or spam; some were very brief; others had answered carefully and thoroughly, keenly presenting their arguments. We made a selection of the two main bodies of text (frequent uploaders and those who never upload) in order to have two bodies of text that had a manageable size and had a similar amount of text in them, in order to make them comparable. The documents were cleaned; we carefully removed non-English, and nonsensical or merely phatic entries, such as 'dont know'; 'All Hail TPB =]'; 'dope shit'; 'LEATHER PANTS~!'. We did err on the side of caution, however, and often chose not to remove doubtful entries. When comparing the occurrences of most common words they were fairly similar, implying that they were thematically coherent:

	Frequent uploaders	Occurrences	Those who never upload	Occurrences
1.	share	600	will	590
2.	file	538	share	432
3.	will	517	file	403
4.	sharing	502	sharing	365
5.	have	393	have	357
6.	not	257	not	318
7.	are	255	are	242
8.	can	232	believe	241
9.	people	212	but	224
10.	but	197	download	206

Table 2: *Most common words in each 200,000-character corpus. Third selection: 'will'/'would'*

The three collective processes noted above (I-III) have been observed by Andersson Schwarz (2013b), based on a small number of qualitative, email-mediated interviews with anonymous file sharers, alongside an analysis of the discourses found online and offline. He accounts for how he could see different regimes of justification, both in his interviews and in his analysis of found discourse. There is a central difference, however, between interviews and written testimonies like the ones given by the respondents in the Research Bay questionnaire: In an interview situation, users are allowed to explicate their arguments further, and the researcher is able to probe opinions by asking follow-up questions.

In this chapter, our focus is on the specimens of reasoning found in the Research Bay answers. These respondent accounts were not interactive, but they served as further evidence that the modes of reasoning explored occur spontaneously among file sharers. Although we did not analyze publicly submitted, written discourse here – such as postings in online forums and communities, comments to blog posts and articles and so on – similar arguments appear also abundant in such settings.

The semantic selection was made by eliciting sentences that contained the words 'will' or 'would'. This was for two reasons: firstly, these were some of the most frequently occurring words; and, secondly, because we hypothesized that the sentences containing these words would refer either to *affinities* or to *temporal change or future development.* The sentences extracted would be likely to contain statements or assertions about the future (what will happen), probabilities (what would be likely to happen), or preferences (what respondents preferred would happen).

The common occurrence of 'will' and 'would' was of course an artifact from the way the open question was phrased in the questionnaire. Hence, one would need to heed the results by bearing in mind that the question explicitly asked what the respondent would think 'will be the next big thing'. Examples from from the group of non-uploaders included:

> 'They cant stop it, as they would need to check every Internet connection 24/7.'
>
> 'I wanna experience everything, if I had the money to do so I would have bought all my software, games etc...'
>
> 'If I would pay, I would pay for legal content for a reasonable price.'

The resulting corpus was two documents: the first (12,404 words; 463 entries; 590 instances of *would/will*) containing excerpts from the accounts of people who said they never upload; the second (14,096 words; 385 entries; 517 instances of *would/will*) [3] containing excerpts from the accounts of people who purportedly upload regularly. These documents were blind-tested; no headers or metadata were given to the analyst revealing which document was which.

---

3 The amount of text per entry shows that these respondents (uploaders) tended to be more verbose.

Trope	Never Uploads		Uploads Regularly		Difference
Unstoppability/resilience (technological and/or human)	**63**	**9.52%**	**81**	**11.81%**	**-2.29Δ**
Evolution of technology/progress (fickle, changing nature of p2p)	43	6.50%	27	3.94%	2.56Δ
Social norms will sway towards f-s-ing (stigma lessening)	6	0.91%	10	1.46%	-0.55Δ
Equating f-s-ing w freedom of knowledge / information (+ "everything will be digital")	19	2.87%	31	4.52%	-1.65Δ
F-s-ing will help creating new forms of culture	3	0.45%	6	0.87%	-0.42Δ
Alternative revenue streams (concerts, f-s-ing = advertising the artist/producer)	19	2.87%	31	4.52%	-1.65Δ
Care for producers - artists (incentives for producers / artists)	25	3.78%	4	0.58%	3.19Δ
Purchasing power (poor country / low-income recognition of affordance)	23	3.47%	19	2.77%	0.70Δ
National discourses (reference to nationhood, local context, anti-US etc)	22	3.32%	32	4.66%	-1.34Δ
Convenience (ease, speed, lack of commercial interruptions)	**16**	**4.42%**	**20**	**2.92%**	**-0.50Δ**
Availability / supply	**19**	**2.87%**	**31**	**4.5%**	**-1.65Δ**
Cheapness / expenditure (reference so "free preview," "less to pay" w/o bias)	**24**	**30.63%**	**29**	**4.23%**	**-0.60Δ**
• "Try before buy" (bias towards buying)	39	5.89%	35	5.10%	0.79Δ
• "I will never buy" (bias towards not buying)	18	2.72%	10	1.46%	1.26Δ
Corporate greed (middle-men, fat cats)	21	3.17%	38	5.54%	-2.37Δ
A lot of cultural production = rubbish	9	1.36%	4	0.58%	0.78Δ
Purging the market of bad artists / productions	11	1.66%	7	1.02%	0.64Δ
Artist idealism (people will produce culture without renumeration)	6	0.91%	4	0.58%	0.32Δ
Anti-advertising	5	0.76%	3	0.44%	0.32Δ
Self-directed / autonomous use ("I control my own habits / usage")	10	1.51%	9	1.31%	0.20Δ
Privacy / encryption (acknowledging it, not necessarily endorsing it)	**38**	**5.74%**	**29**	**4.23%**	**1.51Δ**
Anti-govt regulation (anti-law, anti-censorship)	**66**	**9.97%**	**77**	**11.22%**	**-1.25Δ**
Slowness of govt / establishment to adapt	10	1.51%	10	1.46%	0.05Δ
Market will absorb f-s-ing (e.g. by ad-driven models)	**76**	**11.48%**	**48**	**7.00%**	**4.48Δ**
Market failure - established companies or (at least parts of) market will wither	11	1.66%	5	0.73%	0.93Δ
Consensus / compromise (broadband tax or fee)	5	0.76%	14	2.04%	-1.29Δ
Civil rights	5	0.76%	3	0.44%	0.32Δ

Trope	Never Uploads		Uploads Regularly		Difference
Communism (sharing also money and wealth)	1	0.15%	2	0.29%	-0.14Δ
Praxis / habit remembered (once a new behavior is settled)	1	0.15%	1	0.15%	0.01Δ
File-sharing will stop (bleak future for file-sharing)	9	1.36%	4	0.58%	0.78Δ
F-s-ing is transient / ephemeral (will not be missed)	1	0.75%	0	0.00%	0.15Δ
Weight / clout of masses of people (populism)	**15**	**2.27%**	**32**	**4.66%**	**-2.40Δ**
Community / collectivism	6	0.91%	11	1.60%	-0.70Δ
Seeder / downloader differentiated from network facilitator / hub	1	0.15%	2	0.29%	-0.14Δ
Barriers of entry (uneven openness of f-s-ing networks)	11	1.66%	7	1.02%	0.64Δ
Purity / integrity of p2p networks (and bad reputation of unregulated f-s-ing)	3	0.45%	6	0.87%	-0.42Δ
Gender	2	0.30%	4	0.58%	-0.28Δ
TOTAL	**662**	**100.00%**	**686**	**100.00%**	
CLUSTERS					
Negative towards industry	70	**10.57%**	66	9.62%	0.98Δ
Positive towards industry	164	24.77%	132	19.24%	5.53Δ
Optomistic towards f-s-ing (resilience + evolution + norm)	112	16.92%	118	17.20%	-0.28Δ
Pragmatic dimensions (convenience + availability/supply + cheapness)	116	17.52%	125	18.22%	-0.70Δ
Personal resilience re surveillance (privacy + anti-government + autonomy)	114	17.22%	115	16.76%	0.46Δ
“Geist” of technology (market will absorb + evolution of f-s-ing)	119	17.98%	75	10.93%	7.04Δ
“Geist” of technology (market will absorb + evolution of f-s-ing + resilience)	182	27.49%	156	22.74%	4.75Δ

Table 3: *Distribution of tropes (absolute and relative).*

Findings

35 different categories were elicited (see Table 3). Some of these categories emerged based on the justifications noted above, while others were more inductively taken from the text as different sentiments were expressed by the respondents.

Though one critique of our method could be the subjective selection of categories, it should be noted that since the same analysis was performed on both texts, the key factor for reliability lies in this repetition, regardless of the nature of the categories themselves. Many of these different categories are related and somewhat overlap, yet point to distinct arguments expressed by respondents. Altogether, 662 discrete categorizations were made in the first text, 686 in the other. The clustering of these categorizations shows that the most commonly occurring standalone justifications/sentiments were: the notion of *unstoppability/resilience* (9.5 percent of non-uploaders, 11.8 percent of uploaders); *opposition to government regulation* (10.0 percent of non-uploaders, 11.2 percent of uploaders); and, perhaps surprisingly, the notion that *the market will eventually absorb file sharing* (11.5 percent of non-uploaders, 7.0 percent of uploaders).

Three clusters were similarly apparent in both groups:

Optimism towards file sharing:
- the notion that file sharing is unstoppable/resilient;
- the notion that file sharing evolves as a reaction to its environment;
- the notion that social norms will further sway towards it.

Pragmatic dimensions:
- convenience;
- availability/supply;
- cheapness.

Personal resilience regarding regulation/surveillance:
- privacy;
- opposition to government regulation;
- autonomy of personal consumption habits.

There was, however, a clear bias among the non-uploaders of being more positive towards the entertainment industry than the group of frequent uploaders. 24.8 percent of non-uploader sentiments could be tagged as somewhat positive towards this industry, while only 19.2 percent of uploader sentiments could be tagged in this way.

Generally, this surprising *market optimism* among the non-uploaders could be there for a number of reasons. To begin with, it could be related to Boltanski and Thévenot's (2006) *market* order, noted above, or to what Boltanski and Chiapello (2007) have elsewhere defined as *industrial* and *commercial* orders. Here, *efficiency and professional abilities* (industrial order) as well as the capacity of *supplying desirable commodities in competitive markets* (commercial order) are emphasized. Perhaps more interestingly, it could also be related to the notion of a general, non-specific 'evolution' or 'progress' of technology – a vague notion of progress, market adaptation, and emergence that could be labeled a *'Geist' of technology*.

Explicitly noting this evolution of technology was, in and of itself, not a particularly common trope (only 6.5 percent of non-uploader sentiments and 3.9 percent of uploader sentiments). The trope was clearly stronger among the non-uploaders than among the uploaders. This 'Geist,' seeming to suggest a comforting reminder that "it'll eventually work out," could be related to Boltanski and Chiapello's (2007) notion of a *project-oriented network rationality and flexibility*. Since this trope appears to portray the notion of progress as a social fact – a totality without material form but with 'facticity' and thus coercive power (Alexander 1990) – it would lend itself to being interpreted in more explicitly Durkheimian terms. Due to brevity it is not our intention to do so here, although such an analysis would be interesting.

This evolutionary, emergent *force without a center* seemed to be particularly strong among the non-uploaders, compared to the uploaders.[4] This minority of more dedicated uploaders seemed to express a somewhat different stance than the more undifferentiated, larger group of non-uploaders in that their sentiments tended to have more clearly defined subjects: the vernacular file-sharing masses on the one hand, and the entertainment industry and its cultural producers on the other one. In other words, their accounts seemed to more clearly follow the dichotomous template of a 'copyfight' conflict. Regarding the notion of *caring for the producers/artists*, this consideration only appeared in 3.8 percent of the non-uploader accounts, yet it was even rarer among the uploaders, where it was barely mentioned (0.6 percent). Similarly, the notion of *corporate greed* was more common among the active uploaders (5.5 percent) compared to the more general non-uploaders (3.2 percent).[5]

In addition, the uploaders expressed a stronger bias towards *unstoppability/resilience*[6] and *opposition to government regulation*, seeming to more often equate file sharing with the concept of free information or open knowledge. More importantly, they also noted the *weight/clout of masses* that poses file sharing as a popular, vernacular uproar against a corrupt entertainment industry. This last sentiment

4 If we include the abovementioned notions of *market absorption* and *unstoppability/resilience* as part of this cluster, 27.5 percent of the sentiments found included a reference to it. If we include *market absorption* but not the *resilience of file-sharing*, this notion of a 'Geist' was still remarkably apparent among the non-uploaders compared to the uploaders (18.0 percent of non-uploaders as opposed to 10.9 percent of uploaders).

5 The overall cluster of *negativity towards industry* however showed a stronger presence among non-uploaders (10.6 percent) than uploaders (9.6 percent).

6 The notion of *privacy/encryption* was however more apparent among the non-uploaders (5.7 percent vs. 4.2 percent).

is concomitant with Andersson Schwarz's macrosocial process III (above) and with discourses expressed by the more 'dedicated' file sharers participating in his qualitative study (Andersson Schwarz 2010; 2013b). Some quotes from the Research Bay uploaders can serve as typical for these notions:

> 'File-sharing will always exist, theres very little any laws can do to control it.'
>
> 'Filesharing will be around for as long as people are, its inevitable.'
>
> 'If it becomes too difficult to share files on the traditional Internet, a secondary version will pop up.'
>
> 'Thanks i love thepiratebay and no one regulatory service will be able to completely control it i loves Internet ite [sic] a big game for all over the world I mostly download tv shows cause in my country most tv shows are airing delayed and all of them are airing dubbed I mostly use file sharing to share important information to others on the Internet.'

Notions like 'sharing important information on the Internet' are so commonplace today that they are almost truisms. In this sense, any such statement is intertextual in nature: It invokes the larger discourse that stipulates that *interpersonal communication is to be seen as technologically mediated transmission*, a discourse that relies on the ontological understanding of what communication and culture *is*, when enacted through digital mediation. In its strong form, this discourse would arguably translate into a deterministic 'informational idealism' that stipulates that 'everything that can be digitized *will* be digitized' and equates culture with mechanistic models of transmission and dissemination.

Similarly, there is nowadays a plethora of discourses that stress the *evolutionary* nature of not only technology, but of markets and society in general. Hence, it is not surprising that these notions crop up in spontaneous replies like the ones in the Research Bay survey, as means to explain and predict the future of file sharing. What the differences between the respondent groups seem to tell us, nevertheless, is that the more active uploaders tend to be more likely to express discourses that have been noted in previous, more qualitatively oriented discussions and interviews with dedicated file sharers. This both confirms the data from these previous studies, but also shows the danger of believing that what is valid for these smaller sub-groups of activists and fans would be valid also for larger groups of consumers and citizens in society.

A small bias towards *community/collectivism* was also noted among the uploaders, but falls within the range of statistical insignificance. Instead of reading this as a clear difference from the common discourse which stipulates that *file sharing thrives on community formations* (see Andersson 2012 for a critique of this concept), the weak occurrence of this community discourse is probably attributable to the research design. The lack of interaction inherent to the survey method means that tropes that do not appear instantly or spontaneously tend not to appear at all. In a survey where the researcher is able to probe, more respondents might agree on the notion of collectivism, as well as the undisputable *gender bias*, the *barriers of entry*, and the *civil rights* dimension inherent to file sharing. Moreover, since the Research Bay survey took place in a public forum, the likelihood of *community/collectivism* as a trope is additionally decreased, in comparison to research which takes place in more closed, community-like forums, such as invite-only sites or private trackers (cf. Balázs 2013, Andersson Schwarz 2013c).

In general, the small occurrence of tropes like *mass influence*, *civil rights* and *shared community* are notable, and might be surprising: As researchers, we tend to overestimate those tropes that are of great significance to us – a miscalculation that is further worsened the more common these tropes are in the literature. Another source of error might be that a lot of critical scholarship on the topic of file sharing and 'piracy' is based on ethnographic accounts which, by design, tend to have a bias towards more verbose, dedicated and thereby, arguably, more community- and perhaps activist-oriented respondents.

Conclusion

Applying metaphors influences the ways in which one conceptualizes a given phenomenon. The ways in which one conceptualizes reality are tightly connected to what norms control our behavior and how we reflect and justify our actions. For example, the market optimism among the non-uploaders – embodying the notion of how the market can adapt and/or expand – indicates the degree to which media distribution and culture dissemination are still conceptualized in terms of market metaphors. We can contrast this to early attempts in the scholarly literature on digital file sharing to speak of 'gift economies' and 'cyber-communism' (Barbrook 2000). When compared to the smaller, more dedicated group of active uploaders, the non-uploaders (representing the majority of Pirate Bay users) appeared more positive towards market solutions and the entertainment industry. They also appeared to be more disposed towards a non-specific, generic belief in the progress, evolution, and eventual convergence and assimilation of technology.

Since the notion of online piracy as a mainly illegal activity was a predominant perspective in the survey testimonials, the analysis of its justifications is highly relevant for the broader understanding of law and legal development, as a process, in an increasingly digitized society. Each legal order, according to de Sousa Santos, contains an underlying conception, or *view* of the world which he describes as 'grounding fact [...] a supermetaphor' (1987, 291). This defines the specific interpretive standpoint or perspective that characterizes the adopted type of projection. For example, de Sousa Santos argues, the private economic relations in the market would constitute the 'supermetaphor' underlying modern bourgeois legality (1987, 291-292). Where de Sousa Santos is mainly preoccupied with the normative overload – the 'camelization' of law that he sees taking place particularly after the Second World War, drawing on the claims of several legal thinkers such as Habermas, Nonet, Selznick, and Teubner (1987, 280f.) – we find the change between the second and the third shape of law being more relevant here: from the *resistance* of 'the lion' to the *creation of new values* of 'the child'. Online piracy displays both the state of 'the lion' as well as of 'the child', in that the range of discourses is far from homogenous – a fact that a few recent studies have indicated (Larsson et al. 2012b; Svensson et al. 2013; 2014). Yet, consistencies can also be found, as our analysis has shown.

The invocation of 'market logics' can be seen to be both reflective of current conceptualizations and, in its ongoing emphasis on change and protean development, forward-looking. Seeing file sharing as the emergence of new enterprises or markets both breaks with the past and reinforces it. These new enterprises and markets can be interventions, or alternatives – but many of them are arguably so widespread and popular that they become 'the new normal' (Andersson Schwarz 2013a). There is both strong resistance, somewhat reinforcing a polarization between social and legal norms, and at the same time a more innovative approach, perhaps signifying a revival of a norm-pluralist conception of law in a digital society.

References

Alexander, Jeffrey C. (ed.) (1990). *Durkheimian Sociology*. Cambridge: Cambridge University Press.

Andersen, Birgitte and Marion Frenz (2007). "The Impact of Music Downloads

and P2P File-Sharing on the Purchase of Music: A Study for Industry Canada". *Industry Canada, Intellectual Property Policy*, October.
Andersson, Jonas (2009). "For the Good of the Net: The Pirate Bay as Strategic Sovereign". *Culture Machine*, 10, Pirate Philosophy issue.
Andersson, Jonas (2010). *Peer-to-peer-based file-sharing beyond the dichotomy of 'downloading is theft' vs. 'information wants to be free': How Swedish file-sharers motivate their action.* Ph.D. thesis, Goldsmiths, University of London.
Andersson, Jonas (2011). "The Origins and Impacts of Swedish File-sharing: A Case Study". *Critical Studies in Peer Production.* RS 1-1.
Andersson, Jonas (2012). "The Quiet Agglomeration of Data: How Piracy is Made Mundane". *International Journal of Communication (IJoC)*, 6, Piracy Cultures Special Section.
Andersson Schwarz, Jonas (2013a). "Not necessarily an intervention: The Pirate Bay and the case of file-sharing". In Kevin Howley (ed.). *Media Interventions.* New York, NY: Peter Lang.
Andersson Schwarz, Jonas (2013b). *Online File Sharing: Innovations in Media Consumption.* London & New York, NY: Routledge.
Andersson Schwarz, Jonas (2013c; in press). "Catering for whom? The problematic ethos of audiovisual distribution online". Virginia Crisp and Gabriel Menotti (eds). *Besides the Screen: The Distribution, Exhibition and Consumption of Moving Images* (forthcoming).
Balázs, Bodó (2013). "Set the fox to watch the geese: Voluntary IP regimes in piratical file-sharing communities". In Martin Fredriksson and James Arvanitakis (eds). *Piracy: Leakages from Modernity.* Sacramento, CA: Litwin Books.
Barbrook, Richard (2000). "Cyber-Communism: How the Americans are Superseding Capitalism in Cyberspace". *Science as Culture*, 9:1, 5-40.
Barry, Andrew and Don Slater (eds) (2005). *The Technological Economy.* London & New York, NY: Routledge.
Berger, Linda L. (2009). "How Embedded Knowledge Structures Affect Judicial Decision Making: A Rhetorical Analysis Of Metaphor, Narrative, And Imagination In Child Custody Disputes". *Southern Californian Interdisc. Legal Journal*, 18, 259-308.
Boltanski, Luc and Ève Chiapello (2007). *The New Spirit of Capitalism.* London: Verso.
Boltanski, Luc and Laurent Thévenot (2006). *On Justification: Economies of Worth.* Princeton, NJ and Oxford: Princeton University Press.
Callon, Michel (1998). "Introduction: The embeddedness of economic markets in economics". In Michel Callon (ed.).*The Laws of the Market.* Oxford: Blackwell.
Cenite, Mark et al. (2009). "More than Just Free Content: Motivations of Peer-to-Peer File Sharers". *Journal of Communication Inquiry*, 33:3.
De Sousa Santos, Boaventura (1987). "Law: A Map of Misreading. Toward a Postmodern Conception of Law". *Journal of Law and Society*, 14:3, 279-302.
Edwards, Lee, Bethany Klein, David Lee, Giles Moss and Fiona Philip (2014).

"Discourse, justification and critique: towards a legitimate digital copyright regime?". *International Journal of Cultural Policy,* DOI: 10.1080/ 10286632.2013.874421

Feldman Yuval and Janice Nadler (2006). "The Law and Norms of File Sharing". *The San Diego Law Review*, 43, 577–618.

García-Álvarez, Ercili et al. (2009). "A Contextual Theory of Accessing Music: Consumer Behavior and Ethical Arguments". *Consumption, Markets & Culture,* 12:3, 243-264.

Hardt, Michael and Antonio Negri (2004). *Multitude: War and Democracy in the Age of Empire.* New York: Penguin.

Huygen, Annelies et al. (2009). *Ups and downs: Economic and cultural effects of file sharing on music, film and games.* TNO report 34782. Commissioned by the Ministries of Education, Culture and Science, Economic Affairs and Justice; P. Rutten representing Leiden University. February 18. Delft: TNO.

de Kaminski, Marcin, Måns Svensson, Stefan Larsson, Johanna Alkan Olsson and Kari Rönkkö (2013). "Studying norms and social change in digital age". In Matthias Baier (ed.). *Social and legal norms: Towards a socio-legal understanding of normativity.* Ashgate Publishing.

Lakoff, George and Mark Johnson (1980). *Metaphors We Live By.* Chicago, IL: University of Chicago Press.

Lakoff, George and Mark Johnson (1999). *Philosophy In the Flesh: The embodied mind and its challenge to Western thought.* New York, NY: Basic Books.

Larsson, Stefan (2010). "459 miljarder kronor – om metaforer, flöden & exemplar". In Jonas Andersson and Pelle Snickars (eds). *Efter The Pirate Bay.* Stockholm: Mediehistoriskt arkiv.

Larsson, Stefan (2011a). "Den stigberoende upphovsrätten. Om konsekvenserna av rättslig inlåsning i en digital tid". *Retfærd: Nordic Journal of Law and Justice,* 135(2011:4), 122-146.

Larsson, Stefan (2011b). *Metaphors and Norms. Understanding Copyright Law in a Digital Society.* PhD Thesis, Lund Studies in Sociology of Law, Lund University.

Larsson, Stefan (2011c). "The Path Dependence of European Copyright". *SCRIPT:ed. A Journal of Law, Technology & Society,* 8:1.

Larsson, Stefan (2012a). "Conceptions In The Code: What 'The Copyright Wars' Tells About Creativity, Social Change And Normative Conflicts In The Digital Society". *Societal Studies,* 4:3, 1009-1030.

Larsson, Stefan (2012b). "Metaforerna och rätten". *Retfærd: Nordic Journal of Law and Justice,* 137 (2012:2), 69-93.

Larsson, Stefan (2013a). "Conceptions, categories, and embodiment – why metaphors are of fundamental importance for understanding norms". In Matias Baier, *Social and Legal Norms. Towards a socio-legal understanding of normativity,* Ashgate Publishing.

Larsson, Stefan (2013b). "Metaphors, law and digital phenomena: The Swedish Pirate Bay court case". *International Journal of Law and Information Technology,*

21:4, 329-353.
Larsson, Stefan and Håkan Hydén (2010). "Law, deviation and paradigmatic change: Copyright and its metaphors". In Vargas Martin et al. (eds). *Technology for Facilitating Humanity and Combating Social Deviations: Interdisciplinary Perspectives.* IGI Global.
Larsson, Stefan and Måns Svensson (2010). "Compliance or Obscurity? Online Anonymity as a Consequence of Fighting Unauthorised File-sharing". *Policy & Internet*, 2:4, Art. 4.
Larsson, Stefan, Måns Svensson and Marcin de Kaminski (2012a). "Online Piracy, Anonymity and Social Change – Innovation through Deviance". *Convergence: The International Journal of Research into New Media Technologies*, 19:1, 95-114.
Larsson, Stefan, Måns Svensson, Marcin de Kaminski, Kari Rönkkö and Johanna Alkan Olsson (2012b). "Law, Norms, Piracy And Online Anonymity – Practices Of De-Identification In The Global File Sharing Community". *Journal of Research in Interactive Marketing*, 6:4, 260-280.
Lessig, Lawrence (2004). *Free Culture: How Big Media Uses Technology and the Law to Lock down Culture and Control Creativity.* New York, NY: Penguin Press.
Palmås, Karl, Jonas Andersson Schwarz and Stefan Larsson (2014). "The Liability of Politicalness: Legitimacy and Legality in Piracy-proximate Entrepreneurship". *International Journal of Entrepreneurship and Small Business.*
Schultz, Mark F. (2007). "Copynorms: Copyright and social norms". In Peter K. Yu (ed.). *Intellectual Property and Information Wealth: Issues and Practices in the Digital Age.* Greenwood: Praeger Publishers, 651-728.
Svensson, Måns and Stefan Larsson (2012). "Intellectual Property Law Compliance in Europe: Illegal File sharing and the Role of Social Norms". *New Media & Society*, 14:7, 1147-1163.
Svensson, Måns, Stefan Larsson and Marcin de Kaminski (2013). "Professionalization, gender and anonymity in the global file sharing community". In Roberto Braga and Giovanni Caruso (eds). *Piracy Effect.* Milano, Italy: Mimesis Editore, online version.
Svensson, Måns, Stefan Larsson and Marcin de Kaminski (2014). "The Research Bay – Studying the global file sharing community". In William T Gallagher and Debora Halbert (eds). *Intellectual Property in Context: Law and Society Perspectives on IP.* Cambridge: Cambridge University Press.
Thierer, Adam and Wayne Crews (eds) (2002). *Copy Fights: The Future of Intellectual Property in the Information Age.* Washington, DC: Cato Institute.
Winter, Steven L. (2001). *A Clearing in the Forest: Law, Life, and Mind.* Chicago, IL & London: University of Chicago Press.
Winter, Steven L. (2008). "What is the 'color' of law?". In R.W. Gibbs Jr. (ed.). *The Cambridge Handbook of Metaphor and Thought.* Cambridge: Cambridge University Press.
Wingrove, Twila, Angela L. Korpas and Victoria Weisz (2010). "Why Were Millions Of People *Not* Obeying The Law? Motivational Influences On Non-

Compliance With The Law In The Case Of Music Piracy". *Psychology, Crime & Law*, 17:3, 261–276.
Virno, Paolo (2003). *A Grammar of the Multitude: For an Analysis of Contemporary Forms of Life.* Los Angeles, CA & New York, NY: Semiotext(e).
Yar, Majid (2008). "The Rhetorics and Myths of Anti-Piracy Campaigns: Criminalization, Moral Pedagogy and Capitalist Property Relations In The Classroom". *New Media & Society*, 10:4, 605-623.

Set the Fox to Watch the Geese: Voluntary IP Regimes in Piratical File-sharing Communities

Balázs Bodó

There is a short story I need to tell, before I start this chapter. [W] is a highly secretive, elitist, piratical music-sharing network. Born on the ruins of [O], it is rumored to have the finest, most exquisite and most complete collection of music ever written, hummed or recorded. Entry is difficult. Hopeful candidates need to pass an interview to prove that they know the rules of music piracy. Detailed preparation materials discuss such notions as 'lossy' and 'lossless' compression techniques, bitrates, transcoding, and so on. The hopeful candidates need to be prepared on the community guidelines and as well as site-specific etiquette.

The entry exams are conducted on an IRC channel. When I felt prepared, I tried to join the channel. Instead of a merciless examiner, however, the following message greeted me:

> You were kicked from #[W]-invites by ZeroBot (Banned: Your entire country [Hungary] is banned from the invites channel. This is because of the very high proportion of users from this area being bad for the site – either leechers, traders, sellers and/or cheaters.)

I laughed out loud. In the last few years I got used to the black YouTube screens telling me the "This video is not available in your country," but it was completely unexpected to see that the 'pirates' are also locking me out from their musical archives.

All the grand visions of digital information economies describe information as an inexhaustible resource, where users do not compete with each other: instead of scarcity there is abundance. And yet, it seems, even piratical pools of stolen digital property are subject to some of the dangers facing traditional commons. If not over-grazing, then under-provision and abuse are issues, and they are obviously addressed by those who have some control over the entity that is responsible for the collection.

I was greeted by a bot: a simple algorithmic daemon that checked the Internet address of my computer against a blacklist and kicked me out without any further questions. But someone had to write that bot, others have to maintain the blacklist, and still others had to detect that there was something fishy with users from my region. This simple, sobering message is only a sign of something bigger, more complex. It hints at a system of rules and governance mechanisms whose contours are only barely visible in the background.

It is these constructs that are the subject of this text. To begin with, I will bring three different examples of voluntary intellectual property (IP) enforcement in piratical file-sharing communities. I demonstrate that though the emergence of such rules may sound counter-intuitive, they are the logical results of the development of norms in the underground file-sharing scene. I then move to discuss whether or not the long-term consolidation of such norms is harmonious with the default ethical vision of copyright. Here I show that current practices in the IP field are scattered in both the legal and the ethical dimensions, and stable (social, business) practices consolidate not according to their legality but according to whether they comply with the default ethical vision. Finally, I suggest that voluntary IP regimes can be effective enforcement mechanisms that rights-holders should begin to experiment with.

This is not the Sherwood Forest

[W] is not unique in the current peer-to-peer (P2P) file-sharing scene, neither in its secrecy, nor in its rules-based entry regime. Such a site seems odd only for those who think that The Pirate Bay (TPB) is *the typical* site in the P2P piracy scene. The TPB and other *open networks*, however, only represent the public face of file sharing: beyond them there is a whole network of *closed, private trackers* that lurk in the depths of dark-nets (Biddle, England, Peinado and Willman 2001).

This Janus-facedness of P2P file sharing is a direct consequence of the relentless legal pressure on file sharing over the last decade. The pure logic of network effects would suggest the emergence of a natural monopoly (or possible oligopoly) of file-sharing networks. The continuous attacks by law enforcement organizations, however, eroded this emerging single network –née Napster – into a few open and an unknown number of closed P2P networks.

The obvious difference between open and closed networks is that the former serve anyone, while the latter are only accessible to registered users. From this simple barrier to access a number of important differences arise, most importantly that the membership rules of a closed tracker enable the development of a community, with its own set of norms and its own governance mechanisms. An anonymous member of a public forum described the difference between open and private trackers with a vivid metaphor:

> A private tracker is a close-knit community of upper-classes merchants and artisans, while a public tracker is some unsanitary open market with shady Arabian traders in the middle of U.S-infested Iraq.

In the litigation-heavy post-Napster era, a handful of file-sharing hubs willingly accepted the enforcement challenge, and responded to the attacks of rights-holders by a combination of technological prowess, personal sacrifice, the politicization of the debate and a daredevil attitude. The strategy they employed was to provide a free and open platform to exchange everything, for everyone. They were also willing to defend these services technologically, in court and in the public arena. While The Pirate Bay is the poster child of this approach, there are a few dozen other open networks that offer similar services. The success of such a strategy is, however, ambiguous. On the surface, open trackers seem to be indestructible. But in recent years, many sites shut down as soon as their 'admins' (or site administrators) were served with lawsuits and court orders. Others, like The Pirate Bay itself, are blocked by an increasing number of Internet service providers (ISPs), and their admins-owners were handed prison terms and multi-million dollar fines. Though TPB is still defiant, the days of public BitTorrent trackers may soon be over.

Open BitTorrent trackers are, however, an exception rather than the rule. There are only a handful of open trackers that have more than a million peers, or offer more than a million torrents, and there are only a few dozen sites that are in the hundred thousand range in terms of both peers and torrents. On the other hand, as of May 2012, the biggest Hungarian *private* tracker was number 9 globally in terms of the number of torrents amongst open trackers, and number 2 (behind The Pirate Bay) in terms of the number of peers participating in file sharing. The fact that a Hungarian private tracker, catering to a Hungarian speaking audience, specializing in Hungarian speaking content is on par with the most popular global open trackers suggests that there must be a significant underworld within the file-sharing underground. (Zhang, Dhungel, Wu, Liu and Ross 2010) The file-sharing landscape is in constant flux, but the relevance of closed networks is undeniable even if the individual trackers and their relative power changes from time to time.

Tracker Category	Torrents	Members	Seeders	Leechers
thepiratebay.se	1512045		3894707	1537437
Music	1339876	156362	8874254	113885
www.torrentportal.com	1220121		810017	894301
0-Day	1102604	9358610	16418755	1337426
fenopy.com	934843		10976228	11206835
www.mininova.org	867880		571034	709864
btjunkie.org	593640		1451423	600748
archive.org	512849		5685	8226
0-Day	386105	600000		
Music	339611	93596	1326771	27042
0-Day	277553			
torrentreactor.net	268628		1339159	522989
TV & Movies	261139	152636		
www.kat.ph	259896		789034	312326
www.bittorrent.am	252541		953167	369386
bitsnoop.com	214867		3573115	1216281
tokyotosho.info	186542		260510	230195
XXX	182328	1720756		
www.torrents.net	160952		772613	236419
Music	142106	7650	99279	2145
0-Day	138913	100000	1044942	72496
0-Day	136905	2121718	2400176	109054
www.nyaatorrents.org	132078		105626	83726
Music	132076	1906	34259	358
www.hightorrent.to	125832		25956	47661
0-Day	123592	68786		
bt.ktxp.com	120138		46179	79037
0-Day	115960	100255	386599	45110
extratorrent.com	111672		551293	217994
h33t.com	110566		604668	173703

Fig 1&2: The biggest open and closed networks in October 2012. The first table shows open networks and closed networks (in gray) ordered by the number of files (torrents) available through them. Notice that the biggest music-only closed tracker has nearly as many files as TPB, the latter also serving movies, TV shows, software, e-books and porn in addition to music.

Tracker Category	Torrents	Members	Seeders	Leechers	Sum Peers
fenopy.com	934843		10976228	11206835	22183063
TV & Movies	24335	37657	10120612	11477897	21598514
0-Day	1102604	9358610	16418755	1337426	17756181
Music	1339876	156362	8874254	113885	8988139
thepiratebay.se	1512045		3894707	1537437	5432144
bitsnoop.com	214867		3573115	1216281	4789396
www.torrentcrazy.com	98290		1899946	1127780	3027726
0-Day	136905	2121718	2400176	109054	2509230
www.seedpeer.me	55499		1878231	269621	2147852
btjunkie.org	593640		1451423	600748	2052171
0-Day	81866	688529	1710265	154132	1864397
torrentreactor.net	268638		1339159	522989	1862148
www.torrentportal.com	1220121		810017	894301	1704318
www.torrentdownloads.net	35713		918999	593216	1512215
torrent.cd	62454		1134760	272294	1407054
Music	339611	93596	1326771	27042	1353813
www.bittorrent.am	252541		953167	369386	1322553
1337x.org	81621		1045979	247842	1293821
www.mininova.org	867880		571034	709864	1280898
limetorrents.com	41477		670741	468081	1138822
0-Day	138913	100000	1044942	72496	1117438
www.kat.ph	259896		789034	312326	1101360
0-Day	73699	243533	973665	51556	1025221
www.torrents.net	160952		772613	236419	1009032
0-Day	100422	100000	915891	26737	942628
TV & Movies	85303	98000	798651	13626	812277
0-Day	67142	1992973	740123	40912	781035
h33t.com	110566		604668	173703	778371
extratorrent.com	111672		551293	217994	769287
0-Day	109047	300000	456759	287845	744604
0-Day	86176	233655	580278	70860	651138

The table on the right shows the same trackers ordered by the number of peers simultaneously participating in a file-sharing swarm. TPB hardly made it to the 5th place in this case.

The response of closed networks to enforcement efforts has been to retreat into obscurity and maintain a low profile. This obscurity makes the systematic study of such networks almost impossible – meaning there is a risk of losing crucial information on the actual social practices around file sharing. The numbers suggest that these closed networks – much like their more visible counterparts – play an important role in educating many on what IP is, how it works, what fairness is, and how cultural markets should and do operate. Every day millions negotiate complex rules which not only govern the life of these piratical communities but also shape their users' expectations on the future of cultural marketplaces.

Most closed networks are highly regulated spaces. Most of the rules are there to ensure the long-term survival of the common resource pool of shared files in an increasingly hostile legal and technological environment. They also make sure that the collection is as comprehensive as possible and maintains the highest achievable standards in terms of technical quality. Other rules establish internal administrative hierarchies, decision-making processes and conflict resolution methods: in other words, they establish the foundations of a self-governing community. And in at least some communities, we also find some rather unexpected rules, such as seeds of voluntary copyright regimes complete with restrictions on the exchange of certain works, informal notice and takedown processes and enforcement capabilities. But before discussing this aspect of the communities any further, I will outline three examples and discuss how they operate.

Example 1: specialized, international file-sharing community

[K] is an international torrent tracker catering to film 'buffs'. It has a detailed set of rules on what can be shared via the site. In the manifesto of the site the first rule of [K] makes it clear that:

> ***[We d]o not allow Hollywood/Bollywood mainstream.*** *From its inception, [K] was designed as a source for non-mainstream and off-beat movies. We try to distance ourselves from the pervasive and easily available Hollywood (and Bollywood) mainstream and show people that a huge and exciting world of cinema exists beyond that. Therefore we do not allow any mainstream movies on the tracker. The definition of "mainstream" is very elusive and almost impossible to state precisely. It is within the discretion of the tracker moderators to decide on each specific case. As a general rule, we limit our definition of mainstream to Hollywood and Bollywood movies made after the 70s. Classic Hollywood movies are allowed and welcome - even though some of them may enjoy mainstream popularity, we have high respect for their artistic quality and importance in cinema history. We draw the line with the advent of the big-budget*

> *Hollywood blockbuster (with movies like Jaws and Star Wars) which brought on a rapid deterioration in the quality of movies. Modern independent productions are allowed and we might make special exceptions for new Hollywood movies from special directors. Also allowed are most "mainstream" movies from other countries - what might be a common mainstream movie in Hungary might be totally unknown elsewhere.* For further information, see this collective forum thread for the discussion of the "mainstreamness" of specific movies. We are well aware that the enforcement of this rule makes a subjective judgment on the artistic quality of a movie that some people are bound to disagree with. However, this rule is the very foundation which has made [K] such a distinguished source for high-class world cinema.

This general rule is the source of much complex debate. In the forums dedicated to the topic, there is a detailed list of authors whose specific works are not to be shared. It is, for example, forbidden to share Steven Spielberg's whole oeuvre, but it is OK to share the Coen Brothers pre-2001 films (but not films after 2001). Sam Mendes is forbidden, but pre-1998 Christopher Nolan is OK. Milos Forman is generally acceptable, but his 1999 film *Man on the Moon* is prohibited.

Some of these bans are there because the work is seen as mainstream. But other works are put on the list at the request of their producers. One of the administrators described the process in an email interview. When asked whether works are banned from the site on the request of certain rights holders, the following response was given:

> The short answer to that question is Yes. We have been asked on a number of occasions if we could remove a file by the producers of the work. Only earlier this week did I receive a request to remove something. Most often the producer will ask for it to be removed until a certain date or until they break even on the film. We have also 'paid' (in ratio) producers to keep their work on the site.

This response offers valuable insight into the backroom dealings of piratical communities and rights holders. It suggests that at least some authors and producers are willing to engage with pirates directly, and instead of asking lawyers to send takedown notices, they make such request directly and politely. In return, these pirates seem to respect these requests, and attempt to negotiate deals that are mutually beneficial for all the parties involved.

Furthermore, the final sentence confirms a long suspected detail: some authors/rights holders are not only victims but also beneficiaries of the cultural black markets. These rights holders are willing to tolerate some (actual or perceived) losses in exchange for some of the benefits they receive in their capacity as users/consumers.

Example 2: specialized local community

[B] is a now defunct Hungarian file-sharing network that catered to the political extreme-right. It was organized along the political values of nationalism, national-socialism and social conservatism. It had a rich supply of Nazi propaganda, military history, anti-Semitic and racist literature, as well as cultural products from the local national-conservative music scene. Its manifesto stated:

> The aim of the tracker is to share content that is nationalistic, or due to political reasons is banned elsewhere. Our aim is not to hurt the authors and producers of nationalistic works, so certain restrictions are in place to prevent that.

Its uploading rules made it explicit that:

> What you upload should conform to the nationalistic (Christian conservative, nationalistic/radical) values. You can upload works that contradict these values, but you should explain why you think the material is worthy for sharing (ie: it has some informative or deterrence value). If what you upload confronts our values, and no explanation is provided as for why it is worthy of sharing, the material will be deleted. The reason for this rule is to suppress content that advertises deviance and other liberal values. **All nationalistic works are banned in the six months following their official release.** If the six months passed, sharing these works is permissible. (This rule is in place to ensure that the livelihood of nationalistic authors is granted, and to make sure that the tracker does not hurt them financially. Six months should be enough for you to buy these works.). For works beyond the six months limit, please provide a link where the work can officially be bought, and add the following lines: 'Support our nationalistic artists! If you like this CD/DVD/book/work, please buy it, and so support their work!' (This rule is also to support the nationalistic artists.)

In this case we see a fan community that also happens to be piratical. But in this case, such as in many other online fan communities,

> ...subcultural demands may construct conditions under which other goals predominate over consumer desires at either a micro or a macro cultural level. In other words, status within a subculture may be dependent not on consuming goods through any means possible but instead on consuming them 'legitimately'. (Downing 2011, 768)

Example 3, local, mainstream file-sharing community

Székelys are ethnic Hungarians living in eastern Transylvania, Romania. They have been struggling to maintain their traditional cultural distribution channels. Despite the significant financial support of the Hungarian state, bookstores selling Hungarian language books and cinemas playing Hungarian dubbed films are few and apart. To address these issues, Székely youth have set up their own file sharing service – [C] – to supply themselves with films, music and e-books in Hungarian. [C] includes the following rule in its section dealing with copyright:

> [C] does not support the sharing of works, whose gifted authors are active in Transylvania and who created something worthy of remembering in music or in film. Uploaders of such content have to have the proper authorization to share, unless the author authorized the sharing by him/herself. Such content will be immediately removed upon request of the author or rights-holder. If the content does not meet the aforementioned limitations, its sharing is supported without further limits.

The administrators of [C] also attempt to formulate what constitutes 'legitimate' consumption, and the threshold is the active presence of an artist in the life of the local community. It is arbitrary, and it is formulated in a language that only badly imitates copyright legalese, but again, nothing really forces them to make *any* distinction. It is also worth noting that, similarly to the two examples presented above, the users of [C] are willing to deny themselves important cultural products to protect the livelihoods of the producers.

Though these three file-sharing networks differ in almost every dimension, they have similar voluntary restrictions on sharing certain works. [K] is a highly specialized, prestigious, international network catering to 30,000 film professionals and fans. [B] was used by a few thousand political extremists to obtain and spread Nazi paraphernalia, military history and nationalistic rock music, while [C] has 50,000 users and is a general service defined by age, ethnicity and geography. Yet all three arrived to a point in their development where they felt there was a need to address intellectual property issues, and made important distinctions between certain authors and works – offering protection to some and not others.

What might be the reason behind such behavior? Why would the technologically sophisticated file-sharing pirates, safe behind layers of IP address filters, anonymization services and privacy guarding Virtual Private Networks (VPNs) with servers hosted in far away countries and confronting only inefficient domestic law enforcement, voluntarily restraint themselves in *anything*? It is this question that I attempt to answer next.

Open v closed, public v private: The benefits of limited access

In order to answer these questions, we must first understand the role that such rules serve in private tracker communities. Closed, private trackers are relatively small communities whose most important goal is to *maximize the value of the library of shared files.* The value of the collection is a function of at least three separate factors: (1) the 'completeness' of the collection as a whole; (2) the technical quality of the individual files; and, (3) the robustness of the community that supports the collection. Every action, taken in each of the aforementioned dimensions is to protect and nurture the collection, even if that (significantly) reduces the usefulness of the network for the individual user.

Protecting the collection

The mechanisms that serve to maximize the value of the collection are similar to the layers of regulation described by Lessig (2006) in *Code 2.0.* Some of the rules are embedded in the file-sharing technology, creating an architectural layer of regulation. This layer enables the development of a second, economic system upon itself; while a third layer of social norms and hierarchies makes the system complete.

On the level of technological control there is the capacity to measure the amount of data up- and downloaded by each user. This measurement enables site administrators to detect and punish free-riders, who would rather just download and not seed the content for others. Such a feature, which is hard-coded into the technological layer, opens up the opportunity to set the thresholds for punished, tolerated and rewarded levels of user contribution, effectively introducing a price for consumption (download) and a price for labor (upload) into the system. Such a process turns "private BitTorrent communities [...] from computer systems into economic systems" (Kash, Lai, Zhang and Zohar 2012, 1).

It is important to note that these P2P markets are not free-markets, and the prices are not automatically defined by supply and demand. On the contrary, prices are set by the not so invisible hands of the site administrators to signal preferred behavior and to address certain shortcomings of the P2P activity. By rewarding the sharing of certain content and penalizing the sharing of others, such pricing mechanisms are able to ensure that older, less popular, niche, fringe or otherwise *archival* content stays accessible at all times within the community. By setting download prices to zero these sites play an important role in directing attention to certain works and authors. Such mechanisms help admins to 'curate the collection' and shape the cultural canon within the network.

The accessibility of long-tail content is a strong differentiating factor amongst file-sharing networks. In general, open networks can only rely on chance: that is, the commitment of individual users to sharing, or the law of large numbers when it comes to making content in the long tail available. A strict 'ratio rule' – for example, where one is expected to upload 1 megabyte for each megabyte downloaded – may incentivize sharing in general, while ratio rewards for sharing marginal content and for fulfilling requests boosts the availability of niche content. Such measures help to maximize the completeness of the collection as a whole. The same rules, on the other hand, severely restrict the freedom of the individual to download anything they wish, and therefore limit nomadic, explorative consumption patterns (Bodó and Lakatos 2012), just like any other market mechanism.

In the case of P2P file sharing, technology and logics would suggest a lack of scarcity and a subsequent freedom in consumer choices. Though this image may be somewhat true for open trackers, in closed networks, especially with strict ratio rules, we see the re-emergence of artificial scarcity. This is in part in response to the perceived problem of free riding and the under-provision of certain parts of the content commons. Of course secrecy and access barriers also serve a number of other important goals, such as (a sense) of protection from enforcement, and the maintenance of what Dent describes as,

> ...ritual, political, and material power [...] The capacity of some social groups to keep others from finding out about those discursive practices and then employing them is nonetheless what helps to maintain the given social hierarchy. (2012, 665)

The P2P digitization machine

The second factor that defines the value of the collection is the technical quality of individual files. File-sharing networks are not only highly efficient content distribution networks, but also vast digitization machines. Most networks rely on the contributions of individual users to build an impressive catalogue of content not accessible anywhere else. The technical infrastructure to create digital copies is more-or less accessible, but the production of high quality copies is far from trivial. Closed networks thus have to solve three closely related problems: the encouragement of users to create digital copies in the first place; help users so these copies will be of high quality; and filter low quality entries from user's contributions.

Closed trackers mobilize the community's resources to address all these issues at once. These community efforts include very detailed and self-explanatory guides on the know-how of producing good digital copies; a multitude of forum threads where technical questions are asked and answered; and, an army of community members ready to lend a helping hand to anyone asking. Sophisticated user feedback mechanisms are coupled with administrative control to identify and remove sub-par files. Closed file-sharing networks have the important role of coordinating and organizing some of the anarchic and uncoordinated digitization activity happening all the time on the Internet by setting digitization standards and providing quality assurance mechanisms.

No commons without a corresponding community

The library of shared files, which is at the core of a closed P2P network, is a prime example of a regulated, peer-produced, common property regime, with "particular institutional forms of structuring the rights to access, use, and control resources" (Benkler 2006, 60). The rights, described by Hess and Ostrom (2003) regarding the use of common-pool resources, are all well defined in closed P2P file-sharing communities. It is easy to identify within such networks what Elinor Ostrom identified as the preconditions for a successful common property regime (1990, 90): clearly defined access barriers; locally relevant, context-specific rules; collective choice arrangements; institutions to monitor and sanction behavior; arrangements to resolve conflicts; and, relative autonomy. Most of these institutions are established and operating through the community forums which become a crucial component in the closed file-sharing infrastructure.

Each underground knowledge commons relies on four separate, but closely intertwined technological infrastructures: (1) the resources (storage capacity, bandwidth) of individual users; (2) the torrent tracker, which coordinates the shared individual resources; (3) the search engine, which provides the meta-information on the shared resource; and, (4) the online forums and other communication channels which enable interaction between group members. Most open trackers have one or both of the second and third infrastructures, but offer little in the fourth domain. This latter infrastructure is, however, the space where the community and the norm formation take place. It is on this infrastructure where the rules that differentiate ad-hoc, accidental, anarchic piratical libraries from well managed and regulated knowledge commons are negotiated. It is the participation in various online interactions that helps the lone, anonymous file-sharer to become part of a well-defined community, with its own hierarchies, habits, rules and notions of 'legitimate' consumption. A forum commenter described the role of community as follows:

> The casual downloader would not care about community. They just want to go to the tracker, find what they want, download it, and stop the torrent as soon as they complete the download. They're not interested in getting to know other users of the tracker as well. In private trackers, dedicated members will try to maintain a good sense of community. This starts with keeping torrents seeding as long as possible, making good comments on torrents, and participating in the forums and/or IRC. [...] Believe it or not I used to try to post in the Pirate Bay forums, but given the huge number of people who go there, the forum activity is quite lacking."

The community, its rules, its governance mechanisms, its opinion leaders, its discussions, *its collective identity* is what can ensure the long-term survival of not only the commons in question, but also the practices that sustain these commons.

I believe that this sense of community is an often overlooked factor in studies on the motivations of file-sharers. There is a great deal of research that has attempted to identify the source of individual's attitudes on copyright piracy. Most of the studies, however, have focused either on the micro/individual level, such as: peer pressure (Becker and Clement 2006); family/friend/superior influence (Svensson and Larsson 2009); gender (Chiang and Assane 2008); anonymity (Larsson and Svensson 2010); an individual's socio-economic background (Cox, Collins and Drinkwater 2010); and, motivational background (Bô et al. 2004; Goode and Cruise 2006). There have also been a number of studies focusing on the macro societal influences with examples including: global income inequalities (Karaganis 2011); market failures (Bodó and Lakatos 2012); mass litigation (Depoorter and Vanneste 2005); sources of IP norms (Schultz 2006a, 2009); and, the mechanisms of gift economies (Barbrook 1998; Giesler and Pohlmann 2003; Leyshon 2003; Skågeby and Pargman 2005). But so far only a few studies have realized that online communities with their own IP norms and ethics are the most important peer groups to shape the copy-norms of the individual (Beekhuyzen, von Hellens and Nielsen 2011; Cooper and Harrison 2001; Downing 2010 2011; Lee 2009; Rehn 2004).

Current copyright legislation and ramped up enforcement is still unable to prevent mass-infringement. Despite this, it certainly creates a climate where one feels the need to justify one's actions and situate IP related cultural practices within the macro-framework of IP legislation. Likewise, there is also a feeling that one must explain one's individual beliefs about rights and wrongs. Closed file-sharing communities offer a platform to reconcile conflicting values, ethics and legalities, and serve as interpretative communities that distill their own ethics on the use of intellectual properties.

Different file-sharing networks arrive at different conclusions on what they consider both proper and acceptable uses of IP. Some, such as The Pirate Bay take a radical IP abolitionist position: seeing themselves as digital 'Robin Hoods' who take from the 'evil' rich – which are usually American corporations – and freely give the spoils to the 'poor'. But the closed networks I cited seem to have left Sherwood Forest some time ago.

Probably the most important differentiating characteristic of closed file-sharing communities is their common property regime approach to the resources they use and produce. The rules seem to suggest that these networks realized that a parasitical, approach to the 'natural resource' they are using – that is, the wider cultural environment which produces the works they share – would be counter-productive. For this reason they show signs of self-control which serve both the piratical commons *and* the wider cultural ecosystem. I previously defined the borders of the community as those set by the membership rules; and the common resource pool as the files shared by the members of the community. But those networks that have their own notions about 'legitimate consumption' seem to be ready to take the interests of producers, authors and some intermediaries into consideration. By taking non-members' interests into account, these piratical communities are internalizing the externalities of their actions. They also recognize that only if the whole ecosystem thrives can their own closed common resource pool be successful.

It takes two to tango

The voluntary IP regimes in piratical communities are the results of complex background negotiations between pirates, authors, rights holders, and some times even traditional intermediaries. All sides have to have the willingness to engage in the discussions and must be satisfied with the outcomes if they are to keep cooperating. The motivation to reach an agreement is far from trivial, since the parties have cheap and easy alternatives to cooperation. Authors and rights holders have the full support of law on their side and could easily make life difficult for the pirates. The pirates, on the other hand, can always retaliate and/or disappear in the darknets. Why, then, do we see such arrangements appearing?

From the pirates' perspective, one might say that respecting rights holders' claims is a way to avoid more formal scrutiny. By respecting informal requests they can avert the risk of facing more challenging formal legal procedures which can take down the network as a whole. As such, temporary and even permanent bans on certain works are necessary sacrifices to protect the rest of the collection. This is why I argue that the emergence of voluntary IP restrictions is a logical next step in the development of the rules that serve to protect the common resource pool: by cooperating with rights holders, piratical file-sharing communities can avoid devastating general prosecution.

But there is also another, more utopian, explanation. The restrictions on the common resource pool may also suggest that these communities have realized that the P2P library is part of a larger ecosystem, with which it is in a symbiotic relationship. The fate of a collection is dependent upon the well being of that cultural field which nurtures it and vice versa. When it comes to the protection of the resource they directly control – that is, the P2P library – they need to account for the externalities of their actions as well as attempt to protect that part which they do not have control over (or only indirectly). By having sharing restrictions that redirect P2P demand to other, often legal channels, piratical communities imagine themselves in co-existence with legal markets as well as with rights-holders. This is one significant step beyond the usual descriptions of P2P black markets that suggest that piracy is either an autonomous domain, hostile to the legal markets in general, or is simply a response to the failures of legal alternatives (Bodó and Lakatos 2012; Karaganis 2011).

Authors and rights holders may also come to the conclusion that they have a great deal to gain from cooperating with their piratical audiences and customers. Some of them are explicit members of these networks, so they directly benefit from their existence as users. By being a member they also have more opportunities to represent their interests in the informal discussions on what counts as legitimate consumption. Studies on fan cultures show that in the case of transformative uses, the engagement of rights-holders with fans is a necessary component of the successful management of copy-norms and infringement issues (Condry 2004; Fiesler 2007; Lee 2009; Lipton 2010; Schultz 2006). Other rights holders may have arrived at the conclusion that the black market circulation of their works may not have a devastating effect on their livelihood. The arguments here are well known, and in some cases are empirically well documented, such as: obscurity can be a bigger threat than piracy (Bhattacharjee, Gopal and Sanders 2003; Peitz and Waelbroeck 2006; Waldfogel 2010); free access may lead to increased sales (Boorstin 2004; Bounie, Bourreau and Waelbroeck 2006); and, especially if authors have a limited interest in the long-term financial success of the work, they are simply more permissive. Traditional intermediaries can also use these networks to sample demand, test products and maintain an archive of discontinued products.

So both sides (if we treat producers and audiences separate, which is very much the characteristic of the modern, mediatized, commodified culture) may have an interest in cooperating, even if the setting in which they meet is clearly beyond the limits set by law. We have to ask then, how important a factor is legality in the case of bottom-up social practices that enjoy both long term stability and legitimacy from different stake-holder groups?

The ethical foundations of copyright

I would like to argue that, in the aforementioned cases, both consumers and producers are engaged in activities that are clearly illegal but accepted as legitimate. These exchanges are legitimized by the fact that the participants see them as ethical practices, which usurps the issue of their legality. The ethics of these practices may be contextual and ephemeral, but all of them are deeply grounded in the default ethical expectation of copyright.

James Grimmelman defines this default ethical expectation of copyright as follows:

> The basic ethical expectation of copyright is that authors and audiences respect each other and meet in the marketplace. Authors behave well when

> they create and offer works that enrich the audience's intellectual and cultural lives. Audiences behave well when they offer authors the financial support needed to engage in creative work. The exchange is commercial, voluntary on both sides, reciprocal, and respectful. (2009, 2014)

When authors do not exercise the options given by statutory copyright, and tacitly or explicitly tolerate their works being shared on file-sharing networks under certain conditions, they 'behave well'. When piratical networks voluntarily redirect P2P demand to the marketplace, they also 'behave well'. When authors and piratical audiences engage in a mutually respectful dialogue and in reciprocal exchanges, as we could see in the case of [K], they both 'behave well'. The only catch is that this ethics is not universal, and it is not unconditional. It is situational and contextual: it only applies to certain authors, certain works, certain audiences and certain practices.

Statutory copyright, in contrast, is a universal but impersonal construct. It attempts to balance the general authors' rights against the interests of a general public. Its limits, most notably the length of protection, and exceptions are also generalized. This was not always the case though: bottom-up, extra-legal, community based, voluntary IP rules are actually older then the first statutory formulation of copyright. The history of printing, as a case in point, teaches us that early printers soon realized that they needed to curb unfair competition amongst themselves if they wanted the trade to flourish (Bodó 2011a, 2011b; Darnton 2003; Johns 2004; Khan and Sokoloff 2001; Wittmann 2004).

Such 'synthetic copyright regimes' (Khan 2002) were personal or rather, communal. As a courtesy of trade, they reflected the consensus within the printing community on what was both permissible and undesirable behavior. They also defined the conditions under which they applied, and under which they could be suspended. The emergence of formal IP regimes slowly crowded out such self-regulatory solutions. Up until the arrival of the Internet we find such community based, extra-legal IP regimes mostly at the social, cultural and political fringes, such as in bootlegging subcultures, amongst the bands catering to the American counter-culture, or in various non-Western settings at the time when the cassette recorder arrived (Heylin 1995; Larkin 2004; Manuel 1993; Schultz 2006). The rapid and violent changes in technology, cultural markets and social practices in the last decade created a set of practices that became illegal, despite their perceived ethicality. The tools included in the general IP framework (limitations and exceptions, fair use provisions, the three step test) so far fail to provide a truly safe harbor to many of the newly emerging social practices that are in line with the default ethics of copyright. In such cases the constantly re-negotiated informal arrangements are more flexible to adjust to these practices than the statutory IP regimes, anchored in multiple supra-national institutions.

The emergence of voluntary IP regimes in piratical communities is an important signal that even if they have little respect for statutory copyright or are unwilling to honor every claim made by rights-holders, those millions who engage in piratical practices are well aware of their responsibilities as members of a cultural community. Their decisions, however, are less based on laws, and more defined by the ethics negotiated within the community.

This development has at least three important lessons in it. The first one considers the relationship of IP laws and social practices in the near future. I argue that as long as the main question of the IP field is not *how people can be forced to obey the law*, but rather *under what conditions they choose to respect the wishes of authors and ensure the reproduction of different cultural fields*, the survival of different social practices will be a factor of their ethical disposition rather than their legality. In other words we should expect ethically robust practices to persist even if their legality remains in question, and unethical practices will face considerable public opposition even if they are found to be legal.

The system is constantly in a state of flux: File-sharing services come and go; file-sharing technologies emerge, mutate and become obsolete; generations of 'pirates' turn on, tune in and drop out; rights holders' attitudes change, as do market conditions; and, legal alternatives arise, mature and disappear. In this rapidly changing landscape, certain practices and alternatives are closer to the ethical standard while some are farther away. Those that are closer to the default ethical vision will continue to enjoy public support even if they are not legal, and those legal practices that do not conform to the ethical expectations, will face considerable resentment even if they are vehemently enforced.

The second lesson refers to the re-establishment of communality in the mediatized, industrialized and commodified processes of cultural production, distribution and consumption. The rise of formal and impersonal IP regimes was followed by the rise of impersonal, global, media conglomerates that are more focused on financial returns than on any cultural mission (Hesmondhalgh 2007; Turow 2009). These entities not only connect authors and audiences, but also separate them: their interests are different from those of the authors, whose work they market, and from the interests of the audiences they cater to. They have their own priorities and financial interests in the business of cultural production and distribution, and so far they have been very successful in representing them in formal IP frameworks.

P2P networks are heralded sometimes as dis-intermediaries and at other times as new intermediaries between authors and audiences. I suggest that P2P networks create communities where creators and consumers, authors and fans can, and do, interact. Through these interactions a mutual realization of consumers and authors may emerge that there is no 'us' versus 'them' in this conflict: authors, rights-holders and other commercial intermediaries are also part of the community to which users, down-loaders and consumers belong. Piratical networks with voluntary IP regimes have the potential to abolish the artificial separation of producer and consumer, and reunite these two groups in a non-industrial mode of cultural community, so characteristic of a pre-mediated era, where culture is produced by those who consume it, and vice versa. Here cultural artifacts are distributed and transformed through the acts of 'consumption'.

The final point is that voluntary IP restrictions in piratical communities are probably the most effective enforcement mechanisms to date. Closed file-sharing communities have sophisticated tools of social control in spaces where statutory copyright is irrelevant. The enforcement efforts that target these networks destroy not just the resource pools and the communities that built them, but also destroy the social controls that are in place. Paradoxical as this may sound, the aforementioned piratical communities may be the enforcement allies that rights-holders have been seeking all this time. In any case, it is apparent that they both have at least one interest in common: a sustainable cultural ecosystem.

So maybe it is time to ask ourselves: should we set the foxes to watch the geese?

References

Barbrook, Richard (1998). "The high-tech gift economy". *First Monday*, 3, 12.

Becker, Jan U. and Michel Clement (2006). "Dynamics of illegal participation in peer-to-peer networks - Why do people illegally share media files?". *Journal of Media Economics*, 19:1, 7–32.

Beekhuyzen, Jenine, Liisa von Hellens and Sue Nielsen (2011). "Underground online music communities: Exploring rules for membership". *Online Information Review*, 35:5, 699–715.

Benkler, Yochai (2006). *The wealth of networks: How social production transforms markets and freedom.* New Haven: Yale University Press.

Bhattacharjee, Sudip, Ram D. Gopal and G. Lawrence Sanders (2003). "Digital music and online sharing". *Communications of the ACM*, 46:7, 107–111.

Biddle, Peter, Paul England, Marcus Peinado and Bryan Willman (2001). *The darknet and the future of content distribution.* Redmond, WA: Microsoft Corporation.

Bô, Daniel, Claire-Marie Lévêque, Alexandra Marsiglia, Raphaël, Lellouche, Benoît Danard and Caroline Jeanneau (2004). "La piraterie de films: Motivations et pratiques des Internautes." *Perception.* 20–35.

Bodó, Balázs (2011a). "Coda: A Short History of Book Piracy". In Joe Karaganis (ed.), *Media Piracy in Emerging Economies.* New York: Social Science Research Council.

Bodó, Balázs (2011b). *A szerzői jog kalózai.* Budapest: Typotex.

Bodó, Balázs and Zoltán Lakatos (2012). "P2P and Cinematographic Movie Distribution in Hungary". *International Journal of Communication*, 6, 413–445.

Boorstin, Eric S. (2004). *Music sales in the age of file sharing.* Princeton University.

Bounie, David, Marc Bourreau and Patrick Waelbroeck (2006). "Piracy and the demand for films: Analysis of piracy behavior in French universities". *Review of Economic Research on Copyright Issues,* 3:2, 15–27.

Chiang, Eric P. and Assane, Djeto (2008). "Music piracy among students on the university campus: Do males and females react differently?". *Journal of SocioEconomics*, 37:4, 1371–1380.

Condry, Ian (2004). "Cultures of music piracy: An ethnographic comparison of the US and Japan". *International Journal of Cultural Studies*, 7:3, 343–363.

Coombe, Rosemary J. (1998). *The cultural life of intellectual properties: Authorship, appropriation, and the law.* Durham: Duke University Press.

Cooper, Jon and Daniel M. Harrison (2001). "The social organization of audio piracy on the Internet". *Media Culture Society*, 23:1, 71–89.

Cox, Joe, Alan Collins and Stephen Drinkwater (2010). "Seeders , leechers and social norms: Evidence from the market for illicit digital downloading". *Information Economics and Policy*, 22, 299–305.

Darnton, Robert (1982). *The literary underground of the Old Regime.* Cambridge, MA: Harvard University Press.

Darnton, Robert (2003). "The science of piracy: A crucial ingredient in eighteenth-century publishing". *Studies on Voltaire and the Eighteenth Century*, 12, 3–29.

Dent, Alexander Sebastian (2012). "Understanding the war on piracy, or why we need more anthropology of pirates". *Anthropological Quarterly*, 85:3, 659–672.

Depoorter, Ben and Sven Vanneste (2005). "Norms and enforcement: The case against copyright litigation". *Oregon Law Review*, 84, 1127–1180.

Downing, Steven (2010). "Social control in a subculture of piracy". *Journal of Criminal Justice and Popular Culture*, 14:1, 77–123.

Downing, Steven (2011). "Retro gaming subculture and the social construction of a piracy ethic". *International Journal of Cyber Criminology*, 5:1.

Fiesler, Casey (2007). "Everything I need to know I learned from fandom: How existing social norms can help shape the next generation of user-generated content". *Vanderbilt Journal of Entertainment and Technology Law*, 10:3, 729–762.

Giesler, Markus and Mali Pohlmann (2003). "The anthropology of file sharing: Consuming Napster as a gift". *Advances in Consumer Research*, 30, 273–279.

Goode, Sigi and Sam Cruise (2006). "What motivates software crackers?". *Journal of Business Ethics*, 65:2, 173–201.

Grimmelmann, James (2009). "The Ethical Visions of Copyright Law". *Fordham Law Review*, 77:5, 2005–2037.

Hesmondhalgh, David (2007). *The cultural industries* (2nd ed.). London, Thousand Oaks: Sage Publications.

Hess, Charlotte and Elinor Ostrom (2003). "Ideas, artifacts, and facilities: Information as a common-pool resource". *Law and Contemporary Problems*, 66:1/2, 111–145.

Heylin, Clinton (1995). *Bootleg: The secret history of the other recording industry*. New York: St. Martin's Press.

Johns, Adrian (2004). "Irish piracy and the English Market". In *The History of Books and Intellectual History*. Princeton University.

Karaganis, Joe (ed.) (2011). *Media Piracy in Emerging Economies*. New York: Social Science Research Council.

Kash, Ian A., John K. Lai , Haoqi Zhang and Aviv Zohar (2012). "Economics of BitTorrent communities". In *Proceedings of the 21st international conference on World Wide Web - WWW '12*. New York, New York, USA: ACM Press.

Khan, B. Zorina (2002). "Intellectual Property and Economic Development: Lessons from American and European History". London: British Commission on Intellectual Property Rights.

Khan, B. Zorina and Kenneth L. Sokoloff (2001). "The early development of intellectual property institutions in the United States". *Journal of Economic Perspectives*, 15:3, 233–246.

Larkin, Brian (2004). "Degraded images, distorted sounds: Nigerian video and the infrastructure of piracy". *Public Culture*, 16, 289–314.

Larsson, Stefan and Måns Svensson (2010). "Compliance or obscurity? Online anonymity as a consequence of fighting unauthorised file-sharing". *Policy & Internet*, 2:4, 77.

Lee, Hye-Kyung (2009). "Between fan culture and copyright infringement: Manga scanlation". *Media, Culture & Society*, 31:6, 1011–1022.

Leyshon, Andrew (2003). "Scary monsters? Software formats, peer-to-peer networks, and the spectre of the gift". *Environment and Planning D-Society & Space*, 21:5, 533–558.

Lipton, Jacqueline D. (2010). "Copyright's twilight zone: Digital copyright lessons from the vampire blogosphere". *Maryland Law Review*, 70:1, 1–61.

Manuel, Peter Lamarche (1993). *Cassette culture: Popular music and technology in north India.* Chicago: University of Chicago Press.

Ostrom, Elinor (1990). *Governing the commons: The evolution of institutions for collective action.* Cambridge University Press.

Peitz, Martin and Patrick Waelbroeck (2006). "Why the music industry may gain from free downloading - The role of sampling". *International Journal of Industrial Organization*, 24:5, 907–913.

Rehn, Alf (2004). "The politics of contraband The honor economies of the warez scene". *Journal of Socio-Economics*, 33:3, 359–374.

Sano-Franchini, Jennifer Lee (2010). "Intellectual property and the cultures of bittorrent communities". *Computers and Composition*, 27:3, 202–210.

Schultz, Mark F. (2006a). "Copynorms: Copyright and Social Norms". In Peter K. Yu (ed.). *Intellectual Property and Information Wealth: Issues and Practices in the Digital Age*, Vol. 1. Praeger Publishers.

Schultz, Mark F. (2006b). "Fear and norms and rock & roll: What jambands can teach us about persuading people to obey copyright law". *Berkeley Technology Law Journal*, 21.

Schultz, Mark F. (2009). "Reconciling social norms and copyright law: Strategies for persuading people to pay for recorded music". *Journal of Intellectual Property Law*, 17, 59–445.

Skågeby, Jörgen and Daniel Pargman (2005). "File-Sharing relationships–conflicts of interest in online gift-giving". *Communities and Technologies* 2005, 111–127.

Svensson, Måns and Stefan Larsson (2009). *Social norms and intellectual property: online norms and the european legal development.* Lund: Lund University.

Turow, Joseph (2009). *Media today: An introduction to mass communication.* New York. Routledge.

Waldfogel, Joel (2010). "Music file sharing and sales displacement in the iTunes era". *Information Economics and Policy*, 22:4, 306–314.

Wittmann, Reinhard (2004). "Highwaymen or Heroes of Enlightenment? Viennese and South German Pirates and the German Market". In *Paper presented at the History of Books and Intellectual History conference.* Princeton University.

Zhang, Chao, Prithula Dhungel, Di Wu, Zhengye Liu and Keith W. Ross (2010). Bittorrent darknets. In *INFOCOM'10 Proceedings of the 29th conference on Information communications* (1460–1468).

Pirate Economies and the Production of Smooth Spaces

Pavlos Hatzopoulos and Nelli Kambouri

Introduction

Street vending in Athens is organized mainly around the everyday practices of migrants, who sell pirated, counterfeit and stolen goods without an official license. The conditions for the emergence and success of this economy are contradictory: while street-vending requires by definition the hyper-visibility of the street-vendors on the public pavements, squares and pedestrian roads of the city, it is also simultaneously subject to multiple forms of immigration surveillance and control exercised by the Greek police and anti-immigration/racist groups that are an omnipresent threat to them. In this context, migrant street-vending becomes an economy that requires constant awareness and complex mobility as one must be able to skillfully move across the lines that demarcate public/legal from private/illegal urban zones, activities and usages.

This movement remains largely unrepresentable – if not imperceptible – in public discourse. Migrant street-vendors are either portrayed as illegal criminals that undermine Greek entrepreneurship, or as destitute immigrants forced to resort to illegality in order to survive. Moreover, this discourse tends to be reproduced even by social movements and migrant initiatives that struggle against the prevailing economic rules and conditions. By becoming attentive to the spatial tactics of migrant street-vendors, however, we begin to grasp the emergence of a pirate economy in urban space.

This chapter follows the routes, stops, marches, breaks, heterogeneous frequencies of movements, and encounters from public visibility to invisibility and back again. Main carriers of those movements are migrant street vendors, who become 'users' of urban space by selling and exchanging commercial products. The main argument of this paper is that migrant mobilities of this kind produce 'smooth spaces' that penetrate the official demarcations of the private/public urban divide. Rather than a symptom of immigrant criminality that "destroys the productive base of the city" or a sign of the victimization of illegal immigrants, our conception of street vending is based on a perspective which is informed by an understanding of street economies not as 'informal' but rather as *"economies de la débrouillardise"* (Neuwirth 2011, 17). This is a *term with positive connotations, which is translated, according to Neuwirth (ibid.), as* "ingenuity economies," "economies of improvisation and self-reliance," and "do-it-yourself, or DIY economies". This perspective aims to grasp the active participation and creativity of migrants in the production of urban space (De Certau 1984).

This argument will be contextualized through a twofold discussion: first, we look at the bodily practices of migrant street vendors and, secondly, at the ways in which these bodily practices intersected with the indignados movement during the occupation protests of Syntagma Square in summer 2011. By discussing the latter, we do not aim at a critique of social movements, but rather at a potential opening up of contemporary attempts to re-appropriate public space.

We analyze migrant street vending through a particular reading of the concept of piracy that is closely linked to nomadic mobility. We understand the term 'nomadic' not in a strict ethnographic sense commonly used to characterize rural spaces, past historical periods or distant ethnic communities, but rather as a type of mobility that can also be useful to understand present day pirate practices in urban space. In this context, we follow Gilles Deleuze and Felix Guattari's (1998) notion of nomadism that makes a distinction between the migrant and the nomadic acknowledging that the two modes often overlap. While nomads and migrants can mix in many ways, their speed differs following different principles. While the migrant "moves from one point to another," the nomad moves from "point to point" (ibid., 380). In effect, Deleuze and Guattari argue it is not movement but rather stasis that characterizes nomadic practices:

> Whereas the migrant leaves behind a milieu that has become amorphous or hostile, the nomad is one who does not depart, does not want to depart, who clings to smooth space...Of course, the nomad moves, but while seated and he is only seated while moving... (1998, 391)

Our claim here is neither that migrant street-vendors adopt or desire a self-identification with pirates, nor that we should arbitrarily categorize them under the generic term 'pirates'. Instead, we argue that the production of a pirate economy by migrant street-vendors is premised upon the adoption of nomadic bodily practices and tactics that aim to bypass and escape the control of everyday urban mobilities. Along these lines, we attempt to connect pirate practices to a specific kind of nomadic spatial politics.

The main concepts that inform our analysis are Deleuze and Guattari's (1998) 'smooth' and 'striated' spaces: while the term 'striated' refers to the spaces established by the State apparatus, 'smooth spaces' are established by the war machine. Striated space produces order through the organization of heterogeneous elements; it corresponds to the state logic of imposing the model of labor as the ultimate principle for the production of space. Smooth space lies outside the logic of the state. Smooth space is characterized by continuous variations, by the continuous transformation of forms; it corresponds to the exteriority of the war machine in relation to the state apparatus, to the war machine's direction to untie the organization of urban space as it is implemented by the state. Although the nature of these two spaces is different and conflicting, they are in a constant mix and interaction since they cannot be clearly distinguished in practice. Smooth and striated spaces constantly transform themselves and each other, entering into each other's domain and transmuting into their opposite.

Pirate practices, the smooth, and the striated

Some recent analyses have attempted to connect discussions of piracy, past and present, to the notions of smooth and striated space (see for example Selmann 2008). Even in the text that informs the usage of these terms by Deleuze and Guattari, there are specific references to the open sea and the struggles around its transformation to a state governed space:

> This is undoubtedly why the sea, the archetype of smooth space, was also the archetype of all striations of smooth space. (1988, 480)

This type of association has prompted some authors to discuss piracy – particularly piracy during the Golden Age (though this is not explicitly mentioned by the authors) – through the concepts of smooth and striated space. Pirates, in these narratives, are seen as the guardians of smooth space, the embodiments of the social forces producing the open sea. Brianne Selmann captures this in the following passage:

> This movement to striate the sea was *fundamentally* a movement against the pirates, just as the attempt to striate space by the State can be seen as an attempt to 'displace' the nomads. Empires exercised their power to try to make the sea a 'safe' place – to rid it of the wild, the deterritorializing, they attempted to carve it into routes and passageways of security. (2008, 33)

In a similar fashion, Kuhn (2010) extends the analysis of the subjectivities of Caribbean pirates to Deleuze and Guattari's notion of nomadism. In so doing, Kuhn finds that, "interesting parallels can be drawn to nomads who inhabit the same natural environment as the golden age pirates, namely the sea, or, more specifically, 'an extensive and diversified world of islands'" (ibid., 26).

Taking cue from these analyses of piracy and pirates, we attempt to relocate the focus by transposing it into urban space. What primarily concerns us here is an understanding of pirate practices under the prism of a politics for the appropriation of space, or rather for the production of space. We are concerned, in other words, both with the ways in which pirate practices are produced in relation to the control of urban space, but also to the forms of active resistance that emerge within this process. Somewhat departing from previous analyses, we do not insist on the existence of a clear, rigid dichotomy amongst smooth spaces (being directly linked to piracy, nomadism, deterritorialization, and striation or being directly linked to state power and the annihilation of piracy). From our perspective, the articulation of such dichotomies tends to reproduce the romanticization of piracy (and nomadism), by locating it outside the matrix of contemporary forms of power.

The approach adopted in this chapter is closer to the studies of pirate urbanisms in postcolonial cities (such as those by Liang 2005 and Sundaram 2010). What interests us, along these lines, is how piracy destabilizes in practice the liberal vision of the city: how pirate networks and practices proliferate across urban spaces by tapping into the existing technological infrastructures of the city; how piracy challenges the liberal notions of the divide between public/private and legal/illegal as they are inscribed in the organization of urban space. What distinguishes this chapter from the above studies is twofold: firstly, its focus on Athens, Greece – a city vastly different from the postcolonial Delhi or Bangalore that Sundaram and Liang analyze both in terms of the sheer size of the pirate economy and in relation to how the pirate economy interconnects with the formal circulation of capital; and secondly, the much more limited scope of our study, focusing primarily on the mobilities of a specific social group involved in the pirate economy of Athens: migrant street vendors.

Our intention is not to treat piracy as outside to state power or to the logic of control, nor to claim that contemporary pirates are produced as subjects outside the dominant processes of subjectivation: that is, that they are pure nomadic subjects. Instead, we will insist on the notion of the "patchwork" (Deleuze and Guattari 1998, 474): pirate economies in Athens produce space as a patchwork consisting of both smooth and striated aspects. Smooth and striated spaces do not intersect, do not converge and do not diverge: they are asymmetrical. In this sense, we will focus on the practices of migrant street-vendors as practices of rupture with the specified segmentations and uses of the Athenian urban space and time.

The use of the notion of smooth space in an analysis of piracy in an urban setting, however, might seem puzzling. Even Deleuze and Guattari initially seem to caution us against such an approach when stating: "In contrast to the sea, the city is the striated space par excellence" (1988, 481). Our discussion of smooth spaces views them, however, as spatial ruptures: not as end products of an evolutionary process, but as ephemeral and excessive, rising out of cracks, aberrations that creep out in the dominant urban fabric. Along these lines, it is interesting to see smooth urban spaces – again in Deleuze and Guattari's terms – as a "counterattack" against the forces of striation, as "a hack" against the dominant organizations of urban space (1988, 481).

Before moving on to our analysis, the final point we want to make clear is that this chapter does not take sufficient issue with the notion of subjectivity. Our primary focus here is on spatial bodily practices rather than on the processes of production of subjectivities. We are not, thus, trying to depict migrant street-vendors as full blown articulate pirates, but as carriers of practices that exceed any process of self-identification. Pirate practices, in other words, are not seen as reflecting the identities of pre-defined subjects, nor as necessarily embodying the desires of migrant subjects. They are produced, instead, through an adoption of spatial tactics that remain largely unrepresentable, and non-articulable in public discourse. Rather than focusing only on the declarations that some of their representative or solidarity initiatives have published, and the discussions we had with some of them during the past two years, we try to also read their traces on the streets of the city, to observe their performances, and study their equipment.[1] It is through these observations that we come to understand how

1 Our insights are based (a) on interviews and exchanges with African migrant street vendors who work in Nea Smyrni Square, Athens, in 2009 for the purposes of an open discussion organized in the occupied space of Galaxias and (b) on a series of informal interviews with migrant street vendors conducted for the purposes of the Mig@Net research project (see www.mignetproject.eu) in the centre of Athens – mainly in Victoria Square and the pavement outside the Economic University of Athens in 2011-12. It should be noted that all the interviewees wanted to be kept anonymous.

the pirate economies of migrant street vending in Athens emerge.

Transversing space

Migrant street vendors appeared on the streets of Athens in the 1990s and ever since have multiplied and diversified their practices. The evolution of migrant street practices has been characterized from the beginning by its incommensurability to mainstream commerce. Contemporary public debates on the issue in Greece focus either on the criminality of migrant street selling practices and the damage that this kind of illicit trade causes to Greek business, or on the exploitation of migrant street vendors by large transnational illegal networks trading pirate goods. In spite of its salient presence and its over-visibility in the open spaces of the city, the only existing statistics of migrant street vending are based on police records of arrests and confiscations of goods that over-emphasize the role and efforts of the Greek police to combat illicit trade (The Press Project 2012). This emphasis on police statistics is coupled with a lack of more critical analyses discursively anchoring such policing practices to the securitization of public space. As a result, particularly in the 2000s, a series of speculative and impressionistic estimations have appeared in the press and in new media outlets emphasizing the 'massive' profits that this type of pirate business generates.

Particularly since the beginning of the socioeconomic crisis in Greece and the rise of far right politics, migrant street vending has become a main target of racist popular rhetoric and policies. From 2011 to 2012, the police escalated their efforts to arrest and confiscate the goods of migrant street vendors (thus boosting the relevant statistics) while the far right-wing group, Golden Dawn, has organized systematic violent attacks against migrant street vendors particularly in the wider centre of Athens. In response to these violent attacks, most human rights based organizations have adopted the position that migrant street vendors are only the victims of a multimillion-dollar business that produces cheap goods and forces illegal transit migrants to travel all over Greece to sell them illegally with a very small margin of profit and a very high security risk (Hellenic League of Human Rights 2011). Ironically, this type of humanitarian defense of migrant street vendors is also based on police statistics of arrests and confiscations of goods and arbitrary arrests, and on apocalyptic estimates of the immense illegal profits that this business generates reproduced from mainstream press clippings. In both cases, migrant street vending appears as a phenomenon that cannot be counted or categorized and is precisely because of this feature subject to hyperbolic and dramatic representational practices.

Migrant street-vendors in Greece operate in a state of precarious semi-lawlessness. Even when they have managed to obtain legal status as migrants, their work remains a grey area in relation to state policies. Greek street-vendors selling their goods on the streets and in open-air markets obtain their permits from the municipality. However, through a series of overtly discriminatory acts, the introduction of impossible selection criteria, and extremely high permit fees, the Greek state has made it practically impossible for migrants to obtain such permits (Kourkoulas 2011). In spite of these legal barriers, in practice migrant street vending has been steadily proliferating since the 1990s. The precarious nature of migrant labor has accentuated since 2005, as all regularization procedures have ceased and migrants entering the Greek territory have no access to legal residence permits or work. Simultaneously, there has been an explosion of counterfeit, pirate and stolen goods bought and sold on the street. This has been fueled in recent years, especially after the beginning of the recession in 2009, because of the boom in consumerist demand for cheap products and the rise of migrant unemployment in other sectors of the economy such as construction, domestic work, cleaning, care and agriculture. For many migrant street vendors, particularly those operating in the centre of Athens, street vending has become the only means of generating the necessary funds in order to move to a desired European destination. It has, therefore, become a form of labor inscribed in transit migrant practices.

The rise of the pirate economy was marked by a shift from leisure/entertainment goods such as pirate CDs, fake brand jewelry, watches, bags, shoes, clothes in the 1990s and early 2000s, toward 'the basic necessities' and the 'recycling of stolen goods' in the 2010s. It was also marked by a diversification of the spots in which migrant street-vendors operate. Alongside the commercial avenues and streets, the public squares and entertainment venues, migrant street-vendors have also contributed significantly to the development of gigantic open air markets that are organized during the weekends in central spots of the city, where Greek and migrant unlicensed street-vendors sell all kinds of pirate and stolen products: from PCs and bicycles, to toilet paper and food cans (Hatzopoulos et al. 2012).[2]

2 A relatively new pirate trade concerns recycling. Migrant mobilities are again central to the development of this trade, which consists mostly in collecting metals, glass, paper and other goods from garbage bins or simply stealing them from existing buildings and infrastructures and selling

The pirate economy of street vending is not striated: it does not proliferate through the processes of continuous measurement and control of goods that characterize formal economies. The fake bags and watches, the fake-branded clothes, the CDs and DVDs that have been copied, the mobile phones and bicycles stolen and sold in the street are not fully registered, taxed, controlled. The street-vending pirate economy is based on the reproduction of the product potentially innumerable times making it, thus, something that cannot be officially counted. This resistance of pirate economies to official measurement is reminiscent of Deleuze and Guattari's articulation where smooth space becomes a space where "someone can occupy without having to count," whereas striated space constitutes the space "where someone counts in order to occupy" (1988, 477).

The persistence of this pirate economy rests on its versatility and on the mobile tactics developed by migrant bodies. Unlike Greek street-vendors who carry their goods in large vehicles operated with engines or pushed by hand, the equipment of migrant street-vendors consists of large plastic bags, blankets and other pieces of cloth that can be easily and quickly folded and carried away. Light equipment is indispensable for two reasons. First, it allows migrant street-vendors to carry their goods around in order to become visible *within* other non-commercial and commercial spaces such as cafes, restaurants and bars, without competing with their owners. By 'invading' these licensed and clearly demarcated places, migrant street-vendors usurp their clientele, mesmerizing potential buyers into purchasing their cheap goods without an effort. Second, light equipment makes it possible for them to move quickly during the usual police 'sweep operations' in the center of Athens: here, escaping does not require a road, but can be easily made through small alleyways and public transport making it possible to become temporarily invisible, and move to different locations in order to reappear again often on the same spots.

The itineraries of street vendors are, thus, as versatile as their equipment, scheduling their days in order to capture the space and time of the city without compromising to its logic of control. This versatility accounts for the fact that even the largest commercial streets in Athens, which are filled with security cameras and are regularly policed by municipal and national police, are populated by large numbers of migrant street-vendors that appear and disappear in non regular

them to scrap industries. This type of economic activity is currently booming and one can observe all over Athens migrants with supermarket trolleys carefully selecting these materials from the garbage and carrying them to recycling centers for sale.

intervals. It also accounts for the fact that one can meet migrant street-vendors in their 'regular spots' but also in other unpredicted locations around the city.

Here it is necessary to specify that street vending does not *take place*, rather it *occurs or happens in specific spots and through wisely calculated itineraries* that are always versatile, but not without their own time specificity and spatiality. This requires skillful prediction. For example, one can observe the strategic positioning of umbrella selling migrants in front of the Metro stations and bus stops even before the rain starts and their immediate disappearance once the rain stops. The pirate economy has its own rules that are not subject to the private/public divide: one cannot become visible everywhere, because spots are 'taken' or are reserved for specific groups of vendors at specific times of the day. To take over a spot requires negotiation with the migrant vending-community. However, although one has to respect these 'spots', wandering around public and private spaces to attract potential clients tends to be unlimited. One can 'invade' spaces, one can move across all kinds of spatial borders, as long as one does not interfere with spots or itineraries that are taken by other street vendors.

Control, as is exercised by the municipal and state police, is equally dispersed, as are the practices of migrant street-vendors. Sometimes the municipal or national police attempt to chase them, to confiscate or deface their products, or even to imprison those who do not have residence permits. In other cases, however, the police simply check their permits and let them go, while most of the time the police simply pass them by and leave them alone.

Since 2011, there has also been a devolution of control from police and state authorities to various ultra right-wing groups that violently attack migrant street-vendors, destroying their merchandise in a paradigmatic way (Human Rights Watch 2012). Police and ultra right-wing violence extends beyond the public domain and enters into homes and rented dwellings. The threat of violence is always omnipresent although not exercised in a systematic manner as racist attacks may happen anywhere and everywhere. In a collective text, migrant street vendors working in one of Athens' central squares write:

> We face everyday an aggressive racism from a part of society and especially from the police. The policemen invade our houses and take our money and merchandise. The fascists and the police chase migrants all the time. Especially at night they go round the neighborhoods searching for migrants to hit them. Usually they turn up with a civil identity card, presenting themselves as policemen, they ask our papers and afterwards

> they tear them apart and batter us. In reality, we can never know if those in front of us are fascists or policemen. (Migrant Street Vendors' and Solidaires of Victoria Square 2012)

Migrant street-vendors, in response, invent and perform dispersed practices that allow them to move quickly, becoming visible/invisible according to the circumstances to avoid this form of control and violence. Their movements between visibility and invisibility are also movements between legality and illegality inscribed in their ambiguous relationship to the Greek state: they legalize their presence in Greece through buying social security stamps, an expense that they can cover by selling pirate goods. Through an illegal activity, they manage to become legal. In some cases, a legal status emanates from collecting the necessary fees to move to a new European destination, where they can apply for asylum or a residence permit. In other cases, it means collecting the necessary amount of money to buy the necessary security stamps to renew a Greek residence permit. This is something that completely escapes the public reactions toward this 'informal form of trade' that oscillate between, on the one hand, public outcries about the failure of policing and the economic losses caused to state and 'proper' private enterprise and, on the other hand, a public discourse calling for the normalization of this pirate economy, envisaging the creation of open air ethnic markets set up, licensed, and controlled by municipal authorities (Hatzopoulos et al. 2012).

Interestingly both of these standpoints desire the uninterrupted visibility of migrant street-vendors in specific places in the city. Ultra right-wing initiatives against migrant street vending have set the task of counting, documenting and categorizing migrant street-vendors by photographing them. Relevant blogs are set up in order to publish daily pictures of migrant street-vendors with precise locations and characteristics of each one of them. Marches are organized by seemingly 'concerned citizens' to photograph them in specific places in the centre of the city and publish their photographs online (Doumas 2012; Ios Press 2010). Similarly, several anti-racist and pro-immigrant initiatives play with visual anthropology tactics in order to document their presence in public space (Muñoz 2012).

This process of capturing migrant street-vending in order to denounce it through the photographic lens is inscribed in a desire to arrest movement, to challenge versatile tactics, to stop mobility, to impose a striated logic over a smooth space. However, by being circulated online, such images become objects of mutation and transformation. The same images that are produced by newspaper photographers in order to criticize migrant street vending as a criminal activity are used by anti-racist bloggers to denounce police aggression against them.

And yet there is always something that escapes the attempts to count migrant street-vendors, to position them, to document them, to interrupt their mobility and arrest the versatility of their pirate economy. As noted above, the pirate tactics pursued by migrant street-vendors rest on ephemeral visibility that allows for fast translocation and constant relocation in new spots or even in mobile dislocation within existing places. This practice does not only serve for the self-evident protection from policing authorities that perform checks and patrols, but also helps the more effective promotion of products that are not counted. The tendency of migrant street-vendors to break existing spatial boundaries at regular intervals in order to sell makes them both unpredictable and effective. This is simply because they are trying to sell everywhere: in the spaces of free circulation, in the commercial spaces of gathering, on playgrounds, even on beaches, ships and trains.

This commercial activity is, therefore, connected to a different strategy of production of the space and time of the city, a strategy that does not directly oppose commercialization but contests its existing rules. The practices of migrant street-vendors push commercialization to its limits, refusing to accept that transactions must be defined according to the place it is performed, refusing to accept that commercialized space must be demarcated. To the strategy of 'more and more extended commercial uses of public space', which results in the occupation of the public by the private, the practices of migrant street-vendors counterpoise a strategy of 'commerce everywhere and for all', as long as this activity is pirated.

It is in that sense that migrant bodies produce smooth spaces: a set of ephemeral, disjointed nomadic practices. They perform mobilities that "no longer go from one point to another but instead pass between points" (Deleuze and Guattari 1998, 498). Such mobilities are "constantly changing direction," constantly mutating without a demarcated 'outside or inside': in effect they constitute the main producers of 'a smooth space' within the striated city (ibid.). The mobility of migrant street-vendors results in a smoothness that penetrates the official demarcations of Athenian public and private spaces and denies the logic of the prevailing commercialization that orders the life of the city. If we could map public squares, streets and pedestrian routes following their movements a line would emerge. Drawing on Deleuze and Guattari, this would be a line that:

> …delimits nothing, that describes no contour, that no longer goes from one point to another but instead passes between points, that is always declining from the horizontal and the vertical and deviating from the diagonal, that is constantly changing direction, a mutant line of this kind that is without outside or inside, form or background, beginning or end and that is alive as a continuous variation – such a line is truly an abstract line, and describes a smooth space. (1988, 498)

Nonetheless migrant street-vendors are not nomads, strictly speaking, or at least they are not nomads all the time:

> The nomad is not at all the same as the migrant; for the migrant goes principally from one point to another, even if the second point is uncertain, unforeseen, or not well localized. (Deleuze and Guattari 1988, 380)

The desires of migrant street-vendors are striated. A collective text written by migrant street vendors operating in an off centre square of Athens makes this point clear: "We left from there to come to Europe with the purpose of protecting our lives because our countries were not safe enough to live in and survive" (Migrant Street Vendors of Nea Smyrni 2009). What the migrants desire and are seeking are better living conditions, opportunities, chances to become wealthier, more educated, more independent from political, social and financial constraints. Their text continues:

> We looked for jobs but it was very difficult to find something. We became street-vendors not because we want to be on the streets but because we were searching for a way to survive. (Migrant Street Vendors of Nea Smyrni 2009)

In these narratives, nomadic practices stem out of the inability to fulfill one's primary migratory desires. One is forced to move into smooth spaces in order to fulfill striated dreams. In effect, in migrant lives the smooth and the striated become inter-connected. As one migrant street vendor notes: "Our activity is simply to wander round the streets for petty-commerce" (Migrant Street Vendors of Victoria Square 2012). But this wandering around is a process of change and transformation that has very little resemblance to the romantic notions of piracy manifesting that smooth spaces are not idyllic and utopian. As Deleuze and Guattari note, "Voyaging smoothly is a becoming, and a difficult, uncertain becoming at that" (1988, 482).

Occupying public space

On 25 May 2011, Syntagma, the central square of Athens situated in front of the Parliament building was occupied by a multitude of protesters. This move was envisioned as the beginning of an 'indefinite occupation' of the squares across Greece. The initial open call of the occupiers was addressed to those who want to "take their life in their own hands," who "refuse to acknowledge the debt as [their] own" and who are willing to "bring down the institutions responsible for the debt" (Resolution of the Syntagma Assembly – 25 May 2011). The occupation of the square lasted for approximately six weeks (depending on when you mark its termination date). In addition to some specific days of mobilization which were connected either to national days of strike or to the voting days of the austerity measures by the Greek parliament, the square became a battleground between riot police aiming to disperse protesters and protesters refusing to disperse and re-occupying the square again and again. The occupation enforced the establishment of certain spatial structures that transformed the square.

The occupation ran 24 hours per day as a camping site was established in the green areas and some temporary building structures were set up in shady parts of the square used for organizational and campaign purposes. In the mornings, the square largely continued to function as usual, mainly as a transit space for people going to and from work and for consumers shopping. In the evenings, the same space was transformed in a parallel and often conflictual splitting up of the square. An open assembly was organized at the bottom part, where decisions about the organization of the occupation and the mobilizations against the government were taken through direct democratic procedures. At the top of the square, however, a diverse crowd of mostly nationalist protesters gathered every evening in the street outside the parliament: singing the national anthem, waving Greek national flags, and chanting slogans against the politicians inside the parliament.

Whilst this amalgam of indignados transformed the space and time of the square, the group of mainly migrant street-vendors who were present in the square before the occupation began to proliferate. After all, the occupied square became a 'safer' place for them, since police control was temporarily suspended. In this context, a parallel pirate economy could operate. Migrant street-vendors continued to sell their pirate merchandise: pirate CDs, stolen mobile phones, fake Gucci bags and Nike shoes. Several of them began to diversify their trade to include other counterfeit goods that were useful to the occupiers of the square: including gas-masks protecting demonstrators from chemicals used by the police, Greek plastic flags for the nationalist protesters, and laser flash lights used by demonstrators to temporarily blind the riot squad guarding the parliament, the journalists and TV cameras residing at the five star hotels located around the square, and the residents of the expensive flats of the area. Certain spots were also occupied by a group of mobile cantinas on wheels, where mostly Greek licensed street-vendors were selling hot dogs, souvlaki, soft drinks and beer to the protesters.

The assembly addressed the presence of the migrant and Greek street-vendors in a twofold manner. The migrant street vendors were addressed by the occupiers first, as street vendors and second, as migrants, maintaining though, a somewhat clear distinction between these two identifications. The question of migration and the participation of migrants in the mobilizations became a topical issue for the politics of the occupation. This was a slow process, coupled with the growing radicalization of the open assembly at the bottom of the square, which was partly based on its counter-positioning against the 'nationalists' on the upper part of the square. The assembly, along these lines, articulated the politics of anti-racism and of solidarity with migrants as inherent to their struggle against the forces of the existing political and economic exploitative system. Although the assembly eventually organized an anti-racist day of action, it is mainly the daily debates over racism that are our focus here.

The assembly, about two days following its first meeting, voted in favor of a minor formal recognition of the presence of migrants in the occupation by hanging a banner with the slogan: "All power to local assemblies, Greeks and migrants united" (Resolution of the Syntagma Assembly – 13 June 2011). This first move was followed by the inclusion of the category 'migrant' in the ensuing open calls of the occupiers of the square, which had previously referred to several other social groups, such as the unemployed, precarious workers, farmers, and so on, in relation to the question of 'who the occupiers are' (Resolution of the Syntagma Assembly – 15 June 2011). Later, the assembly voted for organizing a day of deliberation on racism and xenophobia (Resolution of the Syntagma Assembly – 18 June 2011). This day of deliberation was slightly delayed, but materialized with the participation (for the first time officially during the open assembly) of members of migrant associations as speakers (Resolution of the Syntagma Assembly – 16 June).

The attempts to express solidarity with migrants remained, however, an empty gesture towards the majority of migrants who were actually present in the occupation: the street vendors. The migrant street vendors did not directly respond to the calls of the occupation. They were never invited to speak in the open assembly, nor did they show any desire to do so. Solidarity was clearly expressed against violent racist acts, as for example when a member of the security committee of the occupiers violently attacked a migrant street vendor. The Greek, who committed this act, was forced to leave the occupied space and racist violence was denounced (Resolution of the Syntagma Assembly – 22 June). Similar reactions were repeated when rumors circulated that some 'nationalists' on the top of the square were attacking migrant street-vendors and the open assembly again intervened to denounce these acts and to discuss how they could protect other migrants from similar racist attacks.

The debate over the presence of street-vendors in the occupied space was kept distinct from these politics of solidarity. In the debate, there was no distinction between the food sellers slowly moving licensed cantinas in the square and the migrant street-vendors who moved with and in-between the crowds of protesters. The open assembly reached the decision that an occupied space should be free of all commercial activities, even if those activities were organized by migrants, since profit making was recognized as being by definition in direct conflict with the aims of the anti-austerity movement (Resolution of the Syntagma Assembly – 12 June). The migrant street vendors were asked by members of the assembly to leave the occupation – a decision that was never respected by the street vendors themselves. The diversification of the goods for sale by the pirate economy to meet the needs of the occupiers and the resilience of the street vendors to stay in Syntagma together with the occupiers even when the situation turned violent did not transform the decision of the open assembly. In spite of the resolution of the assembly, however, migrant street vendors continued to sell their counterfeit goods until the end of the occupation and persisted even in the most adverse circumstances: such as when chemicals were used by the riot police, who attacked, beat up and arrested protestors.

The end of the occupation meant also the return of the square in its pre-occupation pirate economy. The number of migrant street-vendors decreased, there ceased to be gas masks and laser flash lights for sale or hot-dogs and souvlaki, just counterfeit Gucci bags and pirate CDs and DVDs.

During the Syntagma occupation, two different forms of alternative production of space met. Although both of them questioned the existing boundaries and organization of public/private space, they were not necessarily compatible. On one hand, the distributed movement of the migrant street-vendors in the open space of the square, seeking occupiers/customers and, at the same time, trying to avoid the control of the local police and the racist attacks of far-right nationalist protestors. On the other hand, the practices of occupation that primarily aimed at suspending the existing spatial uses of the central public square of Athens. This was an attempt to produce an open space of encounter amongst the multitude, while denouncing the increasing commercialization of public space and creating zones of anti-commercialization inside it.

The striated aspects of the occupied space (the stratification between a nationalist top and a leftish bottom of the square) were radically challenged by the smooth practices of the migrant street- vendors who moved towards different directions within and outside the square. Their movement redefined the square in terms of nodes: possible selling points, meeting points, and lines of flight. This remapping of the square by migrant mobilities bypassed striation: to sell gas masks, laser flash lights and flags one had to move across the lines separating the nationalist protesters from the open assembly. The migrant vendors were those who were primarily impervious to the striations of the occupied space: they were the ones who distributively moved across Syntagma as if the spatial demarcations reflecting its political heterogeneity were only there to be by-passed.

The pirate practices of the migrant street-vendors were not primarily viewed in spatial terms by the occupiers, but mainly through the lens of the politics of anti-commercialization. Paradoxically, however, there were moments when the movements of both occupiers and migrant street-vendors co-aligned. At times, when riot police attempted to evacuate Syntagma with the use of massive amounts of chemicals, the mobilities of the occupiers and of the migrant street-vendors became synchronized. Both were dispersing around the square and around the nearby streets for a while to catch their breath and then coming back again and again to re-capture the occupied space. One protestor exclaimed in the midst of a tear-gas cloud of chemicals during one of those days: "You know when the chemicals will soon become suffocating and you will have to move elsewhere, when you see that the street-vendors are moving".

When the square was re-occupied, however, their movements became again asynchronous: the occupiers trying to revert the space back to its previous state. In so doing, they attempted to re-establish the ephemeral building structures that had been destroyed by the police or to clean the square from the smell of chemicals; while the migrant street-vendors started to move around and outside the square to identify how their pirate products would be best sold in a space under construction.

Conclusion – Patchworks

In this chapter, we have traced the simultaneous production of smooth and striated spaces in the Athenian urban landscape in a period of intensification of social struggles and of multiplication of sites of contestation. Our main argument can be phrased like this: spatial practices that develop around the pirate economy by migrant street-vendors lead to the production of urban spaces as a patchwork of the smooth and the striated.

The mobilities of migrant street-vendors are "nomadic transits in smooth space": they make "the city disgorge a patchwork, differentials of speed, delays and accelerations, changes in orientation, continuous variations..." (Deleuze and Guattari 1998, 482). The spatial tactics of migrant pirates stand in tension with the predominant control and policing of urban space, but also with the spatial politics of the occupation movements of the squares. It is not our intention to romanticise migrant street-vendors as nomadic pirates or to attribute to them a kind of radical politics.

What we have tried to do, instead, is to sketch out some of the trajectories of migrant street-vendors and to show the unrepresentability of smooth practices within existing social movements. The mobilities of migrant street-vendors are shaped by the conditions of the pirate economy that they produce and the forces of control that act against it. The re-invention of piracy in an urban setting, however, represents a challenge for contemporary social movements: its unmeasurability, its unrepresentability, its defiance of the private-public divide, even its radical over-commercialisation, are not incommensurable with on-going social struggles.

In a way, the tactics of migrant pirates can be located at the exact opposite end of the protestors' aims. They aim at profit: illegal, untaxed profit made through exploiting existing consumerist desires. The decision of the Syntagma assembly to ban migrant street-vendors from the occupation manifested this opposition. From a different perspective, however, pirate practices, by the mere negation of the spatial stratification of space, do not meet but tend to constantly cross the lines of occupy movements. Even the most striated city gives rise to smooth spaces: to live in the city as a nomad, or as a cave dweller. Movements, speed, and slowness are sometimes enough to reconstruct a smooth space. Of course, smooth spaces are not in themselves liberatory. But the struggle is changed or displaced in them, and life reconstitutes its stakes, confronts new obstacles, invents new paces, and switches adversaries. As Deleuze and Guattari note, however, "never believe that a smooth space will suffice to save us" (1998, 500).

References

De Certeau, Michel (1984). *The Practice of Every-day Life.* (trans. Steven Rendall). Berkley: University of California Press.

Deleuze, Gilles and Felix Guattari (1988). *A Thousand Plateaus: Capitalism and Schizophrenia.* London: Athlone Press.

Hatzopoulos, Pavlos, Dimitris Parsanoglou and Carolin Philip (2012). Report on Social movements: Athens Case Study. Mig@Net *research project.* Retrieved 20 September 2012, from http:www.mignteproject.eu

Hellenic League of Human Rights (2011). "On Illegal Trade and Street Vendors" (in Greek). Retrieved 20 September 2012, from http://www.hlhr.gr/details.php?id=607

Human Rights Watch (2012). "Hate on the Streets Xenophobic Violence in Greece". Retrieved 20 September 2012, from http://www.hrw.org/reports/2012/07/10/hate-streets-0

IOS press (2010). "The 'Revolution of the Merchants': Organized against African Street-Vendors". Retrieved 19 May 2012, from http://www.iospress.gr/ios2010/ios20100418.htm

Kourkoulas, Thanasis (2011). "Illegal Trade and Migrants: Racist Lies under Conditions of Crisis". Retrieved 15 May 2012, from http://bit.ly/LmO83s

Kuhn, Gabriel (2010). *Life Under the Jolly Roger: Reflections on Golden Age Piracy.* PM Press.

Liang, Lawrence (2005). "Porous Legalities and Avenues of Participation". *Sarai Reader.* 2005: 6-17. Retrieved 25 July 2013, from http://www.sarai.net/publications/readers/05-bare-acts/02_lawrence.pdf

Migrant Street Vendors of Nea Smyrni Square (2009). Declaration. Retrieved 20 March 2012, from http://eleftherosgalaxias.blogspot.gr/2009/05/blog-post_31.html

Migrant Street-Vendors of Victoria Square (2012). Declaration of 9 March.

Retrieved 21 March 2012, from https://athens.indymedia.org/front.php3?lang=el&article_id=1384598

Muñoz, Lorena (2012). "Latino/a Immigrant Street Vendors in Los Angeles: Photo Documenting Sidewalks from 'Back-Home'". *Sociological Research Online*, 17:2, 21. Retrieved 5 April 2012, from http://www.socresonline.org.uk/17/2/21.html

Neuwirth, Robert (2011). *Stealth of Nations: The Global rise of the Informal Economy.* Pantheon Books.

Panayotis Doumas blog, Retrieved 29 May 2012, from http://doumas.wordpress.com/

Resolution of the Syntagma Assembly 25 May, (2011). Retrieved 15 May 2012, from http://real-democracy.gr/votes/2011-05-25-psifisma-laikis-syneleysis-plateias-syntagmatos

Resolution of the Syntagma Assembly 12 June, (2011). Retrieved 15 May 2012, from http://real-democracy.gr/votes/2011-06-12-psifismata-laikis-syneleysis-syntagmatos

Resolution of the Syntagma Assembly 13 June, (2011). Retrieved 15 May 2012, from http://real-democracy.gr/votes/2011-06-13-psifismata-ls-136

Resolution of the Syntagma Assembly 15 June, (2011). Retrieved 15 May 2012, from http://real-democracy.gr/votes/2011-06-15-psifisma-laikis-syneleysis

Resolution of the Syntagma Assembly 16 June, (2011). Retrieved 15 May 2012, from http://real-democracy.gr/votes/2011-06-16-psifismata-laikis-syneleysis-plateias-syntagmatos-1606

Resolution of the Syntagma Assembly 18 June, (2011). Retrieved 15 May 2012, from http://real-democracy.gr/votes/2011-06-18-psifismata-laikis-syneleysis-plateias-syntagmatos-18-ioyni-2011

Resolution of the Syntagma Assembly 22 June, (2011). Retrieved 15 May 2012, from http://real-democracy.gr/votes/2011-06-22-psifismata-laikis-syneleysis-22062011

Selmann, Brianne (2008). "Pirate Heterotopias". In *Deptford.tv Diaries II - Pirate Strategies.* London: Liquid Culture.

Sundaram, Ravi (2010). *Pirate Modernity: Dehli's Media Urbanism.* London & New York: Routledge.

The Press Project (2012). "Fascism in our Living Room" (in Greek). Retrieved 20 September 2012, from http://www.thepressproject.gr/folder/21531/o-fasismos-sto-saloni-mas

The Collaborative Production of Amateur Subtitles for Pirated TV Shows in Brazil

Vanessa Mendes Moreira De Sa

The focus of this chapter is the *Legenders* – a group of Brazilian fans who collaboratively produce amateur subtitles for (illegally) downloaded television shows, operating in an online fandom community. After downloading an episode of a television show in English from a file-sharing platform, most Brazilians require Portuguese subtitles, which are voluntarily produced by a group of fans named *Legenders* (Bernardo 2011). Although they present practices similar to fansubbers, which is an abbreviation for fan-subtitlers, the Brazilian amateur subtitlers identify themselves as *Legenders* simply because they translate Western TV shows mostly from the US and UK; whereas the fansubbers focus on Asian TV productions.

In Brazil, there are over thirty teams of *Legenders* cooperating with an indeterminate number of independent translators building informal working relationships over the Internet (Mizukami, Castro, Moncau and Lemos 2011, 265). Although federal law in Brazil states that the copyright holders must authorize translations of copyrighted material, the *Legenders* do not consider their work as an 'act of piracy', but rather a hobby and even a community service (Calazans 2010; Magalhaes Silva 2009; Mendes Moreira De Sa 2011; Sayuri 2011). Previous research has confirmed that the key motivations are the building of online friendships created within the networks and a feeling that they become 'part' of their favorite television series (Bernardo 2011; Leal 2010).

A great deal of earlier research has explored the work of amateur communities undertaking subtitling work (see Barra 2009; Jenkins 2008; Lee 2011; Leonard 2005; Perez Gonzalez 2007; Prado Alves Silva 2009; Tian 2011). Most of these studies focus on amateur subtitlers translating the dialogue from Asian television productions into English. However, there is limited research on the Brazilian *Legenders'* free and affective work. Considering that Brazil, along with Russia, India and China, is a country with an increasingly important position on the global economic and political scene it deserves cautious attention. These 'BRIC' nations, an acronym created by economist Jim O'Neill (2001), are identified as increasingly important and rapidly growing economies in global affairs.

The purpose of this study is to understand how the *Legenders* develop and establish a sense of community between the team members, the audiences who download TV shows and subtitles in Portuguese, and www.legendas.tv – a Brazilian fandom website that provides subtitles. The www.legendas.tv site is more than a database of Brazilian Portuguese subtitles, it is also the platform where the *Legenders* meet, interact and publish their work (Mizukami e.al. 2011). The administrators of www.legendas.tv utilize the website to establish quality standards for subtitles, release a subtitle distribution schedule, and organize the allocation of upcoming television shows among the teams of subtitlers (Bernardo 2011). According to the web information company *Alexa*, www.legendas.tv has operated since 2006 and in November 2011, it was the 150th most visited website in Brazil and ranked 120th in Portugal (Alexa 2011).

To gain insights into the online work relations and interactions with the fans, I undertook a qualitative analysis of interviews via email and Skype with five *Legenders* between December 2011 and June 2012.[1] Each one of the interviewees belongs to a particular team: *Maniacs*, *Queens of the Lab*, *Insanos*, *Darkside* and *Subsfreak*. Additionally, I examined previously published work that while strongly descriptive, lacks sufficient academic analysis (see Bernardo 2011; Bold 2012). The limited research on the work of the *Legenders* also comes from online news media publications and interviews with the *Legenders* on fan-based websites (see for example Calazans 2010b; Olhar Digital 2010, 570; Leal 2010; Pagano 2010; Series Freaks Team 2011a; and, Series Freaks Team 2011b). Through an in-depth analysis of original and secondary sources, I apply the concepts of both fan and digital labor to gain an understanding of the similarities and differences that the Brazilian *Legenders* present in comparison to previous research on fansubbing.

In order to further comprehend the dynamics of the *Legenders'* practices, this chapter begins by presenting an overview of previous fansubbing literature. This is followed by an analysis of the *Legenders'* work in the 'fandom world' and a discussion of the working dynamics of the group. Next, I examine symbolic power and hierarchy in these communities, exploring how the *Legenders* negotiate their working practices among members and the www.legendas.tv administrators. This is followed by an overview of the affective labor practices, contrasting these to their external relations with the individuals that 'consume' their amateur subtitles. Finally, I discuss the sense of community, and how this group of fansubbers show

1 In order to protect the participants' identities their names were changed in this research.

resistance to anti-piracy organizations and laws.

Fan labor and the digital environment

This section aims to situate the *Legenders* practices within the digital environment by exploring previous literature on 'fan labor' and 'fan subtitling'.

According to Napoli (2001), television audiences are moving away from being passive observers to active participants in a virtual world: "virtually anyone with the capacity to receive content also has the capacity to produce and distribute content" (2011, 12). As such, if an episode of a television show is not locally available soon enough after its original release, determined audiences will find alternative ways to access it on the Internet. As impatient viewers search the Internet for desired shows, other viewers make them available by feeding the network with videos or facilitating access through fandom websites that provide links for downloading these shows. Such practices confirm that fans are segments of audiences and their enthusiasm motivates an active position in regard to the object of affection (Bielby and Harrington 2005).

This degree of interaction, however, does not apply to all audiences and fans, as not everyone has such a degree of computer literacy, interest or Internet access. For instance, according to the Brazilian Institute of Public Opinion and Statistics (IBOPE 2012), some 79.9 million Brazilians have access to the Internet, which is less than 50 percent of the total population. Yet, recent research indicates that approximately 41 percent of those download media content from unauthorized platforms (IPEA 2012).

For enthusiastic fans, the Internet has become a platform where they can act together to produce and distribute content. As the television shows and movies being downloaded are in their original languages, it becomes difficult for international audiences to watch these if they cannot understand the language of production. Nonetheless, there are fans all over the world that utilize technological tools and online communities to collaboratively produce subtitles for these shows. Bruns (2008) uses the term *produsage* to describe collective practices of production such as fansubbing. Moreover, peer-to-peer (P2P) practices are based on "free cooperation of producers" and "governed by the community of producers themselves" (Bauwens 2005). As discussed in this chapter, such features can be applied to the communities of amateur subtitlers in Brazil.

This is not necessarily a new practice. As Nightingale (2011) argues, many amateur audience practices that have existed for decades in more traditional media are now being enhanced by the Internet. A similar point is made by Benkler who explains that before the Internet, "the practical individual freedom to cooperate with others in making things of value was limited by the extent of the capital requirements of production" (2006, 6). The increasing access to the Internet has given many people "the capital capacity necessary to" be producers, "if not alone, then at least in cooperation with other individuals acting for complementary reasons" (Benkler 2006, 6). As the Internet facilitates the development of such practices, the collaboration among individuals towards shared production goals has also expanded.

On a practical level, trading television content and creating subtitles are activities that emerged prior to the advance and popularity of the Internet. Since the 1980s, fans have been utilizing new technologies to trade television series that are not aired in their countries (Leonard 2005). Initially, this practice mostly happened in the US with Japanese anime through exchange of VHS tapes in fan clubs (Jenkins 2006; Prado Alves Silva 2009). Since many of the fans did not understand Japanese, other fans would create subtitles in English and integrate them into the videos – a process known as 'fansubbing'. As Jenkins explains one of the outcomes of fansubbing practices was that the market for such Japanese shows grew exponentially in the US:

> The global sales of Japan's animation industry reached an astonishing $80 billion in 2004, 10 times what they were a decade before. It has won this worldwide success in part because Japanese media companies paid little attention to the kinds of grassroots activities – call it piracy, unauthorized duplication and circulation, or simply file-sharing – that American media companies seem so determined to shut down. Much of the risk of entering Western markets and many of the costs of experimentation and promotion were borne (sic) by dedicated consumers (2006, 78).

The expansion of the Internet and the increasing availability of free software for translation and subtitling have enhanced fansubbing practices (Bold 2012). Ito explains that, after "the advent of digital distribution, the digisubbing scene exploded, and fansubtitled works reach millions of fans around the world in multiple languages" (2010, 28).

Fansubbing is a form of 'fan labor' and work practice grounded in fan culture that unites amateur subtitlers in digital labor activities. Fan labor is an activity that consists of fans working for pleasure on a not-for-profit basis. This is a type of "affective or immaterial labor" that Hardt and Negri describe as "labor that produces or manipulates affects such as feeling of ease, well-being, satisfaction, excitement, or passion," but also "communication, social relations, and cooperation" (2006, 108, 113). Milner relates this position to fan studies, arguing that this occurs, at least in part, due to the "increased connectivity and community afforded by Information and Communication Technologies" (2009, 495).

Fansubbers originally related to amateur subtitlers who translated various Asian television shows and movies, particular Japanese anime, into their national language. During the past decade, scholarly research has identified a number of emerging patterns in Japanese fansubbing practices: firstly, they are not-for-profit (Hu 2005; Ito 2010; Milner 2009); secondly, this not-for-profit exchange is undertaken within a 'gift economy' where valuable services are being exchanged in a social context with no formal agreements (Barbrook 2003); thirdly, they are grounded in fan culture and often associated with social media (Hu 2005; Milner 2009); and, fourthly, the fansubbers communities rely on hierarchical structures and reputation recognition amongst their peers (Ito 2010). Moreover, previous research has also indicated that one of the outcomes of these fansubbing practices is that they promote content in places where the shows have not arrived yet (see Jenkins 2006; Leonard 2005; Milner 2009; Perez Gonzalez 2007). While these communities of fansubbers appear chaotic, evidence indicates that they are organized in correspondence to Milner's (2009) concept of new organization: that is, it consists in non-traditional labor as members contribute with knowledge and skills driven by their willingness to participate.

The amateur subtitlers in Brazil who translate Western television shows and films, mostly from the US and UK, into Brazilian Portuguese, reflect these characteristics within their fansubbing community. However, as previously stated, they do not consider themselves as fansubbers, but as *Legenders*. This is specifically done so the community can differentiate themselves from fans that translate the various Asian television shows and movies. While it was possible to conclude that the *Legenders'* work reflect many similarities to the broader fansubbing communities described above, they also present their own particularities – something that I explore in the following section.

The *Legenders* and www.legendas.tv

As I argue elsewhere (Mendes Moreira De Sa 2011) the Legenders are Brazilian fans who form communities of practice consistent with Wenger, McDermott,and Snyder's (2002) definition: they are connected by a passion – in this instance television shows – and they meet regularly with the purpose of sharing information and forming a community. These practices also meet previous definitions of social network such as "a common commitment to a shared project" (Knox, Savage and Harvey 2006, 117). The Legenders not only share a commitment among themselves to take part in a collaborative work to facilitate access to television programs, these work practices are also reflected in their interactions with the administrators of www.legendas.tv.

In a digital economy, their work can be classified as free and affective cultural labor (Terranova 2004). The *Legenders*' affective and amateur labor presents features that can be found not only in previous research in Asian fansubbing practices, but also in work relations in offline environments. By analysing my discussions with the *Legenders*, as well as previous interviews available in online news media (Calazans 2010; Olhar Digital 2010; Leal 2010; Pagano 2010; Series Freaks Team 2011a; Series Freaks Team 2011b), it is possible to identify three prominent characteristics that underpin the working dynamics of the *Legenders*: labor division, quality and reputation, and receiving credit for their work.

Labor division

As confirmed by the *Legenders* I interviewed, the www.legendas.tv website is the most popular source of amateur subtitles in Brazil. Although several *Legenders* work solo – as identified by Mizukami et al. (2011) – there are also over twenty teams that provide subtitles for the www.legendas.tv site including groups such as Insanos, InSUBs, Maniacs, theLoneGunners, Queens of the Lab, Subsfreak, United, Darkside and Hellsubs. While most of the *Legenders* teams use their own websites – such as Darkside (http://darksite.tv/) and Hellsubs (http://hellsubs.forumfacil.net/forum.htm) – to provide subtitles to fans and recruit more members, www.legendas.tv acts as a type of 'hub'. Figure 1 shows the website of the Insanos team which is responsible for creating the subtitles for popular US television series, such as *Once Upon a Time* (ABC, 2011-present).

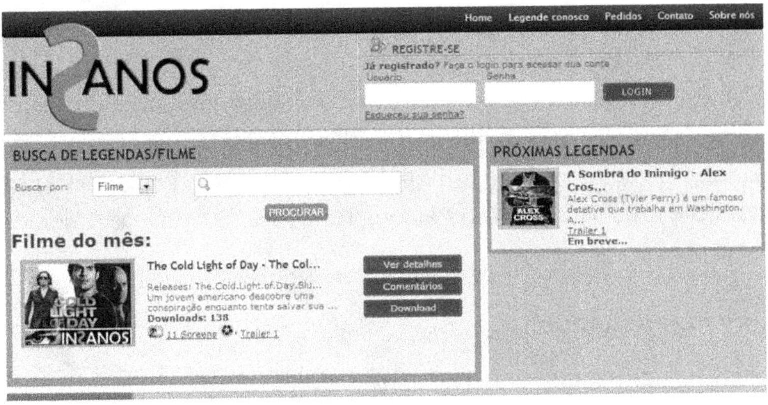

Figure 1. Screenshot of the Legenders' team Insanos website. The team creates subtitles for US TV shows and a range of US films. Retrieved from http://insanos.tv// on November 2012.

Previous research on *Legenders* by Bernardo (2011), Bold (2012) and Olhar Digital (2010), as well as my own interviews with Roger (male, 20, Insanos team) and Kenia (female, 31, Queens of the Lab team), reveal a specific production process from creating to publishing subtitles. Before the show is aired the leader of a *Legenders* team recruits the volunteers for an episode. During or even after the live streaming – which they watch through online channels such as *Justin. TV* – the volunteers discuss the episode and work out the details in online chat rooms. As soon as the video file is available for downloading through file sharing platforms, it is divided into parts by the team administrator and distributed to team members for translation. The process is facilitated by the English subtitles that already come with the video files because of closed caption technologies. Finally, one member is responsible for compiling the subtitles and publishing them on www.legendas.tv.

This type of division of labor is evident in other fansubbing communities too. As Ito explains in her work on Japanese anime fansubbers:

In fansub groups, there is a high degree of specialization and collaboration within each production team as well as in the community overall (2010, paragraph 32).

Moreover, a further division of labor emerges amongst members based on their professional and personal backgrounds. Some of the *Legenders* are students while others have established careers, such as doctors, engineers and IT-professionals.

Their professional and academic background may entitle them the responsibility for specific series. For instance, in the team that creates subtitles for *The Big Bang Theory* (CBS, 2007-present) – a television show about 'geek' culture – there are engineering students who take the lead, as they are able to provide more accurate translations of the humor (Sayuri 2011). As such, the *Legenders'* backgrounds can affect the distribution of tasks among team members, just as it would in an offline day job.

Quality and reputation

My research also found that the *Legenders* display a high level of commitment as team members often work throughout the night to create the subtitles and ensure that the program can be watched as soon as possible. The process of creating subtitles will vary depending on the TV show's popularity and audience demand. For instance, in order to make the subtitle for a popular show such as the US televisions series *Lost* (ABC, 2004-2010) available as soon as possible, more than one team of *Legenders* collaborated during its final season (Calazans 2010a).

Despite the hours, commitment and demands of the work involved, members of the *Legenders* view their involvement as a hobby and a passionate pursuit rather than any type of labor (Mendes Moreira De Sa 2011; Calazans 2010b; Magalhaes Silva 2009; Sayuri 2011). The involvement and commitment to subtitling activities may even develop as Zico (male, 24, Maniacs team) describes:

> [...] it starts as a hobby, and then it stops being a hobby and it becomes addiction, it is an activity to socially interact with others, to make friends, and there are all kinds of people from all over the place, it is a huge culture exchange (Personal communication, Skype, 5 June 2012).

The involvement also creates a type of community of *Legenders* that provides a sense of belonging and safety to its members. Drawing on Arvanitakis' conceptualisation of the "cultural commons," the interactions happen because, "... if I feel safe within my community, even when surrounded by strangers, then I am likely to cooperate with them" (2006, 2).

The *Legenders* are also adamant that just because this is something that they enjoy and do in addition to their paid work, they do not compromise on the quality of their work, maintaining that they act professionally, providing coherence with the subtitles and aiming for accurate synchronization with the scenes (Calazans 2010; Olhar Digital 2010). Ensuring and maintaining high standards of quality seems to be one of the main goals for organized amateur subtitling communities. Ito (2010), for example, identified both quality and reputation as significant and directly linked to anime fansubbing. In the case of the *Legenders*, I also found that they work hard to maintain their reputation among their audiences as well as the administrators of www.legendas.tv. In fact, the www.legendas.tv has policy guidelines regarding quality standards and, according to my interviewees, only the teams that strictly follow this will make it to the website's front-page highlights.

Linking the above two points, there is an overlap between the passionate pursuit of a hobby and the quality of the work undertaken. This is echoed by Benkler, who explains that "non-market collaborations can be better at motivating effort" (2006, 7). As such, while the *Legenders* claim to have no financial return for their voluntary work, they argue that cooperating in the production of subtitles is mostly about the friendships established and the positive feedback from fans that enjoy the programs. As Zico (male, 24, Maniacs team) explains:

Yes, yes, [compliments] are our salary. If I go to the legendas.tv website and check one of the [TV episode's] subtitles I created I will see that it had 10,000 downloads and only 40 people saying thank you. But at least there are [compliments] and they mean a lot to us (Personal communication, Skype, June 2012).

Moreover, prestige seems to be a great non-commercial incentive (Mizukami et al. 2011). As *Legenders* previously declared in interviews, they enjoy becoming what they call "anonymous online celebrities" in the fandom world and to see their names associated with the show which thousands of other people will see (Bernardo 2011; Sayuri 2011; Series Freaks Team 2011a ; Series Freaks Team 2011b).

In the process of producing the subtitles, the team of *Legenders* ensure they receive credit for their efforts. After analyzing subtitles created by different teams from www.legendas.tv, certain patterns emerge such as the inclusion of the name of the team, the participating members' nicknames and even team's slogan. The team InSUBs' slogan is for instance "Qualidade inSUBstituivel" or "irreplaceable quality". Moreover, many teams have their own websites with links and logos displayed on www.legendas.tv (see Figure 1). The different groups also promote their work through various forms of social media such as YouTube (see Figure 2), Twitter and Facebook (see Figure 3).

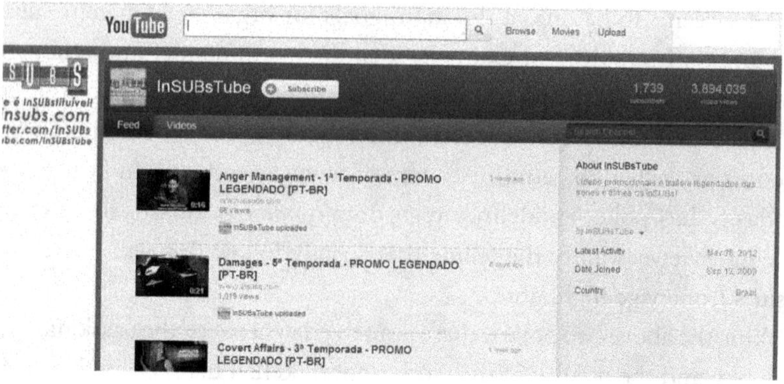

Figure 2. The figure shows promotions of series which the team of InSUBs Legenders creates subtitles for – Retrieved http://www.youtube.com/user/insubstube in 26 May 2012.

Figure 3. Legenders Insanos' Facebook page where announcements regarding subtitles are made: Retrieved from https://www.facebook.com/inSanosTV, 26 May 2012.

It is important to note that the reason the *Legenders* go to great lengths to promote their work is that 'downloads' are the currency in the amateur subtitling world: the greater the amount of downloads, the more motivation the *Legenders* have to continue engaging in the activity. In contrast, as Roger (male, 20, Insanos team) explains, a decline in downloads may reduce team members motivation to produce subtitles which may result in team activities ceasing. Further, the number of downloads is a way of recognizing the quality of a team's work, which will generate further work from the www.legendas.tv website administrators. The latter is important when a team makes a request to the administrators to create subtitles for a specific show - something that I return to in the following section.

As the *Legenders* work in teams and are connected by a network of fans, there is also a need for coordination between members. As explored in this section, this is achieved through the division of labor. Further, the volunteers must produce high quality subtitles in order to maintain their team's reputation among fan-communities and with www.legendas.tv. Finally, they must also ensure they receive credit for their work and promote themselves in the community, seeking recognition to maintain their status. Importantly, a platform such as the www.legendas.tv website is essential to both promote their work as well as to organize the different teams. In the next section I explore how the relations of power and hierarchy emerge between members and the administrators of www.legendas.tv.

Symbolic power and hierarchy in the Legendas.TV website

In their teams, the *Legenders* often present organizational similarities to traditional offline arrangements in regards to the distribution of power. In the offline world, media and popular culture present symbolic power that Bourdieu defines as "the power of constructing reality" (in Couldry 2006, 8). Symbolic power also operates inside digital labor networks, as online communities are "normatively regulated" and "hierarchical" (Baym 2006, 46). Bauwens adds that hierarchy in P2P cultures is more flexible and "based on merit that are used to enable participation" (2005: paragraph 22). In contrast, Benkler believes that P2P production systems "depend on individual action that is self-selected and decentralized, rather than hierarchically assigned" (2006, 62). However, in her work on amateur subtitling of anime videos, Ito (2010) notes the relevance of hierarchy in the amateur media ecology and among fansubbers. In my research, I have also found that hierarchy and symbolic power emerge in the *Legenders'* environment.

In this section I explore both the hierarchy and the internal policies determined by the www.legendas.tv administrators as they manage the teams of subtitlers affiliated with the website. As noted, such an organization is necessary to sustain the quality and reputation of the website as the preferred source of amateur subtitles.

The www.legendas.tv administrators take responsibility for distributing the television series amongst the *Legenders* teams registered on their website (Calazans 2010b). As Diego (male, 18, Darkside team) explains, the administrators of the website allocate the most popular series to the more experienced and qualified teams. Newer teams are not only assigned less popular shows to translate, but also have their subtitles reviewed by the administrators before they are published (Bernardo 2011).

Frequently, an individual's qualifications, including education and professional background, are determinant factors behind the assignment of subtitling for a television show. For instance, the inSUBs team that produces the subtitles for *Greys' Anatomy* (ABC 2005-present) and *House* (Fox 2004-2012), have a physiotherapist, a nurse and a medical student in their team which facilitates the translation of medical terms (Sayuri 2011). As previously discussed, professional backgrounds also affect the internal distribution of tasks among members of the same team. The individual contributions reaffirm the importance of the concept of 'collective intelligence' in these activities:

> ...no one knows everything, everyone knows something, all knowledge resides in humanity. There is no transcendent store of knowledge and knowledge is simply the sum of what we know (Levy 1997, 13-14).

As noted, the administrators have established quality standards and strict rules to be followed when creating subtitles. Each *Legenders* team must follow the rules or they may lose their rights to create the subtitles for a particular television show (Sayuri 2011). The quality standards established by the www.legendas.tv site reflect professional translation standards including the length of exposure and number of characters per page (Bold 2012).

After analyzing discussion forums regarding the *Legenders*, a theme that was continuously re-emphasised by both viewers and subtitlers was the amateur subtitles are of a higher standard than those produced professionally and distributed officially. Similarly, when researching fansubbers, Prado Alves Silva (2009) found that many viewers of Japanese shows in Brazil frequently complained about the quality of professional translations.

My research also confirmed that the administrators establish and manage various deadlines. As noted above, the nature of the deadline depends on the popularity of a specific show. Since the *Legenders* work in teams, if a member delays finishing their individual section, or fails to produce subtitles in accordance with the www.legendas.tv standards, it can jeopardize the work and reputation of all the other members. Two of the interviewees, Diego (male, 18, Darkside team) and Marcio (male, 28, Subsfreak team) had recently stopped producing subtitles in their teams because of their inability to commit to the demanding deadlines. Consequently, time pressure and associated policies in this online community create an environment that, although primarily grounded in a fandom culture, still requires professionalism, responsibility, and commitment. As such, it is possible to argue that symbolic power operates in the community of *Legenders*, where the administrators dictate the rules in exchange for promoting the team's work. Furthermore, this type of relationship between the members and the www.legendas.tv administrators produces specific hierarchies which I noted above.

The motivation for the *Legenders* is not monetary as the work is unpaid. Rather, their various driving forces include the sense of being part of a community, making friends, improving their English skills, and becoming connected to the production process of their favorite television shows. Despite this, there are certain drawbacks to this amateur practice – which I will turn to now.

Free labor and the *Legenders*' relationship with viewers

A key theme that emerged in my research was that the *Legenders* frequently emphasised that they do not receive any financial return for their work. This free labor not only includes their time and effort, but also the expenses associated with Internet connection and electricity. Terranova defines free labor as, an "important, and yet undervalued, force in advanced capitalist societies" (2000, 33). The circulation of immaterial goods is fundamental to these associations of free cooperation in the network (De Araujo Pinheiro 2007, 52). As Lazzarato explains, immaterial labor is "the labor that produces the informational and cultural content of the commodity" (1996, 133). Hardt and Negri (2006) add that immaterial labor can be categorized as affective labor, which results in the establishment and expansion of social networks. As the *Legenders* illustrate through their practices, many fans establish affective engagement with other peers and with media products, increasing their willingness to take part in this collaborative work (Terranova 2004). The affective rewards of reputation and appreciation thus seem to be the compensation that workers enjoy in the fandom world of the *Legenders*.

However, the *Legenders* also admitted that one of the most negative aspects of their affective labor was that they often felt that impatient viewers did not value their efforts. According to the interviewees, there is a great time pressure from fans that demand subtitles as soon as possible. If the production was delayed, the team members even received impolite and abusive messages from fans.

Importantly, Rossiter (2003) has argued that, although such immaterial labor is freely given between peers, it still presents a material dimension that is the commodity object. The fact that the commodity is digital, creates a sense of abundance since its use and redistribution does not affect its original shape or available quantity (Rodman and Vanderdonckt 2006). In the case of the *Legenders*, their non-regulated work may be taken for granted by the viewers that 'consume' the subtitles – a drawback for the *Legenders* that are motivated by an appreciation for both the quality of their work and the efforts they make (Series Freaks Team 2011a; Series Freaks Team 2011b).

Though I did not interview consumers of the subtitles, insights into this impatience is offered by Jacobsen and Poder who explain that people "increasingly perceive the world as a collection of consumer goods and see the aim of life as getting instant gratification" (2008, 106). Thus, the abundance of digital commodities associated with the necessity of instant gratification may affect the notion of value and worth of the *Legenders'* work.

In addition, as the *Legenders'* work is both unregulated and financially unrewarded it also meets the definition of precarious work (Terranova 2000).

Through their unpaid work, the *Legenders* not only benefit many audiences but also the media industry – though the extent of this is yet to be researched. It could be argued that the *Legenders* facilitate access to US television shows to Brazilian audiences, thus promoting the content in a certain way. Yet, it is a topic perhaps unexplored as amateur subtitling may be perceived as a threat rather than an ally, as it also enables users to access content that has not yet been released in their country, hence, being considered a form of Internet piracy (APCM 2012).

Given the possible negative understanding of amateur subtitling practices, many *Legenders* find it challenging to explain their practices in the offline world. They have recorded issues with family members and friends who do not understand such efforts which lack financial gain (Series Freaks Team 2011b).

The file sharing audience's low financial evaluation of cultural commodities does not align with the practices of capitalism. This is reflected in the process of 'gift exchange' where "information is for sharing not for selling" (Barbrook 2003, 91). This is a process that usurps the purpose of a financial exchange of intellectual property. As Castells explains, capitalism is "oriented toward power-maximizing, that is, toward increasing the amount of surplus appropriated by capital on the basis of private control over the means of production and circulation" (2000, 16). Also, if private "property is traditionally based on a logic of scarcity" (Hardt and Negri 2006, 180), the relatively easy and almost costless ability of reproduction and distribution of content on the Internet challenges intellectual property protection. As Arvanitakis states:

> ...under the market logic, a lack of private property rights means that 'resources' are subject to constant dispute. We must be protected from ourselves and our self-interest or all resources, both physical and institutional, will increasingly become scarce and conflict will follow (2006, 5).

Although www.legendas.tv does not publish video files or post direct links for downloading, it can be argued that it still facilitates unauthorized viewing of media content. Thus, it is a practice linked to intellectual property infringement and Internet piracy. According to Brazilian legislation, movies, television series, books or music cannot be translated without the authorization of the copyright owner (Brazilian Copyright Act of 1998; APCM 2012). If caught, the *Legenders* could face up to a year's imprisonment for being involved in unauthorized practices (Magalhaes Silva 2009).

True fans or true pirates

The initial credits at the beginning of any television episode presents an opportunity to not only display the names of the *Legenders* team and individuals responsible for subtitles, but also additional messages. Some teams include messages and claims about 'free culture' – a concept discussed at length by Lawrence Lessig (2004) who however also adds that not all 'free culture' is 'free'. The argument for those who see 'free culture' as 'free' is that cultural products and artefacts should be freely disseminated and shared without external intervention from authorities and copyright holders. This is echoed by one of my interviewees, Roger (male, 20, Insanos team), in regard to the work undertaken by *Legenders,* which he does not see as 'piracy':

> By making subtitles available over the Internet, we contribute in a way that Brazilians are able to watch films and TV shows at the same time as they are released in the US or in any place where it comes from. This way, they [Brazilians] don't need to rely on the networks here and wait

for their distribution (Personal communication, email, 1 June 2012).

It is possible to argue the *Legenders* are part of a particular group of television audiences who feel motivated to provoke social change through their working practices. They are immersed in social relations where participants reject traditional broadcasting processes and find other ways to access and to facilitate access to television programs.

In 2009, Brazil's International Federation of the Phonographic Industry and Cinema and Music Anti-Piracy Association (APCM) – Associação Antipiratária de Cinema e Música – threatened legal action against the webhost of www.legendas.tv causing temporary disruption of its service (Enigmax 2009). APCM represents the interests of major American production companies, such as Universal and Disney. In response to the website's shutdown, hackers hijacked the APCM website adding pop up messages defending downloading (G1 2009). After a few days of disruption and with the dispute remaining unresolved, www.legendas.tv was working again after migrating to a data center in Sweden.

As this process incurred a number of costs, the www.legendas.tv administrators requested financial support from the website's users. Although the donations asked for were not compulsory, the response from supporters was overwhelming. According to different sources (such as Adolfo1349 2009; Garattoni; 2009), the website received 13,000 *Reais* (approximately US$7,500) in donations in the first 33 hours. It exceeded what the website needed for the migration by more than 30 percent. In addition to the financial help, many fans and fandom websites announced their support for the www.legendas.tv website (TB 2009).

In the digital environment, the affective bonds between users have been identified as 'weak' and easily dissolved (Castells 2000). However, the interests that fans share may lead them to reject impositions – making the bonds stronger. Previous studies, such as the Chinese fansubbers of Japanese television dramas, indicate strong bonds and fan resistance to interference by copyright holders (Hu 2005). As I have argued elsewhere (Mendes Moreira De Sa 2011), in Brazil bonds are created among subtitlers who are not satisfied with the limited access to international television shows in the country.

The collaborative production of amateur subtitles may be considered piracy by authorities. Regardless, it illustrates how digital commons challenge the "permission culture" (Brown 2008) shifting into Lessig's (2004) "free culture". The *Legenders'* motivations in social network interactions reflect their rejection of the television broadcasting system while simultaneously creating an organized system based on the affective labor of informal production and distribution of subtitles.

Conclusions: The *Legenders* become legend

The *Legenders* present an example of television audiences moving from simply watching to establishing networks with other fans to facilitate other viewers' consumption. It can be argued that by "combining altruism and self-interest" (Mason 2008, 36), and rejecting the traditional broadcasting system, they attempt to provoke social change through their affective work practices.

The *Legenders'* practices present benefits and drawbacks. Their work is classified as free and affective, as they are part of fandom networks. They work in an organized system where they must follow rules imposed by the www.legendas.tv website administrators, and on many occasions, endure pressure from impatient and unappreciative viewers. Frequently, their work is not appropriately understood by their family and offline friendship networks, or by representatives of copyright organizations who label them as 'pirates'. However, they have attained the appreciation of many Brazilian fans online that otherwise would have to wait for traditional television stations to air their favorite shows. As this research indicates, within these networks, the *Legenders'* practices are not only socially acceptable but actively encouraged.

By mixing work and pleasure, the *Legenders*' practices contribute greatly to illustrate how emerging and evolving audiences are utilizing the Internet as a tool to produce, consume and distribute content. Their collaborative engagement and organization present a kind of commons that is formed and upheld through voluntary labor and engagement.

The *Legenders* amateur subtitling organized system highlights how such a practice is part of a broader movement that aims to promote social change and innovation in global distribution of television and other cultural products and artefacts. Though the case of Japanese Anime fansubbing shows how capitalism finds ways to appropriate the collaborative and collective productions of fansubbers, the same has not yet happened with the Brazilian *Legenders'* work. The end result is unknown and as such, the analysis of the Brazilian *Legenders'* fandom world remains a work in progress.

References

Adolfo1349 (2009). "Legendas.tv is BACK!". *Outerspace.* Retrieved 12 July 2013, from http://forum.outerspace.terra.com.br/showthread.php?p=4205498

Alexa (2011). "Statistics summary for legendas.tv". Retrieved 2 November 2011, from http://www.alexa.com/siteinfo/legendas.tv

APCM (2012). "Pirataria na Internet" [Piracy on the Internet]. Retrieved 6 March 2012, from http://www.apcm.org.br/pirataria_Internet.php

Arvanitakis, James (2006). "The commons: Opening and enclosing non-commodified space". *Journal of Multidisciplinary International Studies*, 3. Retrieved 6 March 2012, from http://epress.lib.uts.edu.au/journals/index.php/portal/article/view/120

Barbrook, Richard (2003). "Giving is receiving". *Digital Creativity,* 14:2, 91-94. doi: 10.1076/digc.14.2.91.27862

Barra, Luca (2009). "The mediation is the message: Italian regionalization of US TV series as co-creational work". *International Journal of Cultural Studies,* 12:5, 509-525. doi: 10.1177/1367877909337859

Bauwens, Michael (2005). "The political economy of peer production". *CTheory.* Retrieved 6 March 2012, from http://www.ctheory.net/articles.aspx?id=499

Baym, Nancy K. (2006). "Interpersonal life online". In Sonia M. Livingstone and Leah A. Lievrouw (eds). *Handbook of new media: social shaping and social consequences of ICTs* (Updated student ed.). London, UK: SAGE.

Benkler, Yochai (2006). *The wealth of networks. How social production transforms markets and freedom.* New Haven, CT: Yale University Press.

Bernardo, Mario Henrique Perin (2011). *Subtitulando: O universo dos legenders e fansubbers no Brasil [Subtitling: The universe of legenders and fansubbers in Brazil].* Post Graduate *Lato Sensu*, Casper Libero, Sao Paulo. Retrieved 1 October 2011, from http://nonameshideout.com/?p=1746&cpage=1#comment-42724

Bielby, Denise D. and C. Lee Harrington (2005). "Global television distribution: implications of TV 'traveling' for viewers, fans, and texts". *American Behavioral Scientist,* 48:7, 902-920.

Bold, Bianca (2012). "The power of fan communities: An overview of fansubbing in Brazil". *Tradução em Revista,* 11.

Brazilian Copyright Act of 1998, 9.610/98 Civil code § 3-Art.29 (IV)

Brown, James J. (2008). "From Friday to Sunday: the hacker ethic and shifting notions of labour, leisure and intellectual property". *Leisure Studies,* 27:4, 395-409. doi: 10.1080/02614360802334922

Bruns, Axel (2008). "The future is user-led: The path towards widespread produsage". *Fibreculture Journal,* 11. Retrieved 12 July 2013, from http://eleven.fibreculturejournal.org/fcj-066-the-future-is-user-led-the-path-towards-widespread-produsage/

Calazans, Ricardo (2010a). "Mercado começa a ver com bons olhos equipes de fãs que legendam séries na Internet" [The industry starts seeing with good eyes the teams of fans that create subtitles for TV shows over the Internet]. *O Globo.* Retrieved 12 July 2013, from http://oglobo.globo.com/cultura/mercado-comeca-ver-com-bons-olhos-equipes-de-fas-que-legendam-series-na-Internet-3012204#ixzz1w9ABAR80

Calazans, Ricardo (2010b). "Um fã conta como é a rotina de uma equipe de 'legenders'". [A fan tells how are the daily activities of a tem of 'legenders']. *O Globo.* Retrieved 12 July 2013, from http://oglobo.globo.com/cultura/mat/2010/05/07/um-fa-conta-como-a-rotina-de-uma-equipe-de-legenders-916532658.asp

Castells, Manuel (2000). *The rise of the network society* (2nd ed. Vol. v. 1). Malden, MA: Blackwell publishing.

Couldry, Nick (2006). *Listening beyond the echoes: media, ethics, and agency in an uncertain world.* Boulder, Colo: Paradigm Publishers.

De Araujo Pinheiro, Marta (2007). "Comunicação, consumo e produção de si" [Communication, consumption and self production]. In Iluska Coutinho and Potiguara Mendes da Silveira Jr. (eds.). *Comunicação: technologia e identidade [Communicarion: technology and identitity]* (51-64). Rio de Janeiro, RJ: Mauad.

Enigmax (2009). "Hackers hit anti-pirates to avenge sub-site takedown" (Web log post). Retrieved 20 October 2011, from http://torrentfreak.com/hackers-hit-anti-pirates-to-avenge-sub-site-takedown-090205/

G1. (2009). "Hackers reagem e atacam página após fechamento de site de legendas" [Hackers react and attack website after subtitles page shutdown]. *Globo.* Retrieved 12 July 2013, from Globo website: http://g1.globo.com/Noticias/Tecnologia/0,,MUL986379-6174,00.html

Garattoni, Bruno (2009). "O Legendas.tv está de volta – e com aliados de peso" [The Legendas.tv is back- and with heavy supporters]. *Super Interessante.* Retrieved 12 July 2013, from http://super.abril.com.br/blogs/rebit/o-legendas-tv-esta-de-volta-e-com-aliados-de-peso/

Hardt, Michael and Antonio Negri (2006). *Multitude: war and democracy in the age of empire.* London: Penguin.

Hu, Kelly (2005). "The power of circulation: digital technologies and the online Chinese fans of Japanese TV drama". *Inter-Asia Cultural Studies,* 6:2, 171-186.

IBOPE (2012). "Número de brasileiros com acesso a Internet chega a 79,9 milhões" [Number of Brazilians with Internet access gets to 79,9 million]. *Nielsen Online*: IBOPE.

IPEA (2012). "Download de músicas e filmes no Brasil: Um perfil dos piratas online" [Music and movies download in Brazil: The online pirates profile]. *Comunicados do IPEA [IPEA announcements],* (147). Retrieved 12 July 2013, from http://desafios2.ipea.gov.br/portal/images/stories/PDFs/comunicado/120510_comunicadoipea0147.pdf

Ito, Mizuko (2010). "Amateur media production in a networked ecology". Paper presented at the Computer Supported Cooperative Work - Savannah, Georgia. Retrieved 12 July 2013, from http://www.itofisher.com/mito/publications/amateur_media_p_1.html

Jenkins, Henry (2006). "When piracy becomes promotion". *Reason,* 38:7, 78.
Jenkins, Henry (2008, May 18th). "Field notes from Shanghai: Fansubbing in China". Retrieved 12 July 2013, from http://henryjenkins.org/2008/01/field_notes_from_shanghai_fans.html
Knox, Hannah, Mike Savage and Penny Harvey (2006). "Social networks and the study of relations: networks as method, metaphor and form". *Economy and Society,* 35:1, 113-140. doi: 10.1080/03085140500465899
Lazzarato, Maurizio (1996). "Immaterial labor". In Paul Virno and Michael Hardt (eds). *Radical thought in Italy: A potential politics* (Vol. 7, 133-147). Minneapolis, Minn: University of Minnesota Press.
Leal, Fred (2010). "Legendadores viram a noite para traduzir seriados" [Legenders stay awake all night to translate TV shows]. *Yahoo technologia.* Retrieved 12 July 2013, from http://br.tecnologia.yahoo.com/article/03022010/25/tecnologia-noticias-legendadores-viram-noite-traduzir.html
Lee, Hye-Kyung (2011). "Participatory media fandom: A case study of anime fansubbing". *Media, Culture & Society,* 33:8, 1131-1147. doi: 10.1177/0163443711418271
Legendas.tv temporariamente fora do ar [Legendas.tv temporarily not available] (2009). (Web log post). Retrieved 30 October 2011, from http://faqlegendastv.wordpress.com/legendastv-temporariamente-fora-do-ar/
Leonard, Sean (2005). "Progress against the law: Anime and fandom, with the key to the globalization of culture". *International Journal of Cultural Studies,* 8:3, 281-305. doi: 10.1177/1367877905055679
Lessig, Lawrence (2004). *Free culture: How big media uses technology and the law to lock down culture and control creativity.* New York: Penguin Press.
Lessig, Lawrence (2008). *Remix: Making art and commerce thrive in the hybrid economy.* New York, NY: Penguin Press.
Levy, Pierre (1997). *Collective intelligence: Mankind's emerging world in cyberspace.*
Mason, Matt (2008). *The pirate's dilemma: How youth culture is reinventing capitalism.* New York, NY: Free Press.
Mendes Moreira De Sa, Vanessa (2011). "Internet piracy as a hobby: what happens when the Brazilian Jeitinho meets television downloading?". *Global Media Journal - Australian Edition,* 5:1. Retrieved 12 July 2013, from http://www.commarts.uws.edu.au/gmjau/v5_2011_1/vanessa_mendes_AA.html
Milner, Ryan M. (2009). "Working for the text: Fan labor and the new organization". *International Journal of Cultural Studies,* 12:5, 491-508. doi: 10.1177/1367877909337861
Mizukami, Pedro, Oona Castro, Luiz Moncau and Ronaldo Lemos (2011). "Brazil". In Joe Karaganis (ed.). *Media piracy in emerging countries* (219-304): The social science research council
Napoli, Philip M. (2011). *Audience revolution: New technologies and the transformation of media audiences.* New York, NY: Columbia University Press.
Nightingale, Virginia (2011). *The handbook of media audiences.* Malden, MA: Wiley-

Blackwell.

Olhar Digital (Producer) (2010, April, 11). Legendadores de torrents: conheça esta mania [Torrents' Legenders: meet this trend] [Video podcast]. Retrieved 12 July 2013, from http://olhardigital.uol.com.br/produtos/central_de_videos/legendadores-de-torrents-conheca-esta-mania/11184

O'Neill, Jim (2001). "Building better global economic BRICs". *Global Economics,* (66). Retrieved 12 July 2013, from http://www.goldmansachs.com/our-thinking/topics/brics/brics-reports-pdfs/build-better-brics.pdf

Pagano, Gabriela (2010, October 10). "Legendadores: por trás dos caracteres que aparecem no vídeo" [Legenders: behind the subtitles that are shown in the videos] Retrieved 20 October 2011, from http://teleseries.uol.com.br/legendadores-eles-estao-por-tras-dos-caracteres-que-aparecem-no-video/

Perez Gonzalez, Luis (2007). "Fansubbing anime: Insights into the 'butterfly effect' of globalisation on audiovisual translation". *Perspectives,* 4:4, 260–277. doi: 10.1080/09076760708669043

Prado Alves Silva, Renata (2009). *Fansub e scanlation: caminhos da cultura pop japonesa de fa para fa via web [Fansub and scalation: the roads of japanese pop culture from one fan to another via web].* Paper presented at the XIV Congress of Communication Sciences of the Southeast Region, Rio de Janeiro, RJ.

Rodman, Gilbert B. and Cheyanne Vanderdonckt (2006). "Music for nothing or, I want my MP3". *Cultural Studies,* 20:2-3, 245-261.

Rossiter, Ned (2003). "Report: Creative labour and the role of intellectual property". *Fibreculture Journal,* 1.

Sayuri, Juliana (2011). "Legendarios" [Legends]. *Super Interessante.* Retrieved 12 July 2013, from http://super.abril.com.br/tecnologia/legendarios-629057.shtml

Silva, Ana Magalhaes (2009). "Os capitães da pirataria. Já pensou em quem disponibiliza o filme ou a música que você baixa?" [The captains of piracy: have you ever thought about who makes available the films and music that you download?]. *Trip.* Retrieved 12 July 2013, from http://revistatrip.uol.com.br/revista/175/especial/os-capitaes-da-pirataria.html

TB (2009, February 3). "O guia de seriados apóia o legendas.tv" [The TV series guide support the Legendas.TV]. *Guia dos seriados* Retrieved 30 October 2011, from http://guiadeseriados.virgula.uol.com.br/2009/02/03/o-guia-de-seriados-apoia-o-legendastv/

Series Freaks Team (2011a, March 18). "Vida de legenders - Parte 1" [Life as a legender- part 1] (Web log post). Retrieved 20 October 20 2011, from http://seriesfreaks.blogspot.com/2011/03/vida-de-legenders.html

Series Freaks Team (2011b, April 12). "Vida de Legenders parte 2 - Queens of the Lab" [The legenders life part 2 - Queens of the lab]. Retrieved 20 October 2011, from http://seriesfreaks.blogspot.com/2011/04/vida-de-legenders-parte-2-queens-of-lab.html

Terranova, Tiziana (2000). "Free labor: producing Culture for the digital economy". *Social Text,* 18:2, 33-58. doi: 10.1215/01642472-18-2_63-33

Terranova, Tiziana (2004). *Network culture: Politics for the information age.* London & Ann Arbor, MI: Pluto Press.

Tian, Yuan (2011). *Fansub cyber culture in China.* Dissertation/Thesis Master of Arts, Georgetown University, Washington, DC. (1491553)

Wenger, Etienne, Richard A. McDermott and William Snyder (2002). *Cultivating communities of practice: A guide to managing knowledge.* Boston, Mass: Harvard Business School Press.

After Piracy: Reflections of Industrial Designers in Taiwan on Sustainable Innovations

Yi-Chieh Jessica Lin

Introduction

This chapter examines piracy within a Taiwanese context where copying and imitation are a significant aspect of cultural and economic life. The chapter focuses on how industrial designers in contemporary Taiwan reflect on issues of piracy analyzing the *Copycat Design* exhibition. This exhibition, held in Taiwan in 2011, asked designers to interpret the phenomenon of 'copycat' and examine the links between copying, imitation, piracy and innovation.

In her book *The Cultural Life of Intellectual Properties*, anthropologist Rosemary Coombe argues that, the postmodern situation should be read as a case for the specificity and multiplicity of "otherness". Here Coombe contends that to engage the "postmodern condition," anthropologists are required to transcend concepts of commodities as transparent symbols of Western hegemonies and understand them as "polyvalent": that is, capable of acquiring new meanings in new contexts.

In her analysis of mimesis and alterity, Coombe traces the history of the industrialization of the US in relation to the installment of trademark laws. The usage of "trademarks" here refers to logos, brand names, advertising images, or other visual forms that condense and convey meaning in commerce. She argues that the introduction of such laws generate conditions for struggles over culture, ownership and property. Coombe criticizes how trademarks in contemporary consumer societies organize the "magic of the mimetic faculty" and entices consumers in its endless uniformity with "promises of both standardization and distinction" (Coombe 1998, 169). Coombe's position is that symbols can never achieve uniformity, and must always be understood as context-specific.

To understand this phenomenon, we can turn to Kedron Thomas (2009), who reminds us that at different locales, brand piracy is situated in complex networks and historical incidences. In her research in Guatemala's apparel industry, she noticed that cultural representations of urban space influence market strategies and moral logics amidst processes of economic and legal restructuring. Among the workshops that produce apparel in Guatemala, Thomas found that pirate producers are often at an economic disadvantage, lacking the financial and cultural capital to build brands for their own workshops (Thomas 2009). These 'pirate producers' are, therefore, often scolded as immoral and illegal by those who own copyrights, patents and trademarks – reflecting an important power dynamic between dominant holders of copyright and those that seek to imitate and innovate.

This issue of 'piracy' has been addressed in many ways, including as simply another 'business model': (see for example, Matt Mason's *Pirate's Culture* (2011) and Kate Raustiala's *The Knockoff Economy* (2012)). It has also been presented as a 'new norm' of capitalist innovation, such as in Kirby Ferguson's (2011) film *Everything is a Remix.* Others see piracy as reflecting and reacting to processes of enclosure that have historically strengthened capitalism (Arvanitakis 2007; Hardt and Negri 2000).

Picking up from Coombe's point that symbols must be understood in context, we can look at different interpretations of 'piracy'. In Indonesia for example, the 'art of piracy' has been motivated by various political agendas. Amidst the Asian Financial Crisis in post-Suharto Indonesia in the late 1990s, counterfeit money became the central theme and the medium for a number of artists to parody the corruption-ridden bureaucracy of the former president and the devaluation of Indonesian moral life. On one piece of counterfeit money, Suharto's portrait was replaced by the artist's own image (Strassler 2009). Other anonymous artists, who supported the politician Megawati Sukarnoputri, reproduced fake money stickers with her image to show their support. In the local language, counterfeit money exemplifies the *aspal:* a neologism that combines the word *asli* (authentic) and *palsu* (false). Thus, counterfeit money became a way for people to voice their protests and was part of the broader actions of anti-government movements that included performance art, cartoons, illustrations, popular songs, and campaign stickers (Strassler 2009).

In light of the above research findings, this chapter then focuses on how piracy is used and conceptualized by industrial designers who work in the cultural and creative industries with the aim of building brands based on new design philosophies: eco-sustainability, ethical consumption and preserving everyday life experience as cultural heritage. By doing so, I aim to understand the mimesis and alterity at the center of Coombe's (1998) work.

Industry designers' reflections on "Copycat"

This research begins with the "Copycat" exhibition held in Taiwan and Tokyo, August 2010 to April 2011. The exhibition was organized by a group of designers affiliated with Public Creative Association (PCA). The Association is a professional organization of designers aged between 20-35 years. The PCA acts as a sharing platform and aims to bring together designers and the general public to explore the interrelationship between consumerism and design from both local and global perspectives.

PCA was founded by Eason Hsieh, who is both a lecturer at Chang Gung University, and the Director of Design for the 3+2 Design Studio in Taipei, Taiwan. While originally encouraged by his parents to study medicine, Hsieh eventually enrolled in industrial design at Tung Hai University, Taichung. After college, he acquired a master's degree at Chang Gung University and started teaching 'creative thinking' in the same faculty, working as a professional designer while organizing exhibitions partially funded by both government and corporate sponsors.

Each exhibition invited designers, who had to pay a fee of approximately NT$100,000 (US$330) to cover excessive costs. In the "Copycat" exhibition, 50 designers took part and 25 works were exhibited in five locations across Taiwan as well as during Tokyo's Designer Week in 2011.

Hsieh outlined two motivations for organizing such exhibitions: the first was his sense of moral responsibility concerning the development of the design industry; and further, he was driven by an aspiration to let everyday life experience inspire design. Eason recruited designers in their 20s or early 30s who shared similar passions and a willingness to commit their own resources to help fund the curation. The ultimate goal, says Hsieh, was to make the works of Taiwanese designers travel to New York and London, highlighting indigenous creativity.

Examples of previous exhibitions that highlight Hsieh's commitment is "Save" – organized amidst the global financial crisis in 2009 and integrated the idea of 'saving' into designs of daily life utensils and wares. PCA also uses exhibitions as a vehicle for providing experiences of curating and creates an environment of 'active learning'.

The Copycat organizers collaborated with one of the largest cultural industry companies, Xuexue, and hosted symposiums on various topics around design and copying. On 27 June 2010, individual designers involved in the Copycat exhibition also called for a conference with the editor of *La Vie Magazine*, Yi-Hsuan Chiu, and other more experienced designers to revise their works at the Taipei UrbanCore Gallery. In this conference, the Deputy General Editor of the fashion magazine *Bella,* Ching-Ling Chang, stated that when fashion brands from the West enter the market in East Asia, they often use large-scale placement marketing to create a sense of status associated with the western brand. Ching-Ling Chang argued that these brands represent more than simply clothing: they have a long history and associated meanings. As such, she argued that the brand spirit, the service and experience in a 'genuine' store do not overlap with the copycat versions.

Further, Ching-Ling Chang stated that, in the Taiwanese fashion industry the trend of copying certain elements from major international fashion shows to design their own works can be traced back over a number of decades. However, this is not simply a 'Taiwanese phenomenon': as Johanna Blakely (2010) has noted, the fashion industry business models based on copying and piracy have long been 'public secrets'. Blakely contends that the culture of copying actually motivates designers to be more innovative, resulting in an acceleration of creative innovation. Furthermore, she feels that piracy and copying promotes a democratization of fashion, faster establishment of global trends, and induced obsolescence.

This seems to capture the feelings and thoughts of many Taiwanese designers. The young designers in the exhibition noted that imported brands and trademarks are symbols of Western hegemony and acquire new meanings in local and new contexts. Reflecting on 'piracy', the designers argued that copying facilitates new ideas of creativity from everyday life experiences. The Taiwanese designers believed that design should be future-oriented and contain a strong sense of mission to improve collective interests of society.

The exhibition

In this section, I discuss the idea of copycatting and the place of Western trademarks, logos and brand names in Taiwan. I will concentrate on piracy, both as remix and as critique of consumerism, as exemplified through a number of objects from the Copycat exhibition.

The first artwork is a Macintosh Notebook remodeled into a lamp (see Figure 1). The popularity of Macintosh products goes well beyond their functionality: the 'bitten' Apple logo has become a sign of fulfilled desire, taste, and a display of wealth. As one designer explained,

> ...the Apple computer is seen as a product of fashion as well as a technology in Taiwan. The message behind it is to question why the life cycle of many electronic products are shorter than we expected; and whether and why the brand name of Macintosh really matter to the consumers in Taiwan, a major production base of laptops.[1]

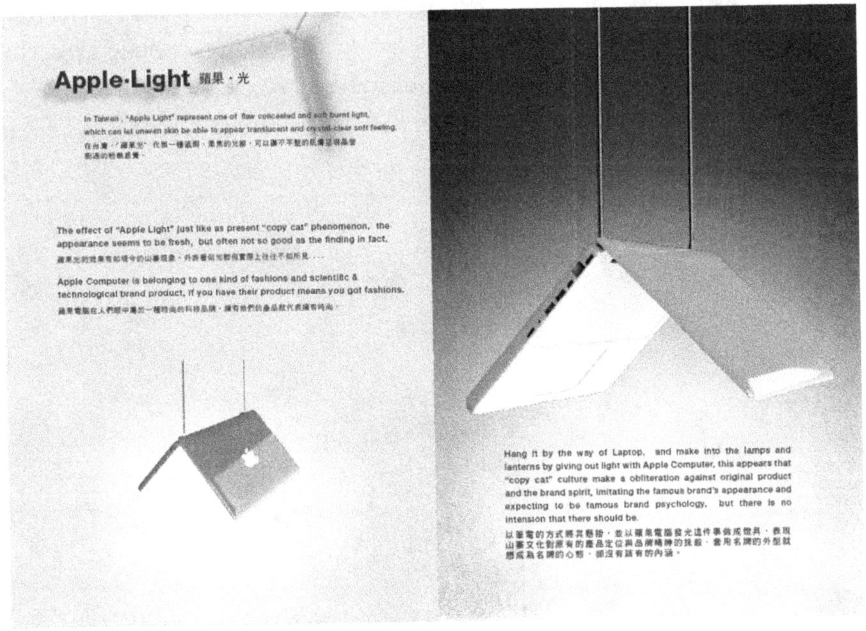

Figure 1: *Apple Light*
Designer: Jamie Wang, Steven Chou and Show Sen
Source: Public Creation Association

The naming of the artwork plays with the connotation of *Apple Light* in the Chinese lexicon: *Apple Light* could also mean a technique often employed in theatrical lighting or studio photography in Taiwan. Specifically, in professional camera studios it refers to the flashlight projected first to a board attached with a thin tin foil paper. When the flashlight is reflected from the tin foil paper to one's face, it enhances the radiation of one's features, creating an instant impression of perfection. The term 'apple light' is also commonly used in cosmetic product

1 Based on interviews conducted in 2010 and 2011.

advertising and where it is associated with words like *perfection, crystal clear, soft feeling and translucent.* Such language in advertising is associated with producing a false myth about the perfection of women's physical appearance.

By making an Apple laptop into a lamp, the designer is also mocking the language of advertising: it is literally an Apple light made with a genuine Mac computer while simultaneously a 'fake' apple light for failing to deliver the effects of perfecting one's appearance.

The works of designer Tai Ling Wu include a number of useful everyday devices in the shapes of repurposed Apple products: examples include a recycled fake *IPhone* case as bill clippers; the cases of an IPod Nano and IPod Classic to be used as spice saucers on the dinner table; and, IPod Shuffles turned into napkin ring holders. Wu gave the work the title *Dinner with Jobs* (see Figure 2).

Figure 2: Dinner with Jobs
Designer: Tai Ling Wu
Source: Public Creation Association

Figure 3: Visualizing copy-'n'-paste culture
Designer: Kelly Lin
Source: Public Creation Association

In another work, designers Walt Wang, Peter Fan, Jacques Ren and Kevin Chang designed a garbage bag named *Trashammer.* When the top part of the paper bag is tightened, this garbage bag turns into an imitation of the Adidas logo (see Figure 4).

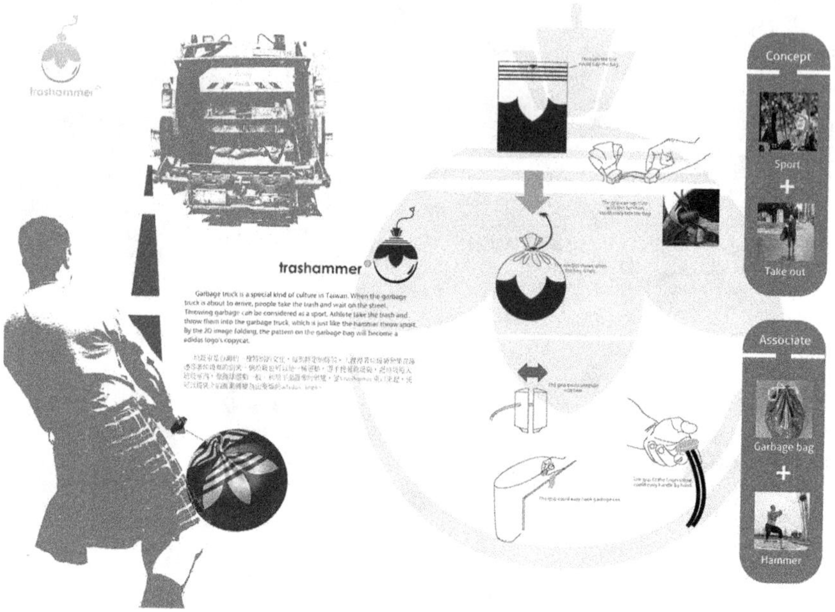

Figure 4: Illustration of the Trashammer Design
Designer: Walt Wang, Peter Fan, Jacques Ren and Kevin Chang
Source: Public Creation Association

The political direction of the exhibition become even more explicit in a cartoon by Song-Chou Wu (founder of Chiang's Talk company) where former President Chiang Kai-Shek and Chairman Mao are depicted as iconic cartoon figures used in fast-food packaging. These two rivals initiated the civil war in 1949, leading to the separation of sovereignty of Taiwan and Mainland China. In the creative design, the designer fantasized that these two political figures became collaborators to kick-start a Chinese fast food chain, which simultaneously criticized the conflict between Taiwan and the Chinese mainland, as well as the introduction of unhealthy fast food chains from the West.

Figure 5: Chairman Mao and Chiang Kai-Shek mugs

Designer: Ajue Wu

Source: Public Creation Association

After the exhibition, a gathering was organized for the designers, artists, local scholars and traders in which Eason Hsieh (half) jokingly said that, during the Expo he could not sleep because he was concerned that copyright holders would show up with the police and accuse them of trademark violations. Such concerns captured a broader dilemma faced by industrial designers in Taiwan, who strive to remix the elements of branded commodities and criticize modern consumerism, while searching for the meanings of commodity and branding.

Such conflicts are captured in Matt Mason's (2008) book *The Pirate's Dilemma.* Mason defines the dilemma in a series of questions about how the people, corporations, and governments react to the changing conditions of privately owned intellectual property. The changing intellectual property laws often result in cultural artifacts leaking out of the public domain.

Mason uses the terms 'piracy' and 'remix' interchangeably, defining the latter term as:

> ...a conscious process used to innovate and create. In fact, it's no exaggeration to say that the cut-'n'-paste culture born out of sampling and remixing has revolutionized the way we interpret the world. As Nelson George said in Hip Hop America, the remix "raises questions about the nature of creativity and originality". (2008, 71)

It is important to note that none of the above-mentioned works were available for sale. At the exhibition, small notebooks were sold for NT$120 (approximately US$4) each, while pamphlets of the works and the ideas behind them were distributed free of charge. The media attention the exhibition received, however, highlights how the act of remixing and jamming commercial culture is critically received.

In contrast to this non-commercial approach, we also see the commercial application of remix and counterfeit culture. For example, an emergent commercial brand name, *Stay Real* (2012), owned by four local designers has been embraced by young consumers in Taiwan. Its specialty is blending existing commercial icons such as Hello Kitty, Astro Boy and Uncle McDonald's with local fashion trends. It has proved so popular that it has extended business to Shanghai and Tokyo. Further, the designers of *Stay Real,* "No2Good" (Po-Liang Chen) and "Ashin" (Shin-Hong Chen), were invited to host a special exhibition of their works at the National Museum of Fine Arts in Taichung, Taiwan for three months in 2010. No2Good (2011) has also been invited to the 54th Venice Biennale. The works of the artists have become collectables whose values now exceed their utilitarian design.

The popularity of remixing was also exemplified by the publication of *The Complete Guide to Fake Toys* (2009) in Japan and Taiwan. This publication documented hundreds of pirated versions of animation cartoon characters, robots and candies and it included articles about the variations of pirated products in Japan, China, Korea, Hong Kong and the Republic of Kazakhstan. The guide also covers the 'original' toys invented in Asian countries outside of Japan, but which are influenced by Japanese animation.

The Copycat exhibition also acted as a forum for the young designers to demystify the argument that copying is 'intrinsic' in Chinese society – something that is often claimed in the West. In *Poorly Made in China,* the author Paul Midler (2009) for example, argues that counterfeit culture runs deep in China and 'Asian cultures' more generally. One of the examples Milder presents is a claim that Toyota's first cars were essentially a copy of Chrysler's AA prototype (Airflow) car of the 1930s and 1940s. The quality of Toyota cars became so superior through innovation rather than originality, however, that Chrysler purchased the design. Hsieh on the other hand points to two examples that actually highlight the reverse. First he argues that some western cultural movements (such as the British Naturalist movement formed by William Edward Godwin (1833-1866) and Charles Greene (1868-1957)) involved learning from the east and took inspiration from Chinese and Japanese porcelains and furniture. A more contemporary example is the 1996 Atlanta Olympic Games theme song "Returning to Innocence" by Enigma, which used popular rhythms from indigenous tribes of Taiwan.

Shanzhai – the mountain fortress!

The Chinese term for Copycat is *Shanzhai,* which literally means 'mountain fortress' and historically refers to bandits in mountain hideaways taking potshots at established power interests in Robin Hood fashion. Today the term is also used to describe practices like commercial TV programs and dramas, fake celebrities, and 'grassroots parodies' that presumably originated from 'ordinary people' (Yang 2011).

The Copycat exhibition itself can be read as an attempt by the local designers to engage in a dialogue with the public discourse of *Shanzhai*. Beyond the Copycat exhibitions, remix and copycatting is a popular genre for making social comments and parodizing the media and cultural industries. One example is the Taiwanese TV show *Chuanminjueidadang*, which started in 2004, where various actors imitate and ridicule politicians and celebrities – with the President, Ying-Jeou Ma, once making a personal appearance. The show has been broadcast across the Taiwan Strait and to the Chinese Diaspora in North America. Even Mingqing Zhang, the spokesman of the Taiwan Office of the People's Republic of China, was ridiculed in the show, though he has become a fan and even exchanged gifts with the actor, Chi-Yuan Tai, in Beijing in 2006. By ridiculing the 'spectacle' of major social events and politics, the show promotes an alternative platform for political participation in civil society. It is also one of the few shows discussing Taiwanese politics that is not banned in Mainland China.

In popular music, the remixing of lyrics with Chinese cultural references and western rhythms is more and more popular and widely accepted by the younger generation in Taiwan, Mainland China and even the population on the west coast in North America. Hip hop singers like David Tao and Alexander Wang, who were born and trained in the US, compose music that incorporates elements of R&B, emphasizes the flows of melodies, but their lyrics often use Chinese cultural references.

After piracy: Efforts of building brands for Taiwanese designs

Despite the fact that many Taiwanese companies began with the model of original equipment manufacturing (OEM) because of historical contingencies (Lin 2011), more and more companies are now focusing on original design and branding. Starting in 2002, Taiwan has been hosting an annual design expo in Taipei and since 2010 it has been held at a newly remodeled fine historical venue, the Taiwan Design Museum. Besides the works of the Public Creative Association, the expo also features works of 50 other designers from various fields, including Taiwanese winners of the Golden Pin Design Award. In recent years, the concept of 'Design Beneficence' has been emphasized to address the issues of environmental protection and cultural diversity. Since November 2011, the Taiwan Design Center (TDC) has been officially stationed in the Taiwan Design Museum, is expected to create a clustering effect and further develop its multiple functions of nurturing, counseling, exhibition, and marketing Taiwanese design.[2]

The cultural and creative industries are defined by the Executive Yuan in Taiwan in 2009 as one of the six important key industries because it enforces the development of 'soft power' (Nye 2004). The government provides a budget of NTD 1 billion (about US$700 million) to develop the content of television, movies, digital media, popular music, design and crafts, in the hope of reaching annual sales of US$30 billon in 2013 at a targeted annual growth rate of 11.6 percent. From 2002 to 2007, the average growth rate of the cultural and creative industries was 7.73 percent, while the annual sales in 2007 reached US$ 20 billion. In 2014, the goal is to reach the sales of NTD 150 billion overseas, and to take over 7.35 percent of market share in Mainland China.

The cultural and creative industries are centralized in Taipei – creating a type of cultural hub. There are eleven assigned creative street blocks in Taipei to promote the development of these industries and increase the city's competitiveness. On average, 14 cultural events take place in Taipei every day, totaling 6,139 events in 2010. The Taipei Award of Industrial Design inaugurated in 2011 received more than 1,000 applications.

In April 2011, I attended the housewarming party of Eason Hsieh's design studio in Taipei. Hsieh made the space facing the street into a community gallery to host different cultural exhibitions. On the night of the housewarming party, a reception was also given for the first gallery exhibition, entitled "The Photo Journey of Maciej Korbas" by a young photographer from Poland. The studio/gallery also served as a hub for artists, agents for international brand names, animation graphic artists and students from Taiwan and overseas to exchange ideas and build connections.

Finally, it is this point that I would like to reflect on here. In some cases, it would appear that processes of globalization – cultural homogenization and consumerism – nourish piracy as discussed by other authors in this volume. This reflects processes of enclosure that have historically strengthened capitalism (Arvanitakis 2007; Hardt and Negri 2000). The industrial designers' reflections on the culture of piracy in Taiwan are not only local responses of cultural resistance against the globalization of brand names, but also attempts to explore alternative choices of sustainable innovation and business models. And it is a model that I feel needs

2 The website of the 2011 Taiwan Design Expo is at: http://www.iccie.tw/

to be supported, not simply dismissed as 'piracy'.

References

Arvanitakis, James (2007). *The Cultural Commons of Hope: The Attempt to Commodify the Final Frontier of the Human Experience.* Berlin: VDM Verlag Dr. Müller.

Barthes, Roland (1990). *The Fashion System.* Berkeley: University of California Press.

Benjamin, Walter (1935). "The Work of Art in the Age of Mechanical Reproduction". In Howard Eliand and Michael Jennings (eds). *Walter Benjamin: Selected Writings, 1935-1938.* Cambridge: Belknap Press of Harvard University Press.

Blakely, Johanna (2010). "Lessons from Fashions' Free Culture". TedxUSC Talk in April 2010. Retrieved 12 July, from: http://www.ted.com/talks/johanna_blakley_lessons_from_fashion_s_free_culture.html

Chan, Chih-Chung (2010). "Design Players' Pavillion". *Design Magazine,* 156, Taipei: Taiwan Creative Design Center, 131-134.

Chen, Franz (2011). *Wanmei Franz.* Taipei: Business Weekly Publisher.

Cheung, Sidney (2013). "From Foodways to Intangible Heritage: A Case Study of Chinese Culinary Resource, Retail and Recipe in Hong Kong". *International Journal of Heritage Studies.* 19:3. DOI: 10.1080/13527258.2011.654237

Coombe, Rosemary (1998). *The Cultural Life of Intellectual Properties: Authorship, Appropriation, and the Law.* Durham and London: Duke University Press.

Christensen, Clayton, Curtis Johnson and Michael Horn (2008). *Disrupting Class: How Disruptive Innovation Will Change the Way the World Learns.* New York. McGraw Hill.

Eisend, Martin and Pakize Schücher-Güler (2006). "Explaining Counterfeit Purchases: A Review and Preview". *Academy of Marketing Science Review,* 2006:12. Retrieved 12 July 2013, from http://www.amsreview.org/articles/eisend12-2006.pdf

Ferguson, Kirby (2011). *Everything is a Remix.* Retrieved 12 July 2013, from http://www.everythingisaremix.info/watch-the-series/

Geertz, Clifford (1973). *The Interpretation of Cultures. New York:* Basic Books.

Harris, Marvin (1976). "History and Significance of the Emic/Etic Distinction". *Annual Review of Anthropology,* 5, 329–350.

Hardt, Michael and Antonio Negri (2000). *Empire.* Cambridge, MA: Harvard University Press.

Harrison, Nate (2010). *Aura Dies Hard (Or: How I Learned to Stop Worrying and Love the Copy).* Retrieved 12 July 2013, from http://nkhstudio.com/#

Hsieh, Eason (2011). *Shanzhai: The Killer of Creative Thinking?.* Lecture delivered in Center for General Education, National Chung Hsing University, March 22.

Inchiki, Bancho and Angura Kato (2009). *The Complete Guide to Fake Toys.* Tokyo: Shakai Hyoron Sha.

Raustiala, Kal and Christopher Sprigman (2012). *The Knockoff Economy: How Imitation Sparks Innovation.* New York: Oxford University Press.

Lin, Yi-Chieh Jessica (2011). *Fake Stuff: China and the Rise of Counterfeit Goods.* New York: Routledge.
Marx, Karl (1992). *Capital: Volume 1: A Critique of Political Economy.* London: Penguin.
Mason, Matt (2008). *The Pirate's Dilemma: How Youth Culture is Reinventing Capitalism.* New York: Free Press.
Midler, Paul (2009). *Poorly Made in China.* Hoboken, NJ: Wiley.
No2Good (2011). "A Fishing Bunny". *54th Venice Biennale.* June 4 – November 27.
Nye, Joseph (2004). *Soft Power.* New York: Public Affairs.
Stay Real (2012). "Stay Real Product Online Catalogue". Retrieved 12 July 12 2013, from http://www.istayreal.com/blog/search.asp?kw=%A4p%B9%AB
Strassler, Karen (2009). "The Face of Money: Crisis, Currency, and Remediation in Post-Suharto Indonesia". *Cultural Anthropology,* 24:1, 68-103. DOI: 10.1111/j.1548-1360.2009.00027.x
Thomas, Kedron (2009). "Structural Adjustment, Spatial Imaginaries, and 'Piracy' in Guatemala's Apparel Industry". *Anthropology of Work Review,* 30, 1–10. DOI: 10.1111/j.1548-1417.2009.01008.x
Veblen, Thorstein (1899). *Theory of the Leisure Class: An Economic Study in the Evolution of Institutions.* New York: Macmillan.
Wong, Wendy Siuyi (2006). "Globalizing Manga: From Japan to Hong Kong and Beyond". *Mechademia,* 1, 23-45. DOI: 10.1353/mec.0.0060

Primary Sources

Transcript of "Copycat" Symposium (1), April 24, 2010, Taipei
Transcript of "Copycat" Symposium (2), May 1, 2010, Taipei
Interviews and fieldwork notes during 2010 and 2011 Taipei Design Expo and in the W Company, February 2012
Two Talks by Eason Hsieh in 2011, Taichung: National Chung Hsing University

List of Figures:

Piracy is Normal, Piracy is Boring: Systemic Disruption as Everyday Life

Francesca da Rimini and Jonathan Marshall

Introduction

What is often called 'digital piracy' is nowadays a mundane and everyday activity. Peukert (2010, 6) points out that millions of ordinary 'good' people who would never steal a book, a CD or a DVD routinely "continue uploading and downloading". Digital sharing "is an everyday practice by millions of people, and in that sense *normal*" (ibid. 15). As such, piracy is a commonplace disorder within the order of information capitalism; it is both created by the ubiquitous orders of information capitalism and suppressed by those orders. In the myriad points of view of its participants, piracy represents an order that is implicit within contemporary life; an order/disorder that we will call 'pirarchy'. For non-corporate producers, it constitutes a way of distributing their work that both threatens their ability to survive off that work, while also potentially opening previously unavailable possibilities of acquiring income or status from their products, or gaining expertise through direct, unmediated contact with fans and audiences. Many corporations see it simply as a disorder that threatens their future. We assert that pirarchy is a non-resolvable part of what we have elsewhere called the 'information disorder' – that is, the way that exchange of information, or the accuracy of information, tends to be disrupted by the political and economic processes of information capitalism (Marshall, Goodman, Zowghi and da Rimini, forthcoming).

There has been little interest in the ways that pirarchy derives from and becomes embedded in everyday social and informational life. This neglect may arise because of illusions of privacy afforded by the software enabling pirarchy, because the drama of landmark legal cases eclipses 'daily life', because prospects of prosecution make practitioners reluctant to share information with researchers, or because most theory assumes that important networks are robust while pirarchy is overtly unstable and uncertain. In this chapter, we attempt to describe some social characteristics of pirarchy, partially through consideration of the literature and news-stories about piracy, but mainly through recent interviews we have conducted with self-identified file-sharers in Australia.

Piracy as scandal: The official position

The flourishing of diverse modes of 'unauthorised' exchange of films, music, text and other materials over the Internet by content-hungry 'peers' has been described by copyright holders as an "unspoken social plague," a "nirvana for criminals," and compared to industrial-scale counterfeiting enterprises (BASCAP 2009; Karaganis 2011a, *i*). Corporations argue that they are losing billions of dollars of potential revenue, and that 'digital piracy' and 'unauthorised downloading' pose a huge threat to the economy in general (BSA 2011). Governments and corporations are exerting pressure on internet service providers to actively monitor and regulate their customers' file-sharing behaviours (Bridy 2011; Hinze 2010). New laws and international treaties are drafted, often cloaked in secrecy until they are leaked, becoming themselves transactions within the pirarchy and demonstrating the difficulties of information enclosure (Anderson 2011; Weatherall 2011). Educational campaigns warn that pirates are evil, socially inept, destroy local film industries, are associated with "drugs, child pornography, weapons, money laundering, child exploitation, fraud, and bikie gangs," and spread infection and destruction (AFACT 2009, 1, 5-6).

With little or no distinction between 'ordinary downloaders', fans/owners of enabling websites, and industrial-scale entrepreneurs, offenders can be prosecuted (Cheng 2010), pay huge fines (Kravets 2011), face extradition (Lee 2012) or jail (Enigmax 2012). Clearly, a massive legal and rhetorical war is being fought against pirarchy.

Despite these efforts at ordering the domain, pirarchy has proliferated, often accompanied by a politicisation and transnational mobilisation of both file-sharers and others around related issues including the right to Internet access, electronic freedom, and digital privacy (Haunss 2011, 1). For others, pirarchy is just a humdrum taken for granted affair, as even if the corporations squash one distribution channel, people expect that others will spring up, and that they can continue to download.

While surveys of unauthorised exchange concur that 'digital piracy' is growing, the means by which people acquire content are shifting. In the classic peer-to-peer (P2P) method, an 'original seeder' digitises a file and then uploads a tracker (or pointer) to its location. While the tracker is stored on centralised indexing and tracker websites, the digitised file remains on the original seeder's computer. 'Secondary seeders' or 'peers' can then download the file by locating the tracker and using a software 'client' to connect to a dynamic distributed 'swarm' for that particular file. The swarm is comprised of other peers who share their bandwidth and processing power to download files in non-contiguous chunks. The P2P protocol ensures that peers automatically upload chunks while they are downloading, thus cooperation is enforced on a technological level, without peers necessarily realising this. People can disconnect from a swarm as soon as they have downloaded a file without seeding back equally – such users are described as 'leechers'. When at least one secondary peer has downloaded the complete file and remains 'seeding' or 'reseeding' it either via their own fixed computers or via a cloud-based 'seedbox', the original peer no longer needs to seed again as, in theory, others keep the file alive or reanimate it upon request.

The most common file-sharing protocol is BitTorrent (BT) with over 8 million simultaneous users and 100 million regular users worldwide. BT generates over 47 percent of all upstream bytes, despite two new trends dominating both legal and illegal downstream Internet traffic: firstly, there is real time streamed entertainment, from sites such as YouTube and Vimeo; and secondly, there were 'cyberlockers' or cloud storage sites such as DropBox and Rapidshare (Envisional 2011), although this "ecosystem" changed dramatically after the Megaupload takedown in 2012.

Ambiguities of the normal domain

The borders between piracy and everyday life in the information society are thin. Originally the purpose of the Internet, apart from the intrinsic interest in building it, was to ease communication and the sharing of information (Hafner and Lyon 1996). Sharing files was fundamental. However, almost from the outset, file-sharing broke boundaries: it was a user-driven activity which occurred in domestic/leisure and work settings. Information and Communication Technology (ICT) has generally enabled domestic/leisure spaces to be permeated by the demands of work and vice-versa. ICT connections at home now approach or exceed the quality of workplace networks. Nowadays, Internet Service Providers offer fast bandwidth and mega-gigabyte or unlimited download plans that ambiguously enable both legal and illegal distribution of online content. Legally available software helps people digitise and copy texts, images, CDs and DVDs; and people require such tools for their own work, personal and social use. Pirarchy needs bountiful data compression, data transmission, the requisite software, and cheap storage options, all of which are now easily available.

Well-known, financially viable sites like YouTube enable forms of file-sharing – despite their disclaimers and their readiness to comply with take-down notices issued by copyright holders. People can upload videos, music clips, music tracks, their own mashups (frequently based on unauthorised sampling), their own music and videos, and watch advertisements, promotional material and so on. It is perhaps necessarily ambiguous how much these sites constitute ways of distributing people's own work, how much they advertise commercially available work, and how much they serve as places where fans can promote the work of those they idolise and support.

DeVoss and Porter (2006, 179) argue that now defunct music-sharing hub Napster (a 'hybrid' P2P system with a central server from which people uploaded and downloaded files) was an important development because it signalled a new 'digital ethic' of text use and file distribution. While we are uncertain it was particularly new, we agree that through normal use of the Internet, users developed the sense that information should be available on demand and usable by the downloader as they chose. Normal experiences promote habits, thus influencing social norms of what is right or natural. Gut-feelings and ideologically-based convictions are reinforced by the sense that a multitude of others share similar positions. As one of our interviewees said, he imagined downloaders as being "people much like myself, people who embrace technology, who are busy, who don't want to actually be told when to watch things and to be bombarded with advertising". These new social norms may conflict both with habits developed elsewhere by others, and with legal norms.

Another contributing factor to this normalisation of piracy is that, in contemporary capitalism, the good consumer is impulsive, impatient and always aiming to own or experience *now*. Not only do marketing experts try to increase impulse purchases but also as Vohs and Faber (2007, 537) suggest, "cash machines, shop at home television programs, and Internet shopping now render urges to act immediately and buy around the clock highly difficult to resist". Information technology weakens the delay between desire and gaining the desired object. Vohs and Faber suggest that this contributes to increasing the "ratio of household debt to disposable income" and causes financial difficulties (ibid, 537); it certainly creates an ambience in which delayed gratification is discouraged.

Attempts by corporations to stop piracy by technological fixes such as copy protection, 'Digital Rights Management' (DRM), or by attempting to monopolise media have led to corporations adding limiting 'features'. Such features are not only resisted by consumers, but also potentially hinder expansion into new markets. Apple is successful with its online iTunes store, but customers are still forced to buy from one seller and originally could only receive only 'lossy compression' format files. As many of today's media corporations fail to provide consumers with what they want, the incentives for pirarchy increase.

David Harvey (2005) is one of many who propose that peoples' lives increasingly reflect neoliberal imperatives: profit maximisation for an elite via privatisation of natural resources and public infrastructure, commodification of the 'knowledge commons', casualised 'flexible' labour, and so forth. If this is accepted, then participation in unauthorised circuits of exchange could offer some relief from the sense of continuous exploitation, loss of one's own production and value, together with what seems like endless work to get socially 'necessary' goods. Similarly, file-sharing and access to information or cultural artefacts can be necessary to perform that work, with people in many employment sectors expected to bring knowledge and social connections to the workplace that they must develop in their own notionally 'free' time.

Finally, in information society people are saturated with commercial media, and it becomes a mode of conversation, of mutual understanding, of storytelling, of sharing in the general cultural milieu or in specific (sub)cultural milieus. Commercialisation of cultural property both promulgates and interrupts that conversation and sharing, by providing what is necessary, but then disrupting the process of taking, or sharing, it.

Piracy is normal

The interviews

Despite the scandal and hype about criminality, the evidence from a small number of in-depth interviews we conducted in 2011-12 with Australian file-sharers aged between 20-55 years suggests that they considered piracy not as theft, but as normal, commonplace, and unadventurous. Many of the interviewees were either professional artists and/or workers in the cultural industries, or people who created cultural artefacts for their own personal enjoyment. This 'casual' attitude towards piracy expressed by the two separate cohorts of respondents seems to be replicated by American and German file-sharers according to Karaganis' recent study of 'copy culture' (2011b, 3-4). Peukert (2010) also reports remarks similar to the ones we describe. Rather than seeing them as expressing the nature of life in our society, however, Peukert understands them as evidence of 'rationalisations' or moral disengagement (2010, 16).[1]

Jonas Andersson (2010), in a study of Swedish file-sharers, reminds us that cultural specificity influences the way that P2P may evolve. Consequently we have to bear in mind that our paper reports on Australian file-sharers, and question to what extent our findings might be universally applicable. Andersson states that broadband came to Sweden early, as did "widespread unrestricted file-sharing, paralleled by a lively and well-informed public debate" (ibid. 8). These circumstances may have produced a relatively high-level of self-reflexivity about the practice, and the social and political contexts in which it is embedded, which may not be present everywhere.

Our interviews reveal that so-called digital piracy has lost its 'novelty value' and is simply what people do to keep in touch, keep current with cultural conversations and consume impulsively: all of which we have suggested may be necessary ways of maintaining status and employability in the 'information society'. Digital piracy has become 'atomistic', mundane and almost withdrawn. Today's cultural exchangers are more likely to share tips with one another than actual files on CDs or USB sticks, further normalising the practice, and making it more of a linguistic than a technological activity. Furthermore, the pervasiveness of file-sharing imparts the sense that risk and blame are distributed, causing individuals to feel relatively safe within the swarming millions; there is only 'bad luck' to blame if one is caught out, much like receiving a speeding ticket or tax audit notice.

---

1 However, Peukert also writes "Copyright might therefore have little support in the mental processes associated with our notions of right and wrong because to follow its rules causes an inherent conflict with basic norms rooted in our emotionally and intuitively grounded sense of justice" (2010, 20).

Before presenting some of the findings, it is important to note the limitations of our research methodology. Specifically, it should be remembered that interviewing is a limited form of research in that it reports what people say they do and what their conscious perceptions are, but it does not necessarily reveal actual dynamics or point to any social unconscious. The flow of the interview is also a matter of a particular moment and the ambience generated by the interaction of interviewer and interviewee. It can, if we are not careful, produce the results the interviewer is aiming for, as people accommodate themselves to each other (Kvale 2007). Hence these interviews, while being semi-structured with a series of possible questions, are open enough for the interviewee to lead the discussion in the direction they find interesting; thus revealing information we had not anticipated, and increasing the pool of questions for future interviews. For this chapter we have coded interviewees by letters of the alphabet.

To illustrate the issues discussed above, we have categorised the interviewees' comments under various headings.

How 'the normal' helps piracy and the unsatisfactory normal promotes piracy.

Our central argument is that piracy grows out of normal trends in the information society. It is not an external or marginal disorder, but is enabled by the factors that make information society possible. The most obvious factor is the presence of the Internet, and the general ability to transfer, copy, and store information. The users' terms for their activity seemed to be 'file-sharing,' 'downloading', 'sharing', or 'torrenting'; no-one talked about 'pirating' per se.

We identify a clear refusal to distinguish between downloading copyright and non-copyright files; to a large degree both types of content are equivalent for file-sharers, which is not to deny the guilty feelings that some people reported. However, this guilt seemed to be assuaged by various rationalisations, mainly to do with the unavailability of desired content via legal means, and through their purchases of other kinds of cultural materials and experiences (achieving a kind of personal balance between licit and illicit goods).

Several interviewees mentioned that having fast cheap bandwidth was essential for piracy as people expected to be able to download large files such as films or entire television series. R mentioned restricted bandwidth as an obstacle to file-sharing. E began downloading because he could purchase good bandwidth and a decent download quota. Y reported that most of his friends could get "very large amounts of quota for a very reasonable price". He had a 150 GB limit that allowed him to get more content than he could "possibly hope to download and watch in a one-month period". However, this expectation of instant access meant that people talked a lot about their problems with legal transmissions. E complained about losing tracks on iTunes or losing them when transferring them to different hardware platforms and mobile devices.

Some mentioned how normal copying software and devices made ripping files and digitising information relatively straightforward. E pointed to the importance of cheap good storage, which allows accumulation of files and good modes of searching for specific items. Several others mentioned that burning CDs or transferring data via portable drives helped them to share materials with non-downloaders (particularly older family members, as with someone's blind mother): this is something which lead us to wonder how many ancillary ICT manufacturing industries profit from pirarchy.[2] Acquiring and using software and data was an everyday part of everyone's work and creative lives. The habits of those lives depended upon freely and instantly available data, examples, and experiences. Consequently restrictions seemed an abnormal interruption.

Frustration with local television companies was high on the list of reasons for downloading, especially the delay in getting programmes after they had first been broadcast elsewhere – which in Australia can be weeks, months, or even years later, at odd or varying times, with programs frequently being shown out of sequence. M talks about "the excitement of... watching it as soon as it hits the screens in the States or wherever… rather than having to wait for whatever broadcast TV does to something and mangles it with ads and blah…" F also remarks that maybe her friends would subscribe to pay TV but didn't because there is "such a long wait often between what's being released in America and when it becomes… commercially available". Y notes that TV stations tend to muck around with their timing, and so viewers end up missing part of a show, and thus 'have' to download it to follow it. Z explains that stations do this deliberately so as to keep people switching to a rival channel. People want to watch a show as soon as it comes out, particularly if they are discussing this show with others

2 Various European countries impose copyright levies on blank media as a way of returning micro-payments to copyright holders. The premise of fair entitlement remains contested, with opponents arguing that individuals frequently copy their own purchases to various media for private enjoyment and should not be subject to further financial impost (Moody 2012). The tax could be seen as more exploitation of audiences and generate further resentment.

who have seen it already and might inadvertently disclose plot developments.

Sometimes the legal barriers do not make sense to users. R specifically mentions that he wants to watch programmes on the BBC website but this option, legal in the UK, was not possible in Australia even though the files were visible. Consequently, he downloaded and configured Tor, a "free software and open network" that helps defend people from threats to "personal freedom and privacy" by routing and encrypting/decrypting communications through a volunteer-provided and managed network of servers distributed around the world (Tor Project, n.d.). So some barriers not only lead to 'piracy' but to a less traceable piracy.

Comparable problems occur with free to air music broadcasts that neither deliver music on demand, nor play the particular type of music that people want to hear. This then leads to further online developments. T remarks that a particular downloading site that stores a mix of illegal files "is like a music community with sound, that shares sound files". People can upload "their own music collations for just streaming; you can share them on… all of the social networks and... there's either a link to buy or download". This site also is used by "established artists like Patti Smith... who are interested in sharing their music in an egalitarian kind of way". T also comments that "it's not just people leeching off the products of capitalism; it's also people who are creating and distributing, producing and distributing stuff from scratch totally outside of all available systems, who are using just making stuff in their lounge room... and then using alternative distribution for it". Creators "can really build up a huge following and a big profile".

Such pirarchy opens up the possibility of an artist moving from the alternative to the mainstream, or at least to more massified niche markets. So these sites provide ways of people getting known, building celebrity and perhaps earning something in the information economy, without being beholden to corporations, or having their earnings diminished by others. In other words, they are normal *and* suggest the possibility of an escape from waged or contract work; they can be sites of imaginative hope, their piracy could be incidental to other forms of sharing and display.[3] Pirarchy depends on the normality of equipment for transmission and copying, of global communication, of making a living or gaining recognition, and the failure of the majority of normal 'legal' delivery mechanisms to provide what consumers have been saying for over a decade that they want.

What is exchanged?

We can hypothesise a little more about pirarchy networks offline from the ways people share files and information with others. In the days before fast broadband, people directly exchanged files whereas today it seems that, unless they are giving something to a non-downloader, they are more likely to exchange information, recommendations, or tips. M says, "I usually tell fellow downloaders about something rather than exchange as it's easier for them than transferring". Y states that in the days before substantial download quota, particular friends in a 'cabal' would be allocated the responsibility for locating particular shows, and periodically individuals would meet up with a flash drive or portable hard drive for a 'swap-over'. Nowadays "it's just easier to get it yourself" and "people give you a tip of something that they feel is worth your time and effort to download". K also states that "it's mostly about just telling your friends about it or talking about it or, I don't very often burn things for anybody any more, they just go and do it themselves".

On the other hand, while disposing of most material, T says that she will download and keep a "certain genre of watchables" so that she can share them with others. At times she and her friends will "do lots of music sharing or movie sharing... series sharing... usually there's an exchange". While E also talks about sharing recommendations rather than "the same physical thing," he also likes to watch certain series with friends as it is "nice to go back to the start with someone else and re-watch it," while F talks about having particular friends whom "you watch one programme with".

Again this indicates a pattern of normality. People do ordinarily share recommendations about programmes, music and books, or converse about particular

3 There is the expected degree of ambiguity here. Piolatto and Schuett (2012) argue that popular artists benefit from piracy and less well known artists suffer from it. There is, however, a long history of recording companies taking advantage of musicians, so the Internet potentially offers a change in the balance of power between the average musician and a corporation. Most musicians earn more from live performances than from recording sales which act as advertisements for performances. The corporation is not needed as much as it was at either the recording or the distribution/promotion end. Neither do the musicians have to fit in with the image the corporation requires.

cultural items and performances, or go and watch or listen to something with a particular subset of their acquaintances. It suggests that the offline networks of piracy are not particularly coherent, nor are they abstractable from people's daily lives as something different. The offline ties are not particularly weak or strong compared to other ties. People who do not download themselves often participate in the benefits of piracy without protest. Piracy is in these senses normal. This is further demonstrated by people's reported motivations.

Motivations

The self-reported motivations of pirates also express normalcy through a desire to share cultural products and engage in work or production of cultural products: that is, they relay the much-hyped aims of information workers. When discussing how she treats other people, M says "share the love, share the load – share the bandwidth" showing that she sees file-sharing in terms of friendly exchange, perhaps harking back to a nostalgia for the early Internet when "there was a sense of community and sharing and the Internet being a resource for everyone". M also sees downloading in terms of research for her everyday work and 'creative practice'. As a student and a writer she needs access to cultural products when she needs them, not at someone else's discretion. Sometimes she just 'needs' to see what something is, or how it was done. Although she experiences no great connection to other downloaders ("I have never uploaded anything... my bit is keeping it going,") her statements do imply obligation: "I will seed something at least until it is [a ratio of one to one]". Some things she considers to be "great," especially those things that few people seed, she will seed for longer; she expresses a "sense of responsibility" to the neglected art and to the people who upload. Some other interviewees similarly reported that they continued to seed "rare" or "classic" works of various genres. Z thought there was a commonly-held idea that "artistic works should belong to everyone"; it followed that he had a personal "duty" to ensure that things "you couldn't buy even if you wanted to" are "available". Hence he had spent hundreds of hours digitising musical rarities from his own collection and uploading the files to a private tracker.

K also sees downloading software as related to her normal experimental art practice: "I never felt any ethical dilemma over those kind of things because I thought they all needed to be distributed because we were the ones that were working out how best to use that stuff". Perhaps her sense of moral right was reinforced by the fact that her own art was not directed at profit. T states that

"I was philosophically opposed to spending money on software and especially if it came from... big companies and also because I was really fucking poor and couldn't afford software but I always wanted to have everything that was available". Some of this was because T needed software for her art and also wanted access to contemporary cultural materials. Similarly, E says "you could argue that any cultural material is part of the work, or some of the works in the cultural industries" and "part of the point that makes me download things is to just engage in the conversation about what it's about or to understand what the popular thing is".

One of R's motivations as an 'amateur' musician was that he would "download ten different versions of some 1930s jazz standard I was learning and you would have this incredible compilation album with ten different artists who had done it... you would be hard pressed to do that, like who's got ten different versions of the same song in their personal collection". This enabled him to get music together in a way that was not otherwise possible.

Again what we see is that access to, and exchange of, cultural artefacts is considered necessary for cultural production. Consequently people don't have an ethical problem with accessing it – especially if they cannot afford the levels and breadth of access they consider essential to experiencing a rich cultural life. Piracy arises within conventional and necessary patterns of sharing culture and participating in cultural life.

Issues of purchasing and profit

S, a sound artist in his late 40s, raises the possibility of generational differences, saying that unlike younger artists he knows he has come to file-sharing "not as a birthright," but rather he has "paid my dues and so I'll download stuff because at the same time I'll still buy". In contrast, the twenty-something crowd he knows "don't buy a single thing," and although they "revere vinyl" purchasing a CD is "not even thought about...it's just purely how they are". M states that while she usually downloads entertainment and only some practical things, she does not get "everything for free" but occasionally buys what she wants: "I actually own my copy of Microsoft Word". In particular she pays "for stuff that I use to earn money". In many cases if she likes a downloaded entertainment product, she claims she will also buy it. Similarly she states, "I delete stuff usually after I've watched it, unless it is something I know I might like to burn and give to somebody who mightn't be a downloader".

In contrast, T says "I have never ever paid for a piece of software ever in my entire life," although later in the conversation this statement turns out not to be quite true. T also states that while she downloads music and films she deliberately buys books: "You probably can't compare, you know, writing and distributing software to writing and distributing a book, yeah, and because I am a writer too – so there is that". Likewise, R did not purchase music digitally but preferred to download, although he did buy printed books. R believes that piracy "hasn't actually influenced record sales a great deal, so the people who are doing it are those that wouldn't be buying the records" contrary to the "assumptions taken by people who are criticising" piracy. Moreover, "in that way it's spreading the music of people," and in any case artists don't get paid that much per disc or song anyway, most of the money goes to the company. Author Del Dryden reflects this attitude about separating books from other forms of cultural products :

> I'm a novelist who has seen decreasing royalties and increasing piracy... If you steal my work... I can't continue to produce it. It's the dismissiveness on the part of people who obviously think this is an unreasonable attitude on the part of writers who apparently are supposed to survive on thin air and the sheer force of their own creativity (Quoted in Gaskin 2011, np).

These positions encapsulate the problem: we cannot survive if everyone downloads without payment, and yet it's hard to stay in the 'cultural conversation' without downloading.

Y occasionally downloads a game, but "these days you can get games … legally in the comfort of your own home with applications such as Steam... they often have a lot of specials on, so [I don't download much], because the availability is there and the price is reasonable". K is accustomed to buying apps [applications] for Apple equipment and music, hoping that money paid to iTunes goes back to the artist, but surprisingly not checking. However K finds the copy protection annoying, as it hampers sharing with friends. E also believes that most of the purchase price "doesn't go to the artist, so I don't feel good about purchasing things; in a way I feel bad that, it's kind of like, I am wasting money". W, who writes and makes art himself without ever hoping "to make money out of it", believes that he makes "some kind of moral judgement" about material he finds online. It is "pretty easy to see who's a struggling independent artist and who's part of some multi-national company," and consequently there is "some hierarchy of who you can steal from and who you can't".

So there is a political edge or rationalisation to the behaviour, but it is not pronounced. This edge could stem from a feeling that their own possibilities of contributing to 'mainstream' cultural production are marginal, even though most of the interviewees are cultural producers. Nevertheless the main paradox here would seem to be the recognition that in the information society people need to be paid for cultural work, plus a reluctance to pay for it, and a feeling that the actual producers do not receive appropriate payment anyway. If there is a radical edge to the actions of these so-called 'pirates', our interviewees do generally not push it, and it is unintentional and possibly self-undermining of their own survival. It is just a habit and people do not have to persuade themselves that they are doing the right thing – rather, it is simply what they do.

Consumerism made free: I need it now

The information society needs consumers, and consequently encourages consumerism, to fund the necessary production. However, if the money is siphoned away from the producers to the owners then there may not be enough money earned to keep the necessary consumption occurring. Given that turnover on speculative currency and derivatives trading dwarfed the rest of the global economy before the late crash of 2007, this siphoning seems to be happening (Marshall 2007, 5). We might also wonder if a whole society can function just by the exchange of information and art: we cannot eat information for example. File-sharing is one of the most direct displays of this cultural and economic incoherence.

Consumerism is widespread even amongst those who reject it. T says, "I definitely wanted and needed to have all that stuff and it's so expensive". E says: "it's just good to have the library to be able to give to someone else or just have that pride of, you know, this is what I have got". Within this society accumulation is good and a matter of status, no matter how it is acquired.

Consequently the ideal consumer is also impulsive to some extent: that is, they see and they buy. E emphasises how good it is to be able to get things the moment he thinks of them: "I remember a film that I have seen and I liked or I really want to watch in the future and I just download that [now]". Similarly the usual modes of free-access, advertising-supported products (such as free-to-air television and commercial radio) are not sufficient for this mode of being:

> I prefer to be able to download it in bulk and watch it in my own time, yeah. I'm not liking the thing of subscribing to this weekly thing where I can only watch one episode.

Y also remarks that, "often I will download a whole season at a time because that's how I now prefer to watch my content… watch an entire season in the course of a week or two… on demand". R and T mentioned lack of money as an incentive to piracy as it obviously retards their ability to experience this type of compulsive consumption.

Here then, piracy is about getting all the benefits of consumerism, and indeed fitting in to consumerist society, without the apparent costs. Although things are never simple and other costs emerge such as the intense accumulation that can lead to both a sense of being overwhelmed and also to 'data-smog' (Shenk 1997). F says:

> My friends and family talk about this feeling of exhaustion and information overload and actual stress. So we're downloading all this stuff but we don't have the time and it sometimes makes us more aware that we are time-poor.

M also captures this sense: "I've got another hard drive full of movies I haven't watched". R says he has a lot of MP3s he has not listened to and is working his way through them. So, while it may seem necessary to have such products to produce cultural outputs, it is quite possible that most of it never gets used, and indeed could act as a potential deferral of production as there is always an extra thing to imbibe.

Overload perhaps implies that people would not have downloaded the material if it was not there – also meaning that they might never actually listened to or watch it. If this is the case, then corporations have certainly not lost the revenues that they claim. Furthermore, if people cannot purchase certain products anyway – such as rare masters of albums, unreleased live tracks, old films, and so on – then there is also no loss. This is a point often made on file-sharing forums. Piracy then, expresses a consumerism that is perhaps out of the control of the producers and copyright holders. Yet in another sense, there is a virtually infinite supply of privately-owned arcane and popular 'second-hand' goods that are populating 'unauthorised' circuits of exchange, feeding a form of consumerism which depends neither on further exchange of monetary tokens nor direct forms of barter.

Politicisation vs. the humdrum

M says:

> I'm a pretty mainstream downloader as a middle-aged person, middle-aged professional... I don't feel like I'm doing anything extreme or radical or anarchic or illegal... [or] unethical – and I have a strong sense of ethics.... not radical at all, just doing my stuff.

M's "whole experience of the Internet has always been one of community and sharing". She does not consider that "copyright law is ethical at all times," and believes it is inevitable that the law is "going to change, it will have to change, it will change". Furthermore, because downloading is "just so incredibly easy," she does not understand "why everyone in the world doesn't do it". Piracy does not mark her self-conception – she is simply doing normal things, sharing normally.

T uses "sharing sites and file-sharing on a daily basis... I've gotten to the stage I think where I just use it as a matter of course and I don't think about it very much anymore". However, she is also "very interested in people who are not only kind of using those systems and creating like an alternative kind of economy". So it is both not worth thinking about and perhaps offers hope – it's a kind of 'humdrum millennialism'.

E also frames the events by normalcy, but with a hint of radicalism, declaring that, "I would only see it as piracy if I was producing it into hard copy and then selling it on". Many interviewees similarly distinguished between 'domestic piracy' and commercial counterfeiting enterprises. Significantly, E doesn't "really see it as sharing. I think it's kind of more just tapping into culture". Hence "it feels more like... going on Wikipedia and looking up information... I think it's the same kind of thing".

Again showing the humdrum and non-involved nature of piracy, K says "I'm pretty practical about it these days – let's just get that movie, get it quick, what's the ratio, have I given enough back yet? It doesn't have a novelty value anymore, it's just this is how I get stuff". Piracy is boring: It is part of daily life, and its politics could be equally humdrum and even not brought into play.

K was the most ideationally radical, saying:

> I'm actually really fascinated by how it's changed the ownership of information and the ownership of immaterial things... and how that's changed the whole landscape of exchange between people. What you get for what you pay for, what you may or may not hold in your hands, how it increases

> wealth and decreases wealth... it's just such a huge area... I've never seen knowledge as property.

However, this latter point might be nostalgic, as knowledge has only recently been seen as strictly private property by some of those involved in artistic or academic life.

Andersson suggests that in Sweden, file-sharers are not "vociferous antagonists" in the "copyfight" but simply "everyday users whose productive agency when consuming and re-distributing media becomes politicised, largely due to the controversial ways in which this agency is currently configured" (2010, 19). Perhaps, P2P, as well as producing what we might imagine as 'unintentional communities', also generates 'unintentional liberationists,' whose daily digital media habits bring them into conflict with capitalism and its copyright laws without any necessary consciousness of the longer-term consequences of the aggregated actions of millions of others similarly engaged.

Swarms and communities

While we have argued that the social forms of piracy are part of the social forms of everyday life, the structures online are contingent, shifting and fluxing. The temporary network crystallises into potential and then dissipates, just as YouTube videos may suddenly attract audiences of millions that then dissipate. As Dejean writes "the distribution of copy does not depend on a particular group of individuals" (2009, 331).

Any fixed community is imagined and largely unintentional. M talks of the "shared action, a shared action that's happening... in apartments and houses... across the world at the same time". However she does not see herself as "an actual active member of community". Some people reject being drawn into the social norms that exist within genre-specific communities that exist around private tracker sites and web boards. S says, "Support your scene, what does that mean? It's just a boy scout attitude". He continues, "Who is this faceless scene? At least with Punk I could go out and see a band and there would be a group of people". His position further supports our suspicion that the social ties binding file-sharing 'communities' are often significantly weaker than those existing within embodied communities and subcultures.

Nevertheless, many people mentioned the various graphic representations of the current swarm as important in their imagining of the social processes around file-sharing. F says of the software client Vuze, "I used to love watching the swarm and the little pieces"; while M notes that "it gives you that real sense of here I am, in the community". E also liked watching the national flags that the P2P clients FrostWire and LimeWire displayed next to peers' IP addresses.

E points to the community of sharing amongst both their friends and amongst specialists: "Say I was looking for an obscure French documentary on bread and then an obscure French documentary on eggs... they would probably come from the same kind of people, so I would probably have more of a sense of community there". But E also adds that this is an amorphous community as the practice of file-sharing becomes increasingly accepted: "It's becoming so mainstream it's not so much community but just society".

In contrast, R has little contact with others: "I was never interested in talking to anyone else, I just wanted their free music (laughter)". In much the same way K says, "I've never used peer-to-peer as a social network, I just use it to get things". K also thinks that the sharing has become less of a factor on these sites as they have become so big, and that most of the site commentary is about "geeky kind of things". T declares herself to be "just a leech" because she does not reseed most of what she downloads. However, this troubles her: "I think about that I don't contribute to that community very much – I just take a lot but you know, if there's opportunities to share then I absolutely share". In the past she shared "all the time on Napster".

For K, while the social aspects occur in more everyday life when she talks with friends, there is a sense of reciprocity: "I do seed back.... Because I feel like I owe it back". Even the anonymous swarm generates quite a strong sense of obligation even though people often do not act upon what they feel is a moral imperative. Perhaps the urge to reciprocate exchange is stronger for those who view the Internet as a web of social relationships. P describes people shifting from participating in a "big media model where you're a customer or a consumer" to a "sharing based model" where they can develop "relationships of trust with others". Here, trust and other affects arise out of material actions and communicative exchange, from "learning how to assess the credibility and durability of a project that's a plug in for your Firefox browser" to "figuring out a good Torrent and then contributing to keeping that piece of culture alive by seeding it". Where problems arise in such scenarios, rather than being "a grumpy customer...you can be part of the solution". It seems that file-sharing – via whatever means (direct download or distributed transmission) – is fuelled by living the normal kind of social life demanded by the system that would make it illegal.

Conclusion

We have argued that pirarchy arises from the very nature of capitalist information society. When people have grown up viewing the Internet as a 'resource for everyone' in which they "share the love, share the load, share the bandwidth," they become less likely to distinguish between what are defined as legal and illegal forms of content. The boundaries of enclosure of information property become fraught. What exists in the cloud and the nets is deemed to be 'public knowledge' and cultural or intellectual capital that should be available to all. As a result, a person does not need to overtly subscribe to pirate or digital commons ideologies to engage in file-sharing. The Internet also furthers the kinds of long term but continually precarious social structures typified by the "swarms" the BitTorrent protocol creates. These swarms join the 'peers' in anonymous functional pirarchy.

In this regime of pirarchy, P2P has transformed from a conscious 'radical' practice to something more intuitive, implicit, pervasive and conventionally humdrum. It is part of ordinary life furthered by the tools of work and cultural creation within information capitalism. Ease of communication, ease of replication, ease of transmission, and ordinary use of cultural items to maintain one's position in an ongoing cultural conversation or to produce artefacts for work, all imply that pirarchy will continue, and disrupt models of property which are based upon easy exclusion and difficulty of replication. If this is a type of radicalism, it is one whose radicalism is unintentional, emerging out of the same forces that try to shut it down. As such, it is a disorder that arises out of information order.

As such, a key theme that emerges here is that an ordering leads to a disorder, which leads to another ordering, as the order's problem-solving either fails to solve problems for everyone, or creates new problems for some. This continual cycle drives social-technical processes. It is possible that breaking the cycle to retain an impossible order, through over regulation, could lead the system to collapse. Each imposition of order leads to further disorder, and not necessarily in a 'logical', reciprocal or linear fashion. Events in one domain can trigger responses extending across other domains, disordering processes that produce cascades of new attempts at ordering the instability, unpredictability, and volatility.

The contradictions of the system are clear: when every idea can be commodified, autonomous popular culture may become impossible. If nothing can be commodified then cultural producers may not survive without other income or without engaging in non-monetary forms of barter and exchange. Those in the pirarchy, and those opposed to it, are all trying to deal with these problems and to take advantage of the system as it stands. The outcome is unknown: it is a process that may generate new transnational and anarchic social formations with non-capitalistic ideas or practices of property; collapse and instability; or a regime dependent on continual use of force and monitoring to contain uncontainable property.

References

Anderson, Nate (2011). "Son of ACTA: Meet the *Next* Secret Copyright Treaty". *Ars Technica*, 11 March 2011. Retrieved 12 July 2013, from http://arstechnica.com/tech-policy/news/2011/03/son-of-acta-meet-the-next-secret-copyright-treaty.ars

Andersson, Jonas (2010). *Peer-to-peer-based file-sharing beyond the dichotomy of 'downloading is theft' vs. 'information wants to be free': How Swedish file-sharers motivate their action.* Diss., Goldsmiths, University of London, London.

AFACT (2009). *Movie Piracy and Community Policing: Protecting your community from the impact of copyright crimes.* Retrieved 12 July 2013, from http://www.afact.org.au/assets/research/community_policing_lowrez.pdf

BASCAP (2009). *Research Report on Consumer Attitudes and Perceptions on Counterfeiting and Piracy.* Retrieved 15 July 2013, from http://www.iccwbo.org/Data/Documents/Bascap/Consumer-Perceptions/Consumer-Research-Report/

BSA (2011). *2010 Piracy Study.* Retrieved 12 July 2013, from http://portal.bsa.org/globalpiracy2010/downloads/study_pdf/2010_BSA_Piracy_Study-Standard.pdf

Bridy, Annemarie (2011). "ACTA and the Specter of Graduated Response". *American University International Law Review*, 26:3, 558-577.

Cheng, Jacqui (2010). "OiNK founder free after two-plus years of legal troubles". *Ars Technica*, 15 January 2010. Retrieved 12 July 2013, from http://arstechnica.com/tech-policy/news/2010/01/oink-founder-free-after-two-plus-years-of-legal-troubles.ars

Dejean, Sylvain (2009). "What Can We Learn from Empirical Studies About Piracy?". *CESifo Economic Studies*, 55:2, 326-52.

DeVoss, Dànielle N. and James E. Porter (2006). "Why Napster Matters to Writing: Filesharing as a New Ethic of Digital Delivery". *Computers and Composition*, 23:2, 178-210.

Enigmax (2012). "NinjaVideo Founder Sentenced To 22 Months in Prison" [Blog post]. *TorrentFreak*, 6 January 2012. Retrieved 12 July 2013, from http://torrentfreak.com/ninjavideo-founder-sentenced-to-22-months-in-prison-120106

Envisional (2011). "Technical report: An Estimate of Infringing Use of the Internet". Cambridge: Envisional. Retrieved 12 July 2013, from http://documents.envisional.com/docs/Envisional-Internet_Usage-Jan2011.pdf

Gaskin, John (2011). "Wiley Suing BitTorrent Book Pirates". *ITworld*, 3 November 2011. Retrieved 12 July 2013, from http://www.itworld.com/security/219417/wiley-suing-bittorrent-downloaders

Hafner, Katie and Matthew Lyon (1996). *Where Wizards Stay up Late: The Origins of the Internet.* New York: Simon and Schuster.

Harvey, David (2005). *A Brief History of Neoliberalism.* Oxford: Oxford University Press.

Haunss, Sebastian (2011). "The Politicisation of Intellectual Property: IP Conflicts and Social Change". *The WIPO Journal*, 3:1, 129-138.

Hinze, Gwen (2010, 17 December). "Not-So-Gentle Persuasion: US Bullies Spain into Proposed Website Blocking Law" [Blog post]. Electronic Frontier Foundation Deeplinks Blog. Retrieved 12 July 2013, from http://www.eff.org/deeplinks/2010/12/not-so-gentle-persuasion-us-bullies-spain-proposed

Karaganis, Joe (ed.) (2011). *Media Piracy in Emerging Economies.* New York: Social Science Research Council.

Karaganis, Joe (2011b). *Copyright Infringement and Enforcement in the USA* (Research Note). The American Assembly, Columbia University.

Kravets, David (2011). "Judge Slashes 'Appalling' $1.5 Million File-sharing Verdict to $54,000". *Wired Magazine.* Retrieved 12 July 2013, from http://www.wired.com/threatlevel/2011/07/kazaa-verdict-slashed

Kvale, Steinar (2007). *Doing Interviews: Sage, Sage Research Methods [online].* Retrieved 12 July 2013, from http://www.sagepub.com/upm-data/26302_Chapter3.pdf

Lee, Timothy B. (2012). "Copyright Wars Escalate: Britain to Extradite Student to US Over Link Site". *Ars Technica*, 13 January 2012. Retrieved 12 July 2013, from http://arstechnica.com/tech-policy/news/2012/01/copyright-wars-escalate-britain-to-extradite-student-to-us-over-link-site

Marshall, Jonathan P. (2009). "The Physiognomy of Dispersed Power". *Leonardo Electronic Almanac*, 16:4–5. Retrieved 12 July 2013, from http://www.leonardo.info/LEA/DispersiveAnatomies/DA_marshall.pdf

Marshall, Jonathan P., James Goodman and Francesca da Rimini (forthcoming). *Disorder and the Disinformation Society: The Social Dynamics of Networks and Software.* New York: Routledge.

Moody, Glynn (2012). "EU Copyright Holders Cling To Old Levies, As New Ones Start To Appear On Cloud Storage". *TechDirt.* Retrieved 12 July 2013, from http://www.techdirt.com/articles/20120928/05551020537/eu-copyright-holders-cling-to-old-levies-as-new-ones-start-to-appear-cloud-storage.shtml

Peukert, Alexander (2010). "Why Do 'Good People' Disregard Copyright on the Internet?". Retrieved 12 July 2013, from http://ssrn.com/paper=1660319

Piolatto, Amedio and Florian Schuett (2012). "Music Piracy: A Case of 'The Rich Get Richer and the Poor Get Poorer'". *Information Economics and Policy*, 24:1, 30–39.

Shenk, David (1997). *Data Smog: Surviving the Information Glut.* San Francisco: HarperEdge.

Tor Project *Anonymity Online.* https://www.torproject.org

Vohs, Kathleen D. and Ronald J Faber (2007). "Spent Resources: Self-Regulatory Resource Availability Affects Impulse Buying". *Journal of Consumer Research*, University of Chicago Press, 33:4, 537-547.

Weatherall, Kim (2011). "An Australian Analysis of the February 2011 Leaked US TPPA IP Chapter Text – Copyright and Enforcement". Retrieved 12 July 2013 from http://works.bepress.com/cgi/viewcontent.cgi?article=1022&context=kimweatherall

An Epilogue
Privacy is Theft: On Anonymous Experiences, Infrastructural Politics and Accidental Encounters

Ned Rossiter and Soenke Zehle

Urban piracy, data piracy, cultural and media piracy, oceanic piracy, ecological piracy – piracy abounds across the world today. Whether analyzed in terms of property violations or acts of resistance, invoked by commercial monopolies or citizen alliances, addressed through strategies of criminalization or the invention of new rights, analyses of piracy delineate the boundaries and (il)legitimacies of specific regimes of power. Across legal, governmental, social, cultural and affective articulations of power, piracy involves a wide array of actors in contestations of ownership, new forms of use and alternative politics of the common.

Beyond analyses regarding the informality of origins, we contend that piracy is also a model dynamic because it is so deeply interwoven with techno-cultural practices of anonymity. In order to analyse some of these practices, we provide a gloss on anonymity to extend perspectives on a "movement without a name" to the material infrastructures enabling and sustaining it (Kahn-Harris 2011). While visions of 'data mining' explicitly redefine creative industries as extractive industries, the financialization of commodities as informational entities has already made the distinction between digital and non-digital objects a matter of degree rather than definitive delineation. As the informatization of products and processes increases, more and more piratical practices also become enmeshed with one another, according the information infrastructures that enable and sustain them a key role that extends far beyond the 'digital domain' of contemporary economies of culture.[1]

Technologies of anonymization, decentralization and informalization have not simply framed or favoured these practices. Beyond the conceptual horizon circumscribed by analyses of piracy, they offer elements of an emergent politics

1 See, for example, the use of file sharing platforms to distribute models for 3D-printing, which have already been accorded a key role in 'industry 4.0' policy visions of industrial informatization. In addition to providers such as The Pirate Bay (which created a 'physibles' search category), a global network of digital fabrication labs is officially exchanging such models on the basis of (emerging) open hardware standards, aimed at promoting peer-to-peer technology transfer. See http://freedomdefined.org/OSHW.

of invisibility. What these technologies can help us comprehend are the stakes of (in)visibility and forms of desubjectification. Anonymity registers the possibilities for both individual and collective refusal to turn our communicative relations into generators expected to power the data-driven enterprises of an experience economy. The result, in effect, is a withdrawal of 'free labour' from the institutional settings of a digital economy, its clouds and communication platforms. In supporting personas without profiles, anonymizing technologies offer a more immediate subtraction of value from the extractive economies of search and social media.[2]

These extractive economies, in turn, rest on the twin pillars of surveillance – public and private.[3] For national security agencies, real-time social media networks offer opportunities for "obtaining and disseminating real time open source intelligence" and improving "situation awareness" that complement their traditional approaches to intelligence.[4] Use of data scraping technologies to collect 'open source intelligence' has obvious implications for the maintenance of user privacy rights, with potential institutional collusion between security agencies and social media platforms that have a commercial interest in safeguarding user-generated data. While not yet on a scale that rivals the reach of commercial alternatives, free software attracts renewed attention as the focus shifts from the rights of individual users to modify code to the political promise that the desire to opt out is best protected by communities developing non-proprietary software.[5]

At stake is not simply the (il)legality of sharing, but the autonomy of experi-

2 For an early NSA analysis of the popular anonymization platform TOR, see NSA 2006 (http://apps.washingtonpost.com/g/page/world/nsa-research-report-on-the-tor-encryption-program/501). As users note, "The irony is that TOR was originally developed by the U.S. Naval Research Laboratory. And even now, the project is still partially funded by the US government through both the State Department and National Science Foundation" (ibid.). The politics of anonymity clearly cut across dichotomies such as privacy/surveillance and state/civil society.

3 For sample analyses of public surveillance, see Electronic Frontier Foundation 2013 (https://www.eff.org/deeplinks/2013/09/government-releases-nsa-surveillance-docs-and-previously-secret-fisa-court). For private surveillance, see Beckett 2013 (https://www.propublica.org/article/everything-we-know-about-what-data-brokers-know-about-you). The phrase "privacy is theft" is one of three mottos (sharing is caring, secrets are lies) of a (fictional, of course) Silicon Valley company. See Eggers 2013.

4 In a Request for Information (RFI) published on January 19, 2012, the FBI notes that "a geospatial alert and analysis mapping application is the best known solution for attaining and disseminating real time open source intelligence and improving the FBI's overall situational awareness ... The purpose of this effort is to meet the outlined objectives for the FBI SIOC, in addition to FBI Field Offices, LEGATS (overseas), and Operational Units for the enhancement FBI SIOC's overall situational awareness and improved strategic decision making". Access the RFI via http://www.theguardian.com/world/2012/jan/26/fbi-social-media-monitoring-privacy.

5 See http://prism-break.org, a site maintained by the Electronic Frontier Foundation.

ence. To better grasp this, a mere focus on the need to shift analysis 'beyond representation' to the material registers of communication will not suffice. Acts of communication are now, by definition, acts of surveillance meshed within an economy that aggregates even the affective, non-representational dynamics of relation. Without anonymity, nothing escapes extraction. Experience is tied to technological assemblages or diagrams of power comprised of technical, cultural, social, economic, political and affective forces. And this is why we use the term technology in a broader sense of practices of collaborative constitution, of a technics that literally involves both objects and subjects and can therefore not usefully be exclusively framed in terms of either.

At the same time, such attention to affect and the singularity of refusal does not imply a neglect of collective, geopolitical registers. Quite the contrary. The arrival of such a politics of (in)visibility includes the rise of the piratical whistle-blower as a key figure of civil disobedience. The effects of Edward Snowden's activities, for example, have already been acknowledged in a number of macropolitical initiatives, from European Union proposals to reorganize Internet governance (including the establishment of a Global Internet Policy Observatory) to Brazilian plans to maintain national information and communications infrastructures.[6] The digital experience, it turns out, is both singular and geopolitical.[7]

Pirate infrastructures

The logistical infrastructures of both piracy and the politics of (in)visibility cut across the contours of a geopolitical and geocultural modernity made dominant through global institutions such as the International Monetary Fund (IMF), World Trade Organization (WTO) and World Bank along with the industrial and economic extension of advanced economies coupled with the colonial and imperial legacy of these nations. No longer can European and US power be assured through the exportation of expertise and infrastructure that has marked many post-crisis economies (be they the 'end' of Maoism and the rise of China as an authoritarian neoliberal state, or the reconstruction of so-called failed

6 Discussions of an 'open Internet' maintained mainly under the auspices of the United States are a reminder of much older conflicts, from resistance to the Cold War 'free flow of information' doctrine to 'multi-stakeholder' approaches to Internet governance initiated in the course of the 2003-2005 World Summit on the Information Society. See Zehle 2012, 1-2.

7 This is one reason why assemblage theories have at least made visible the limitations of established micro- and macropolitical frameworks of analysis. See also Stengers, Massumi and Manning 2008, (http://www.senselab.ca/inflexions/volume_3/node_i3/stengers_en_inflexions_vol03.html).

states in Africa and the Middle East). Countries from the 'global south' – China, India and Brazil chief among them – increasingly remodel a global state system in their own image.

For reasons such as these, the question of 'pirate modernities' continues to be relevant, not as a counter-discourse to ('Western') modernities nor as affirmation of 'alternative modernities' as an analytical framework, but as a possible prefiguration of a new generation of infrastructures that is virtually unmappable. As Ravi Sundaram writes: "does the future trajectory of modern government follow the historic Western liberal and neoliberal models of power and property, or, does it acknowledge an actually-existing constellation where the boundaries of visible property and formal economies coexist with those of the informal and un-propertied?" (Sundaram 2010a; see also Sundaram 2010b). Here, the issue of informality is less related to the romanticisation of subaltern agency through piracy than as a mode of relation that underwrites the resilience (and redundancy) of network infrastructures. Complementary rather than simply parasitical, pirate economies undo the cohesion assumed of discourses distinguishing 'the West' from 'the Rest'.[8]

8 See, for instance, the comment on software piracy submitted to the US Trade Representative by the Social Science Research Council (SSRC). Its recommendations include: "Unlike recorded media business models such as the CD and DVD businesses, piracy is not primarily a drain on the software business, but rather a critical part of the business model that allows the building of market share in low-income countries and the effective locking out of open source alternatives. These network effects are enormously valuable to quasi-monopoly providers like Microsoft, but also smaller vendors seeking to establish a foothold in foreign markets; Unlike recorded media business models, the software industry has strong forms of technical protection at its disposal that go mostly unexercised because for fear of inconveniencing paying customers; Unlike recorded media business models, the software industry has an entirely viable business model in developing countries, based on institutional licenses to large businesses and the public sector. The consumer/retail sector is effectively ignored through western-level pricing. This model has allowed Microsoft, for example, to report 100% growth in sales in China in 2010, despite what the 2010 Special 301 report characterizes as a near total lack of enforcement. Enforcement plays a role in this strategy in the form of pressure on institutions to legalize. But the key market factor is the threat of the adoption of open source alternatives, which creates competitive pricing pressure and leads to lower-prices on licenses. The USTR plays an appropriate role in this context by encouraging countries to legalize software in the public sector and to enforce against commercial pirate vendors under the TRIPS agreement. But in our view, given the complex relationship between legal, unlicensed, and open source adoption, that is as far as the evidence of harms goes. The assumption that there are massive overall losses to US software industries from piracy or significant benefits to stronger criminal provisions for end-user infringement should be heavily discounted. The problem of business sector piracy is best left to the technical protection measures of the vendors and the civil courts. The question of software choice, often involving open source adoption as a strategy for combating piracy, should be left to governments". See Social Science Research Council 2011 (http://infojustice.org/wp-content/uploads/2011/02/Social-Science-Research-Council.pdf). See also "Media Piracy in Emerging Economies" (http://piracy.americanassembly.org) and Page 2013 (http://www.

Following the legacy of Giedion, Mumford and Benjamin, Brian Larkin notes: "Infrastructures create a sensing of modernity" (Larkin 2013, 337). The material qualities special to infrastructure "produces sensorial and political experiences" (ibid.). There was a certain palpability to infrastructure in the age of modernity and industrialisation. Concrete and steel, asphalt and railways, shipyards and factories, electric illumination and flying machines – all provided an index of progress that fuelled utopian dreams of technological prowess and the centrality of human agency.

Network infrastructure in the age of pirate modernities produces experiences (aesthetic sensations) more often abstracted from the logic of the machine. Modernity's meta-narrative of progress became less tenable as a proposition in part due to the dislocation between informatization and action in the world. Progress, in other words, lost its indexical relation once communication departed from its infrastructural supports. Temporality nowadays is all about waiting for the next software update. The result is a sort of perpetual present in which immediacy becomes serialised across the time of expression, experience and, occasionally, action.

Sovereign logistics

Communication and transport infrastructure provides the architecture for global circuits of trade and economy. The extent to which interoperability occurs across these systems depends upon coherence at the level of standards. Bowker: "each layer of infrastructure requires its own set of standards" (Bowker 2005, 111). The universality of infrastructure – its capacity to relate organized practices with material and technical agencies – corresponds with a political economy of standards.[9] Here we see the instantiation of governance and sovereignty beyond the state. International standards are achieved through a combination of national and surpranational institutions, state and non-state actors (private corporations and civil society organizations), reaching some form of agreement which is then implemented.

The political economy that conditions the possibility of infrastructural regimes on a universal scale signals the imperial ambition of both standards and

---

theinquirer.net/inquirer/news/2301622/breaking-bad-creator-says-piracy-helped-the-shows-success).

9 Lampland and Star: "infrastructure is fundamentally a relational concept, becoming real infrastructure in relation to organized practices". Lampland and Star 2009, 17.

infrastructure. It therefore comes as no surprise that sovereign powers attach themselves to infrastructural projects. Because sovereignty is effectively and materially distributed across a wide range of governance dynamics, its reaggregation (in the name of a democratic politics of information, for instance) requires an awareness not only of the logistics of networks (which include the operations of pirate networks), but of the logistics of sovereignty. We see this most obviously in the case of Chinese infrastructural interests in various African countries, along with port leaseholds and factory acquisitions in Europe and the US.[10]

Whether it is the materiality of ports, warehouses, airports, intermodal terminals, railways, satellites and fibre optic cable or the immateriality of digital code, infrastructural protocols tend to be driven by proprietary systems that regulate access and manage sociality within an economistic horizon. Whether it is experts engaged in consultation, management and engineering oversight, or semi-skilled labour undertaking the work of construction or maintenance, infrastructure is always accompanied by labour power. As such, the economic productivity surrounding infrastructure is coincident with the surplus value underpinned by the scale and cost of labour. Deliberately downplayed in enthusiastic visions of globalization-as-dematerialization, the labour of bodies and minds continues to trace the trail of infrastructural development and the redistribution of sovereignty.

Designing autonomy

The political economy of enclosure inspires wilful acts of piracy, and it does not come as a surprise that privacy and property have been the conceptual twins of critical analysis. Misappropriation of data, IP infringement, sabotage, highjacking, hacking – these variants of piracy cross from oceans to information, from cable to dirt. Their actual or apparent illegality is relative to the concept of property and its concomitant juridical regimes designed to protect private ownership. Shifting our focus to the infrastructural practices of a politics of anonymity, we begin to find ourselves preoccupied more with techniques of invention and the politics of intervention.

If we hold on to the term 'piracy' to describe a collective dynamic, pursued by a multitude of actors whose modes of relation are not based on principles of identity but linked through their usage of overlapping logistical infrastructures,

10 Related to this is the link between standardization and the sovereign influence of US-based rating agencies, registered through the mechanisms of development finance.

piracy is neither adequately nor exhaustively comprehended by way of framing it in terms of the legality/illegality of its practices. Given the continued (if romanticized) connotations of a democratization beyond representation, piracy requires instead that we continue to revisit and reframe concepts of collectivity.

It makes no sense, neither conceptually nor politically, to pit 'material' (migrant workers) and 'immaterial' (creative class) labour against one another (nor to rest one's hopes for change with only one of them). As the processes of globalization and informatization transform our communicative relations into networks of social production powered (and made profitable) by free labour, the pursuit of anonymity has to be understood in terms of such a deliberate de-linking from networks designed to capture value through lifestream logistics. The desire for anonymity is not (only) a result of the simultaneous disappearance of privacy and the public. It is, above all, an indication of the growing interest in self-determined uses of social production and technologies of the common that may have been developed and distributed across commercial infrastructures, but whose modes of relation already outgrow the imaginative scope of economies of scarcity and rival goods.

How to design a movement? This is not so much an idle speculation as a question central to the work of political organization. It is a question all too often side-lined by those on the frontlines, squares and encampments of social-political change as they log into their Facebook and Twitter accounts to communicate and organize the urgency of our times. The over-design of user-experience (UX) is so totalising that we find it near impossible to operate outside of aesthetic regimes of computational clouds. Strategies of commercial communication are already engaged in 'primitive accumulation' on the terrain of affect, from 'people-centred' design approaches to the use of real-time biometrics.[11]

Experience these days is so heavily formatted at both design and hardware levels. Contra Virilio, there is rarely an occasion for the 'accident' in experience when mediated through predictive technologies and, increasingly, 'big data' profiling. To begin, then, we suggest that autonomy, here, relates to the status of the accidental encounter, of modes of relation not yet framed by the technics of pre-emptive government and targeted marketing.[12] Piracy, however, has always

11 To the extent that a new generation of natural-interface-based gaming consoles records and stores the interaction and movement profiles of players engaged in cloud-hosted multiplayer games, the notion of bio-piracy might acquire an entirely new meaning. See http://news.xbox.com/xbox-one.

12 For an approach that comprehends our relations to and in technological networks not simply

understood the accidental encounter.

References

Beckett, Lois (2013). "Everything We Know About What Data Brokers Know About You". *Pro Publica*, 13 September. Retrieved 27 October 2013, from https://www.propublica.org/article/everything-we-know-about-what-data-brokers-know-about-you

Bowker, Geoffrey C. (2005). *Memory Practices in the Sciences.* Cambridge, MA.: MIT Press.

Eggers, Dave (2013). *The Circle.* New York: Knopf.

Electronic Frontier Foundation (2013). "Government Releases NSA Surveillance Docs and Previously Secret FISA Court Opinions In Response to EFF Lawsuit", 10 September. Retrieved 27 October 2013, from https://www.eff.org/deeplinks/2013/09/government-releases-nsa-surveillance-docs-and-previously-secret-fisa-court

Kahn-Harris, Keith (2011). "Naming the Movement". *Open Democracy*, 22 June. Retrieved 27 October 2013, from http://www.opendemocracy.net/keith-kahn-harris/naming-movement

Lampland, Martha and Susan Leigh Star (2009). "Reckoning with Standards". In Martha Lampland and Susan Leigh Star (eds). *Standards and their Stories: How Quantifying, Classifying and Formalizing Practices Shape Everyday Life.* Ithaca: Cornell University Press.

Larkin, Brian (2013). "The Politics and Poetics of Infrastructure". *Annual Review of Anthropology*, 42.

Munster, Anna (2013). *An Aesthesia of Networks: Conjunctive Experience in Art and Technology.* Cambridge, MA: MIT Press.

NSA (2006). "Report on the TOR Encrypted Network". Retrieved 27 October 2013, from http://apps.washingtonpost.com/g/page/world/nsa-research-report-on-the-tor-encryption-program/501/

Page, Carly (2013). "Breaking Bad Creator says 'Piracy' Helped the Show's Success". *The Inquirer*, 8 October. Retrieved 27 October 2013 from http://www.theinquirer.net/inquirer/news/2301622/breaking-bad-creator-says-piracy-helped-the-shows-success

Social Science Research Council (2011). "RE: 2011 Special 301 Review / Docket Number USTR - 2010-0037," 15 February. Retrieved 27 October 2013, from http://infojustice.org/wp-content/uploads/2011/02/Social-Science-Research-Council.pdf.

Stengers, Isabelle, Brian Massumi and Erin Manning (2008). "History through the Middle: Between Macro and Mesopolitics. Interview with Isabelle Stengers". *Inflexions*, 3. Retrieved 27 October 2013, from http://www.senselab.ca/inflexions/

in terms of use and embeddedness but as co-constituted experiences, see Munster 2013.

volume_3/node_i3/stengers_en_inflexions_vol03.html
Sundaram, Ravi (2010a). "Externalities, Urbanism and Pirate Modernities: India". Rising Powers Working Paper, ESRC Rising Powers Programme, Goldsmiths, University of London, July. Retrieved 27 October 2013 from: http://www.compas.ox.ac.uk/research/dynamics/social-externalities-china-india-africa/.
Sundaram, Ravi (2010b). *Pirate Modernity: Delhi's Media Urbanism.* Oxon and New York: Routledge.
Zehle, Soenke (2012). "Internet Corporation for Assigned Names and Numbers". In George Ritzer (ed.). *The Wiley-Blackwell Encyclopedia of Globalization.* Chicester: Blackwell Publishing.

Contributing Authors

Jonas Andersson Schwarz holds a Ph.D. from Goldsmiths, University of London, and studies the ways in which digital media consumption takes place and is conditioned by regulation and infrastructure. His current post-doc position is funded by Swedish research foundation Riksbankens Jubileumsfond in collaboration with the advertising agency Forsman & Bodenfors.

Sean Johnson Andrews is Assistant Professor of Cultural Studies at Columbia College, Chicago. He holds a PhD. in Cultural Studies from George Mason University. He teaches classes on media and cultural studies theory, methods, and methodology. His current research centers on the intersection of political economy, culture, and the law.

James Arvanitakis is Professor of Social and Cultural Analysis with the University of Western Sydney and a member of the University's Institute for Culture and Society. He is also the Head of the Academy at UWS. His research areas include citizenship, the commons, hope, and piracy. James is also recognised for his innovative teaching style - labelled 'Teaching Like a Pirate' - and has received various awards including Australian Prime Minister's University Teacher of the Year Award. A former banker turned human rights activist, he has worked in conflict zones throughout the Pacific and Asia.

Balázs Bodó, PhD (1975), economist, piracy researcher and Marie Curie Fellow at the Institute for Information Law (IViR) at the University of Amsterdam. Previously he has been Visiting Researcher and Fulbright Fellow at Stanford University's Center for Internet and Society and at the Berkman Center for Internet and Society at Harvard University. His academic interests include copyright and economics, piracy, media regulation, peer-to-peer communities, underground libraries, digital archives, and informal media economies. His most recent book is on the role of P2P piracy in the Hungarian cultural ecosystem."

Virginia Crisp is Senior Lecturer in the Media Department at Middlesex University, UK. She is part of the Besides the Screen research group (www.bts.re) and has published articles on piracy, file sharing and film distribution.

Danielle Drozdzewski is a lecturer in Human Geography at the University of New South Wales, Sydney, Australia. Her main research areas are cultural geography, geographies of identity, national identities, multiculturalism and cultural memory. Other research interests include qualitative and ethnographic methodologies. She has conducted researched in Kraków, Poland, Phang Nga, Thailand, as well as in Australia.

Martin Fredriksson is assistant professor at the Department of Culture Studies (Tema Q), Linköping University, where he runs a research project on the ideology of piracy and the formation of Pirate Parties in Europe, North America and Australia. He is also executive editor of *Culture Unbound: Journal of Current Cultural Research* (http://www.cultureunbound.ep.liu.se/).

Pavlos Hatzopoulos is currently a senior researcher at the Centre for Gender Studies of Panteion University. He has published several articles on space/time and urban social movements, has co-edited the volume *Religion in International Relations: The Return from Exile* (Palgrave 2003) and has authored the book *The Balkans beyond Nationalism and Identity* (IB Tauris 2007).

You Jie, PhD, is a lecturer at the Department of Journalism and Communication in the School of Film and TV Art & Technology, Shanghai University, China. His main research area covers media policy, journalism ethics, copyright law, and the Chinese participatory media.

Nelli Kambouri is currently working as a senior research fellow at the Centre for Gender Studies of Panteion University and as a scientific advisor on research in the General Secretariat of Gender Equality, Athens. Her publications in Greek and English focus mostly on gender, migration and social movements.

Louise Kiddell has extensive experience working in community and environmental organisations, including Greenpeace Australia Pacific and The Nature

Conservation Council of NSW. Her background is in Medical and Agricultural Science and she is currently completing a Masters of International and Community Development at Deakin University in Melbourne, Australia.

Stefan Larsson is head of Lund University Internet Institute (LUii) and a researcher in Sociology of Law. He is a member of the Cybernorms research group and generally studies conceptual, legal and social change at the intersection of digitization and society.

Yi-Chieh Lin received a Ph.D. in Anthropology from Harvard University and now teaches at the Center for General Education of National Chung Hsing University, Taiwan. She is the author of *Fake Stuff* (Routledge 2011) and "counterfeiting in Italy" (NCKU Law Review June 2013). She now studies food frauds and education in the USA, Japan and Taiwan.

Lucas Logan is a doctoral candidate in telecommunication and media studies at Texas A&M University. His research interrogates the social and cultural consequences of international intellectual property policy. His work has appeared in *The International Encyclopedia of Media Studies: Media Production* (2013).

Jonathan Marshall inhabits the University of Technology Sydney. This research was supported by the Australian Research Council. He is the author of *Living of Cybermind: Categories, Communication and Control* (Peter Lang), *Jung, Alchemy and History* (Hermetic Research), and editor of *Depth Psychology, Disorder and Climate Change* (JungDownunder Books).

James Meese is a doctoral student at the Institute for Social Research, Swinburne University. A media and cultural studies scholar, his research interests include intellectual property, piracy and cultures of innovation in sports media. Recent work has been published in the *European Journal of Cultural Studies* and *Computers and Composition.*

Vanessa Mendes Moreira De Sa is a PhD candidate at the University of Western Sydney in Australia. In Brazil, she has an honours degree in communication studies and a degree in television and radio production. Also, she studied entertainment media management in the US. Her research interests are fandom, Internet piracy and new media audiences.

Yiannis Mylonas is a researcher, writer and lecturer. He has a background in philosophy, social psychology and media studies, and teaches at Copenhagen and Lund Universities. His research interests depart from Critical Theory and Post Structuralism and relate to the study of media, culture and politics. He has published studies on discourse analysis of war and crisis representations, political subjectivity, civic cultures and the political economy of copyrights. His current research concerns the political aspect of the EU's economic crisis.

Ned Rossiter is Professor of Communication in the School of Humanities and Communication Arts at the University of Western Sydney where he is also a member of the Institute for Culture and Society. He is the author of *Organized Networks: Media Theory, Creative Labour, New Institutions*, NAi Publishers, Rotterdam (2006). Ned is currently working on two books entitled *Logistical Nightmares: Infrastructure, Software, Labour* (New York: Routledge, forthcoming 2014) and (with Geert Lovink) *Urgent Aphorisms: The Politics of Network Cultures* (London: Minor Compositions, forthcoming 2014).

Francesca da Rimini is a post-doctoral researcher at the Cosmopolitan Civil Societies Research Centre, University of Technology Sydney, and co-author of *Disorder and the Disinformation Society: The Social Dynamics of Networks and Software* (Routledge 2013). She is also an established artist, creating videos, installations, zines, curiosities, and collaborative Internet projects.

Dr. Daniel Robinson is a Senior Lecturer at UNSW in Sydney. His background is in geography, environmental law and environmental science. Related to biopiracy he has done research for several organisations including UNDP, ICTSD-UNCTAD, DSEWPAC, and Natural Justice. He is currently working with the GIZ-led ABS Capacity Development Initiative in the Pacific.

Sonja Schillings is a PhD candidate with the Graduate School of North American Studies at the Freie Universität Berlin, Germany. In her dissertation project, she analyzes narrative constructions of civilization and legitimacy in the legal fiction of hostis humani generis, “the enemy of all humankind”.

Mariacristina Sciannamblo is a Ph.D. student in Sociology and Applied Social Sciences at the University of Rome “La Sapienza”. Her PhD research project investigates the relationship between gender and computing, with a particular focus on computer systems design. Her research interests concern communication and gender studies, digital culture (especially in relation to user-participatory culture), and Science and Technology Studies (STS).

Soenke Zehle is Lecturer in Media Art & Design and has a long-time involvement in the collaborative conceptualization and implementation of net.cultural projects. Soenke Zehle co-initiated and currently works as Managing Director of xm:lab – Experimental Media Lab at the Academy of Fine Arts Saar, Saarbruecken, Germany. For projects and publications see www.xmlab.org.

Ekin Gündüz Özdemirci graduated from Marmara University, Istanbul with a degree in Communication. She then completed an MA in Film Studies at ESAV (Ecole Supérieure d’Audiovisuel), Université de Toulouse II, and a Ph.D. in Film Studies at Marmara University. Her main research interests are in collective memory, nostalgia films, new media and eco-cinema.

INDEX

www.ingramcontent.com/pod-product-compliance
Lightning Source LLC
Chambersburg PA
CBHW061619220326
41598CB00026BA/3813
* 9 7 8 1 9 3 6 1 1 7 5 9 8 *